W9-CEW-060

SEX & GENDER

The Human Experience

FOURTH EDITION

JAMES A. DOYLE

ROANE STATE COMMUNITY COLLEGE

MICHELE A. PALUDI

CONSULTANTS IN SEXUAL HARASSMENT

Boston, Massachusetts   Burr Ridge, Illinois   Dubuque, Iowa
Madison, Wisconsin   New York, New York   San Francisco, California   St. Louis, Missouri

McGraw-Hill

A Division of The **McGraw·Hill** *Companies*

SEX AND GENDER: THE HUMAN EXPERIENCE, FOURTH EDITION

Copyright © 1998, by The McGraw-Hill Companies, Inc. All rights reserved.
Previous edition © 1995 by Brown & Benchmark Publishers, a Times Mirror Higher Education
Group Inc. company. Printed in the United States of America. Except as permitted under the United
States Copyright Act of 1976, no part of this publication may be reproduced or distributed in any
form or by any means, or stored in a data base or retrieval system, without the prior written
permission of the publisher.

✪ This book is printed on recycled, acid-free paper containing 10% postconsumer waste.

1 2 3 4 5 6 7 8 9 0 QPF/QPF 9 0 9 8 7

ISBN 0–697–25282–5

Publisher: *Jane Vaicunas*
Sponsoring editor: *Beth Kaufman*
Marketing manager: *Jim Rosza*
Project manager: *Ann Morgan*
Production supervisor: *Sandy Hahn*
Designer: *Mary L. Christianson*
Cover image: *August Macke, "People by the Blue Lake," 1913*
Cover designer: *Lesiak/Crampton Design, Inc.*
Compositor: *Shepherd, Inc.*
Typeface: *10/12 Garamond Light*
Printer: *Quebecor Printing Book Group/Fairfield*

Library of Congress Cataloging-in Publication Data

Doyle, James A.
    Sex and gender : the human experience / James A. Doyle, Michele A.
Paludi.—4th ed.
        p. cm.
    Includes bibliographical references and index.
    ISBN 0–697–25282–5
    1. Sex role. 2. Identity (Psychology) 3. Feminism.   I. Paludi,
Michele Antoinette.   II. Title.
HQ1075.D69   1997
305.3–dc21   97–12938
                                             CIP

http://www.mhcollege.com

SEX & GENDER

For Nan, the one person who is always there with total encouragement and sage advice. The one who has taught me a most valuable lesson: Life is not to be lived in solitary pursuit nor selfish endeavor. This is your work as well as mine.

James A. Doyle

For William Dember, my mentor, who helped guide my thinking on the psychology of sex and gender and to students who I mentored for sharing with me their insights on the psychology of sex and gender.

Michele A. Paludi

Contents in Brief

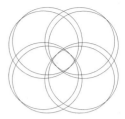

Table of Contents

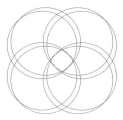

For the Students

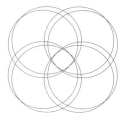

While writing this fourth edition of *Sex and Gender,* we became very pleased to see the many changes that have taken place in research, teaching, and advocacy in areas related to gender since the publication of the first edition of this book in 1985. Even a brief comparison of the table of contents and indices of the first and fourth editions suggests the many new areas of scientific inquiry that have evolved in the ensuing twelve years: e.g., sexual harassment, feminist research methodologies, meta-analyses, and, most notably, the interface of sex, race, ethnicity, and gender.

With this fourth edition we celebrate the twelfth birthday of this text on sex and gender. And as with most twelfth birthdays, this edition signals the adolescence of the field. Developmental psychologists write that adolescence means "to grow to maturity." Like adolescence, we see the field of sex and gender in a period of transition. With new meta-analytic statistical techniques, researchers are learning how to separate well-documented gender comparisons from gender differences that are artifacts of the measurement instrument and/or represent conceptual biases on the part of the researchers.

With guidelines for conducting sex-fair studies, researchers are becoming actively involved in the research process and carefully examining the underlying values and assumptions in their work. Thus, similar to the life stage of adolescence, new conceptual skills have emerged during the adolescence of the field of sex and gender.

With more research on the psychological impact of rape, battering, sexual harassment, and incest, psychologists are educating attorneys, judges, and jurors about the influence of gender and power in interpersonal relationships in the family and at work. Like the life stage of adolescence, the field of sex and gender is encouraging its researchers to make a more conscious commitment to the society.

We are excited to see such changes in positive directions in the ways women and men are valued in this country. We hope this fourth edition can be useful for this important societal change.

We acknowledge and thank the faculty and students who wrote to us with their comments and suggestions based on their reading of the third edition. We have incorporated their valuable ideas in this current edition.

We would like to thank our families for their support and encouragement during the revision of *Sex and Gender.* Writing can be an isolating activity. It was comforting to know our families were right there waiting when we'd leave our computers and stacks of papers.

We also thank the students who have participated in our courses on sex and gender. We appreciate your insightful comments.

We would like to thank the following individuals for reviewing the manuscript and providing us with helpful feedback toward improving the text:

Toby Silverman, William Paterson College
Lauren J. Pivnick, Monroe Community College
Nancylee Koschmann, Elmira College
Pat Lin, California State Polytechnic University
Terry Hatkoff, California State University, Northridge

We want to acknowledge the assistance of many colleagues at Brown & Benchmark. Being encouraged to write the kind of book we wanted to write has been empowering.

In this fourth edition we have updated each chapter with recent research and theoretical perspectives. Following an introductory chapter that deals with the definitions of sex and gender, the illusion of scientific objectivity, and the infusion of androcentric biases in studies of sex and gender, we discuss the biological, psychological, social roles, and anthropological perspectives to understanding sex and gender. For each discipline, we examine the traditional theories and research and explore current findings, issues, and controversies.

In the "Issues" section of this edition, we discuss several social institutions that play a central role in understanding sex and gender: language, education and work, religion and politics, and health fields. We examine each of these institutions by focusing on interpersonal power and the ways that different power bases affect women and men.

Each chapter contains some questions for you to answer as you read the material. We also provide an end-of-the-chapter summary, a list of suggested readings, and boxes within the chapter that will keep you involved with the material.

We invite you to write to us and share your attitudes and feelings about the study of gender roles and our text in particular. We value this dialogue! We believe this is an exciting time to study sex and gender. We hope this fourth edition will encourage you to pursue research and teaching in this discipline.

Acknowledgments

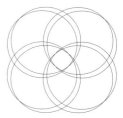

Michele Paludi would like to thank students in her Winter 1997 course on the Psychology of Gender for their insights and support: Katherine Barnett, Megan Collins, JoEllen Cowger, Laura Green, Michael Hamilton, Carrie Heroth, Stephanie LaVine, Deborah Loffredo, Kurt Martel, Jodi Meisler, Alison Mohr, Sarah Moss, Nicole Nacamuli, Jennifer Pool, Leslie Rhein, Elisabeth Sand-Freeman, Christine Schrader, and Allison Williams.

Special thanks and appreciation to Karen Bankston and Ann Morgan for their support and assistance in making this fourth edition become a reality.

Michele Paludi would also like to acknowledge the following family, friends, and colleagues for their support during the writing of this edition: Rosalie Paludi, Lucille Paludi, Fr. John Provost, JoAnne Christensen, Darlene DeFour, Paul Tonko, Anne Levy, Martha Huggins, and Paul Rieschick.

PART ONE

Perspectives

Sex and Gender: An Overview

What are little boys made of?
What are little boys made of?
Frogs and snails
And puppy dogs' tails,
That's what little boys are made of.

What are little girls made of?
What are little girls made of?
Sugar and spice
And all that's nice,
That's what little girls are made of.

Anonymous

Talking about gender for most people is the equivalent
of fish talking about water. Gender is so much the routine
ground of everyday activities that questioning its
taken-for-granted assumptions and presuppositions is like
thinking about whether the sun will come up.

Judith Lorber

Did you know that

In Latina cultures, marianismo demands that women model themselves after
the Virgin Mary and see themselves as spiritually superior to men and
capable of enduring great suffering?

Women and men with emotionally close relationships may also have good
senses of humor?

Men are likely to be seen as group leaders unless power-related cues help
identify women as leaders?

Racial and ethnic minority women trail behind white women in access to top
government jobs?

Men typically focus language skills in the parietal lobe and women tend to focus their language skills in the frontal lobe?

The number of AIDS cases in women is rising so rapidly worldwide that by the year 2000, the number of women with AIDS will equal the number of men with AIDS?

African American men have the lowest cancer survival rate while white women have the highest?

Women's preference for Democrats persists even when a Republican woman runs against a Democratic man?

The social status of American Indian women increases with age but decreases for other U.S. women?

By junior high school, boys perceive themselves as more competent in mathematics than girls do, even though boys receive similar or lower grades?

Physical attractiveness is emphasized for adolescent and young adult women, and the emphasis on thinness can lead to eating disorders?

In this book we will focus on these issues as we discuss sex and gender, integral features of the human experience. The human experience begins at conception, when sex is determined as either female or male, and expands after birth to include one's gender, which arises from the experience of being raised to behave and think of oneself in terms of femininity or masculinity. Inquiry into one's sex and gender is a wondrous study but one that can be filled with misconceptions, prejudice, and bias. To begin our discussion of sex and gender, then, we need to discuss these terms and some of the misunderstandings that may exist about their meanings.

A Basic Distinction: Sex or Gender?

The terms *sex* and *gender* are often used interchangeably. However, this synonymous usage can lead to confusion. Thus, we need to begin our discussion with some basic definitions.

The word *sex* has become a catchall term meaning different things to different people. In everyday usage, most people define sex as one of two mutually exclusive and unchangeable biological categories—female or male—into which most living species fit. The term *sex* can also designate aspects of sexual behavior. Sex, as used in the first way, that of two dichotomous and unchangeable biologically based categories, can be a problematic concept.

Sex: The Dichotomy Inference

Many living species exhibit anatomical evidence of a biological *bisexuality* in their reproductive structures, at least during the early weeks of fetal development (Money, 1975a; Tobach & Rosoff, 1978). For example, during the first six weeks of uterine development, human fetuses of both genetic sexes (i.e., either XX or XY sex chromosomal patterns) possess special sex tissues called *anlagen,* which have the potential to develop into either female or male sex structures. An extreme example of biological bisexuality can be found in the rare cases of true hermaphroditism when a person is born with both female and male reproductive and genital structures.

Compounding the confusion about sex even more are some common misconceptions about hormones. Most people talk as if women and men are dichotomous hormonally, as noted by the frequent references to estrogen and progesterone as being "female hormones," while referring to androgens as "male hormones." In fact, all three hormones are found in the bloodstreams of all women and men (Crews, 1987). Thus, an individual's sex is determined by the amounts of hormones, not by the kinds of hormones.

Even the supposedly dichotomous secondary sex characteristics have been shown to vary widely among individuals. Interestingly, most people determine a person's biological sex category (i.e., female or male) solely on the basis of visible (and highly variable) secondary sex characteristics. However, not all women nor all men have the secondary sex characteristics thought typical for their sex. What all of this means is that when the word *sex* is used to mean one of two strictly separate biological categories, it is being used incorrectly. Rather, biological sex is better understood to mean a continuum whereon the reproductive structures, hormones, and physical features range somewhere between two end points.

Sex: The Unchangeable Inference

Among humans, we now have the surgical ability to change a person's genital and secondary sex features, as found among those who have opted for sex-reassignment surgery (Money, 1975a; Walters & Ross, 1986). These findings suggest that sex is not simply a biological fact based on only two possible categories, nor is it immutable for life, at least not for all living species. In fact, some people have persuasively argued that sex is a social construct and not merely a biological given. It makes more sense to think of the word *sex* as referring to the reproductive structures, hormones, and physical characteristics that exist along a continuum ranging from extreme femaleness to extreme maleness, rather than as comprising a set of biological features of a strictly either/or and unchangeable kind. As we can see, the term *sex,* rather than being a straightforward, unambiguous word, can be fraught with confusion.

Gender: A Needed Concept

Some years ago, psychologist Rhoda Unger (1979) urged social scientists to use the word *sex* only when referring to specifically biological mechanisms (e.g., sex chromosomes or sex structures) and to use the term *gender* only when discussing the social, cultural, and psychological aspects that pertain to the traits, norms, stereotypes, and roles of women and men. Thus, Unger views sex as a biological construct; she defines gender in terms of its social, cultural, and psychological components. Again, however, we must be cautious if we wish to avoid burdening the word *gender* with the same either/or meaning as the word *sex*. Rather, gender and its components (gender role stereotypes, gender norms, gender roles, and gender role identity, all discussed in chapter 3) also vary along a continuum of femininity and masculinity. Furthermore, gender should be thought of as independent of a person's biological sex.

Carolyn Wood Sherif noted some of the inherent problems the word *sex* has brought to the study of gender. With special reference to the construct of sex roles, Sherif (1982) wrote that it "has become a boxcar carrying an assortment of sociological and psychological data along with an explosive mixture of myth and untested assumptions" (p. 392). One of the problems Sherif has with the term *sex roles* is that it

> *uncritically couples a biological concept (sex) with a sociological concept (role). Thus, the concept suffers double jeopardy from myths about sex smuggled in uncritically and from denotative confusions in the sociological concept of roles.* (p. 392)

Although a majority of researchers apparently still prefer the designation *sex roles* rather than *gender roles,* we agree with Unger, Sherif, and others; throughout our discussion, we will use the term *gender* rather than *sex* when referring to the nonbiological features resulting from a person's ascribed status of either female or male.

One might suggest that preferring *gender* over *sex* or vice versa is a small point. However, we must be as precise as possible in our terminology to disentangle some of the confusion that often exists in this field.

Bias: A Fundamental Issue

All of us hold personal values, beliefs, attitudes, and assumptions that influence our perception of the world around us. These personal biases cause us to focus our attention on certain features while avoiding others. In other words, our personal biases act like screens that distort our perception of the world in which we live.

Few areas of inquiry are so fraught with personal biases as the study of women and men and characteristics related to gender role. A number of biases are especially noteworthy if we are to understand why so many people believe what they do about sex and gender, even in the face of contradictory evidence. In this section, we will discuss two biases that influence our views: *scientific bias* and *researcher bias.*

Scientific Bias: Value-Free vs. Value-Laden Research

The sciences, particularly, have an aura of being objective and value free, but this has never been the case (Stanovich, 1986):

> *Each science has gone through a phase when there was resistance to its development. Hypatia of Alexandria, the last scholar to work in the great library, was murdered by members of the early Christian church because her interest in science and learning was associated with paganism. Learned contemporaries of Galileo refused to look into his new telescope because the existence of the moons of Jupiter would have violated their philosophical and theological beliefs. For centuries, the understanding of human anatomy progressed only haltingly because of lay and ecclesiastical prohibitions against the dissection of dead human bodies. Darwin was denounced by the Bishop of Oxford and, of course, by countless others. Broca's Society of Anthropology was opposed in France because knowledge about human beings was thought to be subversive to the state.* (p. 14)

One of the basic tenets of science and its scientific method is its insistence on objectivity. The objective scientist supposedly is detached from her or his topic and, through the scientific method, only observes, controls, measures, and analyzes external events as they happen, letting the accumulated evidence speak for itself. According to this view, a scientist is like an outsider allowing the topic of study to unravel and show its orderly arrangements for all to see. Scientists typically use a single research paradigm that leads to studying human behavior from a linear, predetermined model. The research paradigm favored by most contemporary scientists includes the following steps:

Statement of the Problem
Survey of the Literature
Hypotheses
Design
Statistical Analyses
Results
Conclusion

This linear model is incomplete because (1) it does not encourage any modification in the ongoing research process; (2) it is based on "objectivity" while ignoring biases in the research process; (3) its preselection of statistical analyses does not encourage using alternative analyses of the data; and (4) it overemphasizes the search for differences and only defines differences statistically (Campbell, 1988).

A basic assumption inherent in science is that it is *value free*. That is, a scientist's personal biases supposedly are absent or removed from the study and are not allowed to interfere with the scientific process. Therefore, the perception of the world formulated by science is alleged to be a faithful and valid representation of reality.

But can science, or more precisely a scientist, ever be totally value free? Just because scientists say they approach their subject without personal biases does not make their scientific efforts truly value free. In the past few years, several social scientists have argued persuasively that a value-free science is neither possible nor desirable (Landrine, Klonoff & Brown-Collins, 1995; Rabinowitz & Sechzur, 1993).

Advocates of a value-free science, on the other hand, argue that only by removing one's personal bias can one be sure of a truthful rendition of the event(s) being studied. Such a view implies a value-free observation is more valid than an observation made under the influence of a *value-laden* approach, or one where a scientist openly admits to holding certain biased viewpoints. However, those who believe a value-laden approach distorts an observation of reality, whereas a value-free perspective reflects a truer version of reality, are themselves guilty of letting a particular bias influence their thinking. Thus, the belief that a value-free science affords a more valid account of reality is nothing more than another value-laden perspective for which there is no *a priori* guarantee to its claim of greater truthfulness of its findings.

We will note later how the study of gender may be better served with a value-laden approach rather than a purportedly value-free perspective.

Researcher Bias: Getting What One Looks For

Thus, one of the more basic forms of bias may be the belief that simply by following certain scientific methods or procedures one is assured that all biases have been thoroughly put to rest. In reality, there is little assurance that a researcher is not allowing some personal bias to enter into the research. For example, a researcher who is gathering data on nurturant behavior may systematically and precisely count the number of times a mother talks to or smiles at her baby while she is holding the child. But why did the researcher study the baby's mother? The culturally influenced belief that mothers are the best infant caregivers or that women and not men are normally expected to perform nurturant activities may have played a role in the selection of whom to study. Such culturally influenced assumptions on the researcher's part may affect the outcome and interpretation of such a study.

The classic theories and research on morality (Kohlberg, 1966) and achievement motivation (McClelland et al., 1953) were based on boys and men only. In addition, in research on aggression, nearly 50 percent of the research was conducted using boys or men only, 10 percent using girls or women, and 40 percent using both sexes. This 50 percent is higher than the percentage of male-only research in psychology in general (Rabinowitz & Sechzur, 1993), supporting the conclusion that when scientists investigate a stereotyped "masculine" behavior, they are less likely to include girls and women as participants.

Scientists bring their own personal biases with them to their particular field of study. This fact is no less true and, in fact, may be more true in the field of gender-related topics than in other fields of study. Naomi Weisstein

(1971) made a persuasive case that social scientists, especially male psychologists, have allowed their personal biases about women to color their research endeavors. She concluded:

> *Until psychologists begin respecting evidence and until they begin looking at the social contexts within which people move, psychology will have nothing to say of substance to offer in this task of discovery. I do not know what immutable differences exist between men and women apart from differences in their genitals; perhaps there are some other unchangeable differences; probably there are a number of irrelevant differences. But it is clear that until social expectations for men and women are equal, until we provide equal respect for both men and women, our answers to this question will simply reflect our prejudices.* (p. 222)

Another bias is that the results of research using boys and/or men would likely be generalized and discussed as "individuals are . . . ," while research based on girls and/or women was likely to be generalized only to this sex (Schwabacher, 1972).

In addition, researchers have typically issued conclusions about individuals in general, when in fact only one group, typically white, middle-class men, have been observed (Landrine, Klonoff, & Brown-Collins, 1995; Reid & Paludi, 1993). Furthermore, most researchers describe ethnic minority individuals collectively. This approach contributes to making the same error that occurs when one collectively describes any group. Ethnic minority women and men are as varied and differ as much among themselves as do white individuals. Thus, individuals' experiences are extremely diverse; there are significant differences in the socialization experiences of ethnic minority individuals. The choice to ignore the differences and to pretend that universality is the rule appears increasingly unacceptable. Carla Golden (1987) made a similar argument with respect to studying sexual orientation and concluded:

> *One of the most important insights of both feminist psychology and the women's movement is that our being born female does not mean that we automatically and naturally prefer certain roles and activities. We have recognized that the category* woman *has been socially constructed, and that societal definitions notwithstanding, women are a diverse group with interests, attitudes, and identities that do not always conform to what is traditionally considered feminine . . . sexual feelings and activities are not always accurately described in either/or terms, nor do they exist in a simple one-to-one relation to our sexual identities . . . we must be careful in our social construction of sexuality not to construct categories that are so rigid and inflexible that women's self-definitions put them at odds with the social definitions. To do so only limits the expression of the diversities and variabilities in women's sexual identities.* (p. 33)

A researcher is just as likely to be influenced by her or his cultural beliefs, values, and expectations as is anyone else in society. Such bias is referred to as *experimenter bias*. Unwittingly, experimenter bias may cause a researcher to look at a problem in only one way, while avoiding other possibilities. For instance, the exclusion of lesbian couples, fathers, nonmarried heterosexual couples, single women, or gay couples in parent-infant studies suggests a bias on the researcher's part. Experimenter bias may also show itself in the way a researcher words her or his questions. For example, requesting information about a participant's "marital status" denies lesbian and gay relationships as well as nonmarital heterosexual cohabitation. Even the types of questions a researcher asks may bias the results in favor of the researcher's hypothesis (Rosenthal, 1976). Omitting information about participants' sexual orientation, ethnicity, and age is also indicative of the researcher's biases. Too often, the questions we ask (and don't ask) and the way we ask them can determine the answers we find. If our questions are embedded with our personal bias, we are more likely to find answers that support our bias. This argument was expressed by Karen Briefer (1987), who pointed out that heterosexist bias has largely been unexamined in psychological research:

> *The problem is not one of explicit anti-gay prejudice, or even one of a lack of non-biased research. Heterosexist bias in recent work is found in more subtle forms: in the structuring of texts, use of language and grammatical constructions, through veiled anti-gay statements that imply undesirability, and through the omission of a lesbian/gay perspective entirely. . . . Negative attitudes toward homosexuality run deep, and are rooted in basic assumptions about women, men, and what constitutes "appropriate" sex-role behavior. But precisely because these attitudes run deep, and can be traced to such basic notions of what it means to be female or male, challenging heterosexism should become an important and explicitly acknowledged part of the task we have set for ourselves as feminists.* (pp. 2–3; 13)

The ethnicity, sex, sexual orientation, and age of the researcher and participants should be considered when reviewing and conducting research. As Hope Landrine, Elizabeth Klonoff and Alice Brown-Collins (1995) argue:

> *. . . the traditional psychological experiment never has yielded or entailed objective observations or brute behavioral data; rather, it always has entailed and yielded interpretations of interpretations of interpretations, each level of which is part culturally determined and situated.* (p. 72)

Statistical Treatment of Women's and Men's Responses

Psychologist Stephanie Shields (1975) reported that psychologists have considered women "as a special group" since the mid-nineteenth century. Researchers believed that they could distinguish between women's and men's brains in terms of differences in gross structure. The location of these differences varied according to the popular theory of the time. For example, when psychologists believed the frontal lobe was responsible for intelligence, men's frontal lobes were assumed to be larger than women's. When it became in

Box 1-1

Ferreting Out Research Bias in Your Academic Field

Now that you've read through the section on research bias, you might want to see if you can find research bias in your major field. Not only will this exercise give you practice in spotting research bias, you'll also learn more about the researchers (and the journals) in your chosen field of study.

To get started, head for your university's library and select several recent journal issues from your major field. Every academic field (e.g., history, communication, psychology, literature, nursing, etc.) has numerous journals highlighting current research. If you're not sure where to find your major's academic journals in your library, ask your professor or a librarian at the information desk.

Once you have several issues, look through the table of contents and find an article that deals with some aspect of gender (Hint: look for words in the title like "femininity," "masculinity," "parenting," or "gender").

Once you have selected an article, read it carefully. As you read, identify the article's main issue or topic. For instance, say you're a business major and you have a research article in a business journal dealing with successful managers' leadership styles. Who did the author select to study as successful managers? Are all the participants male? Are there any female managers in the study? Does the author explain how s/he selected the participants? How does the author define "success"? Does success seem more characteristic of one sex than the other?

What if you selected a sociology journal and found an article studying different parenting styles and all the participants are female? What does that suggest? Possibly, researcher bias against males as parents? After going through several articles, you'll begin to find research bias is much more evident than you first thought. Good hunting.

vogue to consider the parietal lobe as the repository of intelligence, however, women's and men's frontal lobes were assumed to be equivalent, but women were now described as having smaller parietal lobes than men.

Thus, early research was focused on "differences" and "similarities" between women and men rather than avoiding any direct discussion of women without comparisons to men. Hollingworth, for example, devoted considerable research to investigating the "variability hypothesis", the assertion that "women as a species are less variable among themselves than are men; all women are pretty much alike, but men range enormously in their talents and defects" (Hollingworth, 1943, p. 114). This variability hypothesis, first discussed by Havelock Ellis, flourished in the early 1900s and was used to explain the greater frequency of men on lists of distinction and a wider range of intelligence for men than for women.

From this variability hypothesis psychologists derived implications about gender differences in perceptual-motor abilities and emotionality. Shields (1975) pointed out that the variability hypothesis was used against women in the areas of social policies and education.

If this tendency to mediocrity was natural to the "fair" sex, as the variability hypothesis would hold true, then it would be wasteful of public and private resources to train or encourage women to high levels of achievement. (p. 6)

This focus on gender similarities and differences was used in the 1970s by psychologists Eleanor Maccoby and Carol Nagy Jacklin (1974). They used the "voting method" of analysis (see chapter 3) in which they tallied the number of research studies reporting statistically significant gender differences (in each direction) in addition to the number of studies reporting no gender differences. In their classic text *The Psychology of Sex Differences,* Maccoby and Jacklin examined over 1,600 published studies ranging over a broad spectrum of human behavior, including cognitive functions, personality traits, and social behaviors. Their goal was "to sift the evidence to determine which of the many beliefs about sex differences have a solid basis in fact and which do not" (p. vii). Their analyses revealed that many of the presumed gender differences were more myth than fact, whereas a few differences appeared to stand up. Maccoby and Jacklin's research will be discussed in greater detail in chapter 3; a summary of their findings follows.

Some of the studies reviewed by Maccoby and Jacklin (1974) and Jacklin (1989) point to several areas where there seems to be some gender differences with respect to specific abilities and to one personality trait:

Girls have greater verbal ability than boys.
Boys excel in visual-spatial ability.
Boys excel in mathematical ability.
Males are more aggressive than females.

Maccoby and Jacklin concluded that girls' verbal abilities mature more quickly than boys'. While girls' and boys' verbal abilities are similar during the early school years, beginning in high school and beyond, girls take the lead. This includes a better understanding and fluency of the complexities of language, better spelling and creative writing abilities, and better comprehension of analogies.

Beginning in early adolescence, boys are better able to rotate an object in space and pick out a simple design or figure that is embedded within a larger more complex design. Again, beginning in adolescence, boys show a greater facility with math than girls. However, in those studies that use verbal processes in mathematical questions, girls do better than boys; on those that require visual-spatial abilities, boys do better than girls. Furthermore, Diane Halpern (1995) has noted that the conclusion that there exists a gender universal in mathematical ability is shown to be incorrect when one includes data from non-Western cultures.

And finally, beginning in the early preschool years, boys are more physically aggressive than girls. Boys exhibit more mock-fighting and other forms of aggression than girls. Also, boys direct their aggression during these early years more toward other boys than toward girls. Boys continue to be more aggressive than girls throughout adolescence and the adult years.

Many of these conclusions have been challenged in studies of race and ethnicity correlates of these behaviors (Landrine, 1995). And, in many cases it was noted that in the initial Maccoby and Jacklin study, they simply counted up the studies that found a gender difference (no matter which sex the results favored) from those that did not. If there were more differences than similarities, Maccoby and Jacklin concluded a significant gender difference. Jeanne Block (1976) has argued that such a procedure is questionable: many of the studies Maccoby and Jacklin reviewed contained relatively few participants, leading to the possibility of finding little or no gender differences with respect to the topic under study. Sherman (1978) re-reviewed many of Maccoby and Jacklin's studies and found that many times the magnitude of the differences was quite small.

Janet Hyde (1981; Hyde & Frost, 1993) also reanalyzed Maccoby and Jacklin's verbal, quantitative, visual-spatial, and field articulation studies. She summarized her research:

> *The main conclusion that can be reached from this analysis is that the gender differences in verbal ability, quantitative ability, visual-spatial ability, and field articulation reported by Maccoby and Jacklin (1974) are small. Gender differences appear to account for no more than 1%–5% of the population variance. . . . Generally, it seems that gender differences in verbal ability are smaller and gender differences in spatial ability are larger, but even in the latter case, gender differences account for less than 5% of the population variance.* (pp. 894–896)

Hyde used meta-analyses to arrive at her conclusions. *Meta-analysis* is a statistical procedure that permits psychologists to synthesize results from several studies and yield a measure of the magnitude of the gender difference. It is a statistical method for conducting a literature review. Psychologists who use meta-analysis proceed in the following way:

1. They locate as many studies as they can on the particular topic of interest. They use computerized database searches in this phase of the analysis.
2. Psychologists perform a statistical analysis of the statistics reported in each of the journal articles or conference presentations. They compute an effect size statistic, *d,* for each study. This *d* statistic explains how far apart the mean of the women's scores and the mean of the men's scores are in standard deviation units. This statistic also yields information about the variability of women's and men's scores, recognizing that each sex is not homogeneous.
3. Psychologists average the *d* statistics obtained from all the studies they reviewed. Then, variations in values of *d* are analyzed.
4. Finally, psychologists group the studies into categories based on logical classifications (e.g., mathematical reasoning, arithmetic computation). Psychologists can then determine the gender difference based on the classifications assessed.

Meta-analytic studies have been conducted in a variety of areas, including cognition (Hyde, 1981; Hyde & Linn, 1988), influenceability and conformity (Eagly & Carli, 1981), visuospatial ability (Masters & Sanders, 1993), and nonverbal behavior (Stier & Hall, 1984). In their review of meta-analytic studies, Janet Hyde and Laurie Frost (1993) concluded that meta-analysis can advance the study of psychology of gender because it indicates not only whether a significant gender difference exists, but also the magnitude of the gender difference.

One criticism of meta-analytic techniques and Maccoby and Jacklin's "voting method" concerns the belief that continued emphasis on gender differences and gender similarities encourages us to exaggerate those differences we do find. A major problem with this perspective is that sex is treated as the explanation rather than as the starting point for scientific investigation (Rabinowitz & Sechzur, 1993). And, like the early research that focused on differences in brain size, the tendency persists to use research data about women to formulate social policies that would be harmful to women (Eagly, 1995). And, all because the focus is on viewing women as individuals separate from men!

According to Rachel Hare-Mustin and Jeanne Marecek (1988), one consequence of focusing on difference is:

> *the tendency to view men and women as embodying opposite and mutually exclusive traits. Such a dichotomy seems a caricature of human experience. For example, to maintain the illusion of male autonomy at home and in the workplace, the contribution of women's work must be overlooked. Similarly, the portrayal of women as relational ignores the complexity of their experiences. Rearing children involves achievement, and nurturing others involves power over those in one's care. . . . Gender dichotomies are historically rooted in an era, now past, when the majority of women were not part of the paid labor force. . . . When gender is represented as dichotomized traits, the possibility that each includes aspects of the other is overlooked.* (p. 459)

Proponents of the gender-as-different perspective view differences between women and men as universal, enduring, and essential. Research along these lines has, therefore, as its goal reaffirming differences between women and men. This perspective can best be illustrated with the literature on moral reasoning.

Lawrence Kohlberg (1966) concluded that moral reasoning could be divided into six stages. Stage one moral thinking is based on rewards and punishment. A girl who displays stage one moral reasoning, for instance, obeys her parents and acts "good" to be rewarded or to avoid punishment. At stage six moral reasoning, a woman espouses a system of generalized ethical principles, such as living one's life according to universal moral principles.

Kohlberg's research has been criticized because it was predicated on boys' and men's responses only. Kohlberg concluded that his six moral stages adequately described the levels of moral reasoning for *all* people. And, he argued that women's moral reasoning is less developed than that of men's.

Carol Gilligan's (1982) research is especially revealing in terms of the differences between women's and men's moral decision making. She views women's morality in terms of an ethic of care. She believes women see "life as dependent on connection, as sustained by activities of care, as based on a bond of attachment rather than a contract of agreement" (p. 57).

Kohlberg and Gilligan both used the following moral dilemma to test moral development:

In Europe, a woman was near death from a special kind of cancer. There was one drug that the doctors thought might save her. It was a form of radium that a druggist in the same town had recently discovered. The drug was expensive to make, but the druggist was charging ten times what the drug cost him to make. He paid $200 for the radium and charged $2,000 for a small dose of the drug. The sick woman's husband, Heinz, went to everyone he knew to borrow the money, but he could only get together about $1,000, which is half of what it cost. He told the druggist that his wife was dying, and asked him to sell it cheaper or let him pay later. But the druggist said, "No, I discovered the drug and I'm going to make money from it." Heinz got desperate and broke into the man's store to steal the drug for his wife. Should the husband have done that? (Kohlberg, 1963, pp. 18–19)

Both women and men (and girls and boys) typically desire that Heinz' wife live. But girls' and women's solution is to "find some other way" besides stealing to get the drug. Girls and women see the dilemma in terms of how to gain the drug while preventing any negative consequences that may come from simply stealing it. Boys and men, on the other hand, opt for stealing it, reasoning that life is more important than the druggist's demand to be paid for the drug. Thus, women's moral reasoning revolves around the "connectedness" (Gilligan's term) between Heinz and his wife. Men, on the other hand, are more concerned about the unreasonableness of the druggist's demand to be paid.

Gilligan (1982) thus views women as relational-connected and men as rational and instrumental. She construes women's caring as an essential feminine attribute. However, political scientist Joan Tronto (1987) has argued that women's moral differences may be a function of their subordinate or tentative social position. According to Tronto:

Even if an ethic of care could primarily be understood as a gender difference, however, the unsituated fact of moral difference between men and women is dangerous because it ignores the broader intellectual context within which "facts" about gender difference are generally received. Despite decades of questioning, we still live in a society where "man" stands for human and where the norm is equated with the male. Gender difference, therefore, is a concept that concerns deviation from the normal. Given the conservative nature of our perceptions of knowledge, evidence of a gender difference in and of itself is not likely to lead to the widespread questioning of established categories, such as

*Kohlberg's. Instead, it is likely to lead to the denigration of "deviation"
associated with the female.* (pp. 652–653)

When psychologists focus on why a gender difference exists in moral reasoning, we disregard the question of why domination exists. Also, women
differ widely in terms of ethnicity, age, class, stage in relationship, sexual orientation, stage in career development, and other cultural and social circumstances. Focusing on gender differences ignores within-group variability.

Minimizing differences between women and men and focusing on similarities underlies the construct of psychological androgyny (see chapter 3). *Androgyny* was initially considered an ideal personality pattern wherein a person
combined the socially valued stereotypic characteristics associated with both
femininity and masculinity. An androgynous person exhibits both feminine and
masculine traits, depending on the situation. An androgynous woman/man can
also show socially valued feminine and masculine traits when appropriate. According to the concept of androgyny, women/men are no longer expected or
encouraged to restrict their behaviors to traditional gender-role-specific traits
(Kaplan & Sedney, 1980). Sandra Bem (1977) and Jeanne Marecek (1978) prescribed androgyny as a liberating force, leading women to fuller lives.

However, Bernice Lott (1981) pointed out that while androgyny is an improvement over the view that femininity and masculinity are opposite and
mutually exclusive ends of a personality dimension, the androgynous perspective still holds that personality comprises feminine and masculine elements. The androgyny perspective implies the equivalence of femininity and
masculinity, however, in fact, the masculine traits are more highly valued.
Hare-Mustin and Marecek (1988) noted that "when the idea of counterparts
implies symmetry and equivalence, it obscures differences in power and social value. . . . Arguing for no differences between women and men, however, draws attention away from women's special needs and from differences
in power and resources between women and men" (pp. 458, 460).

Androgyny ensures that attention is drawn away from women's unique
needs and the power imbalance between women and men in this culture.
"Difference" is a problematic way to construe gender and the psychology of
women. If differences are exaggerated (as is illustrated by the research on
moral reasoning), the findings may serve as a basis for discrimination against
women, who are "different." On the other hand, if actual differences (e.g., in
wages) are ignored or minimized, women may also be discriminated against
(e.g., through inadequate child support). Thus, in both the "gender as difference" model and the "minimizing difference" model, white middle class, heterosexual men and masculinity are the standards of comparison, the norm
against which women and femininity are judged.

The overemphasis on differences provides confirmation of the stereotype
that women and men are "opposite," and that the male is normative and
the female is a deviation from the norm (Deaux & Kite, 1993). Finding no
difference in a study may even cause a researcher to file the study's results
away in a file drawer because the researcher believes it has little chance for

publication (Rosenthal, 1979). One possible reason that so many early studies reported many gender differences may have been that, all too often, studies finding no differences were unceremoniously put away and forgotten in researchers' file drawers.

We must keep in mind that sex and gender are topics laden with value judgments, assumptions, and biases. Even when there are "large" gender differences, the differences within each sex are larger than the differences between women and men. Researchers may want to announce their particular biases openly so that others may know right from the start what those biases are. This approach will be our next issue for discussion.

The Study of Gender: Sharing Perspectives with Colleagues

Critical voices have been raised over the limitations of science's purported value-free orientation and its reliance solely on certain supposedly objective methods (Halpern, 1995; Landrine, Klonoff, & Brown-Collins, 1995; Rabinowitz & Sechzur, 1993). A major assertion is that science, rather than being value free as it professes, is really value laden. If scientists' research contains an unstated value system or biased viewpoint, they should state it openly so that others could judge its findings for what they are—a biased view of the world. Others may then choose to accept or reject its findings. If rejected, the critics then have a responsibility to come up with an alternative approach. Barbara Wallston (reported by Wallston & Grady, 1985) typically provided a section describing herself and her own biases in her review articles so that the reader could evaluate her conclusions.

In this section we will first examine the unstated or implicit biases embedded in a strictly defined, empirically based, scientific study of gender. Next we will outline an alternative model, one with certain stated values and one that, in the words of Evelyn Fox Keller (1982, p. 589), may "carry a liberating potential for science."

Science: An Androcentric and Antifemale Institution

Science is embedded in a particular culturally influenced world view that often restrains and suppresses alternative or contrary world views (Kuhn, 1962). Science is no more immune from certain culturally influenced biases than any other social institution. Science is not simply a set of methods separate from the scientist. Rather, science is a dynamic process of inquiry growing out of the interaction between a culturally influenced scientist and the topic of her or his inquiry. Yet, many modern-day scientists believe their research is devoid of bias (value free) by virtue of their reliance solely on supposedly objective scientific methods. Even if science were value free—and it is not—there is no logical justification for believing knowledge acquired by its methods to be more valid than a value-laden approach (Kukla, 1982).

The question remains, what culturally influenced value system or set of biases can be singled out as infusing the so-called value-free science? Our contention is that science is deeply embedded with our culture's all-pervasive antifeminine and androcentric world views.

Even the language typically used in experimental procedures conveys the masculine-biased nature of the field. Terms like *subject, manipulate,* and *control* imply dominance, status, and power on the part of the researcher while placing the participant in a subordinate position. DeFour and Paludi (1988) reported that it is important to avoid the use of value-laden language so as not to legitimize negative stereotyping of ethnic minority women. For example, the labels used to describe various lifestyle choices depends on the socioeconomic class and/or ethnicity of the individual being discussed. Unmarried black mothers have been described in the context of a "broken home," while single white mothers have been frequently discussed in the context of an "alternative" or "contemporary" lifestyle.

Woman can be thought of as one from whom *man* must separate if he is to develop a sense of his own personhood (Chodorow, 1978; Dinnerstein, 1976). Furthermore, *woman* has become a personification or embodiment of nature (e.g., "mother nature"), which man seeks to control. We may infer that to control nature is to control woman. Keller (1982) makes just this point:

> *To see the emphasis on power and control so prevalent in the rhetoric of Western science as projection of a specifically male consciousness requires no great leap of the imagination. Indeed, that perception has become a commonplace. Above all, it is invited by the rhetoric that conjoins the domination of nature with the insistent image of nature as female, nowhere more familiar than in the writings of Francis Bacon. For Bacon, knowledge and power are one, and the promise of science is expressed as "leading to you Nature with all her children to bind her to your service and make her your slave," by means that do not "merely exert a gentle guidance over nature's course; they have the power to conquer and subdue her, to shake her to her foundations."* (p. 598)

Underneath science's goal of the ultimate domination of nature and its ("her"?) erratic forces lies the antifemale bias and a male-as-normative, or androcentric, world view.

Science's antifeminine bias is not only found in the rhetoric of early scientists like Bacon; it can be found in more recent views about women's and men's natures and in the way in which scientific findings have been used to justify the so-called natural order. For instance, Mary Brown Parlee (1975) charged the science of psychology with furnishing support for many of society's antifemale practices. She notes that "the body of 'knowledge' developed by academic psychologists happened (apparently) to support stereotyped beliefs about the abilities and psychological characteristics of women and men, and such beliefs happen to support existing political, legal, and economic inequalities between the sexes" (p. 124).

Further, economist Julie A. Nelson (1996a & b) argues that the "objective" field of economics contains a masculine-biased view of reality. She writes:

> *[F]ar from guaranteeing objectivity, the current definition of economics reflects deep-seated, gender-related biases. Defining economics as the study—using techniques based in mathematics—of rational choices made by autonomous individuals assumes views of human identity and of the nature of knowledge that are closely linked to our culture's notions of masculinity.* (1996a, p. B3)

Journalist Susan Faludi (1991) also outlined several ways the popular culture (media in particular) has produced images of women that are misleading and harmful and produce a "backlash." Her main message is that social science research about women's issues is slanted to make it appear that women have achieved equality with men and that this equality is not worth the price in terms of their relationships with men, children, and their colleagues at work:

> *The truth is that the last decade has seen a powerful counter-assault on women's rights, a backlash, an attempt to retract the handful of small and hard-won victories that the feminist movement did manage to win for women. This counter-assault is largely insidious: in a kind of pop-culture version of the Big Lie, it stands the truth boldly on its head and proclaims that the very steps that have elevated women's position have actually led to their downfall.* (p. xviii)

Faludi cited several news stories: the "man shortage" that caused women not to marry and the sharp decline of women's opportunities to marry after age 30, the "infertility epidemic" that affects professional women who postpone childbearing, the depression and burnout that affects career women and never-married women, and the devastating economic impact of divorce on women compared with men. All of these "facts," however, were based on single research studies that were subsequently shown to be seriously flawed or entirely incorrect. Reputable research on these issues, however, received little or no media attention.

Furthermore, science can be thought of as a nearly all-male club with a sign at its entrance that states boldly, "Women not welcome" (Walsh, 1977). The number of women who have been allowed entrance into the various natural and social sciences is small compared to the percentage of women in the population. Throughout history, women who sought knowledge have been cast as evil incarnate (Eve's eating from the tree of knowledge) or as witches seeking alchemy's secrets (Garrett, 1977). In the last century, women stood on the periphery of science (Kohlstedt, 1978), and in this century, few have made it into science's august inner circle of influential policy makers (Russo, 1984).

In the late 1960s, women organized in psychology and formed the Association for Women in Psychology in 1969. The Division of the Psychology of Women in the American Psychological Association was formed in 1973 "to promote the research and study of women . . . to encourage the integration of this information about women with current psychological knowledge and beliefs in order to apply the gained knowledge to the society and its institutions" (Russo, 1984). The Committee on Women in Psychology was formed in 1973. The goal of this committee was to "function as a catalyst, by means of interacting with and making recommendations to the various parts of the Association's governing structures . . ." (Russo, 1984).

The American Psychological Association today also includes divisions on the Psychological Study of Lesbian and Gay Issues and the Society for the Psychological Study of Ethnic Minority Issues. Divisions on women's issues exist in most professional organizations today (e.g., the American Medical Association, American Educational Research Association, and the Modern Language Association).

Science's androcentric bias finds still further expression with the omission of the female-as-participant from study, as we have discussed earlier. Male researchers may have had many "logical" reasons for this exclusionary policy in human research, but finding that "virtually all of the animal-learning research on rats has been performed with male rats" (Keller, 1982, p. 591) seems ludicrous and more than a little telling of a male bias against female participants that extends even to the animals. Such a selection bias favoring males can be explained by an implicit, if not explicit, bias that many male scientists have toward viewing the male-as-normative for all species. Within the biological sciences, such male bias may explain why biological constructs and theories have a peculiarly male slant.

A number of male-oriented academic/professional associations have begun openly to challenge androcentric assumptions within academia and various professions. For instance, the American Psychological Association's newly formed Division 51 ("The Society for the Psychological Study of Men and Masculinity") encourages psychological researchers to study men not as humanity's norm but rather as psychological individuals shaped by the same historical, social, and cultural influences that influence women (see Levant & Pollack, 1995).

Another organization founded in 1992, the American Men's Studies Association, is a multidisciplinary group of academics and professionals who, among their many stated goals, seek "to develop methodologies [for] the study of masculinities, from an ethical perspective which eschews oppression in all forms (namely, sexism, racism, homophobia, anti-Semitism)" (excerpted from the American Men's Studies Association's Mission Statement). Time will tell if these and other professional men's organizations will succeed in reducing, if not eliminating, the androcentric bias found within most academic disciplines.

A Feminist-Oriented Social Science: An Alternative

Several social scientists have called for a new value-laden approach—a feminist orientation that will eliminate the androcentric and antifemale biases from the study of gender (Denmark, 1994; Rabinowitz & Sechzur, 1993). Feminist research insists that the researcher become actively involved in the research process. It is not enough to simply administer more tests or introduce more participants; rather, the researcher must constantly ask herself or himself the question: "How does that which I propose to do reflect my own experiences in the real world, the world of my own experiences?" Such questions and attention to one's own experiences can lead to further refinements of the methods or design of the study. For example, before interacting with research participants, a feminist-oriented psychologist may ask herself or himself how she or he would feel on the other end of the investigation. "What would I feel or experience if I were asked to do this task?" Furthermore, by asking questions of the research participants during and after the study, one can gain additional information that might have been missed. Above all, the feminist researcher is not detached from the investigation but rather becomes an integral part of the whole research procedure.

Feminist research also emphasizes the ways that information gained from the research can be used to help the participants themselves. Overall, research should prove helpful, certainly not harmful, to those who share themselves with the researcher (Rabinowitz & Sechzur, 1993).

McHugh and colleagues (1986) and Florence Denmark and colleagues (1988) have offered suggestions for nonsexist research, including interpreting without bias, avoiding excessive confidence in traditional methods, and examining explanatory models. These suggestions, presented in box 1-2, provide the beginnings for an alternative approach to the study of human behavior. First and foremost, research is viewed as taking place within a well-defined cultural and social context, never totally free from the concerns and values of the larger society.

Halpern (1995) has provided researchers with a set of recommendations when planning, reading, and interpreting research. Among these recommendations:

Are main effects being moderated by unidentified interactions? For example, is the main effect of gender or ethnicity really the effect of socioeconomic status on gender or ethnicity? Would the effects of gender, for example, change if different age groups had been included as subjects? What other variables are confounded with gender and ethnicity? For example, African Americans in the United States take fewer college preparatory courses in high school than White students. Given the confounding of these variables, would at least part of the differences that are found be attributable to differential course-taking patterns?

Were tests of significance followed with effect size statistics? Were results that were not in accord with the researcher's worldview labeled as "small" and those that were in accord with the researcher's worldview described as "large" when they were, in fact, quite similar in size?

Are you careful to distinguish between research results and interpretations of research results? For example, the finding that women and men show different patterns of scores on the SATs does not necessarily mean

Box 1-2

Suggestions for Nonsexist Research

These suggestions for sex-fair research are from Maureen McHugh and colleagues.

Avoiding excessive confidence in traditional methods:

Carefully examine the underlying values and assumptions in all research and state them explicitly.

Encourage the use of alternative and nonexperimental research methodologies directed toward exploration, detailed description, and theory generation as well as experimental and quasi-experimental approaches designed for hypothesis testing.

Engage in ongoing debate about the strengths and weaknesses of all research techniques, focusing attention on the capacities and limitations of experimental and nonexperimental research as procedures for studying processes and systems and for permitting generalizations to particular contexts.

When undertaking literature reviews, examine past research for both methodological rigor and unexamined sexism in procedure or interpretation.

Be aware of factors other than methodological soundness that may influence the publishability or distribution of results.

Remember that the convergence of established findings with experience and the convergence of results based on different methods add to their credibility; divergence should prompt renewed study.

Examining exploratory models:

Exercise care in the terminology employed to describe or explain results in order to avoid (a) confusing sex with gender, (b) confusing description with explanation, and (c) reducing complex or interactionist explanations to overly simple ones.

Consider all possible explanations for sex-related phenomena, including social-cultural, biological, and situational factors.

Consider alternative explanations even if they have not been investigated.

Recognize that many consistently demonstrated sex-related behaviors may result from either consistent and pervasive cultural factors or biological factors. Often empirical tests differentiating competing explanations are unavailable.

Become aware of, consider, and devise studies of alternative and more complex models of causation.

More detailed models that incorporate and specify relationships involving both physiological and sociocultural variables.

Increased effort toward developing common terminologies and providing more elaborate tests of competing explanatory models.

Equal emphasis in publication to findings of "sex similarities," rather than biasing journal policy toward findings of "sex differences."

Source: McHugh et al., "Issues to Consider in Conducting Nonsexist Psychological Research: A Guide for Researchers," *American Psychologist,* 41:879–890, 1986. Copyright © 1986, American Psychological Association, Arlington, VA.

that there are gender ability differences. All it does mean is at this time and with this test, there are "on the average" between-gender differences. Results of this sort indicate nothing about the cause of the differences.
*Have you maintained an amiable skepticism? Do you scrutinize new research carefully and require independent replications before you are willing to place too much faith in the findings? (pp. 88–89)

As Alice Eagly (1995) commented:

Contemporary psychology has produced a large amount of research revealing that behavior is sex differentiated to varying extents. The knowledge produced in this area of science can be beneficial both in helping women and men to understand their natures and their society and in suggesting ways to enhance gender equality. (p. 155)

An Invitation to Study Sex and Gender

A feminist perspective urges one to be wary of any viewpoint "that makes unwarranted claims to be the sole source of truth" (Unger, 1983, p. 26). Thus, we will begin our discussion by examining from several different perspectives the dynamic interweave between sex and gender, noting cultural concerns and issues. We will initially discuss biological sex similarities and sex differences (chapter 2). After birth, we begin to develop psychologically; one of the more important psychological features of our personality is our view of ourselves in terms of femininity and masculinity (chapter 3). We are not born in isolation, nor do we develop without others' help. Parents, teachers, and peers help to shape us in the ways that society believes essential (chapter 4). And last, the culture we are born into reinforces certain values and rules that also influence how women and men will live out their lives in terms of their gender roles (chapter 5).

After discussing the various perspectives and their views of sex and gender, we will discuss several social institutions that help to shape our views of what women and men should be like. We will start by examining the issue of power on the individual level (chapter 6). Next, we will cover several specific social institutions, such as language (chapter 7), education and work (chapter 8), religion and politics (chapter 9), and the health field (chapter 10), to see their influences on gender.

In our last chapter we will discuss the women's and men's movements and address issues that many think will shape our thinking about gender in the near future (chapter 11).

Summary

Sex and gender are two of the most fascinating features of the human experience. As defined in this chapter, sex pertains to certain reproductive structures, hormones, and physical characteristics that exist along a continuum ranging from extreme femaleness to extreme maleness. Gender refers to those social psychological features associated with the status of either female or male. Many people have misconceptions about sex and gender. For example, they believe that sex and gender represent two mutually exclusive and unchangeable categories.

All of us have certain personal biases that can influence our view of the world around us. Personal biases are noteworthy when discussing sex and gender. Three types of bias are especially prominent: scientific, researcher, and publication. Sex and gender are topics laden with value judgments. Even when there are "large" gender differences, the differences within each sex are larger than the differences between men and women.

Traditional science is presented as being value free and thus a more valid way of studying our world. However, traditional science, especially the social sciences, is not value free and, in fact, is influenced by certain androcentric and antifemale biases. Several researchers have called for a feminist-oriented approach to the study of gender, which challenges the male-dominated sciences to look at the world in a new way, one that among other goals incorporates girls' and women's perspectives and gives respect to their ethnicity, race, sexual orientation, age, and socioeconomic class.

Suggested Readings

Eagly, A. (1995). The science and politics of comparing women and men. *American Psychologist, 50,* 145–158.

Hyde, J. S., & Frost, L. A. (1993). Meta-analysis in the psychology of women. In F. L. Denmark & M. A. Paludi (Eds.), *Psychology of women: A handbook of issues and theories.* Westport, CT: Greenwood Press.

Landrine, H., Klonoff, E., & Brown-Collins, A. (1995). Cultural diversity and methodology in feminist psychology: Critique, proposal, empirical example. In H. Landrine (Ed.), *Bringing cultural diversity to feminist psychology: Theory, research and practice.* Washington, DC: American Psychological Association.

Lorber, J. (1994). *Paradoxes of gender.* New Haven, CT: Yale University Press.

Rabinowitz, V. C., & Sechzur, J. A. (1993). Feminist perspectives on research methods. In F. L. Denmark & M. A. Paludi (Eds.), *Psychology of women: A handbook of issues and theories.* Westport, CT: Greenwood Press.

2

The Biological Perspective

The French say vive la difference, facetiously applauding the differences between the sexes. Unfortunately, la difference has lost something in translation, and has been interpreted as implying an unfavorable comparison with men in the intrinsic value of the female and in her value to society. In order to use biology to support the premise of the inferiority of women to men, the physiological attributes common to the human species have been ignored or minimized and the differences between the sexes have been exaggerated and misrepresented.

Anne M. Briscoe

What's Your Opinion?

Do you believe that good health is the most important thing in your life?
Would you do whatever it takes to look better?
What are the major health problems you believe women and men face today?
What recommendations can you make for women and men to learn more
   about their physical health?
What do you believe are the major health problems of minority women and
   men?

Even the most casual observer can see that women and men differ. They look, move, and sometimes even act differently. Many people believe the differences make for a more interesting world, proclaiming, "Vive la difference!" It's not enough, however, to note that women and men differ. Rather, by how much, in what areas, and more important, why do they differ? Looking at women and men from a biological perspective can afford us with much valuable information.

In this chapter we will begin our discussion of biology by briefly noting why the biological perspective remains controversial. We then will focus on the prenatal period. Chromosomes and hormones play a large part in shaping our physical makeup, and we need to be aware of their contributions. Next, we will describe sex similarities and differences across the life span. We will also examine hormones and behavior. And, we will discuss one of the more controversial topics in this area, namely, sociobiology.

The Politics of Biology

Why should there be such a struggle between those dedicated to explaining sex and gender differences? The debate over biology (nature) and cultural forces (nurture) seems to intensify when, according to Ann Oakley (1972), "the existing roles and statuses of male and female are changing." Certainly, women's and men's statuses and roles have been changing in the last several years. Thus, we shouldn't be too surprised that the nature-nurture debate seems to be at fever pitch nowadays.

Another reason for the continuing controversy is that, historically, biology has been used to defend the so-called "natural order" of certain social systems. For instance, during the Middle Ages, gross injustices and oppression were justified by what was called "the divine right of kings." Many proclaimed the naturalness of these systems with their inequities, stating that nature deemed that some had the right to oppress others. Today, we are becoming aware that many in the past used biological differences to keep women in a subordinate and powerless position.

As a matter of record, during the last century and into the early part of this century, biological differences were used to rationalize women's unequal status in society. About 100 years ago, for instance, it was commonly believed that a woman's "fragile" nature required her to be protected, that a woman's menses destined her to periodic bouts of uncontrolled emotions, and that her small brain limited her intellectual horizons. Consequently, women were prevented from pursuing certain professions such as medicine or law, were not allowed to vote, and were subjected to numerous other restrictions all by virtue of their "fragile" biology (see chapter 8). Furthermore, because women gave birth, most believed they were forever destined for child raising as well as household duties. Even when early researchers found women superior to men in certain abilities (e.g., verbal abilities), little was made of such talents. An even more blatant use of a biological principle employed against women was the *variability hypothesis* (Shields, 1975, 1982. Also see chapter 3).

Stemming from Darwin's theory of evolution, the variability hypothesis stated that the more varied and widespread a species' behaviors, skills, and talents were, the more likely that species was to survive and develop. In other words, a species that possessed wide-ranging and adaptive abilities was more likely to survive and pass on its genes than a species whose abilities were more restricted or more rigidly expressed. Those who applied the variability hypothesis to humans thought that men, as a rule, showed more variability in their abilities than women showed. For example, one reason given for the greater number of men geniuses throughout history was men's greater intellectual variability. Men, according to this line of reasoning, were thought to be naturally predisposed to greater heights of intellectual achievements (and greater deficits as well, though that was never discussed) than women, whose achievements were limited—neither gifted nor retarded—to a more narrowly defined range of intellectual endeavors. If women were constrained by their lack of great intellectual achievements, they had little need or reason for more than a cursory or basic education. This is only one example of a supposed biological difference used to prevent women from gaining educational opportunities equal to those of men. It is not surprising, then, that biology and biological principles have taken on a controversial air in the discussion of sex and gender differences.

We should also note that there has been criticism of the methodology and reporting of research on the biology of sex and gender differences. Many studies dealing with brain development or hormone function have been done on animal populations and the results generalized to humans (Goy, 1978; Phoenix, 1978). In some research studies, average differences are likely to be statistically significant even when the differences themselves are quite small (see chapter 1). Furthermore, researchers have tended to overemphasize biological causation and neglect the importance of cultural values on physical functioning, such as the impact of religious views. The search for biological underpinnings of girls' and women's behavior are frequently interpreted as an attempt to set unchangeable limits on their opportunities. On the other hand, attempts to explain all of girls' and women's traits in terms of environmental factors may be seen as a denial of the genetic realities of human behavior. Obviously, an understanding of both the biological concomitants of female and male behavior and the external influences on that behavior are necessary for a psychology of sex and gender.

Prenatal Events and Sex Differences

The *prenatal period* of development is the time elapsing between conception and birth. It averages about 266 days, or 280 days from the last menstrual period (see discussion below). The prenatal period is divided into three stages: the germinal period, embryonic period, and fetal period.

The *germinal period* is characterized by the growth of the zygote and the establishment of a linkage between the zygote and the woman's support system. The *embryonic period* lasts from the end of the second week to the eighth week. This period is characterized by rapid growth, the establishment of a placental relationship with the woman, and the early structural appearance of all major organs. Development begins with the brain and head areas and then works its way down the body. This growth trend is referred to as *cephalocaudal development*. The cells in the central portion of the embryo thicken and form a ridge that is referred to as the *primitive streak*. This streak divides the embryo into right and left halves and becomes the spinal cord. The tissues grow in opposite directions away from the axis of the primitive streak. This growth trend is referred to as *proximodistal development*.

The *fetal period* begins with the ninth week and ends with birth. This period is characterized by the continuous development of major organ systems. The organs also assume their specialized functions.

Determination of sexual characteristics begins at conception. When a woman's ovum (the female reproductive cell with 23 single chromosomes) is

Prenatal
Development

© Lennart Nilsson, *A Child
Is Born,* Dell Publishing

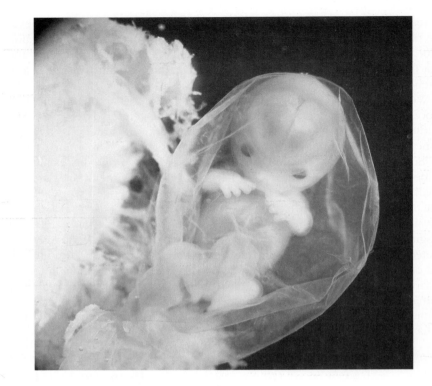

fertilized by a sperm cell (the male reproductive cell with 23 single chromosomes), the result is expected to produce the characteristic human cell with a total of 46 chromosomes (23 pairs). Of these pairs only one pair, "the sex chromosomes," controls the genetic sex of the child (Rathus, 1988). The woman's ovum possesses an X chromosome for sex, while the man's sperm cell may contain an X or Y. When an X-bearing sperm cell fertilizes the X-bearing ovum, the genetic pattern is established for a female (XX). When a Y-bearing sperm cell fertilizes the X-bearing ovum, the genetic pattern is established for a male (XY). This explanation of the development of sexual characteristics allows one to conclude that the male sperm cell controls the sex of the offspring and that chromosomes are the determinants of sexual characteristics. While these conclusions are basically correct, other factors may mediate the outcome: female viability and hormonal factors in sex development.

Female Viability

The environment through which the sperm cell must pass to reach the ovum must be considered a factor in sex determination (Rathus, 1988). Genetic researchers have found that the X-bearing sperm appear more viable than the Y-bearing sperm. Women who conceive during times when their vaginal environment is likely to be strongly acidic are more likely to produce girls. This suggests that a strongly acidic environment is detrimental to the Y-bearing sperm.

Hormonal Factors

While the chromosomal pairing of XX or XY occurs in most cases, anomalies in which too many or too few chromosomes connect result in physical differences. The female pattern of development is the standard. While male development needs the secretion of male hormones from the testes to stimulate the growth and development of the male reproductive system (approximately the sixth week), female development occurs spontaneously, even in the absence of ovaries and their hormonal secretions (Money, 1987).

Adrenogenital syndrome is a hormonal abnormality. This condition seriously affects genetically normal female fetuses. The adrenogenital syndrome can have several causes. First, some women develop tumors on their ovaries or on their adrenal glands that in turn produce a surplus of androgens. If such a condition develops during pregnancy, some excessive androgen may reach a female fetus via the bloodstream. A second cause may be the fetus' own adrenal cortices. Normally, a fetus's adrenal glands produce a hormone called cortisol, which is similar to an androgen. Some female fetuses have a defective adrenal cortex that produces an abundance of cortisol, which can affect its body much like an androgen. Finally, during the 1940s and 1950s, many women with histories of miscarriages were prescribed a synthetic drug (progestin) that affected female fetuses much like androgen. Thus, some female fetuses have suffered the masculinizing consequences of being exposed either naturally or medically to an overdose of androgen or androgenlike chemicals during fetal development.

The outcome and extent of adrenogenital syndrome depends on the amount of the androgen substance in the fetus' bloodstream and the time at which exposure occurs, leading to various degrees of masculinization of the external sex structures. The external genitalia of the female appear masculine despite the XX chromosomal pair. These girls may be labeled and raised as boys. Although surgical procedures may be necessary at puberty to facilitate development as a boy, these individuals will adjust to the sex designation they were given at birth (Money & Tucker, 1975).

Psychologists Susan Baker and Anke Ehrhardt have conducted several studies on girls with adrenogenital syndrome (Baker & Ehrhardt, 1978; Ehrhardt & Baker, 1978). The adrenogenital girls observed in these studies were all treated soon after birth with cortisol, which prevented further masculinization of their bodies and allowed them to develop normal female secondary sex characteristics. Boys can also be classified as adrenogenital when they are exposed to extremely high androgen levels before birth (Ehrhardt & Baker, 1978).

Androgen-insensitivity syndrome is an abnormal hormonal condition affecting a genetic male and is caused by an X-linked, recessive condition. Because the fetal gonads develop as testes, the Mullerian-inhibiting substance prevents the development of internal female sex structures. However, the androgens produced by the testes do little if anything to foster the development of a male's internal or external sex structures because these tissues, for some yet unknown reason, do not respond to the masculinizing effects of the androgens. But the small amounts of estrogen produced by the testes are able to stimulate female sex characteristics such as a vaginal opening. Consequently, at birth, most of these individuals have what appears to be external female sex structures.

If this condition is not noticed at birth or shortly thereafter, these infants will be labeled as girls and, more than likely, accept the prescribed feminine gender role behavior (Money & Ehrhardt, 1972). Because they lack the internal sex structures of the female, however, they will not menstruate. Thus, the person who suffers from the androgen-insensitivity syndrome is a genetic male who usually grows up as a female because the embryonic sex tissues did not respond to the masculinizing effects of androgens.

These hormonal abnormalities show the dramatic influence that androgens have on either a male or female fetus. Without androgen and its masculinizing effect, or if the body's sex tissues are immune or insensitive to androgen, the fetus will develop as a female. If, somehow, excessive amounts of androgen or other androgenlike substances happen to occur during the female fetus' development, she will have varying degrees of masculinization of her sex tissues. The key issue in all of these conditions is that androgens, especially testosterone, play a pivotal role in the development of the internal and external sex structures.

The results of studies of individuals with abnormal genetic or hormonal conditions clearly indicate that biological factors are necessary but not sufficient to produce the characteristics that we attribute to sex. Even in the prenatal period there appears an interaction between physical and social conditions, which will be repeated again and again.

Sex Chromosomal Abnormalities

In the prenatal stage of development, as throughout life, there is an interaction between social and physical conditions. The sex chromosomes' contribution to fetal development is also important. To learn more about the effects sex chromosomes have on the physical structures, we will now turn our attention to three abnormal chromosome patterns: Turner's syndrome, Klinefelter's syndrome, and the double-Y syndrome.

Turner's Syndrome

In approximately 1 in every 10,000 infant girls an abnormal sex chromosome pattern is found in which the second female sex chromosome is either defective or missing (Hamerton et al., 1975). This condition is referred to as *Turner's syndrome*. Since it is the second sex chromosome that directs the development of the gonadal tissue into either functioning ovaries or testes, girls with Turner's syndrome always develop a female body with either underdeveloped ovaries or no ovaries whatsoever. Consequently, they will not menstruate at adolescence, nor will they develop breasts. Their bodies do not produce the estrogen necessary for the development of secondary sex characteristics during adolescence.

Administration of estrogen will contribute to breast growth. In addition, an artificial menstrual cycle may be produced by administering estrogen for three weeks followed by one week without this treatment (Golub, 1992). This treatment has been reported to be beneficial for girls' self-esteem and self-concept (Ehrhardt & Meyer-Bahlberg, 1975).

Girls with Turner's syndrome usually have a short stature, a weblike configuration around the neck, eyelid folds, and a rather broad or shieldlike chest (Money & Granoff, 1965). Also, they show little or no impairment in intellectual ability; some even have IQs significantly above normal (Money, 1964).

Klinefelter's Syndrome

One type of sex chromosomal abnormality results from a surplus of sex chromosomes. For example, there can be too many X or Y chromosomes. We will first discuss those boys with a surplus of Xs (either 47, XXY, or 48, XXXY), who have what is called *Klinefelter's syndrome*. Approximately 1 or 2 out of every 1,000 infant boys have Klinefelter's syndrome (Hamerton et al., 1975). Boys with Klinefelter's syndrome are usually taller than average and appear rather gangling because of their long arms and legs. During adolescence, their chests usually take on a female-like appearance by becoming larger than normal. Their testes are infertile and produce abnormally small amounts of testosterone (Money & Ehrhardt, 1972).

1 or 2/1,000

Boys with Klinefelter's syndrome usually have some impairment in intellectual functioning, and many are classified as mentally retarded. In prison populations, men with Klinefelter's syndrome have been found in greater numbers than expected by chance alone. However, this finding may be attributed to their committing more minor crimes and getting arrested more often rather than to some genetic predilection for criminal activity (Witkin et al., 1976).

The Double-Y Syndrome

Approximately 1 of every 1,000 infant boys has one or more extra Y chromosomes, which is designated as the *double-Y syndrome* (Hamerton et al., 1975). In adulthood, these men are taller than even men with Klinefelter's syndrome. Other than their above-average height, few other obvious physical features set these men off from chromosomally normal men (Owen, 1972). A major psychological feature of the double-Y man, however, is a marked increase in his impulsivity and lack of tolerance for frustration (Nielsen & Christensen, 1974). Intellectually, he shows a slightly below-average overall ability (Witkin et al., 1976).

1/1000

The issue that first caught the public's attention with respect to the double-Y syndrome was the much publicized research that found these men in greater numbers in prison populations than would be predicted by chance alone (Jacobs et al., 1965). The press highlighted this, and soon the public was convinced that the extra Y chromosome somehow predisposed such men to a life of violence and crime. However, the relationship between the extra Y and criminality has proved tenuous. In fact, male prisoners with an extra Y have less violent criminal histories than genetically normal male prisoners (Witkin et al., 1976). Rather than indicting the extra Y chromosome as the cause of violent and criminal behavior, it makes just as much sense to point to the fact that the XYY male's greater impulsivity and excitability, coupled with frequent emotional outbursts, may contribute to many of these men committing crimes. Their psychological profile, rather than their genetic abnormality, may be the more important factor (Noel et al., 1974).

Infancy and Childhood

Boys are more vulnerable to most every type of physical disease, environmental insult, and developmental difficulty (Jacklin, 1989). Approximately 125 boys are conceived for every 100 girls. By the end of the prenatal period, however, there is a significant loss of male concepti: The ratio of boys to girls is 106 to 100 (Strickland, 1988).

In addition, females experience fewer difficulties during the birth process and consequently, fewer birth defects. Carol Nagy Jacklin and Eleanor Maccoby (1982) reported that even in unproblematic deliveries, the births of girls are on average an hour shorter than the deliveries of boys. This shortened length of labor has been correlated with fewer problems in infancy. Girls are thus more viable than boys.

Research has supported this greater *female viability* even after birth. For example, women have an overall life expectancy that surpasses men at every decade of life, regardless of race (Jacklin, 1989; Strickland, 1988). Girls have fewer congenital disorders, are less likely to succumb to *sudden infant death syndrome* (the death, while sleeping, of apparently healthy infants who cease breathing for unknown medical reasons), and are less prone to hyperactivity (Rathus, 1988). All of these findings suggest genetically determined strength.

Infant girls are more mature at birth than are infant boys. Girls have more advanced skeletal and neurological systems (Hutt, 1978; Rathus, 1983). Girls continue to mature between 2 and 2.5 years faster than boys. Their skeletal development at birth is approximately one month ahead of boys'. Development for boys and girls follows the cephalocaudal principle and proximodistal principles. Growth thus progresses from the head region to the trunk and then the leg region. Motor development also follows the cephalocaudal principal. Infants learn to control the muscles of their head and neck, then their arms and abdomen, and finally their legs. Thus, infants learn to hold their heads up before they can sit, and they learn to sit before they learn to walk. Infants' large muscle control develops before fine muscle control.

Height remains equal for both girls and boys until age seven, when girls are, on the average, taller than boys. This difference reverses at age 10. While, as a group, boys are physically stronger and weigh more than girls after puberty, there is considerable overlap. Many girls are physically stronger and weigh more than the average boy.

In early and middle childhood, boys are overrepresented among children who have speech, behavior, and learning disorders. Approximately twice as many boys than girls exhibit articulatory errors; three times as many boys as girls stutter (Bentzen, 1963). In addition, the incidence of reading problems is almost five times more prevalent in boys than in girls (Knopf, 1979). Mental retardation is higher among boys than girls. And, more boys than girls are autistic and hyperactive.

No consistent differences have been observed in the average of onset of certain developmental tasks, e.g., eruption of teeth, walking, sitting up, or thumb-and-forefinger grasping. Many studies report sex as a factor in performance of motor tasks, but they frequently give the advantage to boys. This assignment of advantage contradicts the fact that girls have more accelerated physical development. It is illogical that biological acceleration may be given as an explanation of girls' rapid acquisition of language skills (Maccoby & Jacklin, 1974) and their ability to excel in fine motor skills, while an expectation of inferior performance in gross motor activities remains. Sandra Bem (1981) concluded that differences in motor performance appear to be influenced by both biological and environmental factors. The low expectations that parents and teachers have with respect to girls' motor performance, in addition to the lack of rewards given to girls for such activities, apparently combine to produce low motivation and low performance levels for girls in the behaviors that have been societally defined as appropriate for boys (see chapters 3 and 4).

Adolescence and Early Adulthood

The period of adolescence is marked by changes in physical development that are part of the passage from childhood to adulthood. These physical changes occur during the stage of development referred to as *pubescence,* which is the period of rapid growth that culminates in *puberty,* or sexual maturity and reproductive capacity.

Pubescence technically begins when the *hypothalamus* (part of the upper brain stem) signals the pituitary gland to release the hormones known as *gonadotrophins*. This usually occurs during girls' and boys' sleep a year or so before any of the physical changes associated with pubescence appear (Schowalter & Anyan, 1981). The obvious physical differences among adolescents of identical chronological age underscore an endocrinological issue: the hypothalamus does not signal the pituitary to release the gonadotrophins at the same time in every adolescent. The exact factors that activate the hypothalamus are not determined. However, researchers (e.g., Frisch, 1984; Katchadorian, 1977; Tanner, 1962) have argued that the hypothalamus monitors adolescents' body weight and releases the necessary hormones when the body is of sufficient weight. In the United States, the age when puberty is reached has steadily decreased with the trend now leveling off. Most adolescent girls in the United States begin pubescence at approximately 11 years of age and reach the end of their growth by 17. Their growth spurt starts between 9.5 and 14.5 years. Girls grow fastest in height and weight at approximately 12 years of age. They reach 98 percent of their adult height at 16.25 years. Girls typically mature on the average of two years earlier than boys. As a group, boys are physically stronger, are taller, and weigh more than girls after puberty.

During adolescence girls and boys undergo common physical changes. For example, their lymphatic tissues decrease in size; they lose vision due to rapid changes in eyes between the ages of 11 and 14, and their facial structures change during pubescence. Also, their hairline recedes and the facial bones mature in such a way that the chin and nose become prominent. Adolescents' weight nearly doubles during pubescence; girls weigh 25 pounds less than boys as a result of their lower proportion of muscle to fat tissue. There is considerable overlap in the distributions, however (Petersen & Taylor, 1980). By the time they are 15, adolescents have lost 20 deciduous teeth. The number of bone masses during pubescence drops from approximately 350 to less than 220 as a result of epiphyseal unions (Petersen & Taylor, 1980).

Middle and Later Adulthood

Men's greater vulnerability holds true from conception to old age, and the death rate for American men is higher than that for women in every decade of life. Women have an overall life span expectancy that surpasses men at every age regardless of race (Klonoff, Landrine, & Scott, 1996).

Approximately 33 percent more boys than girls die in their first year of life. An equal sex ratio does not occur until 18 years of age, when 100 men are alive for every 100 women. However, the ratio steadily decreases throughout adulthood: By age 87, one man is alive for every two women (Williams, 1983). The life expectancy for women in the United States is 78.2 years; for men 70.9 years. Black women live longer (73.8 years) than both black men (64.8 years) and white men (71.4 years).

In adulthood, the mortality rates for men exceed those of women for most disorders, especially heart disease, malignancy, accidents, and chronic pulmonary disease (Strickland, 1988). Lung cancer surpasses breast cancer as the leading cause of cancer death for women. While more men than women die from pulmonary causes (perhaps because of the greater rate of smoking among men than women), there has been a leveling off in deaths of white men whereas for white and African American women and African American men there has been an increase (Klonoff, Landrine, & Scott, 1996). Smoking interacts with the use of oral contraceptives; consequently the risk of heart attack for women who use oral contraceptives increases 10 times if they smoke. Women have a higher death rate than men for strokes since they live longer and are thus more likely to suffer cerebral accidents.

Breast cancer is the second leading cause of cancer deaths among women between 35 and 55 years old. Cancer of the prostate accounts for 10 percent of the malignancies that occur for men.

In adulthood, the number of women with Alzheimer's disease is twofold to threefold that of afflicted men. In addition, women are more likely than men to be subject to chronic and disabling diseases, e.g., arthritis, rheumatism, hypertension, and diabetes.

The highest male-to-female death ratios occur for AIDS (approximately eight times more men than women), suicide (approximately four times more men), homicide (three times more men), accidents (twice as many men), and chronic liver diseases (twice as many men).

Prevailing wisdom once held that as women participate in more male-populated (considered "high stress") careers, they would increase their chances of heart disease. However, research has indicated that women in executive career positions do not show a higher incidence of heart disease than women not in these positions (Haynes & Feinleib, 1980). Heart disease is more likely to be found among women in clerical or low-status jobs where they have poor or no support systems. Role strain is increased for women in low-income jobs with many child care demands and no assistance with housework. And, illness and poor health are more likely to be found among individuals of lower socioeconomic status.

Research does point to the negative effects of socialization practices of boys and men. Anxiety associated with conforming to the masculine gender role, including the emphasis on competitiveness and achievement, may lead to the development of compensatory behaviors that are hazardous to men's health: exhibitions of violence, smoking, excessive consumption of alcohol, drug abuse, risk-taking behavior. African American men in particular are vulnerable to physical illnesses and death (Klonoff, Landrine, & Scott, 1995). They may have inadequate access to affordable health care and suffer the added stress of racism. African American males have higher rates of infant mortality, low birth weight, sickle cell anemia, nonfatal and fatal accidents, elevated blood pressure, and sexually transmitted diseases. Among African American men homicide is the leading cause of death.

Elizabeth Klonoff, Hope Landrine, and Judith Scott (1995) pointed out that across many cultures with different stressors men still die earlier and have a greater incidence of chromosomal abnormalities than do women. A biological predisposition seems to interact with cultural factors to make men more physically vulnerable than women. Research does suggest that female hormones may be protective (Rodin & Ickovics, 1990; Travis, 1993). Girls' and women's ability to withstand infection may be transmitted via the X chromosome, or their lower metabolic rate may contribute to their viability.

Klonoff and colleagues (1995) also point out the need to continue to research the interface of sex and race in health psychology since this field has relatively ignored the problems of people of color in general and women of color in particular. As these authors argue:

> *Differences in beliefs, religion, foods, customs, traditional folk remedies, and so forth, all may have significant implications for research with minorities. When ethnicity is ignored, the potential role of these factors is therefore artificially obscured.* (p. 355)

Hormones and Behavior

Let's now proceed with our discussion of some of the effects that hormones have on certain behaviors.

Aggression

One of the most frequently mentioned gender differences is that boys and men are more aggressive than girls and women. Maccoby and Jacklin (1974) concluded that, "Aggression is related to levels of sex hormones and can be changed by experimental administration of these hormones" (p. 243). Let's review some of the research on men and see the relationship between aggression and testosterone.

The first correlational study between aggression and testosterone levels using a sample of men was conducted by Persky, Smith, and Basu (1971). Two groups of physically healthy men were selected for the study. The first group consisted of 18 college men between the ages of 17 and 28, and the second contained 15 men between the ages of 33 and 66. Each of the men took a battery of tests, including the Buss-Durkee Hostility Inventory, a paper-and-pencil test that asks the respondent to check off statements, such as the frequency of losing one's temper and getting into fights, that apply to himself. A significantly positive correlation was found between levels of testosterone and aggression scores among the younger men but not among the older ones. We could argue that aggression on a paper-and-pencil test is one thing, but what about the testosterone levels for those men who actually lose their tempers and get into fights?

In a study of prison inmates, Leo Kreuz and Robert Rose (1972) studied testosterone levels between those inmates who were classified as fighters and those classified as nonfighters. Interestingly, Kreuz and Rose found no difference between these two groups of men with respect to their testosterone levels, nor did they find a relationship between their testosterone levels and their scores on the Buss-Durkee Hostility Inventory. Others who have used different groups of men and different measures of aggression have found equivocal results, at best, between testosterone levels and male aggression (Doering et al., 1975; Persky et al., 1977; Tieger, 1980; Udry & Talbert, 1988).

In an extensive review of the literature on aggression and testosterone levels, Joseph Pleck (1981) remarked that:

> *Given the social importance of aggressive behavior, it is clear that research on its possible biological sources will continue to receive serious attention. At the present time, the evidence in animals for hormonal factors in male aggression is strong (albeit complex). But comparable evidence for human male aggression is much weaker and less consistent.* (p. 170)

We will also discuss aggression in chapter 6 when we address violence against women.

The Premenstrual Syndrome

Women's testosterone levels remain relatively stable, but their estrogen and progesterone levels show considerable fluctuation during their menstrual cycle. Menstruation occurs in most women between the ages of 12 and 45 or 50. Although menstruation is a normal feature of a woman's life, many ancient peoples believed a menstruating woman was unclean. Others believed the menstruating woman unfit to handle food or even dangerous to others' safety and well-being (Delaney et al., 1988). Today, few people think of menstruation or menstruating women as dangerous, but many view menstruation as hindering women from taking on certain responsibilities and being treated fairly in many situations. Karen Paige (1973) noted as much when she wrote:

> *Women, the old argument goes, are eternally subject to the whims and wherefores of their biological clocks. Their raging hormonal cycles make them emotionally unstable and intellectually unreliable. If women have second-class status, we are told, it is because they cannot control the implacable demands of that bouncing estrogen.* (p. 41)

Menstruation carries with it a burden of cultural beliefs, and stereotypes by many men and some women (Golub, 1992; Klonoff, Landrine, & Scott, 1996). In the last several decades a new element has been added to the issue of the menstruating woman, namely, *premenstrual syndrome* (*PMS*).

First described by an American physician (Frank, 1931), the premenstrual syndrome, or tension, as it was originally called, is thought to occur during the preceding week or two before the onset of menstruation. PMS's symptoms vary among women, but there seems to be a fairly consistent pattern among most who report suffering from PMS. The prevalent psychological symptoms are tension, depression, anxiety attacks, and irritability. Physical symptoms include headaches, backaches, fatigue, tenderness of the breasts, water retention, and cold sores (Hopson & Rosenfeld, 1984).

A considerable amount of controversy has surrounded the premenstrual syndrome. Researchers have failed to agree upon the characteristics of PMS (Golub, 1992; Parlee, 1993). The lack of a definition for PMS makes it difficult to investigate women's symptoms carefully. Furthermore, PMS is controversial because some experts report that all women experience the syndrome while others state that PMS doesn't even exist, that it is a myth. Both sides of this issue discriminate against women.

One attempt at defining PMS for research purposes was a conference at the National Institute of Mental Health in April 1983. The criteria agreed to at this conference were that there must be a change of at least 30 percent in the intensity of symptoms measured in days 5–10 of the cycle as compared with the premenstrual phase, and that these changes must be prospectively documented for at least two consecutive cycles.

Research does indicate that some women have mild to severe mood swings that are related to their menstrual cycles. However, certainly not all women experience PMS. The data simply demonstrate a correlation between cycle phase of hormone levels and mood. Thus, it is questionable to infer that hormones *cause* mood changes. We could just as well argue that the mood change associated with a woman's menstrual cycle "appears to be related . . . to a woman's current psychosocial experience and more enduring features of her psychological makeup such as attitudes about menstruation and personality factors" (Friedman, Hurt, Arnoff, & Clarkin, 1980, p. 726).

Jacklin (1989) summarized the literature on hormones and behavior in the following way:

> *A word of warning: Correlations between hormones and behavior are typically interpreted as cases in which the biological causes the psychological. It fits our predispositions to assume that hormones cause behavioral outcomes. The hormone system is an open system. Much more empirical work is needed before the direction of the causal arrows are understood.* (p. 130)

The causes of PMS are not clear nor agreed upon by most researchers. Some point to fluid retention, brain changes, or a decrease in progesterone levels during the premenstrual period as possible factors in negative moods (Dalton, 1964; Janowsky, Berens, & Davis, 1973). Others, however, point out that stress-producing social factors—being fired from one's job or getting a divorce, for example—may play a decisive role in PMS symptoms (Parlee, 1993). Whatever the causes for the premenstrual syndrome, few can deny that the culturally defined negative social attitudes about menstruation can seriously influence a woman's perceptions of her own bodily states.

Attitudes about Menstruating Women

Cultural factors contribute to mood shifts. For example, in many cultures and many religions, menstruating women are seen as unclean. The words of Leviticus 15:19–33 speak most clearly of this belief:

> *And if a woman have an issue, and her issue in her flesh be blood, she shall be put apart seven days: and whosoever toucheth her shall be unclean until the even.*

In this culture, many women may abstain from sexual intercourse during menstruation. Since all women have the same hormone cycles while the correlated psychological cycles are different, the latter must be influenced by cultural attitudes. Girls' and women's attitudes and feelings about menarche are most important.

Brook Gunn and Anne Petersen (1984) reported that adolescent girls who have such negative attitudes toward menstruation will experience the most depression and discomfort in their own menstrual cycles. Adolescent girls with the most liberal attitudes about gender roles and sexuality experience less menstrual pain than adolescent girls with more conservative attitudes. Research has also suggested that girls who reach menarche prior to age 12 feel the most "abnormal" about menstruation.

Many adults as well as media emphasize only the hygienic aspects of menstruation, thus perpetuating the belief that menstruation is unclean and should be hidden from others in an ashamed manner (Gunn & Petersen, 1984). Negative attitudes about menstruation have been found to be related to health problems. Adolescent girls, while attempting to rid their bodies of what they have been socialized to believe are unclean odors, will use vaginal deodorants, deodorized tampons, and douches. These products irritate their genital tissues and may create vaginal infections.

The importance of cultural factors on menstruation and the cease of menstruation is notable. For example, to what extent are "hot flashes" biologically mediated? One study (Beyene, 1986) investigated hot flashes in rural Mayan Indian women on the Yucatan peninsula and a group of rural Greek women on the island of Evia. It reported that 72.7% of the Greek menopausal and postmenopausal women reported hot flashes. However, the sole symptom of menopause identified by the Mayan women was the irregularity and eventual cessation of their menstrual periods. Thus, there may be cultural differences in what constitutes physical symptoms.

Sociobiology: A Brewing Storm in the Social Sciences

For some time now, there has been a battle over the issue of the relative importance of one's biology versus the impact of one's environment as determinants of human behavior. In the last several years, since the introduction of a new perspective on human social behavior called *sociobiology,* the debate has become especially strong.

Most will agree that our evolutionary heritage has played a significant role in the development of our human species. Some suggest that our early ancestors have more in common with us than many might think. Beatrix Hamburg (1978) suggested this when she wrote:

> *The evolution of human behavior and its relation to social organization are best understood in the context of early man in the period of hunting-and-gathering societies. The best available information indicates that out of the roughly 2 million years that hominids have existed, over 99%*

*of this time has been spent in hunting-and-gathering societies. Agricul-
ture as a major way of life was instituted only 5,000 to 6,000 years ago.
The Industrial Revolution is a recent development of the last 100 years,
and only the most minute fraction of humans have lived in an industrial or technological society. Our biological heritage chiefly derives from
the era of man the hunter. The long period of man's existence in the
challenge of a hunting-and-gathering way of life has afforded the opportunity for those adaptations to become firmly established in the gene
pool. It has been postulated that our intelligence, interests, emotions,
and species-specific patterns of social interaction are all the evolutionary residue of the success of Homo sapiens in the hunting-and-gathering
adaptation. In effect, modern man carries essentially the same genetic
heritage as early man.* (p. 378)

Sociobiology has become an established alternative view for explaining
human social behavior (de Waal, 1996a & b). We will examine its tenets and
then some of the major criticisms directed against it.

The Case for Sociobiology

Edward Wilson (1978), a major proponent of sociobiology, defines this new
science as "the systematic study of the biological basis of all forms of social
behavior" (p. 16). In their attempt to understand the biological principles underlying social behaviors, sociobiologists draw data from several different
disciplines: genetics, anthropology, psychology, and sociology. Thus, sociobiology can be considered an interdisciplinary science.

Basically, sociobiologists believe that certain behaviors are inherited
through one's genes, much like one inherits skin color or hair texture. The
reason for certain behaviors having a genetic link is simply that these behaviors proved advantageous to the species' survival throughout the evolutionary period.

Sociobiologists, for example, believe that among early human groups,
when men banded together and dominated women, there was a greater likelihood of the group's survival and development to higher levels (Tiger, 1969;
Tiger & Fox, 1971). The key to sociobiology's view of social behavior is simply that certain social behaviors have "become genetically encoded in a
species if they contribute to the fitness of those individuals that have them"
(van den Berghe, 1978, p. 20).

With an eye to their genetic basis, several specific human social behaviors
have been examined, such as altruism, aggression, homosexuality, and even
ethics. One area that is especially interesting with respect to our preceding
discussion of gender differences is that of maternal or nurturant behaviors. A
common belief is that women are somehow predisposed to act more nurturant and have special feelings toward the young. In most societies we find
that women also act as the primary, if not the sole, caretaker of the newborn
infants. But is there anything preventing a man from taking over after birth

and performing many of the caretaking duties? Or are women directed by their genes or something called a "maternal instinct" after birth to continue their care of the young?

Anthropologist Lila Liebowitz (1989) argued that the early division of labor was molded by socioeconomic considerations, not biological imperatives:

> *The "common sense" explanation of the division of labor by sex that is usually offered is that it is related to differences in size and strength between early, proto-human women and men and to the lengthened "biological" dependency of the young. This implies that the sexual division of labor is protocultural and, therefore, "natural." But this notion does not bear up under close inspection. . . . Early hominids of both sexes, despite their difference in size after reaching sexual maturity, engaged in the same kinds of productive activities. Adult females just combined these activities with bearing and nursing the young.* (p. 3)

Sociologist Alice Rossi (1977) believes that biology plays a significant role in the development of a strong mother-infant bond. Rossi believes that, historically, women who have had a greater involvement with and in their children's growth are predisposed for such behaviors. Accordingly then, because men lack the biological bond with their offspring, they never develop the same attachment to the young. Rossi thinks that new mothers exhibit many responses toward their newborns that are not learned. For example, many mothers will automatically hold their infants in their left arms, which brings their infants close to their hearts where the infants can be comforted by the soothing and rhythmic sounds.

Rossi's views have been challenged (Chodorow, 1977, 1978). Rossi, however, believes that biology is far too important a factor in the human experience to dismiss outright because of past misuses by individuals who used biological constructs to oppress others. Other sociobiology proponents argue that their critics have been too quick to frame their condemnation of sociobiology's tenets in illogical either/or terms. Frans de Waal (1996a), for one, has pointed out:

> *The debate is no longer about whether a particular [human] trait is learned or innate—which is basically a nonsense question—but about how variable a trait is and where its variability, or invariability, derives from. What is it in our species, for example, that makes people everywhere develop art and religion? Why are some societies more hierarchical than others, but, also, why are status hierarchies so common? Why are certain individuals more aggressive, depressed, or timid than others?* (p. B2)

The Case against Sociobiology

Sociobiology has been criticized as "opening the door to justifying the oppression of one group by another on the basis of biological inferiority" (Rogan,

1978, p. 85). Furthermore, there are several obvious flaws in its propositions (Kitcher, 1987), not the least of which is what some consider sociobiology's failure "to be minimally scientifically rigorous" (Marks, 1996, p. B3).

First, the basis of sociobiology rests on the existence of some as yet unidentified genes. Wilson and others have outlined a whole realm of social behaviors ranging from altruism to xenophobia (i.e., fear of strangers) without so much as identifying even one possible gene that affects these behaviors. It seems somewhat unreasonable, then, to postulate that a set of social behaviors are caused by genetic material and then not be able to point to the material in order to study its effects.

The second and most telling criticism of sociobiology, however, is the extreme difference in terms of time when we compare biological evolution to cultural evolution. Several tens of thousands of years are relatively few in terms of biological evolution. But a decade or two can witness preliterate societies whisked into a technological age and the social behaviors of those involved completely revamped. Social customs and rituals thought appropriate only 10, 50, or 100 years ago would today be seen as eccentricities at best, if not evidence of aberrant mental states.

Pointing to the contention that women, by virtue of their biological makeup, make better parents, researchers studied the fathers of first-borns and found evidence of a strong attachment or a bond between the fathers and their newborns that the researchers called *engrossment* (Greenberg & Morris, 1974). Although the existence of a father-infant bond has been seriously challenged (Palkovitz, 1985), others have found that fathers do, in fact, give considerable attention to and show affection for their newborn infants (Parke & O'Leary, 1975). Thus, research doesn't support the popular belief that women have some biological edge over men when it comes to nurturant social behaviors.

A major problem with sociobiology, then, is that it relies too much on an overly simple or reductionistic explanation for some very complex issues (Brittain, 1996). Also, sociobiology tends to dismiss alternative explanations for social behaviors as if it were the final authority on such topics (Gould, 1976). Maya Pines (1978) states the argument against sociobiology as follows:

> *Sociobiology may give the illusion of offering new insights into the human condition. Yet its methods are still so gross, its notions of "fitness" so primitive (can fitness really be measured by the frequency of copulation or the number of offspring?), our information about animal behavior still so meager, and human culture so complex that sociobiology can provide very little enlightenment about the behavior of real people at this time.* (p. 24)

Time will tell if sociobiology becomes an accepted part of mainstream social science. For the moment, there appear to be too many scientists who fear that its tenets could be more of a hindrance than a help in trying to make sense out of the issues that surround gender differences. Ethel Tobach and Betty Rosoff (1978) argued:

The recent publication of . . . Wilson's sociobiology . . . strengthened the "scientific" legitimacy of "hereditarianism." By hereditarianism we mean the dogma that genes determine an individual's life history in the most significant ways. In other words, each of us has a "genetic destiny" that programs our behavior according to race and sex. Defenses of sexism and racism in the name of evolutionary theory have been used to support the continuing attacks on the few victories won by women in the United States, such as antiabortion legislation, ERA defeats, and legal actions against affirmative employment programs. These events and the attempts to pit women against Blacks, Hispanics, and other minorities in a period of increasing unemployment have made it clear that it is necessary to expose the myth of genetic destiny. That myth says that women are doomed to exploitation because their genes determine their anatomy, physiology, and behavior. This then limits their societal activity and prevents them from overcoming their oppression. (p. 7)

Summary

Human development begins with our sex chromosomes and hormones. Several abnormal conditions exist that show the degree to which our biology influences later development, namely, Turner's, Klinefelter's, the double-Y, androgen-insensitivity, and adrenogenital syndromes.

Controversy continues over the effects that hormones have on individuals' behavior, such as aggression and premenstrual syndrome.

In the last decade, the study of sociobiology has caused a stir in the social sciences. Sociobiology has been hailed by some as a new approach to the study of human social behavior using biological constructs; others see it as little more than a scientific way of justifying inequality and discrimination of women.

There are a number of sex differences across the life span, especially in terms of male vulnerability and mortality rates of various illnesses. We need to remember that when sex differences are found, they are to be interpreted as physical only. Biology predisposes but does not predetermine the functions of individuals.

Suggested Readings

Fausto-Sterling, A. (1985). *Myths of gender: Biological theories about women and men.* New York: Basic Books.

Pool, R. (1994). *Eve's rib: Searching for the biological roots of sex differences.* New York: Crown.

Tavris, C. (1993). Women and health. In F. Denmark & M. Paludi (Eds.), *The psychology of women: A handbook of issues and theories.* Westport, CT: Greenwood Press.

3

The Psychological Perspective

Someday soon virility may be the measure of how well a man relates to a woman as an equal, and masculinity will be equated not with money-making prowess but with a man's power to feel, express, and give love. That might just possibly be worth much more than money.

Robert E. Gould

What's Your Opinion?

What personality characteristics do you think of when you hear the words "woman" and "man"?

Do you believe women and men can exhibit identical behavior, depending on the situation in which they find themselves?

What do you think of when you hear the term "machismo"?

How would you feel if you were told that the results of a personality test revealed you are "feminine" in your gender role orientation?

At what age did you learn about "how women are" and "how men are"?

After reading the last chapter, who can deny that women and men differ biologically? Many people have gone beyond these biological differences and suggested that women and men differ in other ways as well. For example, in Chinese cosmology the principles of *yin* and *yang* are thought of as opposite forces that complement each other. Yin is the passive female principle exhibited in cold and darkness; yang manifests itself as an active masculine principle found in light and heat. In Hindu, the duality of nature is stressed by Mother Earth. She is seen as twin goddesses: *Nirrti* and *Prthvi*. As Nirrti she is seen as death and destruction; as Prthvi, she nurtures. They are both seen as dangerous if they do not have a man to control them.

Many individuals associate different characteristics with women and men and from these characteristics go on to see the world in terms of women being controlled and men being in control. In this chapter we will examine the psychological similarities and differences between women and men. We will begin by looking at components of gender role identity: gender role preference, identification, orientation, knowledge of sex-determined role standards, and gender role adoption. We will then discuss the measurement techniques psychologists have used for each of these components of gender role identity. We will also examine gender similarities and differences across the life span. We will discuss some psychological theories that explain children's acquisition of a gender role identity.

Gender Role Identity: Definitions and Measurement Issues

Acquisition of a gender role identity is a fundamental component in the personality development of children (Reid & Paludi, 1993; Reid et al., 1995). The term *gender role identity* is often used parsimoniously to describe a complex developmental process that includes the following: gender role preference, gender role identification, gender role orientation, knowledge of sex-determined role standards, and gender role adoption. By *gender role preference* we refer to individuals' desire to adopt the behavior associated with either women or men, or the perception of such behavior as preferable or more desirable (Brown, 1956b). *Gender role identification* is the incorporation of a feminine or masculine role and the actions characteristic of the behavior of a particular role. *Gender role orientation* refers to individuals' self-definition as feminine or masculine. *Knowledge of sex-determined role standards* refers to individuals' concepts and espousal of gender role stereotypes of both femininity and masculinity. And, *gender role adoption* refers to individuals' overt behavior that is characteristic of a given sex, not to stated preferences per se. It is the activities in which individuals participate in rehearsing and practicing the characteristic modes of behavior of the preferred role.

Measurement of Gender Role Identity: Some Examples with Children and Adults

Gender-Role Preference

The IT Scale for Children (ITSC) (Brown, 1956a; 1956b) has been used frequently to measure children's gender role preferences. This is a projective test that employs a child-figure drawing, "IT," for which children are asked to make choices among drawings of feminine and masculine objects, figures, and activities. The assumption underlying the ITSC is that children will project themselves into the "IT" figure on the basis of their own gender role preferences. Therefore, a child who basically prefers a feminine gender role will project such a preference to "IT." One of the principal findings with the ITSC is that boys exhibit masculine preferences at all ages but girls do not exhibit feminine preferences (Brown, 1956b). For all ages tested (kindergarten through grade 5), girls prefer masculine to feminine items. This result has led several investigators to conclude that girls perceive Western culture to be male-oriented and to provide boys and men with advantages not afforded girls and women (Paludi, 1981b). Girls and boys have learned to make discriminations of sex-typed depictions appropriate to their own sex and to the opposite sex as well (Paludi, 1981b). Therefore, the major findings with the ITSC cannot be attributed to girls' failure to have learned sex-typed discriminations. However, there are several methodological and statistical problems regarding the ITSC that can explain the predominant findings (Paludi, 1982).

For example, the ITSC is open to the criticism that "IT" is not sexually ambiguous but actually resembles a boy. Children may select choices for the "male figure" rather than project their own choices onto "IT." In other words, the ITSC may be measuring knowledge of sex-determined role standards, not gender role preference (Paludi, 1981b; Sher & Lansky, 1968). Therefore, instead of the customary intrapsychic explanation—girls are responding in terms of a preference for the masculine role—a perceptual interpretation may be stated: The majority of girls and boys view the "IT" figure to be male and choose items and activities accordingly (Brinn et al., 1984).

Support for this position comes from studies by Leonard Lansky and Gerald McKay (1963). These researchers asked children to complete the ITSC under standard conditions involving choices for the "IT" figure and also under conditions in which the choices were made for a concealed child named "IT" whose picture was hidden in an envelope. Both studies found that girls exhibited more feminine preference under the concealed relative to the standard conditions. In addition, Michael Sher and Leonard Lansky (1968) and Michele Paludi (1981b) pointed out that the majority of both sexes label the "IT" figure as a boy, while a majority of both label the concealed "IT" as their own sex.

In recent years, investigators have developed alternative measures of children's gender role preference (e.g., Brinn et al., 1984; Edelbrock & Sugawara, 1978; Paludi, 1981a) that are free of the methodological limitations inherent in the ITSC.

Gender-Role Identification

This component of gender role identity has typically been assessed by the Draw-A-Person Test (Machover, 1949). Individuals are expected to draw a figure of their own sex as their first response to the examiner's directions to "draw a person." A consistent difference between the sexes exists in the sex of the first drawn figure (Machover, 1949; Swenson, 1968). Opposite-sex drawings are frequently obtained from early school-age boys and adolescent and adult women (Craddick, 1963; Heinrich & Triebe, 1972). Several explanations have been offered in order to account for why boys draw women first: closer relations with the mother than with the father, uncertainty about gender role identity (Lynn, 1959), and having more women than men teach in elementary schools. Most research concerning the gender difference in sex sequence on the Draw-A-Person Test, however, has focused on why adolescent and adult women draw a man first. A widely cited intrapsychic explanation for this finding concerns women's ambivalence regarding their gender role identification.

However, Paludi and Bauer (1979) found a significant relationship between the first figure drawn and sex of administrator. Of the men who made drawings of women, most drawings were elicited by a woman examiner. A similar finding was obtained for women: Most drawings were elicited by a man. Thus, the extent to which individuals identify with the examiner is reflected as an increase in number of drawings of the same sex as the examiner.

A cultural explanation may also be offered to explain the tendency for women to draw men first. There may be a pervasive learning that "person" is synonymous with "man," not "woman" (Broverman et al., 1970; see chapter 7).

Gender-Role Orientation

Over the past 50 years, most psychologists interested in gender role orientation have developed very different models of how individuals describe themselves in terms of femininity and masculinity (Pleck, 1981, 1984). We will describe two of these models.

The Simple Conception of Femininity/Masculinity

During the 1930s and 1940s, most psychologists accepted the then commonly held notion that the behaviors, attitudes, and interests generally associated with either femininity and masculinity were exclusive features of women and men. In other words, women and men were not only thought to differ in terms of their basic personality characteristics, but also these characteristics were conceived of as opposite of each other. For example, *masculinity* was shown by a person's strong competitiveness, aggressiveness, and independence. The opposite of these would make up what would be called *femininity*. Therefore, a person would show the characteristics of femininity by the lack of competitiveness, aggressiveness, and independence. In terms of behavior, whatever a feminine person did, a masculine person didn't.

Much of the research during these years revolved around developing paper-and-pencil tests that would assess the degree of a person's femininity or masculinity. To accomplish this, large groups of women and men were given items to determine how they differed in their responses. For example, items like the following were found to differentiate between women and men. Women tended to give the answer noted in the brackets more frequently than men.

I do not like sports. (*True*)
Home chores do not appeal to me. (*False*)
I think I would like the work of a building contractor. (*False*)
I prefer a shower to a bathtub. (*False*)
I like mechanics magazines. (*False*)

(Items 1 and 2 come from the Masculinity-Femininity scale taken from the Minnesota Multiphasic Personality Inventory and items 3–5 come from Gough's Femininity Scale.)

The more items a person answered in the "feminine" direction, the more feminine this person was supposed to be. Some of the more common tests incorporating this "simple" conception of femininity and masculinity were Gough's Femininity Scale (1952), the Masculinity-Femininity scale on the Minnesota Multiphasic Personality Inventory (Hathaway & McKinley, 1943), and the Terman-Miles Attitude-Interest Test (Terman & Miles, 1936).

The Androgynous Conception of Femininity/Masculinity

During the late 1960s and the 1970s, the androgynous model was introduced to the field of measurement of gender role orientation. From this perspective, femininity was not thought of as being comprised of personality characteristics that were opposites of masculinity. Rather, the psychological characteristics of femininity and masculinity were viewed as being comprised of two independent dimensions that could be separate but could overlap as well (Gonen & Lansky, 1968; Marsh et al., 1989).

Sandra Bem (1974) developed a test called the Bem Sex Role Inventory (BSRI) that attempted to measure androgyny. Consisting of 60 socially desirable "feminine" (e.g., shy and warm), "masculine" (e.g., aggressive and self-reliant), and "neutral" (e.g., happy and sincere) adjectives, people taking the test indicated the extent to which each item was true for themselves in terms of a 7-point scale ranging from 1 (i.e., never or almost never true) to 7 (i.e., always or almost always true). The test gives separate femininity and masculinity scores that can be combined into one of four types: (1) androgynous (high on both the feminine and masculine); (2) feminine (high on the feminine items and low on the masculine ones); (3) masculine (low on the feminine items and high on the masculine ones); and (4) undifferentiated (low on both the feminine and masculine). Others have also developed androgyny scales, such as Berzins, Welling, and Wetter's (1975) PFO Andro Scale, and Spence, Helmreich, and Stapp's (1974) Personal Attributes Questionnaire.

Knowledge of Sex-Determined Role Standards

A stereotype is an oversimplified set of descriptive components about a visible group of people who are thought to share certain characteristics (Ashmore & DelBoca, 1979, 1981). What comes to mind when you think of a "typical" woman? After a moment's pause, did you think of words like "gentle," "talkative," "passive," "tactful," and of course, "emotional"? Now, what about a "typical" man? This time, did you think of "confident," "aggressive," "independent," "dominant," "worldly wise," and "unemotional"? Don't be surprised if these personality traits came to mind when you thought about a typical woman and man. The early research in knowledge of sex-determined role standards found that most people thought of women and men in such terms (Fernberger, 1948; McKee & Sheriffs, 1957, 1959). Each sex supposedly had its own set of components or clusters of traits, one for women and the other for men (Broverman et al., 1972; Rosenkrantz et al., 1968). Let's now examine the personality traits that we most generally associate with each gender role stereotype. To do this we shall highlight the research of Paul Rosenkrantz and colleagues (1968).

Rosenkrantz asked a group of college women and men to examine a list of 122 bipolar items, such as *very aggressive* versus *not at all aggressive* and *very dependent* versus *not at all dependent,* on a 7-point scale. The scale used in the study looked something like this:

Not at all aggressive						Very aggressive
1............2............3............4............5............6............7						

Very dependent						Not at all dependent
1............2............3............4............5............6............7						

Students then were told to imagine that they were about to meet either a woman or man for the first time and all they knew about this person was her or his sex. Using the scale, the students checked off the degree to which each of the bipolar items reflected what they thought characteristic of each sex. Overall, the students thought of a man as more typically aggressive, independent, dominant, ambitious, etc. A woman was thought of as showing a relative absence of the characteristics associated with a man. These students saw a typical woman as emotionally expressive, talkative, and concerned with security. A man was seen as exhibiting a relative absence of these characteristics. Upon further study, the stereotypic characteristics for women and men fell into two broad categories or clusters: a warmth-expressiveness cluster for women and a competency cluster for men. Other researchers have found much the same with their measures of gender role stereotypes (Spence et al., 1974).

Other researchers, however, have taken the position that the gender role stereotypes comprise more than only certain personality traits (Deaux & Kite, 1993; Eagly, 1995, Helgeson, 1994; Ricciardelli & Williams, 1995). Specifically, Kay Deaux and Laurie Lewis (1984) suggest that:

> *a number of separate components of gender stereotypes can be identi-*
> *fied: specifically, traits, role behaviors, occupations, and physical ap-*
> *pearance, each of which has a masculine and feminine version. Al-*
> *though no component is seen as the exclusive province of one or the*
> *other sex, masculine and feminine components are significantly more*
> *strongly associated with males and females, respectively. The like-sex*
> *components (e.g., male role behaviors and masculine traits) bear some*
> *relationship to each other, but correlational analysis suggests that they*
> *are best viewed as separate factors that can vary independently.* (p. 992)

An important feature of this new multicomponent approach to gender role stereotypes is the emphasis on the relative versus absolute assignment of characteristics to women and men. For example, although one of the role components of the masculine gender stereotype is that of financial provider for the family, many women also perform this role. Thus, people do not define the various gender role stereotypic characteristics in terms of their being only associated with one sex and not the other.

Note that when people assign the role of financial provider to either women or men, there is a much higher degree of relatedness to men than to women. No longer are men seen as the exclusive financial provider. Many of the characteristics once thought to be the sole feature of one sex or the other have been found to vary. Men can be thought of as, and are, graceful, caring for children, and warm. Likewise, women can be thought of as, and are, competitive, sexually assertive, and independent. This new multicomponent approach to gender role stereotypes with its emphasis on relative differences rather than absolutes appears more realistic and fruitful for researchers.

This multicomponent approach to gender roles is also supported by research on the interface of gender and race (also see chapter 5). For example, early ethnographic studies of Latino family life promoted the themes of "machismo" of men and the passivity of women (Ginorio, Guttierrez, Cauce, & Acosta, 1995). However, more current research suggests that even in "traditional" Mexican American families, women hold much more power within the private sphere of the family. In addition, most Latin American cultures assign the "healing" role to women. These healers, *espiritistas,* are viewed as powerful and have gained high status in the Latin American cultures. Thus, the generalization of Latinas as subservient masks the very powerful roles they play within the family and community.

Theresa LaFromboise and colleagues (1995) also highlighted that the Spirit World is essential to American Indian life, especially to American Indian women. In American Indian cultures, women are viewed as extensions of the Spirit Mother and as keys to the continuation of their people. As LaFromboise and colleagues stated:

> . . . *American Indian women's lives are enriched by caring that is expressed in a variety of ways. These expressions range from being cared for as a daughter to caring for the spiritual well-being of the community as a wise woman.* (p. 225)

Furthermore, Latinas hold the value of *respeto* very dear. *Respeto* means respect. For Latinas, respeto means that one's demeanor with older individuals should be respectful and subordinate. Confrontational behavior with one's grandparents would not be culturally supported (Ginorio et al., 1996). *Respeto* would not be viewed as Latinas having no status or power within the family.

When do we begin to perceive each sex in relatively stereotypic ways? Deanna Kuhn and associates (1978) observed a group of two- and three-year-old preschoolers. These children's parents were students and faculty members at Stanford University. We might expect then that these children would perceive women and men in less than traditionally gender role stereotypic ways. However, even at this early age, these children already thought that girls were more likely to play with dolls, help their mothers, clean house, become nurses, and ask for help. Boys, on the other hand, were thought more likely to help their fathers, become bosses, and express aggression. Others have found that preschoolers typically stereotype each sex's actions in play activities by having boys go off to work, while girls stay home and cook (Garvey, 1977). By age five or six, children apparently have a thorough knowledge of the gender stereotypes (Reid & Paludi, 1993). Thus, an awareness of the contents of gender role stereotypes begins in the preschool years and is rather well-developed by the time a youngster goes off to first grade.

Gender-Role Adoption

Gender-role adoption has been measured by observing individual's behavior in their daily activities at home, school, and work, as well as in the research laboratory. In 1974, psychologists Eleanor Maccoby and Carol Nagy Jacklin published their now classic text *The Psychology of Sex Differences*. In this work, Maccoby and Jacklin examined over 1,600 published studies ranging over a broad spectrum of human behavior, including cognitive functions, personality traits, and social behaviors. Their aim for such a massive undertaking was "to sift the evidence to determine which of the many beliefs about gender differences have a solid basis in fact and which do not" (p. vii). Their analyses revealed that many of the presumed gender differences were more myth than fact, whereas a few differences appeared to stand up. Let's begin by examining briefly some of their findings.

The Myths and Realities of Gender Comparisons

Myth: Girls are more social than boys.

Reality: Maccoby and Jacklin could find no convincing evidence that girls are more social than boys. During early childhood, both girls and boys played with others with about equal frequency. Boys were no more apt to play with inanimate objects than girls were, and at certain times, boys actually played with their playmates more than girls did.

Myth: Girls are more suggestible than boys.

Reality: Girls are just as likely as boys are to imitate others' behavior spontaneously. When there is pressure to conform to an ambiguous situation, both sexes are equally susceptible to persuasive face-to-face communication.

Myth: Girls have lower self-esteem than boys.

Reality: Overall, girls and boys are similar in their personal views of self-confidence and self-satisfaction. They do, however, differ in the

By the age of five children are well aware of gender role stereotypes.

© Bob Kalman/The Image Works

areas within which they feel self-confident. For example, girls are more likely to rate themselves as higher in social competence whereas boys see themselves as powerful and dominant. During most of their early school years, girls and boys believe they can influence their own fate. During the college years, however, women are less likely to believe that they can control their destinies and are less optimistic about their futures than similarly aged men are. We should not interpret this to mean that young women have lower self-esteem than young men. Maccoby and Jacklin suggest that young men are perhaps overconfident. Women may also be realistically appraising the attitudes and attributions men make about women's abilities.

Myth: Girls lack motivation to achieve.

Reality: Girls and boys can be equally motivated to achieve, but both are influenced by different factors that push their achievement levels (see chapter 8). Girls are motivated to achieve in situations where there is less competition or social comparison. Boys, on the other hand, apparently require a sense of competition or ego-involvement in order for them to achieve the same levels of achievement as girls.

Myth: Girls are better at rote learning and simple tasks.

Reality: Both girls and boys perform equally well on simple, repetitive tasks. Neither is more susceptible to simple conditioning on somewhat automatic processes.

Myth: Boys are more analytic than girls.

Reality: To analyze, one must disregard unimportant aspects of a situation in favor of the important features of a task. Both women and men are as apt to pay attention to unimportant details as to the important ones.

Myth: Girls are more affected by heredity, boys more by environment.

Reality: Both before and after birth, boys are more vulnerable to a variety of harmful agents. However, we cannot conclude from this that boys are more affected by their environments than girls are. Both girls and boys learn with equal facility in many different situations, and if learning is a measure of the effects of the environment, then both are equal in this regard.

Myth: Girls are auditory; boys are visual.

Reality: Both infant girls and boys respond equally to sights and sounds in their environments.

Some of the studies reviewed by Maccoby and Jacklin (1974) pointed to several areas where there seems to be some gender differences with respect to specific abilities and to one personality trait.

Gender Comparison: Girls have greater verbal ability than boys.

Explanation: Girls' verbal abilities mature more quickly than boys'. During the early school years, girls' and boys' verbal abilities are similar, but beginning in high school and beyond, girls take the lead. Girls' greater verbal abilities include a better understanding and fluency of the complexities of language, better spelling and creative writing abilities, and better comprehension of analogies.

Gender Comparison: Boys excel in visual-spatial ability.

Explanation: Beginning in early adolescence, boys are better able to rotate an object in space. Boys also are better at picking out a simple design or figure that is embedded within a larger, more complex design (Baenninger & Newcombe, 1989; Hyde, 1990).

Gender Comparison: Boys excel in mathematical ability.

Explanation: Again, beginning in adolescence, boys show a greater facility with math than girls show. However, in those studies that use verbal processes in mathematical questions, girls do better than boys; on those that require visual-spatial abilities, boys do better than girls (see Jackson, Fleury, Girvin, & Gerard,1995; Taal, 1994).

Gender Comparison: Males are more aggressive than females.

Explanation: Beginning in the early preschool years, boys are more physically aggressive than girls. Boys exhibit more mock fighting and other forms of aggression than girls. Also, boys direct their aggression during these early years more toward other boys than toward girls. Boys continue to be more aggressive than girls throughout adolescence and the adult years (see chapter 6).

Reanalyzing the Data: 1993

As we discussed in chapter 1, some of Maccoby and Jacklin's conclusions have been challenged because, in many cases, they simply counted up the studies that found a gender difference (no matter which sex the results favored) from those that didn't. If there were more differences than similarities, Maccoby and Jacklin concluded a significant gender difference. Some researchers have argued that such a procedure is questionable. Others noted that many of the studies Maccoby and Jacklin reported contained relatively few participants, leading to the possibility of finding little or no gender differences with respect to the issue under study. Julia Sherman (1978) reviewed many of Maccoby and Jacklin's studies and found that many times the magnitude of the differences was quite small. Along the same line, Janet

Hyde (1981) reanalyzed Maccoby and Jacklin's verbal, quantitative, visual-spatial, and field articulation studies using meta-analysis. Maccoby and Jacklin had suggested that based on their analyses these abilities showed "well-established" gender differences. However, Hyde's analysis of these same studies prompted a note of caution for such a generalization. She concluded:

> *The main conclusion that can be reached from this analysis is that the gender differences in verbal ability, quantitative ability, visual-spatial ability, and field articulation reported by Maccoby and Jacklin (1974) are small. Gender differences appear to account for no more than 1%–5% of the population variance. . . . Generally, it seems that gender differences in verbal ability are smaller and gender differences in spatial ability are larger, but even in the latter case, gender differences account for less than 5% of the population variance.* (pp. 894–896)

Measurement of Femininity and Masculinity: A Critique

Psychologists have spent countless hours researching gender differences, as testified by the innumerable studies that have been published in the last 50 years. As found in reviews such as Maccoby and Jacklin's and Hyde's, few genuine differences of any substantial nature can be found. Psychologists have conceptualized and measured femininity, masculinity, and androgyny in several different ways. However, most measures developed to tap femininity and masculinity have focused on what can be seen as merely different variations of expressive (femininity) and instrumental (masculinity) traits. Such a limited view is thought of as less than useful to analyze the various features associated with gender role identity (Deaux & Kite, 1993).

Much of the confusion surrounding femininity and masculinity is caused by the vastly different definitions presented. As long as researchers cannot agree on what they are measuring or come up with a straightforward scale for its measurement, the future doesn't look bright for these constructs.

Cultural lag may also be an important contributor to the results with tests of gender role identity. Although it is evident that item content does interact in gender role identity tests, it is still unclear as to how to control for those effects (Constantinople, 1973). A related issue concerns the fact that some test developers (e.g., Brown, 1956b), defined the component of gender role identity in terms of their preconceived cultural standards of femininity and masculinity. It is more meaningful, both theoretically and methodologically, to define the components of gender role identity in terms of the modal response of individuals of the same age as those for which the test is designed. Thus, when girls rejected "feminine" items in the IT Scale for Children, they may not have rejected the feminine role as they conceived of it.

Furthermore, evident is the need to develop measures of gender role identity that are ethnically sensitive since the age at which components of gender role identity become stable varies for girls and boys of different ethnic backgrounds and socioeconomic classes (Landrine, 1995; Reid et al., 1995). And,

Anne Constantinople (1973) suggested that multiple forms of tests of gender role identity be developed since test scores vary with developmental age. Susan Thomas (1979) developed the Adolescent Sex Role Inventory to measure adolescents' gender role orientation, since the adjectives that comprise the BSRI were too abstract for individuals younger than the age of the standardization sample.

Psychological Theories of Gender Role Acquisition

Several theories have attempted to describe how a child acquires her or his gender role identity. The differences in theoretical perspectives are due to the initial assumptions made about human behavior. We will discuss two assumptions: *nature/nurture* and *activity/passivity*.

Nature vs. Nurture

The question of whether gender role acquisition occurs due to the forces of *nature* (genetic, biological, and inherited factors) or *nurture* (learned, experiential, and environmental factors) lies at the root of almost all theories of gender role acquisition. While it seems that it is reasonable to recognize the contributions of both nature and nurture, the debate remains strong concerning which contributes more significantly (see chapter 2).

Sigmund Freud (1927, 1959a, 1959b, 1965) theorized that basic gender differences were rooted in biology, and this thinking gave rise to his famous statement that "anatomy is destiny." He theorized that each infant goes through a series of *psychosexual stages* that follow an invariant sequence and are based on physical growth. These psychosexual stages are linked to the child's level of cognitive and social development and to her or his feelings about her/his parents.

The concept of *identification* is the basis for Freud's theory of gender role acquisition. By identification, Freud meant the child should acquire the personality traits, behaviors, attitudes, and roles of the same-sex parent and recognize the similarities she or he shares with the same-sex parent.

Social-learning theory, by contrast, views gender role acquisition in terms of nurture (Bandura, 1969). The major constructs of social-learning theory are reinforcement, imitation, and modeling. The simplest mechanism for learning behavior appropriate to gender role is that of a reward or reinforcement given to a person for performing a certain behavior. For example, when a father praises (i.e., a powerful reward) his daughter for helping him with the dishes, according to social-learning theory, the daughter is likely to help her father with the dishes in the future. On the other hand, if a son is scolded (i.e., a form of punishment) for crying over a skinned knee, the boy may not cry the next time he hurts himself. Thus, parents teach their children gender-related behaviors (i.e., girls do dishes, boys don't cry) by reinforcing or punishing the children's gender-related behaviors.

In addition, social-learning theory suggests that observational learning and imitation play a part in children acquiring a gender role identity. A crucial element in the social-learning perspective is that for children to learn their gender-related behaviors, they need to imitate same-sex models more than opposite-sex models (see chapter 4).

How does social-learning theory deal with race? According to Pamela Reid and colleagues (1995):

> *Social-learning theory is flexible enough that it appears to be applicable to minority groups. In the abstract, experiences common to each ethnic group or social class segment determine what should be expected from the females in that group. However, as with other theories, there have been few empirical attempts to demonstrate the relevance of different cultural practices to . . . behavior. Thus, the recognition that gender-appropriate behavior for females in one cultural group may be considered gender inappropriate in another has been relatively unexamined.* (p. 96)

The *cognitive-developmental theory* of gender role acquisition (Kohlberg, 1966, 1976) contains a mixture of the biological and environmental views. Its concepts of stages of cognitive development and readiness to accept gender role identity allows for individual differences. This theory also establishes the importance of the child's environment, in particular, the importance of societal models in addition to the parents.

Activity vs. Passivity

Activity vs. passivity refers to the role which people play in their own development. The cognitive-developmental theorists, such as Barbel Inhelder and Jean Piaget (1958) and Lawrence Kohlberg (1976), believe that children actively engage the environment. In this perspective, children are biologically prepared to organize their world. Other theoretical views, social learning, for example, see children as more passive recipients and reactors to stimuli (Bandura, 1969).

Kohlberg (1966) suggested that a child moves through three stages in the process of learning appropriate gender-related behaviors that make up the child's gender role identity. During the first stage, beginning around two years of age, the child learns that there are two sexes and comes to understand how to apply the labels "girl" and "boy." As the child develops during these preschool years, she or he learns to attach the appropriate sex label to herself (girl) or himself (boy). Thus, the first stage is for a child to become aware of her or his sex. The child also learns to associate certain features, such as dress styles or hair lengths, with each sex. For example, a three-year-old child learns to associate dresses with girls and short hair with boys. One feature that stands out during this first period is how rigid, or what Kohlberg calls concrete, a child's thinking is. By concrete, Kohlberg means that a child does not allow for exceptions to the things that she or he sees around them. A three-year-old boy who sees a Scottish gentleman clad in a kilt is apt to say that this person is a girl because only girls wear "dresses." As the child grows and develops through the next few years, the components of the child's gender role identity become more stable and extend out to include most of the expected behaviors related to gender role.

The second stage finds older children (from approximately five years to six or seven years) beginning to develop a system of values associated with their sex. That is, during this period, children learn to value or find more desirable the behaviors associated with their own sex and begin to imitate other same-sex persons more so than other-sex persons. For instance, according to Kohlberg, the reason a six-year-old boy won't play with dolls is that he feels that playing with dolls is for girls, and whatever girls do can't be as good (i.e., valued) as what boys do.

Finally, during the third stage, children develop an emotional attachment to the same-sex parent, which reinforces that they will learn the complex set of behaviors associated with their sex.

Gender Schema Theory

Gender schema theory contains features of the cognitive-developmental theory of gender role acquisition and social-learning theory (Bem, 1981). Gender schema theory proposes that gender role acquisition derives in large part from gender-schematic processing as well as a generalized readiness on the part of children to encode and organize information. This theory further proposes that gender-schematic processing is derived from the sex-differentiated practice of the social community. Thus, by observing the distinctions made between women and men in their culture, children learn the specific content of gender role related behavior and that distinctions based on sex are important. A girl may observe that girls are generally described as "nice," while boys are described as "brave." This girl learns that there is a difference between girls and boys and that certain attributes are more relevant for girls than for boys and vice versa. Matching one's behaviors against the developing gender schema results in the child's evaluation of her or his adequacy as a person.

Gender schema theory assumes that since gender-role typing is learned, it can also be modified; therefore, stereotypes can be eliminated if children engage in one or more of the following (Papalia & Olds, 1990):

> *Discard all schemata, distinguishing the sexes only by anatomical and reproductive differences. (Young children usually fail to do this, basing their decision about a person's sex on other external signals like clothing or hairstyle.) Learn the individual-differences schema, that there is great variation within groups. For example, some girls do not like to play base-ball, but others do—and that some boys do not.*
>
> *Learn the cultural-relativism schema, the understanding that people in different cultures and at different historical times hold different beliefs and customs about what is appropriate for males and females.*
>
> *Learn the sexism schema, the conviction that gender-stereotyped roles are not only different but wrong, no matter how common they are.*
> (p. 363)

Gender schema theory has received empirical support (Bem, 1983). Individuals do process their world in terms of schema, and some individuals use a gender schema as their primary way of organizing their world as well as self-concept. Furthermore, gender schema theory has been hailed as the most useful of theories for explaining the development of gender behavior in individuals of color (Reid et al., 1995).

Sex-Role-As-Rule Theory

Constantinople (1979) described the acquisition of a gender role identity as being similar to the way in which rigidly adhered-to norms become the basis for how a child learns her or his gender role identity. First of all, she suggested that gender roles are not simply mental rules of gender-related behaviors divorced from a person's feelings or emotions. Gender roles, according to Constantinople, have both a cognitive and an emotional side to them. Blending both the cognitive and emotional elements in gender role acquisition is especially noteworthy in Constantinople's model. For example, when a father chastises his four-year-old son for putting on his sister's dress and looking like a girl, the father is not only providing information to the son—boys shouldn't wear dresses—but he also is causing the boy some pain in the sense that the boy feels bad as a result of his father's scolding. Thus the little boy learns what is expected of him in terms of the masculine gender role (i.e., boys don't wear dresses—a cognitive element) and also learns that if he is to avoid future pain (caused by his father's scolding), he must not wear dresses.

This model makes certain assumptions about the nature of young children. The first assumption is that children are motivated to avoid pain and maximize pleasure in their dealings with the world. Second, Constantinople suggests that a child's brain works in such a way as to allow it to create schemata of all the incoming information or stimuli the child receives from the sensory world. Constantinople believes that these early schemata or categories constantly expand to include additional information gained through experience. A child does not create a new category or schema for each new stimulus, but rather adds this to an already established schema for which the new stimulus seems best fit. As a child learns the specific behaviors associated with each sex's gender role, the child shifts this new information to other situations. The information the child learns at home transfers to school, for example.

The Psychological Perspective: A Critique of Personality Theories

Psychologist Judith Worell (1990) suggested that theories of personality may be described as "traditional" when they reflect the following themes in their conception of human behavior: androcentrism, gendercentrism, ethnocentrism, and heterosexism. *Androcentrism* refers to the theories of personality that use boys and men as the prototype of humankind and girls and women as variants on the dominant theme. *Gendercentrism* in personality theories is evident when separate paths of life span development are suggested for women and men as a result of the biological differences between them. *Ethnocentrism* refers to personality theories assuming that development is identical for all individuals across all racial, ethnic, and class groups. And, *heterosexism* is evident in personality theories that assume that a heterosexual orientation is normative, while a lesbian or gay sexual orientation is deviant and changeworthy. We will illustrate these themes with two classic theories of personality, those of Erikson and Freud.

Erik Erikson's "Eight Stages of Man"

We discussed androcentrism in chapter 1 when we addressed research methods in psychology. We noted that the theories on achievement motivation and moral development were based on boys and men only. Personality theories (as well as the theories of achievement motivation and morality) view women as "less than" men in terms of intelligence, rationality, morality, and in taking responsibility for their lives. One example of an androcentric theory of personality is the work of Erik Erikson (1963; 1968).

Erikson proposed a model of development that was based on his concept of the "eight stages of man." According to Erikson's model, development proceeds throughout life according to stages in which polarities determine the formation of an individual's personality. He theorized that growth proceeds from conflict and cast each of his stages of development in terms of unique crises. The eight stages, accompanied by the ages and "successful outcomes" Erikson believed individuals dealt with these polarities, are as follows:

Trust versus Mistrust (birth–1) security and predictability
Autonomy versus Shame and Doubt (2–3) self-control
Initiative versus Guilt (4–5) responsibility
Industry versus Inferiority (6–12) competence and self-esteem
Identity versus Role Confusion (13–19) coherent sense of self
Intimacy versus Isolation (20–24) establishment of mature relationships
Generativity versus Stagnation (25–64) guiding the next generation
Ego Integrity versus Despair (65–death) wisdom

Two of these stages, identity versus role confusion and intimacy versus isolation, posed problems for Erikson as he attempted to understand how women's development fit his theory. Let's look at these two stages in more detail to address each of the biases.

In the identity versus role confusion stage, Erikson theorized that adolescents either achieve a sense of personal identity by embracing a philosophy of life and commitment to a career or by being confused and uncommitted to a career. In the intimacy versus isolation stage, individuals, according to Erikson (1963), must meet the following standards if their development is "healthy:"

mutuality of orgasm
with a loved partner
of the opposite sex

with whom one is able and willing to share a mutual trust
and with whom one is able and willing to regulate the cycles of work,
   procreation, and recreation
so as to secure to the offspring, too, all the stages of a satisfactory
   development. (p. 266)

Individuals who cannot develop a capacity for intimacy, according to Erikson, experience a sense of isolation, an inability to take chances with one's identity by sharing true intimacy. Erikson described these individuals as self-absorbed and able only to engage in interpersonal relationships on a very superficial level.

There is a danger of overinterpretation when considering stage theories. Erikson questioned these stages for women's development. He reasoned that women defer dealing with the identity versus role confusion polarity until "they know whom they will marry and for whom they will make a home" (1968, p. 123). There are several biases inherent in this theory. For example, "normal" intimacy is translated into heterosexual intimacy, thus denying lesbian and gay relationships and considering them "abnormal." In addition, Erikson viewed sexual relationships in terms of procreation. One result of this assumption about development is that women and men who choose to remain voluntarily childless have been ignored, denigrated, and regarded as less than human.

Erikson's position on women's identity suggests that women's identity is not defined by career commitment, as in men's, but rather by their commitment to the roles of wife and mother and their relationship to a man who will give them direction. Erikson's theory thus posits very important prescriptive guidelines or mandates for women: to be a wife and, especially, a mother. This latter mandate is what Nancy Felipe Russo (1976) labeled the *motherhood mandate.*

In the first stage, trust versus mistrust, Erikson believed that if a mother acts in a loving and consistent way, the infant will develop a sense of basic trust. In contrast, a baby will develop a sense of basic mistrust if the mother has a "poor attitude and therefore acts in an unreliable, aloof, and rejecting way." Mothers are assumed to be the sole caretaker and the cause of the child's problems in infancy and throughout life. Mothers are also assumed to be "natural" caretakers and not interested in a career in addition to or instead of providing care for children.

Gendercentrism is also illustrated in Erikson's theory in its division of life goals between women and men to career versus intimacy, with intimacy not as valued as career identity. This theory is ethnocentric as well: Erikson believed that children develop best when in the care of a nurturing, biological mother. This position disregards evidence from a variety of cultures (even within the United States) that suggests children socialized in gay and lesbian families, extended family arrangements, in dual-earner couples, or single parent families are well-adjusted. In fact, as research by Marjorie Hill (1988) suggested, lesbian mothers perceived their daughters and sons to be more similar in characteristics than did heterosexual mothers. Lesbian mothers held less stereotypic ideas relating to the feminine role. Daughters and sons of employed mothers perceive woman's role as involving freedom of choice and satisfaction. Sons and daughters of employed mothers perceive a smaller difference between women and men in terms of warmth and expressiveness than do children of unemployed mothers (Hoffman, 1989; Reid et al., 1995; see chapter 8).

Research also suggests a greater flexibility and permissiveness in middle-class homes (regardless of ethnicity) that leads to the availability of a wider range of activity choices for boys and girls. In many working class homes, parents are more concerned that their daughters and sons adhere strictly to stereotypic feminine behavior (Reid & Paludi, 1993).

Sigmund Freud: "Anatomy Is Destiny"

We will illustrate androcentrism, ethnocentrism, gendercentrism, and hetero-sexism in another personality theory, the psychoanalytic theory proposed by Freud (1948, 1965). This theory illustrates gendercentrism, since personality development was posited separately for women and men as a result of the biological differences between them (specifically, the presence of a penis in men and the capability of women to bear children).

Freud believed that young girls, when noticing they have vaginas, not penises, blame their mother for this anatomical difference. Freud believed girls develop "penis envy" and consequently a basic sense of inferiority. They resolve this "genital loss" by passively accepting it from a man and bearing sons. For a girl, therefore, this process involves identifying with her mother, accepting the feminine gender role, and thereby rejecting the masculine gen-der role. However, this process does not adequately capture how most eth-nic communities operate. For example, in African American families, multiple generations of women share in child-rearing duties (Reid et al., 1995).

Freud maintained that girls' identification with their mothers only develops out of their competition for their father as well as a fear of losing their moth-ers' love altogether. Freud viewed women as less ethical than men, as having a lesser sense of morality, and being more influenced by emotions than by logical reasoning. Why? Because girls' identification process is never as strong as that of boys' and, as a result, they have less well-developed con-sciences. Consequently, women are passive, emotional, masochistic, narcis-sistic, and in competition with other women for men's attention. According to Freud (1968):

> *I cannot escape the notion . . . that for women the level of what is ethi-cally normal is different from what it is in men. Their super-ego is never so inexorable, so impersonal, so independent of its emotional ori-gins as we require it to be in men. Character traits which critics of every epoch have brought up against women—that they show less sense of justice than men, that they are less ready to submit to the great neces-sities of life, that they are more influenced in their judgments by feelings*

of affection or hostility—all these would be amply accounted for by the modification of their super-ego which we have already inferred. (p. 193)

Freud maintained that girls' and women's moral inferiority is due to the fact that they lack a penis. Because they do not have to worry about being castrated (retaliation from their father for loving their mother), girls and women are not as motivated to become obedient rule followers.

No research evidence exists to support the concept of penis envy and castration complex (Jacklin, 1989).

Freud's theory is also ethnocentric. Many ethnic minority women, for example, view themselves not as the passive and submissive women Freud described, but as strong, independent, and self-reliant. These positively valued characteristics, however, have been misnamed as deviant in African American women, as the "matriarchal structure" responsible for the alienation of black men! However, several factors contribute to the greater rates of female-headed households among African American families, including the lower marriage and higher divorce rates among African Americans and the obstacles African American men have encountered when seeking and maintaining jobs to support their families (Dickson, 1993).

Furthermore, the stereotype of the black matriarchy ignores one important fact: if the current statistic of 47 percent of African American households are headed by women, then 53 percent must be headed by men and women together or by men alone.

Freud viewed white male/female power structures as normative and thereby cast ethnic minority families in a deviant framework. DeFour and Paludi (1988) found that single white mothers are frequently described in the psychological literature as being in an alternative or contemporary lifestyle; the same family constellation for black women is described as a "broken home." What would Freud say if he saw current statistics that suggest that there is a trend toward an increase in the number of female-headed households among white families?

Is Androgyny the Answer?

An individual's sex is not only a biological fact, it is a social fact as well. People react in specific ways that depend on an individual's sex. Stereotypes about women and men, however, are not highly correlated with individuals' actual behavior. Stereotypes do not accurately reflect social reality. They are representations of cultural inventions that are woven around biological facts. For example, in actuality, girls and women are more competent than the stereotype implies, and boys and men are more expressive than the stereotype suggests.

Androgyny was hailed as the exemplar for child rearing and teaching children. Androgyny implies an integration of positive feminine and masculine personality traits in one individual. Androgynous individuals would be expected to be maximally effective in a wide range of situations because they would not be constrained by stereotypic feminine and masculine behaviors. However, it is unclear as to the impact of androgyny on individuals' interpersonal relations.

As we get older, our behavior increasingly depends on context. Adolescents, for example, are more likely to behave in gender role stereotypic ways when on a date than when alone. There is no research support to date to suggest that highly stereotyped children become highly stereotyped adults.

However, gender role stereotypic behavior is intensified during the adolescent years in order for adolescents to "fit in" with the peer group. Among boys, for example, the pressure to be tough is greatly intensified; they are likely to engage in fights with their peers. This behavior may be exhibited so they can gain status among other adolescents in their peer group (AAUW, 1993; Paludi, 1996).

Adolescence for girls may be experienced as anxiety as they learn to value "feminine" gender role stereotypic behaviors, such as popularity and attractiveness, over which they have little or no control. As Elizabeth Douvan and Joseph Adelson (1966) concluded:

> There is not one adolescent crisis, but two major and clearly distinctive ones—the masculine and feminine. . . . The tone and order of development that begins in adolescence and concludes in maturity . . . differ sharply for the two sexes. . . . The areas of achievement, autonomy, authority, and control focus and express boys' major concerns and psychological growth; the object relations—friendship, dating, popularity, and the understanding and management of interpersonal crisis—hold the key to adolescent growth and integration for the girl. . . . (p. 350)

Thus, exhibiting gender role stereotypic behavior is related to popularity among peers in childhood and adolescence. Moreover, it is an important aspect of self-esteem. The question remains to be answered whether androgynous children and adolescents would be able to maintain their status in the peer group and have a favorable self-concept.

Androgyny does not mean the same thing as "liberal," as in having liberal attitudes about gender roles in society. One individual may believe he is less stereotypic in his attitudes about women and men than his peers and yet have traditional beliefs about gender roles. Also, androgyny does not mean homosexual. The concept of androgyny does not refer to sexual orientation. Knowing a woman scores androgynous on a personality test in no way tells us about her sexual orientation. This independence between androgyny and sexual orientation holds true for other classifications of gender role orientation (i.e., feminine, masculine, undifferentiated).

Finally, androgyny isn't a substitute for social change. Instead of socializing children and adolescents to exhibit both feminine and masculine behaviors, it would be to society's advantage to value all positive behaviors, regardless of their "appropriateness" for one sex or the other. This gender role transcendence characterizes many women and men in middle and later adulthood (Burger & Solano, 1994).

Jean Sinnott (1984) suggested that successful aging may depend on exhibiting feminine personality characteristics, such as attachment rather than isolation, and intimacy instead of nondisclosure. For children this would also mean flexibility in behaving, without incurring punishment. As Bem (1983) concluded:

> *Focusing on androgyny organizes both our perceptions and our social world. . . . If gender schema theory has a political message, it is not that the individual should be androgynous. Rather, it is that the network of associations constituting the gender schema ought to become more limited in scope and that society ought to temper its insistence on the ubiquitous functional importance of the gender dichotomy. In short, human behaviors and personality attributes should no longer be linked with gender, and society should stop projecting gender into situations irrelevant to genitalia.* (p. 616)

Reid and colleagues (1996) agree with Bem. They noted:

> *. . . although girls and women in White American families have traditionally been socialized to be passive, dependent, conforming, expressive, and sexually receptive, African American women have been found to behave independently and to expect more egalitarian relationships. . . . On the other hand, Latinas, including Puerto Rican and Mexican American women, appear to be extremely submissive and indulgent toward men. . . . Chinese American women similarly appear to be submissive in public; however, they are vocal and demanding in private. . . .*
>
> *Which of these groups represents the "American ideal," or the norm?*
>
> *Our response is all of them and none of them. All, because every American group must be included and represented in Americans' image and none, because one, alone, is not adequate to convey the complexity of developing gender behavior in the context of family and community.* (p. 103)

Summary

Psychology has proved a fertile ground for the study of gender role identity. A person's gender role identity has been especially difficult to study because of the continuing debate over what factors—biological, social, or a combination of both—contribute to its development.

For centuries, scholars have assumed that women and men differ in countless social and psychological ways. The encyclopedic study made by psychologists Eleanor Maccoby and Carol Jacklin put most of these presumed differences to rest. However, several other psychologists have questioned even the few differences that Maccoby and Jacklin found. They noted that when gender differences were found, they were quite small.

Traditionally, femininity and masculinity were seen as mutually exclusive: one set for girls and women (emotional-expressive) and the other for boys and men (instrumental-competency). We now have a multicomponent model of femininity and masculinity where behaviors, personality characteristics, appearances, and roles are seen to be related and where an individual's cultural heritage is acknowledged and valued.

While the concept of psychological androgyny has proven interesting, research has not substantiated the benefits of androgyny.

Suggested Readings

Beall, A. E., & Sternberg, R. J. (Eds.). (1993). *The psychology of gender*. New York: Guilford Press.

Belenky, M., Clinchy, B., Goldberger, N., & Tarule, J. (1986). *Women's ways of knowing*. New York: Basic Books.

Hare-Mustin, R. T., & Marecek, J. (1990). *Making a difference: Psychology and the construction of gender*. New Haven, CT: Yale University Press.

Hyde, J. S., & Plant, E. (1995). The magnitude of psychological gender differences: Another side to the story. *American Psychologist, 50*, 159–161.

Marecek, J. (1995). Gender, politics, and psychology's ways of knowing. *American Psychologist, 50*, 162–163.

The Social Roles Perspective

I was raised the Chinese way: I was taught to desire nothing, to swallow other people's misery, to eat my own bitterness. And even though I taught my daughter the opposite, still she came out the same way! Maybe it is because she was born to my mother and I was born a girl. All of us are like stairs, one step after another, going up and down, but all going the same way.

Amy Tan

There is only one complete unblushing male in America: a young, married, white, urban, northern, heterosexual Protestant father of college education, fully employed, of good complexion, weight, and height, and recent record in sports.

Erving Goffman

What's Your Opinion?

From whom have you learned gender stereotypic behavior: your mother? father? friends? teachers? television?

Read through a magazine designed for women (e.g., *Glamour, Cosmopolitan, Leers, Mirabella, Allure)*. What images of women do the advertisements in these magazines suggest? How are overweight women portrayed? Are there women of color in these advertisements? How are men depicted?

Listen to your favorite music. Do the lyrics suggest any images of women and men? Are these images positive or negative?

With its focus on the patterns of human interaction among various groups, the fields of sociology and social psychology have much to offer to a discussion on behavior related to gender role. Nineteenth-century sociologists like William Graham Sumner and Lester Ward saw women's and men's gender-related behaviors as extensions of their biology. These early sociologists perceived women as being destined to care for infants by virtue of their "maternal instinct"; men were seen as more aggressive because of their belligerent impulses.

The disciplines of sociology and social psychology had an androcentric focus (Rabinowitz & Sechzur, 1993). The reemergent women's movement of the late 1960s and early 1970s contributed to many feminist-oriented researchers focusing their attention on the stratification of and discrimination against women and other related issues that were seen as integral parts of Western society's social structures (Paludi & Steuernagel, 1990). Areas of interest included the socialization process and the important socializing agents (e.g., parents, teachers, and peers) who taught the individual what was expected of her or him in terms of gender role related behavior. Sociologists and social psychologists also examined the social institutions (e.g., education and politics) that perpetuated the inequality of status, prestige, and power between women and men. In the past decade or so, sociologists and social psychologists have played a large role in analyzing sex and gender from the perspectives of how we learn about what is expected of us and how society through its powerful institutions reinforces and supports a basic inequality between women and men.

In this chapter we will examine how individuals learn what is expected of them in terms of their sex label as either female or male. First, we will discuss several sociological constructs that make up the basis of social interaction, namely, status, roles, and norms. Next, we will focus on the feminine and masculine gender role norms. Then we will discuss the socialization process and several socializing agents, such as parents and peers, who act as major social forces shaping our gender role related behavior. We will discuss social institutions (e.g., education, religion, politics, the health field) that perpetuate unequal status for women and men in Part Two of this book.

Status, Roles, and Norms: The Building Blocks of Gender Roles

All human groups are made up of people who occupy a position or rank within the group. A person's position in a group is called a *status.* Some common examples of statuses are woman, husband, son, daughter, soldier, mother, physician, minister, TV celebrity, and senior citizen. A status is a social label that identifies a person's position in a particular group.

A status not only serves as a social label, it also allows people to be ranked in terms of other people's statuses. For example, the status of mother has a higher rank in a family than that of son or daughter. Some statuses are more highly valued or ranked in our society than others: Teachers have more status than students, managers more than employees, physicians more than nurses, and, in general, men more than women (see chapter 8).

Sociologists distinguish two types of statuses: ascribed and achieved. *Ascribed status* refers to a person's position in a group over which she or he has little or no control. Some common examples of ascribed statuses are a person's biological sex, a person's ethnicity, and a person's age as in the ascribed age-related statuses of *adolescent* or *older adult*.

Achieved status refers to those social positions over which an individual generally has more control. The statuses of student, mother, quarterback, scientist, and rabbi are all achieved statuses because they are social positions or statuses that a person earns or chooses to become through personal effort.

Everyone has several ascribed and achieved statuses. Sociologists refer to the number of individual statuses held by one person as a *status-set* (Merton, 1968). A college student could list a number of ascribed and achieved statuses like woman, Hispanic, young adult, daughter, sister, lesbian, chemistry major, and student government president. All of these statuses give others who relate to this person some indication of how they should interact with her, and they give others an indication of the rank she holds in a particular group. For example, an adolescent daughter knows that she should defer to her mother's judgment about her curfew on the weekend.

Every status carries with it a set of *norms* or prescribed behaviors that combine to make up a role. (Actually, a status may have several sets of prescriptive norms, which means a status may have several roles associated with it.) A person who occupies a certain status is usually expected to act in certain ways, perform certain obligatory behaviors, and, quite often, enjoy special privileges related to a particular status. For instance, the achieved status of father carries with it certain normative obligations like contributing to the support of his children, teaching them how to behave as members of society, being available to help them when they have problems, and if necessary, getting them out of difficult life experiences. A father has certain privileges like seeing his children's accomplishments in interpersonal relationships and school achievements. The norms a society prescribes for a particular role usually provide a type of blueprint of how a person should act.

One question sociologists and social psychologists are particularly interested in is how we learn the norms that make up our various roles. They generally believe that role behaviors are learned from the people around us (our parents, peers, teachers, and other influential people in our lives), as well as from various media (television, movies, books, and magazines). Although most norms and their consequent roles associated with various statuses are not normally written down, some statuses are so important to a particular society that certain prescribed role behaviors may be entered into the basic documents of a country. The Constitution of the Republic of Ireland, for example, prescribes that mothers should not work outside of the home:

> *In particular, the State recognizes that by her life within the home, woman gives to the state a support without which the common good cannot be achieved. The State shall, therefore, endeavour to ensure that mothers shall not be obliged by economic necessity to engage in labour to the neglect of their duties in the home.* (Article 41, Section 2, Subsections 1 and 2)

The ascribed statuses of woman and man and their accompanying roles are, to many people, the most important social structures that each of us must contend with. These specific social structures literally give definition to each person's daily life.

Gender Norms

All societies prescribe certain behaviors, beliefs, and attitudes for girls, women, boys, and men. These prescriptions make up the *gender norms.* The gender norms taken together comprise the *gender roles.* In other words, gender norms are the prescriptive guidelines that form the gender roles. But what does our society prescribe for women and men in terms of their gender norms? Society's gender norms are somewhat generalized in their prescriptive weights, and there are exceptions to them, but we can outline what is generally prescribed for both women and men. Let's begin with women's gender norms.

Women's Gender Norms

Women's primary gender norm is what Nancy Felipe Russo (1976) labeled the *motherhood mandate.* Little girls are encouraged to play with dolls. Doll play is perceived as an important way for little girls to learn appropriate nurturant behaviors that will supposedly be necessary in their adult lives. For example, in adolescence, girls are considered to be more capable of handling baby-sitting activities and responsibilities than are boys of a similar age. And, one of the first questions asked of the newly married woman is when she is going to have a baby. Thus, having a baby and becoming a mother can be seen as the central feature or gender norm of a woman's life and the very core of a woman's identity as a person. According to Russo (1976):

> *Characterizing motherhood as prescribed, however, does not adequately communicate the centrality of this behavior to the definition of the adult female. "Being pretty" is also prescribed, but one can compensate for not being pretty (by being a "good mother," for example). Motherhood is on a qualitatively different plane. It is a woman's raison d'etre. It is mandatory. The mandate requires that one have at least two children (historically as many as possible and preferably sons) and that one raise them "well." As long as this situation exists for the vast majority of women in Western society and the world in general, prohibitions may be eliminated and options widened, but change will occur only insofar as women are first able to fulfill their mandate of motherhood. (p. 144)*

The motherhood mandate also includes the injunction that a woman should strive to be a "good" mother—good in the sense that she devote a majority of her time and energy to caring for the children. For women, then, becoming a mother is the central gender norm. Although most women are influenced by the motherhood mandate, there are several problems associated with it. Sociologist Jessie Bernard (1988) describes some of these problems:

> *Even if the young woman is in sync with the institutional timing for entrance into the world of mothers—early twenties—she may not be prepared. Although it has been taken for granted from her birth, by the girl herself as well as others, that she will become a mother and although she has been surrounded by books, pamphlets, articles, old wives' tales and lore, she is, as Alice Rossi pointed out some time ago (1968), quite*

unprepared for it. She can prepare her body for childbirth, but how can she prepare it for the sleepless nights, the fatigue, the anxieties, the feelings of helplessness in the face of a crying infant that cannot communicate its pain? for the nameless fears? the unlimited responsibilities? the endless duties and obligations? the pervasive guilt? (p. 166)

Second only to the motherhood mandate in prime importance is what may be called the marriage mandate. Marriage is for many women a *rite de passage*, an entrance into the world of adults, freedom from parental control, and a means of fulfilling an expectation of femininity. In marriage a woman takes on the role that many see as one of her primary responsibilities, that is, becoming a homemaker. As with the motherhood mandate, the marriage mandate does not fully prepare most women for many of the less than ennobling activities prescribed for the woman-homemaker: the cleaning, caretaking, and countless other tasks that fill a homemaker's day (Lopata, 1971) and the additional duties (and stress) that come with caring for elderly loved ones (Doress-Worters, 1994). Generally speaking, a woman finds herself faced with two major mandates or socially prescribed gender norms, those of becoming a mother and a married woman. More and more women are challenging these two gender norms and seeking other alternatives to fulfilling their place in society.

Cultural research on women's gender norms has suggested several similarities and differences to the discussion we just presented. For example, in American Indian cultures, the central theme is caring for others; this cycle of caring includes being cared for, preparing to care for, and caring for (Red Horse, 1980). According to Theresa LaFromboise and her colleagues (1995):

Whether their well-being is deemed effective functioning, adaptation, and competence or living a peaceful (Hopi), artfull (Acoma), or beautiful (Navajo) life, the path each takes is guided by a commitment foremost to family and community and the universal Indian values of wisdom, intelligence, poise, tranquility, cooperation, unselfishness, responsibility, kindness, and protectiveness of all life forms. (pp. 197–198)

As another example, Latinas' values include marianismo. Marianismo demands that women model their life after the Virgin Mary. They are reared to see themselves as spiritually superior to men and able to endure great suffering. According to Ginorio and colleagues (1995), marianism is "a value that some Latina women interpret as placing one's children's needs before one's own."

We discuss additional cultural prescriptions for women in chapter 5.

Men's Gender Norms

Men's gender norms do not focus on the elements of parenting and marriage as they do for women. Fathering does not carry the same impact for the man's identity as mothering does for the woman's. Being a father is something most men find personally satisfying and a significant feature in their lives (Doyle, 1995; Palm, 1993). However, most men's sense of identity is not as totally focused on parenting as is the case for most women. When it comes to specific men's gender norms, we find a series of loose-knit prescriptive elements or themes that men should evidence in their lives.

Robert Brannon (1976) has grouped the male's gender norms into four categories:

1. *No Sissy Stuff:* The stigma of all stereotyped feminine characteristics and qualities, including openness and vulnerability.
2. *The Big Wheel:* Success, status, and the need to be looked up to.
3. *The Sturdy Oak:* A manly air of toughness, confidence, and self-reliance.
4. *Give 'Em Hell!:* The aura of aggression, violence, and daring. (p. 12)

James Doyle (1995) added a fifth, the sexual element, to Brannon's normative categories. According to Doyle, the five men's gender norms are the antifeminine element, the success element, the aggressive element, the sexual element, and the self-reliant element. Let's examine each in turn.

Men are admonished never to act in any way that may be interpreted as feminine. The *antifeminine element* is basic to the men's gender norm. If women are thought of as too emotional, dependent, or nonassertive, men must be the opposite to prove themselves masculine in the ideal sense. The antifeminine bias in most men's attitudes and behaviors has been pointed out by several authors who have written extensively about men's lives (Brod, 1989; Farrell, 1974; Jourard, 1974; McCreary, 1994).

Being number one or the best is another prescription and is referred to as the *success element*. Here we find the injunction that men should prove their masculinity by doing better than others at work and sports. Men may strive to outdo others and by doing so prove themselves more masculine than others. There are many ways a man can show himself to be a success, for example, by having a bigger office, a bigger car, or even by being able to outdrink a colleague. It is not surprising that many men measure their success in terms of the size of their paychecks (Gould, 1974). The amount of money a man earns seems a convenient and easily quantifiable measure of both his success and his masculinity.

Men are expected to fight for what they consider right. Down through the centuries, men have been pictured as naturally more aggressive than women. The *aggressive element* is the third norm prescribed in varying degrees for men. Most men prefer to use force as a way of dealing with public disturbances rather than nonviolent, or what many men think of as "feminine," means (Miedzian, 1991).

The *sexual element* is the fourth norm prescribed for men. Sexual conquest is for many men one of the strongest proofs of masculinity. Many men see themselves as the initiators of sex, whereas most women define themselves in terms of being objects of sexual advances. For both women and men, sexual knowledge, sexual attitudes, and sexual activities play an integral part in their self-concepts. However, the man-as-sexual-initiator/controller is an important norm to which men live up.

The last gender norm is the *self-reliant element*. Men must be cool, unflappable, in control, and tough—in other words, self-reliant in most situations.

Although this last element is difficult to achieve, a man may feel the pressures to be, or rather, to act as if he is in control of himself and of whatever situation in which he finds himself.

Thus, we see that in our society and others both women and men have very explicit gender norms. Not all women and men continuously fulfill all the prescriptive gender norms placed on them, but that in and of itself does not deny the presence of such gender norms. We now need to ask how we learn the specific gender norms that constitute our gender roles.

Although no systematic study has been undertaken to see if the above five male norms find expression in cultures outside of North America, the antifeminine element appears as a common feature among men from numerous cultures. For instance, antifemininity is a prime male prescription among men living in a small Australian town (West, 1994), among those attending Chinese universities (Chia et al., 1994), and those identified as Filipino labor migrants (Margold, 1994).

Interestingly, the stereotypic "machismo" associated with Mexican men and its connotation of virulent antifemale sexism and hypersexuality is more myth than reality, at least among many urban Mexican men (Gutmann, 1994, 1996). Describing his recent ethnographic research on gender roles among Mexican men, Matthew Gutmann writes: "In Mexico in the last 20 years, . . . the entire society has witnessed rapid and widespread upheavals involving . . . gender roles" (p. 31). Testifying how Mexican men's supposed "hypermasculine" concern with fathering (i.e., the sexual element) is not universally characteristic, Gutmann quotes one 27-year-old man, "For me, having a lot of kids to prove you're really macho is a bunch of bulshit (*sic*)" (p. 28).

The Social Mold: Shaping the Gender Roles

Passing by a hospital nursery, one can observe just how similar most newborn babies really are in their appearance and, more important, in their behaviors (see chapters 2 and 3). Why is it that so many people earnestly see infant girls as being so different from infant boys? An answer may be simply that most parents see their children through "gender-role-colored" glasses that focus on presumed gender differences where few exist. Because parents see their infants differently, there may be a tendency to treat each sex differently. Treating infant girls and boys differently is just the first step in the long process called socialization, which, among many influences, leads to the creation of two very different gender roles.

But what do we actually mean by the term *socialization?* Socialization is the process by which children, adolescents, and adults learn what is expected of them through their interactions with other individuals. Socialization can be thought of as a social mold that shapes each person to fit into a group. A child, for example, learns certain basic feeding skills, including which utensil to use with which type of food. Depending on the society, a child may be taught to use chopsticks or a spoon and fork. Children and others must learn the ways, traditions, norms, and rules of getting along with others, and socialization is the process by which everyone learns the lessons that others deem necessary for them to fit into their group.

Socializing Agents

When a mother tells her daughter to pick up the dishes on the kitchen table, when a little girl sees a picture in a department store catalog of little girls playing with a miniature stove, or when a young boy recites the Boy Scout oath that he should be "physically strong, mentally awake, and morally straight," we can see different *socializing agents* at work. Any person or social institution that shapes a person's values, beliefs, or behaviors is a socializing agent. Socializing agents are especially effective during childhood. An effective socializing agent usually is respected by the person being socialized.

Some of the most important lessons a child learns and those that are reinforced throughout a child's early years and beyond are her or his gender roles. Let's examine some of the different socializing agents that combine to shape a child's gender role.

Parents As Socializers

Parents are one of the more important socializing agents. But just how early in their children's lives do parents begin to teach their children what is expected of them in terms of their sex label?

In their classic study, Jeffrey Rubin and associates (1974) found that first-time parents described their one-day-old infants in terms of gender role related characteristics. Typically, fathers saw their newborn sons "as firmer, larger featured, better coordinated, more alert, stronger, and hardier," while other fathers saw their daughters "as softer, finer featured, more awkward, more inattentive, weaker, and more delicate." These fathers saw gender-related differences when actually none were obvious: The infant girls and boys were identical with respect to birth weight, birth length, and neonatal activity ratings. More than likely, these fathers' notions of gender role stereotypes played an important role in why they saw their newborn infants so differently. Other researchers have found similar but not as extreme patterns where parents see their children in terms of gender role stereotypes rather than their children's actual behaviors (Karraker, Vogel, & Lake, 1995).

Parents know their infant's sex, and some may suggest that they are reacting to real gender differences and not to something they have preconceived in their minds. What about adults who don't have firsthand knowledge of an infant's sex? Do they also treat infant girls and boys differently? The answer is most emphatically yes! Research shows that one of the more important factors influencing how an adult interacts with an infant is the infant's sex label (Eagly, 1995; Seavey et al., 1975; Sidorowicz & Lunney, 1980). For instance, a helpful toy salesperson (a stranger) will select toys for a child according to a child's sex (Kutner & Levinson, 1978). To highlight just how important a child's sex is for an adult, let's examine one often-cited study to see how adults use the sex label to guide their play with an infant.

Jerrie Will, Patricia Self, and Nancy Datan (1976) asked mothers to play with a six-month-old infant. Mothers played with the infant who was dressed in a pink dress and called "Beth." Some mothers played with the same infant who was then wearing blue pants and named "Adam." (Actually, the infant was a six-month-old boy.) Placed in a room with the infant, the mothers were given toys with which to entertain the child, specifically, a plastic fish, a doll, and a train. When asked to play with either "Beth" or "Adam," the respective mothers generally offered Beth the doll and Adam the train. Not only did these mothers offer different toys on the basis of the "perceived" sex of the infant, they even interacted differently with the infant. The mothers who thought they had Beth smiled more and held her closer to themselves than did the mothers who had Adam. After the observations were completed, the mothers were interviewed, and all stated that mothers should not treat infant girls and boys differently!

Other studies have demonstrated that adults perceived an infant's behavior as "feminine" if it was labeled a "girl" and "masculine" if the infant was labeled a "boy" (Paludi & Gullo, 1986). Discussions with parents of young children suggest a consensus that girls are expected to be verbal, compliant, passive, physically weak, and clean (Basow, 1986). Even before birth parents project fetal activity as representative of assumed gender differences; e.g., very active fetal movement is assumed to be characteristic of a boy rather than a girl.

Parents also play with girls and boys differently. Parents are more likely to interact and talk more with their daughters, while parents with sons are more apt to play more actively with them (Bem, 1993). Infant girls are usually seen as more fragile by both mothers and fathers alike (Reid & Paludi, 1993). There are many reasons for this differential treatment. Beverly Fagot (1978, 1988), for example, suggested that parents want their sons to be rough and tough, or "masculine," and daughters are encouraged to be neat and orderly, or "feminine," in their behaviors.

In addition to holding stereotypic expectations, parents encourage sex-appropriate activities by providing children with sex-typed toys and clothing (Geer & Shields, 1996). Girls are given dolls, doll houses, and miniature household appliances. Boys are provided with building blocks, sports equipment, and models of vehicles. Parents engage in more "rescuing" behavior with girls, e.g., assisting and accompanying girls more often than necessary. Parents' willingness to constantly "help" girls supports high levels of dependency in girls (Geer & Shields, 1996).

Parents also continue shaping their children's gender roles through the kinds of chores they assign them around the house. In a statewide sample (Nebraska) of 669 boys and girls between the ages of 2 and 17, researchers Lynn White and David Brinnerhoff (1981) found distinctive gender differences in the kinds of chores children did. Basically, girls did "women's work": cleaning the house, doing the dishes, cooking, and babysitting for younger siblings. Boys did "men's work": mowing the lawns, shoveling

Box 4-1

> ### *Barbie Speaks, Will Girls Listen?*
>
> In the fall of 1991, Mattel Toys manufactured the latest Barbie doll. What's new
> with this version? When the "Teen Talk" Barbie's back is pressed, she speaks.
> Her message caused concern for two mathematicians at Rennselear Polytechnic
> Institute (RPI) because the phrases include, "Math class is tough." According to
> Professor Joyce McLaughlin: "I think we've worked hard to teach math and one
> of our goals is to have more women enter the field. . . . In order to do that we
> need to change some of the stereotypes out there that girls can't do math. . . .
> This doll certainly doesn't do any good. . . . It's just an old stereotype and we
> object to that."
>
> After reading a letter sent to Mattel Toys by the mathematicians at RPI and
> the American Association of University Women, company spokesperson Lisa
> McKendall announced that future versions of this Barbie will not have the "Math
> class is tough" message. Mattel also agreed to exchange Barbies that have the
> math message for another doll, but refused to recall this version of the doll.

snow, taking out the garbage, and other general yardwork chores. Other researchers have also found similar divisions of labor along gender lines in
their studies of task assignments (Antill, Goodnow, Russell, & Cotton, 1996).

Majorie Hill (1988), however, noted that lesbian mothers perceived their
daughters and sons to be more similar in characteristics than did heterosexual mothers. Lesbian mothers held less stereotypic ideas relating to the feminine role and encouraged more traditionally masculine role expectations of
their daughters. And, daughters of employed mothers perceive a woman's
role as involving freedom of choice and satisfaction. Daughters and sons of
employed mothers perceive a smaller difference between women and men in
terms of warmth and expressiveness than do children of unemployed mothers. Furthermore, African American and Latin American mothers hold higher
expectations for their daughters than white American mothers.

Within the United States the role expectations for girls and those for boys
have many commonalities, but they also vary depending upon social class
and the ethnicity of the family and surrounding community. Research has
suggested a greater flexibility and permissiveness in middle-class homes regardless of ethnicity. This flexibility leads to the availability of masculine activity choices for girls and feminine activity choices for boys. In working-class
homes, parents are more concerned that their children adhere strictly to sex-
appropriate behavior, as it is stereotypically defined (Reid & Paludi, 1993).

Another powerful facilitator of women's and men's career development is
maternal employment (Betz, 1993). Daughters of employed mothers are
more career-oriented (versus home-oriented) than are daughters of homemakers (Hoffman, 1989). Sons and daughters of employed mothers are less
stereotyped in their gender role preferences. And, daughters of employed
mothers are more willing to pursue nontraditional careers than daughters of
homemakers. Employed mothers place considerable emphasis on independence training (Betz, 1993).

Research with ethnic minority individuals consistently has demonstrated that maternal employment is positively associated with academic achievement. In addition to maternal employment per se are the effects of the mothers' feelings about work. Women's primary role decisions of career, noncareer work, or homemaking did not parallel those of their mothers' but were related to their mothers' messages to them. In addition to mothers' encouragement of their daughters' success is their concomitant lack of pressure toward culturally defined expectations of femininity. Mothers who exert less pressure on their daughters to date, marry, and mother have more career-oriented daughters (Betz, 1993).

Besides the influence of parents' socioeconomic and racial statuses on what is taught to children, the sex label, as we have noted, determines to a great extent what kinds of values parents wish their children to learn. We can see this gender-related difference in the emphasis placed on the value of independence. Girls are often encouraged by their parents to show more dependent behaviors. Boys are often encouraged by their parents to exhibit independent behaviors. Parents teach either independence or dependence to a child in many ways, but there are clear differences in what is taught to girls and boys. For example, young boys are more often permitted to leave their yards and play with others than young girls are (Reid & Paludi, 1993). Boys, it seems, are subtly encouraged to roam away from parental supervision, but girls are discouraged from such independence-producing behavior.

Parents are not the only socializing force in a child's life. Other forces present in the child's early life shape the content of behavior related to gender role. Most women and men prefer boys to girls and base their preferences on assumed gender differences (Paludi, 1992). Preference for boys is especially noted in some countries where boys and men have higher status and represent income and financial support. Girls and women are perceived to be a financial burden since a dowry must be paid for a daughter to marry.

Since the use of chorionic villa sampling and amniocentesis (methods that detect the sex of the fetus around the third or fourth month of gestation), a disproportionate number of female fetuses have been aborted. Individuals who prefer sons are most willing to use sex selection technology.

Media As Socializers

The mass media—books, magazines, comics, radio, television, films, and music—play a significant role in people's lives. Mass media provide more than mere entertainment; they teach, persuade, and shape people's lives. A recurrent theme in much of the media is how the women and men should behave. When we see an advertisement in a magazine, listen to popular songs, read a romance novel, or watch a soap opera, the message is often decidedly traditional in content: women should act "feminine," and men "masculine" (Eagly, 1995). Let's examine some of the more important media and focus on just what messages they emphasize in terms of gender roles.

The Printed Word

Children's books with their stories of humanlike animals and humans provide a powerful vehicle for the socialization of gender roles. Sociologist Lenore Weitzman (1979) wrote:

> *Through books, children learn about the world outside their immediate environment: they learn what other boys and girls do, say, and feel, and they learn what is expected of children their age. Picture books are especially important to the preschool child because they are often looked at over and over again at a time when children are in the process of developing their own sex-role identities. In addition, they are read to children before other socialization influences (such as school, teachers, and peers) become important in their lives.* (p. 7)

The gender roles presented in children's books often offer a biased and narrow portrayal of the feminine role. To learn more about the not-so-subtle gender messages contained in these early primers, we need to examine how girls and boys are portrayed. Weitzman (1972), along with several of her colleagues, conducted a content analysis of several prize-winning children's books (i.e., the Caldecott Medal winners between 1967 and 1971). A majority of the books told stories about boys and men, but a few girls and women were present in the stories. The gender bias in these books becomes striking when we note that male characters outnumbered female characters by 11 to 1. The bias becomes even more obvious when animal characters (e.g., rabbits, horses, puppies) are added. The ratio of male to female animals was 95 to 1.

As for the stories themselves, boys and men performed a variety of different and exciting activities and roles that portrayed them as acting competently and in charge of the stories' action. When girls and women did enter the stories, they usually did so in a rather limited and, for the most part, quite passive way. The message in these primers is rather clear: Boys live exciting and independent lives, whereas girls are primarily auxiliaries to boys.

More recent reviews of the Caldecott winners suggested a marked improvement in the stories' sex ratio. Boys and men outnumbered girls and women by only 1.8 to 1. However, if we again include the animal characters, males outnumber females by 2.66 to 1 (Kolbe & LaVoie, 1981). Obviously, recent authors of children's books have tried to improve the representation of female characters in their children's stories. Although the sex ratio has improved, the fact of the matter is that girls and women outnumber boys and men in the real world, a fact apparently forgotten by most authors of children's literature.

Aside from the distorted sex ratios portrayed in these books, just what kinds of activities are the books' characters doing? A majority of the men characters engaged in "masculine" activities, and the few women characters primarily worked around the home doing traditional "feminine" jobs. Surely, many of the children reading these books can't help but notice that their mothers work outside the home, while the mothers in their storybooks stay home all day.

Box 4-2

Are These the Messages We Want to Give Our Children?

Georgie Porgie, pudding and pie,
Kissed the girls and made them cry.
When the boys came out to play,
Georgie Porgie ran away.

Peter, Peter, pumpkin eater,
Had a wife and couldn't keep her.
He put her in a pumpkin shell,
And there he kept her very well.

There was an old woman
Who lived in a shoe.
She had so many children
She didn't know what to do.
She gave them some broth,
Without any bread,
Then spanked them all soundly,
And sent them to bed.

Little Polly Flinders
Sat among the cinders,
Warming her pretty toes!
Her mother came and caught her,
And spanked her little daughter,
For spoiling her nice new clothes.

Textbooks also present stereotyping of feminine and masculine activities. Mathematics textbooks present stereotyping of girls' competencies and abilities. Girls are frequently portrayed as poor in math and confused by complicated math problems. Furthermore, Pamela Reid & Michele Paludi (1993) reported that readers and textbooks predominantly portray white characters. African American girls and white girls are seldom depicted together in the same story. The absence of female models conveys a message that they are not important enough to be represented. This must be the impression given to ethnic minority girls. Ethnic minority characters are rarely depicted in a significant way in readers and textbooks.

Paludi and colleagues (1991) reviewed 33 textbooks that are currently in use in undergraduate and graduate statistics courses (taught in psychology departments) in the United States. Their review of the statistics texts indicated that there are practically no references made to women/girls (the few references that do exist are stereotypical in content), no references to ethnicity of researchers/experimenters, no information on sex bias in psychological research. While some textbook authors used the plural or he/she format (e.g., "when a physical scientist talks about measurement, he or she usually means . . ."), most used men/boys as referents. Paludi et al. found phrases such as:

"If the *English instructor* subtracts . . . if *she* multiplies . . ."
". . . *math instructor* . . . Since *he* has added a constant amount . . ."
behavioral scientist needs to draw *his* conclusions . . ."
"*Senator* Bean wants very much to know what fraction of the voters in *his*
    state . . ."
"The *congressman* receives 1310 pieces of mail on pending gun legislation
    . . . what will you tell *him*?"
"In this sense, each subject serves as his *own* control."
"The basic requirements and primary objectives of the experiment are
    formulated by the *experimenter;* the *experimenter* may or may not be
    aware of the possible alternative approaches that can be followed in the
    conduct of *his* experiment . . ."

And, they found the types of variables used in analyses to include the following:

women's dress size
sex of consumers choosing between two brands of soap
whether blonds (all women) "really have more fun"
women preparing food
change in women's assertiveness following their participation in an
    assertiveness program
rank ordering of women in a beauty pageant contest

Cartoons were also present in statistics texts, supposedly to make the material more fun. However, the cartoons depicted girls as "dumb" in math or husbands as "henpecked." Andrew Jackson, Franklin Delano Roosevelt, Alf Landon, and other "famous" men were mentioned, but no "famous" women were mentioned. Quotes from "famous" statisticians, including Karl Pearson, Sir Francis Galton, and Sir Ronald Fisher, were cited. No quotes from "famous" women statisticians were present, however. In short, women/girls were excluded from the discussion and when they were included, they typically were not viewed as contributing to statistics or to psychology, despite the fact that women now constitute about one-third of psychologists employed and over one-half of those earning Ph.D.'s in psychology each year.

The statistics course, similar to the introductory-level courses, holds a unique place in the career development of students in undergraduate and graduate training programs in psychology. This course is occasionally seen by students as one which will determine future careers in psychology. From a pedagogical perspective, the statistics course is a critical point at which students are introduced to the basic vocabulary and concepts in psychological research. Exclusion of research material on gender and race may not be subsequently questioned if the statistics course does not treat the material from a balanced perspective. Research questions about these issues would, therefore, remain marginal, not central, to the field.

Ellen Kimmel chaired a Task Force for the Division on the Psychology of Women of the American Psychological Association and reported findings similar to Paludi and colleagues in texts dealing with developmental psychology and introductory psychology.

Television and Motion Pictures

Without a doubt, television plays a significant role in the socialization process. When it comes to children's television and its commercials, we find considerable sexism in its content. An early study of the highly acclaimed "Sesame Street" even found its presentation of the gender roles relatively biased in traditional ways (Gardner, 1970).

But children do not limit their viewing habits to children's fare only. Prime-time television draws the largest number of viewers of every age group. In general, TV commercials portray women almost solely in the helping role, waiting on others and living out their lives in service to others, never really taking charge of their own lives. Such a view perpetuates traditional views of women's and men's roles in society (Coltrane & Allan, 1994).

A few television sponsors have made an effort to introduce counterstereotypic gender presentations. For example, we occasionally see "Josephine the Plumber" tackling a stopped-up drain and showing a man what needs to be done. But do such commercials have an effect other than being novel? Joyce Jennings Walstedt and several colleagues (1977) found that women who watched counterstereotypic TV commercials were more self-confident and less likely to conform to group pressure in other situations. Portraying women in counterstereotypic ways may have positive effects for women in the TV audience in terms of their building self-confidence as self-determining and achievement-oriented individuals (Geis et al., 1984).

For the most part, however, advertisers present women and men in stereotypic ways. Men celebrate the end of another day by stopping at a local bar with their pals. If not in a bar, a man is out in a distant woods or by a remote stream all because he chose the right kind of four-wheel-drive vehicle. In contrast, women in most commercials seem interested only in stemming the telltale signs of age, marveling over the softness of bathroom tissue, bemoaning the waxy buildup on their kitchen floors, or standing seductively by some car as a man describes the car. Lucy Komisar (1971) sees the treatment of women in advertising as follows:

> *Advertising . . . . legitimizes the idealized, stereotyped roles of woman as temptress, wife, mother, and sex object, and portrays women as less intelligent and more dependent than men. It makes women believe that their chief role is to please men and that their fulfillment will be as wives, mothers, and homemakers. It makes women feel unfeminine if they are not pretty enough and guilty if they do not spend most of their time in desperate attempts to imitate gourmet cooks and eighteenth-century scullery maids. It makes women believe that their own lives, talents, and*

*interests ought to be secondary to the needs of their husbands and
families, and that they are almost totally defined by these relationships.*
(p. 310)

In the television shows packaged in between the commercials, we find
women generally excluded or portrayed in very narrow and traditional roles.
Two rather exhaustive government-sponsored studies of television programming (U.S. Commission on Civil Rights, 1977, 1979) concluded that television
portrayed most women as having no definable occupation or means of support. Of those women employed outside the home, a majority held occupations associated with traditional "women's work" like nurses and household
workers (Kalisch & Kalisch, 1984). Besides showing women performing traditional feminine tasks, the studies also found that women, for the most part,
were portrayed as being dependent on men for their livelihood; men were
generally portrayed as being more independent and in charge of a variety of
situations (Dominick, 1979; Klumas & Marchant, 1994).

Men TV characters are shown in ambitious, adventuresome, strong, and
dominant roles, whereas women are more often cast in dependent, submissive, and weak or auxiliary roles. Even when women and men are in the
same occupation, they are portrayed as performing gender role related behavior. For example, in the soap opera, "The Doctors," male physicians performed surgery; female physicians filled out hospital admission forms
(Bergmann, 1974).

In the most general sense, men play either heroes or villains, and women
appear as either adulterers or victims of men's actions (Eagly, 1995). Although men occasionally are portrayed in less than flattering ways, they are
usually shown as the "important ones" in the drama. "Dallas's" J. R. may not
have been a likable character nor one most men would have wanted to emulate, but the drama focused on him, a characteristic of TV drama that most
women characters do not share, except for the few women on the prime-
time soaps. For a woman to be the central figure in a TV drama, she must be
calculating and someone who will do anything to get her way (Cantor & Pingree, 1983). Television portrays women as appendages to men's lives but
portrays men as independent, aggressive, and in charge of their lives.

In an early study of this issue, Terry Fruch and Paul McGhee (1975) found
children who were "heavy" television viewers (i.e., 25 or more hours a
week) held more traditional gender role stereotypes than those who were
"light" viewers (i.e., 10 or less hours a week). Others have also found that
"heavy" television viewing, as well as how television portrays gender roles,
has an effect on the viewers' conceptions about gender role stereotypes
among preschoolers and young adults.

The television characters that entertain us each week present us with very
definite pictures of how we should act. In the main, women characters are
the bystanders watching men overcome all kinds of problems. There are far too
few dramas where a woman is presented in a competent and self-determining
way. Granted, we do find an occasional woman character like the attorney

Jill Hennessey played on "Law and Order" or the physician Christine Lahti plays on "Chicago Hope." However, in most of the highly rated TV shows, women are either auxiliary to the action and seemingly there only to add some "sugar and spice" and fulfill the sexual needs of the men, or they are powerful matriarchs who are evil and manipulative.

Ethnic minority women on television are also stereotyped relative to white characters and ethnic minority men characters. In all-white families on television, men are more dominant than women. In all African American families, however, women are more dominant. African American women are portrayed more forcefully than white women. African American women are typically shown within the family, reinforcing myths about black matriarchy (see chapter 5).

Darlene Hine (1993) discussed the way Hollywood portrayed one African American actress, Hattie McDaniel, the first African American woman to win an Academy Award:

> *Character actress Hattie McDaniel presents a troubling figure on the landscape of American race relations. On the one hand, she had a fruitful career in the competitive industry of Hollywood cinema in the 1930s and 1940s. . . . On the other hand, she became famous for portraying mamma-like figures and thus perpetuated one of the most hated stereotypes of Black women. . . . It is also impossible to reconcile these two opinions, because McDaniel was so firmly defined by a paradoxical nature.* (p. 768)

Beverly Goodwin (1996) cited four controlling images of African American women in the media: the mamma, the matriarch, the welfare mother, and the Jezebel. The women have, as their primary responsibility, nurturing somebody other than members of her family or friends or herself. *"Those outside her race get her best; her family and friends get what is left. Probably she is a domestic. But this role has recently been updated to other kinds of service worker, civil servant, or best friend—someone who is generally supportive of a non-Black character" (p. 186).*

The portrayal of lesbian women in television programs is virtually nonexistent. When they are portrayed, they are typically ridiculed, as was the case in episodes of the comedy series, "Roseanne," during 1994 and 1995. Linda Garnets (1996) describes this and other attitudes toward lesbians as a reflection of a perceived threat to the traditional patriarchal power structure. As Garnets noted:

> *Lesbians may be perceived as having greater power than heterosexual women because they live independently of men and do not depend on men for sexual, emotional, or financial support. . . . Lesbians' autonomy and self-sufficiency may be perceived as challenging both the female's subordinate status and the gender role that defines her identity only in terms of her relationship to men. In other words, "autonomous woman" becomes synonymous with lesbian, leading to accusations*

toward independent heterosexual women that they are the most hated kind of women: lesbians. And lesbians are "accused" of not being women. (pp. 140–141)

Women who are physically challenged are even rarer on television. If any disability is discussed, it is usually with respect to mental illness, not physical health problems (see chapter 10).

Stereotypes about women's and men's behavior are clearly observable in rock music videos. Girls and women are depicted as emotional, deceitful, illogical, frivolous, dependent, and passive. Boys and men are portrayed as sexually aggressive, rational, demanding, and adventuresome. Rock music videos depict gratuitous violence against women and women as sex objects. The interface of sexism and racism is also apparent. Susan Basow (1986) reported, for example, that in "All She Wants to Do Is Dance," an ethnic minority woman was depicted as sexual and hedonistic while a revolution is going on. Male characters in the video step on her image in a mirror. Other rock music videos act out women being raped. Frequent exposure to rock music videos increases the probability that subsequent women's and men's behavior will be appraised in the context of the gender role stereotypic schemas (Hansen & Hansen, 1988). This finding has been obtained even for preschool and young children as well as adolescents (Waite & Paludi, 1987). Women rappers challenge the stereotypes by being level-headed and in control. However, women rappers get very little airtime on MTV and other music video channels (Basow, 1992).

Preschool girls have been shown to make sex-typed choices based on television characters they observe, and even identification with the characters depends on their stereotypic portrayal. Bem (1983) suggested that parents should monitor the television programs to which their children are exposed so children can view programs that value women and femininity.

Susan Faludi (1991) noted that Hollywood's depiction of women and men reinforce stereotypes about competency, independence, passivity, and nurturance. In recent years, the backlash against feminism has meant that Hollywood has portrayed a narrow range of female characters. In 1993, for example, Oscar voters had difficulty in finding five roles meaningful enough to fill the best actress category (this is despite the fact that the 1993 Academy Awards had as its theme, "Oscar Celebrates Women and the Movies"). Perhaps a "backlash" resulted from the release of the film, *Thelma and Louise.* Following the release of *Thelma and Louise,* Hollywood offered several movies that shared an image of a woman as crazed killer, including *Basic Instinct, The Hand that Rocks the Cradle,* and *Single White Female.*

This image of women is to the nineties what the marriage versus career dilemma was to the eighties in Hollywood. In the mid and late 1980s Hollywood introduced us to several women characters who at first support feminist principles and then renounce them as evil. For example, in *Working Girl,* the female protagonist, Tess, succeeds in business and has a relationship with a man only by playing dependent and daffy. As Faludi states:

She succeeds in business only by combing the tabloid gossip columns for investment tips—and relying on far more powerful businessmen to make the key moves in her "career." She succeeds in love Sleeping Beauty-style, by passing out in a man's arms. . . . Tess is allowed to move up in the ranks of American business only by tearing another woman down. . . . (p. 128)

Consider the female protagonists in the following motion pictures: J. C. Wiatt in *Baby Boom* and Isabella in *Crossing Delancey*. How did you perceive them? Do you believe they represent real women you know in your family, class, or workplace?

Marvin Moore (1992) examined "successful" television family series across four decades. Moore reported that 94 percent of the family presentations featured white families. In addition, a slightly higher percentage of white families with African American members as African American families were presented (e.g., "Webster"). African American families were portrayed more than all other groups.

Moore's research also suggested that 50 percent of the series featured couples with children while 14 percent featured childless couples. Twenty-nine percent of single-parent families were also presented. Unlike real-life experiences of single parents, a larger percentage of the television single parent families featured men as heads of households.

Moore concluded in his assessment that ". . . successful family presentations have generally ignored or greatly exaggerated the changing roles of men and women and the impact that these have had on both individuals and families. In general, changes in male roles have been exaggerated. . . . The changing roles of women and the consequences of these changes have been largely ignored in the programming" (pp. 57–58).

Teachers As Socializers

As we discuss in more detail in chapter 8, teachers treat girls and boys differently (Sadker & Sadker, 1994). Several years ago, psychologist Lisa Serbin (1973) and several of her colleagues studied how teachers treat preschool children and how this treatment influenced the children in learning their gender roles. In the classroom, Serbin found that preschool girls behaved more dependently, whereas boys generally acted more aggressively. Clearly, these behaviors mirror the commonly accepted gender stereotypes for each sex. Serbin also found that the teachers' behaviors toward their students helped reinforce these gender-specific behaviors. Specifically, when boys acted aggressively, their teachers were more likely to reprimand them than they were to reprimand girls who acted in a similar manner.

Research has shown that reprimanding a child for a particular behavior may have the same effect as reinforcing that behavior; consequently, that behavior is more likely to continue. Thus, the teachers' reprimands may have reinforced the boys' aggressive behaviors. When girls behaved dependently, the teachers' interactions with them can be seen as a type of reinforcement for their dependent behaviors. When girls needed assistance, their teachers often required that the girls come to them for help, which reinforced the girls' dependency on an adult. Boys, however, weren't required to come to their teachers for assistance. In summary, Serbin found that teachers play a decisive role in their students' acquisition of behaviors associated with traditional gender role stereotypes (see chapter 8).

The 1992 report by the American Association of University Women (AAUW) concerning gender comparisons in elementary and secondary education experiences noted that teachers keep girls dependent on them for help with their schoolwork while praising boys for their independence. In addition, the report noted that girls are not asked for their opinions or answers to questions as often as are boys. Girls are required to raise their hand if they have something to say while boys are reinforced for shouting out an answer or statement.

In the AAUW report, "Shortchanging Girls, Shortchanging America," responses of 3,000 students between the ages of 9 and 15 years were summarized. The study provided comparisons among African American, Latina, and white girls. Results suggested that Latinas had the highest levels of self-esteem of all three groups in elementary school but suffered a larger drop in self-esteem by high school than any of the other groups. Ginorio et al., (1995) explain this AAUW finding by the responsibility Latinas carry for child care and housekeeping, even among girls in grade school.

Pamela Reid and colleagues (1995) discussed the other ways the interface of sex and race could be devastating if both expectations on the part of teachers were negative. For example, intelligent African American girls disconfirmed teachers' expectancies about African American children and girls in general; consequently, African American girls received less attention than any other race or sex group. Reid and colleagues (1995) also found that as African American girls advanced through school, they received less attention from their teachers.

Through the early grade school years, girls generally do better scholastically than boys. However, somewhere near the end of high school, many girls' academic performance declines even below that of those boys whose grades were lower than the girls' just a few years earlier (see chapter 8). How can we explain this "turnaround" in girls' academic performance?

During the 1970s, Carol Dweck and colleagues conducted a series of studies looking into the effects of what they termed *learned helplessness* (Dweck, 1975; Dweck et al., 1978). Learned helplessness occurs when people reduce their effort because they assume that failure is inevitable. If, for example, a child perceives that failure at some task is more likely than success because of lack of ability, then the child may concede that she or he can do little to avoid failure.

But what would make a person feel that he or she must inevitably fail? If a person fails and believes the failure was due to a lack of personal effort, then failure is not inevitable but could be avoided in the future by redoubling one's effort. But what about a person who fails and assumes the failure was due to a lack of ability? For this person, redoubling of effort will do little to insure future success. Failure in the latter case is assumed to be due to one's lack of ability, which can't be changed, and in the former case, failure is assumed to be caused by lack of effort, which can be changed. Dweck's research found that girls are more likely to attribute their academic failures to a lack of ability and boys attribute their academic failures to a lack of effort. In Dweck's analysis, girls can fall victim to a sense of learned helplessness. But why is this so?

Dweck suggested that boys generally receive much more negative feedback about their behavior and academic performance from parents and teachers alike. Eventually, boys learn to dismiss much of this negative feedback as irrelevant. Girls, on the other hand, receive much less negative feedback from adults about their behaviors and academic performance, and thus when they do receive it, they tend to take it more seriously. In other words, boys become oblivious to criticism because there is so much of it, whereas girls become oversensitive to it because of the relatively little amount with which they deal. Dweck also found that boys receive relatively less negative feedback about their academic performance than girls do (Dweck et al., 1978). From their observations, boys were more heavily criticized for their conduct or for breaking rules than girls were. Thus, although girls receive less negative feedback than boys do, the negative feedback they do receive is more likely directed at their poor academic performance. Consequently, girls come to believe that poor academic performance is attributable to lack of ability, something over which they have little control. What all of this means is that girls tend to believe that they are less likely to succeed because they have been taught to think of themselves as less capable intellectually than boys. Research on the availability of role models and mentors suggests similar conclusions for college women and men (Haring-Hidore & Paludi, 1989; see chapter 8).

Several researchers, teachers, and employers have suggested that role models and mentors are important, in fact necessary, for individuals' career development. Mentoring has two major functions: psychosocial and vocational (Schockett & Haring-Hidore, 1985). Vocational functions include: educating, consulting/teaching, sponsoring, and protecting. Psychosocial functions include: role modeling, encouraging, counseling, and being a transitional figure. Each of these components can be defined as follows:

Educating:	teaching, challenging, and evaluating.
Consulting/Coaching:	acquainting a protege with the political structures in the academy; implementing the protege's goals.
Sponsoring:	promoting a protege's work to colleagues.
Protecting:	shielding a protege from negative publicity or from damaging contacts with individuals in power.

Role Modeling:	providing opportunities for a protege to observe the mentor interact with colleagues, deal with conflicts, and/or integrate lifestyle and career.
Encouraging:	building a protege's confidence.
Counseling:	discussing the protege's fears about career and/or personal concerns.
Being a Transitional Figure:	becoming a colleague with the protege; reciprocal sharing of ideas and assistance.

Not all individuals who are "mentors" will fulfill all of these vocational and psychosocial functions; not all "proteges" want all of these behaviors to be obtained from only one person (Fleming, 1996). In addition, some styles of mentoring can encompass various psychosocial and vocational functions. Two styles recently receiving attention are "grooming mentoring" and "networking mentoring." Grooming mentoring involves a more experienced person who uses power and/or position to educate, open doors, and sponsor a less mature professional who is seeking to ascend the career ladder. An egalitarian alternative to this type of mentoring is called "networking mentoring" (Swoboda & Millar, 1986).

In networking mentoring, two or more people play the roles of mentor and protege to each other at different times. This is an egalitarian rather than hierarchical approach and is based on the notion of mutual enhancement. Its advantages include that it is open to all individuals, not just a select few who find someone to groom them. Also, there are fewer relational problems that stem from intensity, greater self-reliance, less resentment by colleagues concerning favoritism, an opportunity to learn how to mentor, and no setbacks related to a mentor's career and/or personal problems (Paludi & DeFour, 1992).

Paludi and colleagues (1990) reported incidence data with their new instrument, the Mentoring Experiences Questionnaire. In a national sample of 120 graduate students and faculty members (from the City University of New York schools and from the following organizations: Association of Black Psychologists, Modern Language Association, American Sociological Association, American Association of University Professors, and the National Association of Women Deans, Administrators, and Counselors), they found the following results: (1) mentoring is more common among graduate students than among undergraduate students; (2) more women than men endorse psychosocial functions of mentoring relationships, e.g., receiving advice (mostly from women) on personal problems, receiving information on dealing with role strain involved in combining a career and family life, and being assisted with personal development; (3) more men than women endorse the vocational functions of mentoring relationships, e.g., being guided from one stage of their career to subsequent stages, being coached on submitting a paper for publication, and having a faculty member share their knowledge and expertise (mostly from men); (4) women report not being given instruction to complete their projects, e.g., that a "null environment" has been set up for them in which no information is shared; and (5) more women than men report problems in mentoring relationships (especially with male mentors), including unwanted attempts to be drawn into a discussion of personal or sexual issues and not being included in a mentor's professional network.

Schockett and colleagues (1983) identified the following stages of mentoring relationships:

Initiation: begins as the mentor provides educating and role modeling for the protege;

Cultivation: includes consulting and coaching, encouraging, sponsoring, protecting; the relationship grows stronger;

Separation: ambivalence experienced as mentor and protege begin a process of psychological disengagement;

Redefinition: the primary function of the mentor is one of moving from a transitional figure to friend.

Research by Darlene DeFour (1990) and Yolanda Moses (1988) provides compelling evidence of the importance of African American faculty in the retention of African American graduate and undergraduate students. Contact with African American faculty is associated with better academic performance and psychological well-being. African American faculty may serve as role models for African American students (DeFour & Hirsch, 1990).

As already suggested, boys generally do not do well in school during the early grades, at least not as well as most girls. The boys' lack of early success may be due to their supposedly greater inclination toward rebelliousness toward authority, rather than to any inherent intellectual deficiency. As boys proceed through the school years, they begin to achieve better grades. This may be explained by the increase in pressures to achieve as boys get closer to the college years, or it may be explained by the lack of the debilitating effects of learned helplessness. Boys and men face pressure to work harder once they come to believe they will soon take on the "breadwinner" role (see chapter 8).

According to Nancy Betz (1993), by age 29, the brightest men are beginning to manifest their intellectual potential; the brightest women fall further short of their potential for educational and occupational achievement. Arnold's research (as cited in Betz, 1993) also supports this finding. In 1981, 46 women and 34 men who graduated as valedictorians and salutatorians of their Illinois high school classes were interviewed about their career goals and plans. Additional interviews took place in the years 1984, 1985, and 1988. Results suggested that all but four students (two women; two men) finished college and performed well (mean grade point averages of 3.6 and 3.5 for the women and men respectively). Arnold reported that gender differences started to emerge immediately after high school. For example, there was a decline in the intellectual self-confidence of women, a persistent concern among women about combining career and family, and differences in the extent and level of planned labor force participation. In fact, six women abandoned their career goals of becoming a physician. Two-thirds of the women valedictorians, but none of the men, planned to reduce or interrupt their labor force participation for childrearing.

Arnold (1989) reported that women and men valedictorians were pursuing careers in traditionally male areas of science, business, law, medicine, and academia (as cited in Betz, 1993). A substantial proportion of women (but no men) were pursuing traditionally female caregiving or helping professions. Arnold noted that differences in educational and career achievements among the men can be predicted by individual differences in ability, motivation, job experience, and college prestige. The only useful predictor among women is career versus family priorities.

As we can see, students learn more than the three R's from their teachers. Besides being a place where students learn the basics, school is also a place where students interact with others of their own age, or what most people refer to as a peer group. However, the time the young spend in school does not equal the amount of time they spend with their friends.

Peers As Socializers

By definition a *peer group* is made up of those individuals with whom we share a similar status as well as many similar values and behaviors. One of the main functions of a peer group is to be a sounding board where a person can try on new behaviors and perfect those already learned. During adolescence, the peer group is probably the most powerful socializing agent in a person's life. During this stage of the life span, most teenage girls and boys strive more for the approval and acceptance of their peers than they do for that of their own families. The importance of the peer group is summarized best in the following statement:

> *The peer group provides an opportunity to learn how to interact with age-mates, how to deal with hostility and dominance, how to relate to a leader, and how to lead others. It also performs a psychotherapeutic function for the child in helping him deal with social problems. Through discussions with peers the child may learn that others share his problems, conflicts, and complex feelings, and this may be reassuring. . . . Finally, the peer group helps the child develop a concept of himself. The ways in which peers react to the child and the bases upon which he is accepted or rejected give him a clearer, and perhaps more realistic, picture of his assets and liabilities.* (Mussen, et al., 1974, p. 515)

The next time you are strolling around a shopping mall or walking down a crowded street, notice the groups of young people who are interacting together. What do you notice about the groups? Probably one of the first impressions that will strike you is the similarity in dress and behavior. One area where peers influence their members is that of appearance. Young people generally dress to impress their friends. Much of the interaction that takes place between adolescent peers helps to reinforce their conceptions of gender roles. Young boys show off their "masculine" behaviors for girls, and girls act as if they find the boys' "masculine" behaviors quite appealing. Girls coach each other on the "ways" of boys, and vice versa.

In what ways do peers influence the young as opposed to the family's influence? Research suggests that peer groups are more likely to influence their members in terms of dress, lifestyle, and sexual activities, whereas the family appears to influence basic values and lifelong goals for the young.

Children and adolescents receive information about behavior related to gender role from a variety of sources, including parents, teachers, the peer group, and media. The pressure to conform to traditional gender roles limits the potential of girls, women, boys, and men. As Carol Nagly Jacklin (1989) suggested:

> *Gender roles and the division of labor may play a strong role in causing gender differences. If interacting with infants and children brings forth nurturance in the caregivers, and there is considerable evidence that it does, then we need to rethink who does the child care in our society. Currently women and girls do most of this care while men and boys may even be discouraged from doing it. Why should nurturance be encouraged in only one sex? Nurturing may be an antidote for violence.* (p. 132)

Summary

Sociologists and social psychologists are especially interested in the positions or statuses that people occupy within various groups. Each person has numerous statuses; some we have no control over (ascribed status), while others we must do something to earn (achieved status). Each status carries with it a set of prescriptive behaviors, called norms, that make up a particular role. Our gender norms and roles are some of the most important features of our lives.

The norms associated with being a woman encompass the prescriptions that women should have children and marry in order to fulfill themselves in terms of their femininity. The norms for men usually prescribe that a man should shun acting feminine, be a success, be aggressive when the occasion warrants it, be the initiator in sexual relations, and be self-reliant and tough.

Most sociologists emphasize the importance of socialization as the primary means a group uses to teach the young what is expected of them. Parents, media, teachers, and peers are important socializing agents for teaching children and adolescents their gender roles.

Suggested Readings

Bem, S. (1993). *The lenses of gender: Transforming the debate on sexual inequality*. New Haven, CT: Yale University Press.

Chrisler, J., Golden, C., & Rozee, P. (1996). *Lectures on the psychology of women*. New York: McGraw-Hill.

Cohan, S., & Hark, I. (Eds.). (1993). *Screening the male: Exploring masculinities in Hollywood cinema*. New York: Routledge.

Coltrane, S. (1996). *Family man: Fatherhood, housework, and gender equity*. New York: Oxford University Press.

Jordan, J., Kaplan, A., Miller, J., Stiver, I., & Surrey, J. (1991). *Women's growth in connection: Writings from the Stone Center*. New York: Guilford.

Thorne, B. (1993). *Gender play: Girls and boys in school*. New Brunswick, NJ: Rutgers University Press.

5

The Anthropological Perspective

Femininity unfolds naturally, whereas masculinity must be achieved; and here is where the male ritual cult steps in.

Gilbert Herdt

Many, if not all, of the personality traits which we have called masculine or feminine are as lightly linked to sex as are the clothing, the manners, and the form of head-dress that a society at a given period assigns to either sex. . . . The evidence is overwhelming in favor of the strength of social conditioning.

Margaret Mead

What's Your Opinion?

If you could design a culture that would ensure equal roles for women and men, what would you include? Why?

How do aspects of your cultural heritage get expressed with friends? in college courses? with family?

What have you learned from interacting with peers who are from different cultural backgrounds than you?

How are aspects of culture integrated in your college courses?

Inis Beag is an isolated island just off the coast of Ireland. Little more than 350 live on Inis Beag. The inhabitants of Inis Beag may live in "one of the most sexually naive of the world's societies" (Messenger, 1971). Sexual activity is forbidden to all but married people, who engage in sexual activity only for procreation. On the other side of the globe, in the South Pacific, lies an island, Mangaia. One researcher described the inhabitants of this island being encouraged to explore their own bodies and each other's at an early age (Marshall, 1971).

How can we explain the vastly different attitudes and behaviors of these two island peoples? The cultures of Inis Beag and Mangaia play a decisive

An Apache girl
dances with her
sponsor during her
puberty ceremony
on the Ft. Apache
Reservation in
White River,
Arizona.

© Stephen Trimble

role in shaping these two groups' sexual practices. In this chapter we will discuss the impact of culture on the behavior of women and men. We will begin by examining some of the basic concepts about culture. We then will note the different gender roles found among the individuals in New Guinea. Next, we will describe some of the cultural universals related to gender roles. And last, we will discuss social experiments in which traditional gender roles have been reshaped into what has been considered a more egalitarian social structure.

Culture

Culture is an integral part of all of our daily lives; it helps us to adapt to our environment and gives us continuity with our past. The idea that culture is something that a select few have has its roots in nineteenth-century anthropology. When Charles Darwin published *On the Origin of Species* (1859/ 1967), he speculated that living organisms evolved from simple structures to more complex ones. Soon after, Darwin's theory of evolution influenced many nineteenth-century anthropologists who applied his theory to the development of societies. According to the view of social evolution, human groups could be described as evolving from savages, at the bottom of the human scale, to the civilized, or "cultured," at the top. Consequently, the idea of "low" and "high" culture became a commonly accepted notion (Levin, 1984). Today, however, the common view among anthropologists is that all humans (regardless of their lifestyles) have a culture, and their culture is what sets them apart from other animal species.

The Contents of Culture

Culture is best understood as being comprised of everything that makes up a way of life. Thus, we can say that culture consists of the accumulated knowledge, the values, and the symbolic expressions of a particular group of people.

Knowledge refers to all the information we share about our world. Knowledge can be either empirical or existential in form. *Empirical knowledge* consists of information that is gained and passed on from one generation to the next; it is based on scientific inquiry, common sense understandings, religious teachings, and oral and literary sources. Such knowledge is taught in religious education, schools, at the dinner table, and around camp fires. *Existential knowledge* pertains to more abstract issues and is more likely to deal, for instance, with such questions as "Why are we here?" and "Where did we come from?" Usually, this kind of knowledge is considered the domain of philosophy and religion.

Values consist of socially shared beliefs about what is good or desirable. In the American culture, for example, freedom, individuality, achievement and success, and material comfort are a few of the commonly accepted values. The norms or rules that govern our everyday lives are other examples of some values that help shape our lives.

Culture's *symbolic expressions* range from the music of Hootie and the Blowfish to the music of Bach, from the paintings in an art gallery to the spray-can murals on the side of a building, and from breakdancing to the ballet. All of these cultural expressions reflect the personal experiences of their creators.

As we can see, then, culture takes many forms. Essentially, culture expresses the many sides of people's way of experiencing their world and of the way they effectively deal with their environment.

The Characteristics of Culture

The contents of a particular culture are learned, not passed down from one generation to the next in the genes. A person learns her or his culture from others—sometimes from family members, from peers, or from television (see chapter 4).

Culture is broadly shared among the members of a group. The ideas, the behaviors, and the symbols that comprise a culture are agreed on as to their meanings by the various members of a group. Among some groups, such as the African pygmies, the traditions and common knowledge are generally shared uniformly and agreed upon by all members of the group. In a larger and more complex group, such as American society (where many different ethnic groups and religions come into contact with each other), we are apt to find various subcultures and countercultures. A *subculture* shares many of the same cultural contents of the larger culture but also has its own distinct values, norms, and lifestyle. Such is the case in a distinct ethnic minority concentrated in one location, for example, New York's Chinatown. A *counterculture* is a subculture that is opposed to certain basic features of the larger

A Bar Mitzvah
recognizes a boy's
thirteenth birthday
and begins his
religious
responsibilities to
the Jewish faith.
© Bill Aron/PhotoEdit

dominant culture. For instance, the Hell's Angels (a motorcycle club) are opposed to many of the basic values of American society (Yinger, 1982).

Although we may be fascinated by the Ituri Forest pygmies' hunting spears or the personal computers used by New York stockbrokers, a culture's material artifacts (e.g., spears, computers, music, paintings, and the like) are not the most important feature of a culture. Rather, the important feature of a culture is the underlying meaning these objects have for the people involved. A pygmy's spear and a stockbroker's computer may both be seen by their owners as tools for survival. A spear differs from a computer in many ways; however, they also have similar meanings for their owners.

Ethnocentrism and Cultural Relativism

Culture allows us to make sense out of our world and organize its elements. Culture also may blind us by disposing us to think that our ways are the only ways of understanding and organizing our world. Many of us have a tendency to see our culture as the one way and the right way of viewing the world. The belief that our way is the only way and the best way of perceiving the world is called *ethnocentrism.* When we judge another group by our cultural standards, we fall victim to ethnocentrism. If, on the other hand, we look at other groups with their different values, beliefs, and lifestyles and note that these are just their ways of adapting to their lives' circumstances, albeit strange from our own, we have what is called a *cultural relativistic perspective* (Landrine, 1995).

With this brief overview of the concept of culture, we are now ready to examine its impact on the gender roles as seen in different societies. Women and men have interacted for countless centuries, and we can learn much about present-day gender roles by trying to understand that our ways are not the only nor the "right" ways for such interactions to transpire.

Gender Roles in New Guinea

During the early 1930s, Margaret Mead set off to explore the ways that gender roles were defined among several preliterate societies in northeastern New Guinea. There Mead found the material for what was to become the basis for the now classic study of gender roles entitled *Sex and Temperament in Three Primitive Societies* (1935/1963). Each of the three societies that Mead studied—the Arapesh, the Mundugumor, and the Tchambuli—had very different conceptions of what was expected of women and men. Let's examine each of these three societies in turn to see how differently they defined femininity and masculinity.

The Arapesh

Mead first encountered the mountain-dwelling Arapesh in the area bounded by the sea to the north and extending back into the coastal mountains and grassy plains to the south. Life among the Arapesh, as described by Mead, was "organized . . . in a common adventure that is primarily maternal, cherishing, and oriented away from the self toward the needs of the next generation" (p. 15). Mead used terms like *cooperative, unassertive,* and *gentle* to describe Arapesh women and men. Whether caring for the children or for the crops, both women and men worked cooperatively for the good of the society. Aggressive behaviors were strictly prohibited in Arapesh society. An Arapesh man who displayed aggressive behavior—a major element of the masculine role in virtually every other society—was ostracized from the group for display of "deviant" behavior. Competition in any form—an integral part of the American man's gender role expectation—caused the participants to be regarded with shame. In Arapesh society then, status and prestige were conferred on those who shared and cooperated within the group. Mead described the Arapesh woman and man in terms that Western people have to come to associate with femininity. The traits most admired among the Arapesh were epitomized in the caring, cooperative, gentle, loving, nuturant, sharing, and selfless person. Mead wrote:

> To the Arapesh, the world is a garden that must be tilled, not for one's self, not in pride and boasting, not for hoarding and usury; but that the

*yams and the dogs and the pigs and most of all the children may grow.
From this whole attitude flow many of the other Arapesh traits, the lack
of conflict between old and young, the lack of any expectation of jealousy or envy, the emphasis upon cooperation. Cooperation is easy when
all are whole-heartedly committed to a common project from which no
one of the participators will himself benefit. Their dominant conception
of men and women may be said to be that of regarding men, even as we
regard women, as gently, carefully parental in their aims.* (p. 135)

The Mundugumor

The Mundugumor were known for their cannibalistic practices and for their
penchant for warfare. Speaking of the Mundugumor man, Mead described
life as a constant battle:

> *The Mundugumor man-child is born into a hostile world, a world in
> which most of the members of his own sex will be his enemies, in which
> his major equipment for success must be a capacity for violence, for see-
> ing and avenging insult, for holding his own safety very lightly and the
> lives of others even more lightly. From his birth, the stage is set to pro-
> duce in him this kind of behavior.* (p. 189)

Because the Mundugumor mother viewed her maternal duties as burden-
some and unrewarding, the child quickly learned to fend for herself or himself. The child's early experiences of maternal neglect and rejection fostered
a degree of self-reliance that promoted the personal traits that the Mundugumor cherished most, namely, competition and aggression. Any show of tenderness or kindness toward another was strictly frowned upon by the
Mundugumor. Consequently, the submissive, withdrawn, or gentle Mundugumor was viewed as a misfit and shunned by others. Life among the
Mundugumors was a trial, and only the most fit—the aggressive and unyield-
ing ones—held the positions that brought one honor and respect.

Thus, Mead found a fundamental similarity in both the Arapesh and the
Mundugumor societies: Women and men were both socialized toward identical personality characteristics. The Mundugumor emphasized a harsh self-
centeredness, while the Arapesh promoted a gentler other-centeredness.

The Tchambuli

Living around Lake Aibom, the Tchambuli were a headhunting society in
which the usual gender roles were reversed from what we know in the West.
Tchambuli women, for example, were responsible for the village's business.
The village women earned the money used by the family, were responsible
for the farming, fishing, and manufacturing required by the village, and even
made the decisions that affected the village (e.g., giving their approval of
marriages). Tchambuli women were easygoing, hard-working, and reliable.

Generally, an air of affability existed among the village women. Tchambuli men, on the other hand, were considered the "weaker sex." Men seemed only interested in their own adornment and in self-aggrandizing pursuits. They spent their days in other men's company, discussing their costumes and their body adornments. Around women, Tchambuli men became timid, and they appeared in awe of the opposite sex:

> *The Tchambuli man may be said to live principally for art. Every man is an artist and most men are skilled not in some one art alone, but in many: in dancing, carving, plaiting, and so on. Each man is chiefly concerned with his role upon the stage of his society, with the elaboration of his costume, the beauty of the masks he owns, the skill of his own flute-playing, the finish and elan of his ceremonies, and upon other people's recognition and valuation of his performance.* (p. 245)

Mead's work among the Arapesh, the Mundugumor, and the Tchambuli gave us a richer appreciation of the variety of gender roles practiced in societies. However, we should note that not all anthropologists accept Mead's case in support of cultural determinism as the explanatory concept underlying gender roles. Specifically, some have charged that Mead's research on gender role flexibility is misleading if not seriously flawed (see for instance, Freeman, 1983). Whether we accept Mead's arguments for culture's influential shaping of gendered behavior or not, few would argue (Mead's detractors included) that culture is an important—if not the sole—factor in shaping one's gender presentation.

Cultural Universals and Gender Roles

Thus far, we have emphasized the variety and differences in various cultures with respect to gender roles. However, are there certain gender-related features that are likely to be found among all, or nearly all, groups with vastly different cultural traditions? In other words, are there what anthropologists call *cultural universals* (Murdock, 1945) when it comes to gender-specific behaviors or features of gender roles? The answer to this question is yes. We will now turn our attention to several areas where there appears to be some unanimity among different human groups about expectations of women's and men's behavior.

We will begin our discussion by examining the well-established behavioral patterns in which women perform certain jobs and men perform others. This pattern is usually referred to as the division of labor. Next, we will focus on the pattern of men's dominance over women in vastly different cultural settings. And last, we will examine exceptions to the universal feature of having only two relatively exclusive gender roles by identifying several cultures where there are more than two gender roles.

Division of Labor

Most of us at one time or another have heard someone mention that a job was "women's work" or "men's work." The notion that certain tasks are best accomplished by women rather than men or vice versa is one that appears throughout most societies (Betz, 1993; Landrine, 1995). Anthropologists have long studied what is termed the *division of labor* along gender lines (Kelly, 1981). One of the most extensive studies to focus on the division of labor among preliterate groups was conducted by George Murdock (1937). Murdock studied 224 societies and found strong evidence for a gender-based division of labor. In general, Murdock found that men's activities were generally those that required strength, long periods of travel away from the campsite, and a high degree of cooperation. The activities performed by women were usually those that required less upper-body strength and less travel and that could be performed alone. Biological differences, such as a man's greater physical strength and a woman's greater involvement in child-bearing and child-rearing, may have played a significant role in the differences found by Murdock.

However, when we examine the division of labor dealing with the manufacture of certain items, we find that biological differences play a small role in determining job performance. Women in nearly every society were chiefly responsible for making and repairing clothing. Men in nearly every society made weapons. Weapon making does not require great strength, mobility, or group cooperation. Making clothes is not easier than making weapons, nor does it require one to work alone or to be less mobile. Why, then, is weapon making an activity for men and the manufacture of apparel nearly always an activity for women? Murdock suggests that not only has the division of labor arisen by virtue of some physical differences, but also has included those tasks that are somehow related to physical differences, even if only indirectly. Therefore, because weapons were generally used by men on the hunt, weapon making probably was assumed to be a labor that men should be responsible for.

We must keep in mind, however, that the groups studied by Murdock exhibited considerable overlap of activities among women and men. Although there is evidence that a division of labor along gender lines existed among many early subsistence groups, there also was a great amount of cooperation among the sexes for the work that needed to be accomplished. Both women and men contributed to the groups' sustenance, and according to some, women did more than their share (Dahlberg, 1981). Lila Liebowitz (1989) suggested that the sexual division of labor occurred after our species developed the ability to exchange goods; that "the division of labor itself was a social construct that arose out of new techniques of production" (p. 3). Liebowitz thus viewed the private sphere/public sphere dichotomy as being correlated with certain forms of sociocultural organization. She wrote:

> *Which tasks were assigned to what class of persons undoubtedly depended in part on local circumstances and in part on local traditions.*

Whatever the way the division of labor was institutionalized, the need for dividing tasks ultimately derived from the emergence of new foraging techniques and strategies and from the new processing problems that arose from them. . . . The increase in the birth and survival rates . . . seems to reflect a behavioral change. It is obvious that those adults who did not go out on a stalking-type hunt must have assumed the responsibility for performing hearth-centered tasks and for overseeing the activities of the "dependent" youngsters excluded from the hunt. Women with nursing infants presumably were non-hunters for variable lengths of time. . . . The population increase may, therefore, reflect a change in women's activities. The increase suggests that women in earlier settings, which were not complex enough to generate a sexual division of labor, were not as hearth bound or sedentary as the women in those later cultures where sophisticated forms of projectile hunting were practiced. In the latter cultures, people probably engaged in a "causal" or circumstantial division of labor that to some extent followed sex lines. (pp. 19–20)

In today's society, strength and mobility are usually not required for most jobs, so there really is no need to regard jobs as either women's work or men's work (see chapter 8).

The Dominant Man

In nearly every society studied by anthropologists, we find that usually men dominate and control women (Friedl, 1978; Lorber, 1994). In spite of that, women are not entirely powerless (Landrine, 1995).

We differentiate power from authority. Women wield considerable power or influence in decisions of social importance, but authority is usually vested in men. Anthropologists Kay Martin and Barbara Voorhies (1975) viewed the distinction between power and authority as follows:

Power refers to the ability to coerce others toward desired ends, whereas authority refers to legitimate or legal power. A survey of human societies shows that positions of authority are almost always occupied by males. Technically speaking, there is no evidence for matriarchy, or rule by women, Amazonian or otherwise. Of even greater significance, however, is that the assignment of power and authority may vary independently. Leadership positions are generally occupied by males, but power may attach itself to either sex. This is especially well illustrated by matrilineal societies, in which senior women assign public offices to males, but may reserve the actual decision-making for themselves. (p. 10)

As a rule, men have the more privileged, more valued, and higher status positions in most societies (Blumberg, 1978). As suggested by many researchers, men have a definite edge in almost every group. Although women may have various amounts of power within their groups, they usually are dominated by men. We need to examine some of the various ways that men dominate women in other cultures.

The Traditional World of Male Dominance

Few cultures are as totally male dominant as those in the Middle East, where men are seen as preeminent over women (Wadley, 1977). Fundamentalist Middle Eastern cultures like that found in Saudi Arabia, writes Judith Lorber (1994), "create the greatest gender difference . . . [where] women are kept out of sight behind walls or veils, have no civil rights, and often create a cultural and emotional world of their own" (p. 34). We need only turn to the Hindu code and read that "In childhood a woman must be subject to her father; in youth, to her husband; when her husband is dead, to her sons. A woman must never be free of subjugation." The social structures of most Muslim societies reinforce men's dominance and women's subservience (Beck & Keddie, 1978; Rapoport et al., 1989).

In India, one historic means of reinforcing the women's inferior status was by performing the now prohibited practice of suttee of the act of burning or burying women alive with their deceased husbands (Mazumdar, 1978). On the surface, suttee, outlawed by the British in the early nineteenth century, kept the widow from dishonoring her deceased husband, but it was also a social ritual testifying to the status of women in comparison to men. Dorothy Stein (1978) explained the rationale behind suttee:

> *The orthodox Hindu belief was that the widow was responsible for her husband's predeceasing her, by sin in a previous life if not in the present, for in the normal course of events the wife was expected to die first. A lifetime of austerity was considered scarcely enough to expiate her survival. Suttee, then, was primarily based on the belief that women are by nature sexually unreliable and incapable of leading chaste lives without a husband to control them.* (p. 255)

Purdah, the social practice of secluding women from the public world, is still found in many Middle Eastern countries. The degree to which a woman is secluded from the public's eye varies from class to class. For example, in some societies, a woman may leave her home but must wear the *chador, the head-to-toe garment;* in other societies, she must not leave the home at all (Sharma, 1978). Regardless of the extent of purdah, the intent is always the same: to protect a woman's chastity by keeping her secluded from men (Mernissi, 1975). Women in the Middle East are thought to possess powerful sexual urges that, if allowed to be expressed outside of marriage, would bring shame on the women's families. Although several Middle Eastern observers do not view purdah as oppressive or demeaning to women (Abu-Lughod, 1983; El Guindi, 1981), many Western social scientists see it as a powerful means to reinforce male dominance and keep women inferior and subservient (Paige, 1983; Sharma, 1978).

Besides the institution of purdah, the Islamic religion also condones polygamy. The sacred book of Islam, the Koran, enjoins men not to take a second wife unless he can provide for her well-being. However, among many Islamic cultures taking a second wife is one way that a man can get back at his first wife for her lack of wifely respect. If a Muslim man is too poor to take a second wife but has grown tired of his first wife, he may simply repudiate her, which in effect is the same as divorcing her; he then takes a second wife. Thus the practice of serial monogamy has become quite frequent among less wealthy Muslim men (Leavitt, 1971).

Women in Islamic countries have little legitimate authority over their own lives, but that does not mean they have little or no power over their own lives or the lives of their children. Many ways can be found to circumvent the restrictions placed on women. A common story is told of the Islamic mother who wished to have her daughters vaccinated by a local physician. Because the physician was a man, the woman's husband refused to let her take their children to see the doctor or to allow him to give the necessary shots, which would have required that the daughters expose their arms to an unrelated male. Through messages, the woman contacted the physician and arranged for him to come to her home; she then had her daughters stick their arms out through one of the windows where the physician inoculated each.

Not all Moslem societies are unaffected by the social changes brought about by the infusion of petrodollars. Countries that only a decade or two ago were preindustrial in nature have been pushed into the twentieth century, with all the accompaniments of modern cities, government bureaucracies, and changes in people's lives. A sociologist and specialist in Muslim societies, Fatima Mernissi (1975), believed that in most newly developing Muslim countries, there is considerable tension between the ancient traditions that separate the sexes and exclude women from anything other than their roles as outlined by purdah and the modern social forces that push for change and modernization. Mernissi believed that until women gain a greater measure of personal freedom, many of the changes brought about by the wealth from oil will have little lasting value in the lives of the common folk.

Another example of the ways women are suspect for their supposedly sexual powers in many Islamic countries is the ritual of *female excision*. Female excision consists of cutting the clitoris with a sharp instrument, causing a small incision. In this form, female excision is much like the common ritual of male circumcision, which is sanctioned in most Western societies for infant boys. However, in some Middle Eastern countries, a more radical form of female excision is practiced. Here, an infant girl's entire clitoris and labia are surgically removed for the purpose of "protecting" her chastity in adulthood (Morgan & Steinem, 1980). The thinking behind this extreme form of female excision is that with the removal of the sensual parts of the girl's genitalia, she will remain faithful to her husband rather than be tempted toward other lovers.

The role played out by women in traditional Chinese and Japanese societies was one of total subjugation and dependence on men in the guise of father, brother, husband, and sons, much the same as we saw in the Middle East (Kristeva, 1975). Anthropologist Margery Wolf (1980) pointed out the basic inequalities in the lives of Chinese women and men by describing what she sees as the distinctly different worlds each lives in. She wrote:

> *Few women in prerevolutionary China experience the continuity that is typical of the lives of the menfolk. A woman can and, if she is ever to have any economic security, must provide the links in the male chain of descent, but she will never appear in anyone's genealogy as that all-important name connecting the past to the future. If she dies before she is married, her tablet will not appear on her father's altar; although she was a temporary member of his household, she was not a member of his family. A man is born into his family and remains a member of it throughout his life and even after his death. He is identified with the family from birth, and every action concerning him, up to and including his death, is in the context of that group. Whatever other uncertainties may trouble his life, his place in the line of ancestors provides a permanent setting. There is no such secure setting for a woman. She will abruptly leave the household into which she is born, either as an infant or as an adult bride, and enter another whose members treat her with suspicion or even hostility.* (p. 177)

We need only read Maxine Hong Kingston's *The Woman Warrior* (1976) to get a personal glimpse into the "uterine" world of women in the China of old. Her description of the suicide of her paternal aunt—the "no name woman"—is especially revealing about the treatment of women in a totally patriarchal society.

Only Two Roles?

Most of us, if asked, would probably say there are only two sexes (male and female) and two collateral gender roles (masculine and feminine). Such a bifurcated system is thought by most to be a cultural universal. However, such a view has come under serious challenge among many sex and gender researchers (see Blackwood, 1984; Herdt, 1994; Kennedy, 1993; Tewksbury & Gagne, 1996; Williams, 1986). Presenting the case for multiple sexes and gender roles, Judith Lorber (1994) points out that in Western societies:

> *on the basis of* genitalia, *there are* five sexes: *unambiguously male, unambiguously female, hermaphrodite, transsexual female-to-male, and transsexual male-to-female; on the basis of* object choice, *there are* three sexual orientations: *heterosexual, homosexual, and bisexual (all with trasvestic, sadomasochistic, and fetishistic variations); on the basis of* appearance, *there are* five gender displays: *feminine, masculine, ambiguous, cross-dressed as a man, and cross-dressed as a woman (or perhaps only three); on the basis of* emotional bonds, *there are* six types of relationships: *intimate friendship, nonerotic love (between parents and children, siblings and other kin, and long-time friends), eroticized love,*

passion, lust, and sexual violence; on the basis of relevant group affiliation, *there are* ten self-identifications: *straight woman, straight man, lesbian woman, gay man, bisexual woman, bisexual man, transvestite woman, transvestite man, transsexual woman, transsexual man (perhaps fourteen, if transvestites and transsexuals additionally identify as lesbian and gay).* (p. 59)

Here though we will examine six exceptions to the rule of two gender roles, namely, four found among North American Indians (i.e., the *berdache,* the *nadle,* the *alyha,* and the *hwame*), a group found in India (the *hijras*), and the *xaniths* of Oman.

The Berdache

Among the North American Indians there was a special category of people known as the *berdache* (Forgey, 1975; Jacobs, 1968; Mihalik, 1989). According to anthropologists Charles Callender and Lee Kochems (1983), a berdache was:

> *a person, usually male, who was anatomically normal but assumed the dress, occupations, and behavior of the other sex to effect a change in gender status. This shift was not complete; rather, it was a movement toward a somewhat intermediate status that combined social attributes of males and females. The terminology for berdaches defined them as a distinct gender status, designated by special terms rather than by the words "man" or "woman." Literal translations of these terms often indicate its intermediate nature: halfman-halfwoman, man-woman, would-be woman.* (p. 443)

The berdache suffered neither scorn nor shame for this gender role. Berdaches generally assumed the occupations of the sex whose attire they wore. For example, men berdaches usually became extremely skilled in sewing and cooking. Evelyn Blackwood (1984) reported that evidence from 33 Native American tribes (e.g., Bella Coola, Queets, Atsugewi, Wintu, Apache, Pima, Ute, Kutenai) indicated that an alternative gender role for women was as viable as the berdache role for men.

A common misconception about the male berdache is that he turned to the life of a berdache to avoid warfare. From their analysis of different Indian nations where berdaches were found, Callender and Kochems could find no evidence to substantiate such a claim for cowardice. In the final analysis, the berdache was a separate gender role.

The Nadle

Among the Navajo and the Mohave Indian tribes, infants born with ambiguous genitals were assigned to the gender role of a *nadle* (Olien, 1978). The nadle was treated with extreme deference. Accordingly, the nadle wore women's clothing when engaged in women's work and men's clothing when involved with men's activities. Hunting and warfare were the only two activities prohibited by the nadle.

The Alyha and the Hwame

Among the Mohave Indians, two other gender roles were recognized: the alyha and the hwame. A Mohave man who chose to live the life of a woman was called an alyha. In nearly every respect, the male-turned-alyha dressed and acted like a woman; the alyha even mimicked a woman's menstrual flow by cutting his upper thigh (Olien, 1978). A woman who wished to live as a man was ceremoniously ushered into her new status as a hwame. The hwame dressed and acted out the masculine gender role, with the exception of not being permitted to go into battle nor serve in a leadership role.

Thus, we can see with the berdache, nadle, alyha, and hwame that among some groups of North American Indians there were more than two gender roles that a person could live out. According to Blackwood (1984):

> Neither women nor men had an inferior role but rather had power in those spheres of activity specific to their sex. . . . Gender-assigned tasks overlapped considerably among these people. Many individuals engaged in activities that were also performed by the other sex without incurring disfavor. . . . Engaging in such activities did not make a woman masculine nor a man feminine, because, although distinct spheres of male and female production existed, a wide range of tasks was acceptable for both sexes. Because there was no need to maintain gender inequalities, notions of power and prestige did not circumscribe the roles. (pp. 32–33)

The Hijras

In northern India we find a group of intersexed males, many of whom undergo ritualized castration called hijras (Nanda, 1986, 1990). Anthropologist Serena Nanda has studied this group and noted that many function as homosexual prostitutes. Although hijras dress as women they are not seen as women within their social circles. Nanda (1986) reports that:

> Their [hijras] female dress and mannerisms are exaggerated to the point of caricature, expressing sexual overtones that would be considered inappropriate for ordinary women in the roles as daughters, wives, and mothers. Hijra performances are burlesques of female behavior. Much of the comedy of their behavior derives from the incongruity between their behavior and that of traditional women. They use coarse and abusive speech and gestures in opposition to the Hindu ideal of demure and restrained femininity. (p. 38)

The Xaniths

Next we move to the strictly sex-segregated country of Oman where women live a partitioned life away from all males other than their close male relatives at home. Here we find a group of male homosexual prostitutes known as the xaniths who dress in gaudy and brightly colored men's attire (Wikan, 1982). At social gatherings, the xaniths associate with the women (a practice forbidden non-xanith males). As any contact between non-related (biologically or through marriage) women and men in Oman is forbidden, one of the chief roles xaniths perform is to serve as sexual outlets for unmarried or separated men.

What we see with the hijras and the xanith is how non-Western cultures allow for other gendered groups to fulfill special needs within a society where two gender roles prove insufficient. Apparently, two sexes and two genders are not enough.

The Socialist Experiments

The nineteenth-century social philosopher Karl Marx condemned the male-dominated capitalistic system for its tyranny over the lives of the working person. The writings of Marx and his collaborator Frederick Engels contributed to one of the most elaborate social experiments ever to be conceived, that of a society where women and men were equal. Both Marx and Engels believed that as long as women remained restricted to housework, with its lack of remuneration, and prevented from gainful employment, they would never be men's equal (Sanday, 1973). In this section, we will focus on four societies where equality has been, to greater or lesser degrees, implemented.

First, we will examine the countries of the former USSR and the People's Republic of China, where Marx's ideas were translated most ambitiously (Croll, 1981a and b). Then we will note the social changes brought about in the decidedly socialistic expressions seen in the country of Sweden and those found in the Israeli kibbutz. Let's begin with the much-promised utopian existence ushered into Russian culture with the overthrow of the Czar and the workers' revolution that promised a true egalitarian lifestyle for all citizens regardless of sex.

Former Soviet Union

Few modern-day countries had the constitutional guarantees providing for the total equality of all its citizenry than did the former Soviet Socialist Union (Sedugin, 1973). In 1918, Lenin decreed that women were to be men's equal. The Soviet Union's Constitution guaranteed all Soviet citizens total equality under the law, ensuring them equal pay for equal work and access to and promotion within any job regardless of sex, as well as equal political status before the Soviet Union Supreme Communist party. Some might suggest that the USSR must surely have been a feminist utopia. However, Soviet women found themselves in a type of double-duty bind. Soviet women did find greater occupational opportunities than most other European women or most women in the United States (Scanzoni & Scanzoni, 1981). However, Soviet women still carried the main responsibilities for most of the household chores along with their daily jobs outside of the home. Even Lenin seemed aware of the inequalities foisted on Soviet women for carrying what must be considered two full-time jobs, while for the most part, Soviet men paid little attention to assisting with family responsibilities. With respect to this problem, Lenin wrote: "So few men—even among the proletariat—realize how much effort and trouble they could save women, even quite do away with, if they were to lend a hand in 'women's work.' But no. . . . They want their peace and comfort" (quoted in Scanzoni & Scanzoni, 1981, p. 61).

Since Lenin and the Communist revolution, no Soviet feared that she or he would not be treated equally when it came to the guarantee of the right to work. To work in almost any type of job from construction to the professions was a right and a duty of the good Soviet. However, the pictures of Soviet women serving as physicians as proof of their equality were a distortion. Over half of all Soviet physicians were women, but they predominated in the lower-status specialties (e.g., pediatrics), while the higher-status positions (e.g., surgery) were generally considered men's specialties. As in medicine, the trend in other professions was also for women to occupy the lower-status positions, leaving the higher ones for men (Lapidus, 1978). The fact that women made up over half of the labor force in the USSR only assured them of the tiring double-duty work of running the household along with their job-related responsibilities. Soviet women also spent countless hours every week purchasing the needed family goods and groceries. Soviet women were liberated in terms of the law, but their freedom to work only added duties to those that they already had as primary housekeepers as well. Ludmilla Zemlyannikova, secretary of Soviet trade unions, examined the plight of Soviet women in such terms. She believed that:

> It would be wrong to paint the life of our women in general in rosy colors. Society has created every possibility for their cultural growth. Socialism has emancipated women socially, politically and economically, but it cannot relieve them of household care in one stroke. (quoted in Daniloff, 1982, p. 54)

Let's now examine how women have fared under communism as practiced in the People's Republic of China.

Women in Communist China

In mainland China, women's status has historically been lower than that of men's. For centuries, the teachings of the fifth-century B.C. Chinese philosopher Confucius were employed to condone all kinds of practices testifying to women's inferior status, such as foot binding, legal concubinage, female infanticide, and the selling of infant girls by those families too poor to afford a daughter's wedding. All this changed with the 1949 Revolution and the leadership provided by Chairman Mao. The total subjugation of a woman to her father and then to her husband gave way to an emphasis on the woman's economic freedom and the institution of egalitarian marital relationships (Curtin, 1975; Stacy, 1975; Walstedt, 1978).

However, the rhetoric of equal pay for equal work has not yet been fully implemented into the factory system, which is supposedly the backbone of the new social system of the People's Republic. For example, in many of China's factories, men hold the majority of supervisory positions, technical positions, and semiskilled laborer positions, which earn for these men approximately $47 to $60 a month. In these same factories, women are more often found in the lower-paying jobs, such as assembly work, where the pay is likely to be from 15 to 20 percent lower than those of their male colleagues (Wallace, 1982). In rural areas many of the patriarchal traditions still govern peoples' lives.

Thus, in the two Marxist countries, we see that patriarchal traditions of men's supremacy are not totally uprooted even when the sanctions of these socialist governments push for the reformation of women's status and roles. Next we need to move to the West to examine what has taken place in the roles that women and men are expected to play out in the progressive socialist country of Sweden.

Changing Gender Roles in Sweden

Few countries have made as much effort to change the traditional roles of women as housekeeper and man as provider as has the socialist country of Sweden. Although other socialist countries have moved to eradicate patriarchal privileges and higher status of men, only Sweden has emphasized that changes in the masculine gender role are necessary if the changes in the feminine gender role are to have any permanent effect. Noting the need for a change in men's roles, Alva Myrdal (1971) wrote:

> *In Sweden, the debate has progressed beyond the conventional focus of discussions of family problems, i.e., the conflict between women's two roles—family and work. Its scope has been enlarged to encompass the two roles of men. Men are no longer regarded as "innocents abroad" in family affairs. Instead, it is becoming increasingly recognized even outside sociological circles that their role in the family must be radically enlarged. No longer can they be allowed to confine themselves to the role of "provider," they must begin more fully to integrate the family into their life plans.* (p. 9)

Unlike most Western societies, Sweden has not waited until the last few decades to begin to question the roles played by women and men in the family and in the workplace. The Swedish people have debated the issues of men's double standard of morality since the late nineteenth century (Myrdal & Klein, 1956). Sweden, in fact, had been in the forefront of change in gender roles before American women won the right to vote (Dahlstrom, 1971).

The single biggest social area attesting to Sweden's commitment to changing the gender roles' status quo is that of family policy. The Swedish government has instituted generous benefits for either the mother or the father who stays home with children. Some of these inducements come in the form of generous tax breaks for multiple-child families and, of greater consequence when it comes to changing the traditional gender roles, parental-leave benefits for the parent (be it the mother or the father) who stays home to care for the child. These progressive practices have not been instituted simply to eradicate outmoded gender roles, but rather to encourage parents to have children. Furthermore, the Swedish government has taken the stand that Swedish women will gain equality in the workplace only if Swedish men take an equal share of the duties related to the home and to the raising of the children (Baude, 1979).

Beginning in 1974, the Swedish government adopted a policy to encourage fathers to take paternity leaves during the first months of their infants' lives. However, even with a massive advertising campaign picturing fathers taking care of their children, only about 5 percent of the fathers who are eligible for such paternity leave have availed themselves of this lifestyle (Lamb, 1982). The reasons that so few Swedish fathers take paternity leave are somewhat disconcerting when we remember that the government is publicly behind such a role reversal. Many of the Swedish fathers point out that they fear retribution from their employers—an action prohibited by the government—if they take paternity leave. Other fathers point out that if they did in fact take an extended leave of absence, their jobs and advancement in their work would suffer more so than would their wives' work were the wives to take an extended leave. And still others point out that they believe that a child benefits more from the mother's presence than from the father's.

Thus, in Sweden, where the government has made a concerted effort to bring about real equality between the sexes, patriarchal attitudes seem to die hard. May-Britt Carlsson (1977), Organizing Secretary of the Swedish Central Organization of Salaried Employees, described the problem:

> *The majority of men in Sweden still follow traditional roles. Men still dominate the labor market and do not assume the dual role that working women do in taking responsibility for home and child care. What is needed, then, is an analysis of the male role leading to change and adaptation in both the traditional male and female roles. . . . This is no easy task and no one . . . has offered a blueprint for success. . . . For true equality between the sexes, the traditional masculine role must not become the pattern for women to follow. The roles of both men and women must be transformed.* (p. 270)

The bottom line in the countrywide experiment to change the traditional gender roles of Swedish women and men, at least when it comes to reinforcing greater participation of fathers in the raising of their children, seems to be somewhat of a disappointment if not a downright failure.

For our last look at where a concerted effort has been made to change traditional gender roles, we will move to Israel, where we find a social experiment of dramatic proportions with the agricultural communities known as the *kibbutzim*.

Israeli Experiments with Changing Gender Roles

During the late 1940s, a small group of European immigrants began a bold social experiment in Israel. Initially, the *kibbutz* (the singular form for kibbutzim) was an agriculturally based social commune where gender equality was paramount in the group's ideology (Maimon, 1962; Weithorn, 1975). To accomplish this, the mothers on the kibbutz were "freed" from being the sole caretakers of their children. Rather, the children of the kibbutz's members were raised in a communal children's house, or *creche*, where a caretaker, or *metapelet* (usually a woman), was responsible for the children's socialization (Rabin, 1970). The goal of raising the children in this manner was to ensure that all kibbutz members—women and men—could fully participate in the kibbutz's farming, managing, and marketing activities on an equal basis (Mednick, 1975). However, the goal for full equality of women and men on the kibbutz was more an ideal than a reality, as attested to by many observers (Blumberg, 1976; Talmon, 1972; Tiger & Shepher, 1975). Melford Spiro (1971) wrote of the undermining of the kibbutz's goal of women's emancipation in the following way:

> In view of its emphasis on the economic equality of the sexes, how is it that the women have not become "rooted" in the economic life of the kibbutz? It has already been noted that when the vattikim first settled on the land, there was no sexual division of labor. Women, like men, worked in the fields and drove tractors; men, like women, worked in the kitchen and the laundry. Men and women, it was assumed, were equal and could perform their jobs equally well. It was soon discovered, however, that men and women were not equal. For obvious biological reasons women were compelled at times to take temporary leave from that physical labor of which they were capable. A pregnant woman, for example, could not work too long, even in the vegetable garden, and a nursing mother had to work near the Infant's House in order to be able to feed her child. Hence, as the kibbutz grew older and the birth rate increased, more and more women were forced to leave the "productive" branches of the economy and enter its service branches. But as they left the productive branches it was necessary that their places be filled, and they were filled by men. The result was that the women found themselves in the same jobs from which they were supposed to have been emancipated—cooking, cleaning, laundering, teaching, caring for children, etc. In short, they have not been freed from the "yoke" of domestic responsibilities. (p. 225)

Equality on a broader scale, encompassing the whole of Israeli society, also appears to be more illusory than fact (Tabory, 1984). <u>Although Israeli women must serve in the armed forces, and most people recall the strong political presence of Golda Meir, Israeli society finds women unequal to men.</u> Selma Brandow (1980, p. 403) wrote that "the mass of the Israeli female population exists in the subordinate 'second sex' position which differs little from that of women in other parts of the world." Others do not agree with this perception of Israeli society, noting that although total equality is not yet a reality, it is moving in that direction (Bar-Yosef & Lieblich, 1983).

In each of the social attempts presented above, the heart of the problem of bringing full gender equality has not been one of not trying. In the former Soviet Union, the People's Republic of China, Sweden, and Israel's kibbutzim, the leaders have attempted to change age-old traditions and roles that prejudice women and favor men. The issue is not so much in attempting to change women's role of maternal responsibility, but rather in not doing enough to change men's attitudes and behaviors (Hacker, 1975). Anthropologist Michelle Rosaldo (1974) succinctly stated the underlying problem in unfulfilled attempts to bring about true gender equality:

> *The most egalitarian societies are not those in which male and female are opposed or are even competitors, but those in which men value and participate in the domestic life of the home. Correspondingly, there are societies in which women can readily participate in important public events.* (p. 41)

Summary

Culture plays a large part in what we become. Although we have a tendency to think that women's and men's relationships are similar the world over, anthropologists like Margaret Mead have found that gender roles vary considerably in different parts of the world. Gender and race interact both as social norms are formed and in the way they affect behavior. Gender roles are defined in the cultural context of a particular group of individuals (e.g., race, ethnicity). Thus, there are variations in gender roles from one culture to another.

Although there is a great diversity among various cultures, most cultures find certain universal patterns of women-men relations, such as a division of labor and varying degrees of male dominance. However, among some American Indian tribes, we find evidence of more than two gender roles.

During this century, several countries (i.e., the former Soviet Union, the Republic of China, Sweden, and Israel) have attempted to eliminate the unequal status found between women and men. Their attempts, however, have not been entirely successful. An analysis of these attempts suggests that in order for changes in the feminine gender role to be successful, there must be corresponding changes in the masculine gender role.

Suggested Readings

Castaneda, D. (1996). Gender issues among Latinas. In J. Chrisler, C. Golden, & P. Rozee (Eds.), *Lectures on the psychology of women*. New York: McGraw-Hill.

Chrisler, J., & Hemstreet, A. (1996). *Variations on a theme: Diversity and the psychology of women*. Albany: State University of New York Press.

Gilmore, D. (1990). *Manhood in the making: Cultural concepts of masculinity*. New Haven: Yale University Press.

Gutman, M. (1996). *The meaning of macho: Being a man in Mexico City*. Berkeley: University of California Press.

Herdt, G. (Ed.). (1994). *Third sex, third gender: Beyond sexual dimorphism in culture and history*. New York: Zone Books.

Root, M. P. P. (1996). The psychology of Asian American women. In H. Landrine (Ed.), *Bringing cultural diversity to feminist psychology: Theory, research, and practice*. Washington, DC: American Psychological Association.

Suggested Fiction and Popular Titles

Allen, P. G., *Grandmothers of the Light: A Medicine Woman's Sourcebook*, Beacon Press.

Kingston, M. H., *The Woman Warrior*, Vintage Books.

Marshall, P., *Daughters*, Plume.

Morrison, T., *Tar Baby*, Knopf.

Niethammer, C., *Daughters of the Earth: The Lives and Legends of American Indian Women*, Touchstone Books.

Walker, A., *The Color Purple*, Harcourt Brace Jovanovich.

PART TWO
Issues

6

An Interpersonal Power Perspective to Understanding Sexual Victimization

American boys must be protected from a culture of violence that exploits their worst tendencies by reinforcing and amplifying the atavistic values of the masculine mystique. Our country was not created so that future generations could maximize profit at any cost. It was created with humanistic, egalitarian, altruistic goals. We must put our enormous resources and talents to the task of creating a children's culture that is consistent with these goals.

Myriam Miedzian

What's Your Opinion?

Why are women who have been a victim of sexual violence reluctant to report the incident?

Why do men batter women?

Do you believe that socialization practices in the United States encourage girls to be weak and passive and boys to be strong and aggressive?

Do you believe women lie about being raped, especially when they accuse men they date?

Do you believe sexual harassment is the same thing as flirtation?

What does it mean when sexual victimization is defined in terms of power, not sex?

In this chapter we will focus on the interpersonal aspects of power and suggest that power is a central feature underlying nearly every aspect of relationships between women and men. We will begin our discussion by outlining the different types of power an individual may possess. Next we will note the different ways women and men use their power. And, we will discuss types of sexual victimization, including rape, incest, battering, and sexual harassment. We will continue our discussion of power in chapters 7, 8, 9, and 10 when we discuss power from institutional perspectives.

Interpersonal Power

What is the essence of power at the interpersonal level? *Interpersonal power* refers to the ability to achieve ends through influence. In other words, power enters into a relationship when people (i.e., *powerholders*) have the ability to achieve ends by influencing others (i.e., *target persons*). Feminist scholars have made a distinction between power over and power to. *Power over* expresses a relationship: An individual has power over another if s/he can make this person do something s/he would not have done. *Power to* expresses ability to obtain some good. The term connotes empowerment and is considered less coercive.

How do people get others to achieve certain ends—i.e., have "power over"? One of the first in-depth analyses of this issue was conducted by John French and Bertram Raven (Raven, 1965). French and Raven listed six different types of power that people use in their interpersonal relations: reward, coercive, referent, legitimate, expert, and informational. Let's begin our discussion of power by first examining each of the six power types and their bases and noting some of their consequences for relationships between target persons and powerholders.

Power Over: The Power Types and Their Bases

A person possesses *reward power* when that person has something of value for which another person is willing to do something. Usually, a person with reward power possesses any one of several kinds of resources, or things of value, that others perceive as worthwhile or desirable. Resources can be either concrete or personal. *Concrete resources* are comprised of those valued things that are tangible (e.g., money or gifts). *Personal resources* are less tangible (e.g., a person's friendship, affection, or even pleasant words that cause another to comply with the powerholder's bidding). More often than not, the target person will feel positive toward a powerholder who uses reward power. Although the target person's compliance with the powerholder's wishes will be assured in the short run, long-term compliance is less certain, especially if the powerholder withholds the desired resources.

Coercive power is held by one who threatens to withdraw a reward or punish the target person unless that person complies with the powerholder's wishes. Obviously, coercive power is one of the strongest forms of power one person can have over another. The use of coercive power, however, is likely to instill in the target person a strong dislike or even hatred for the powerholder. Furthermore, the use of coercive power generally does not assure long-term compliance with the powerholder's wishes once she or he is gone.

A person who is admired or liked by others has what is called *referent power*. In other words, if people like or admire you, they are more likely to comply with your wishes than if they didn't like or respect you. According to French and Raven, people with referent power oftentimes don't even know they exercise such power over others. One with referent power normally enjoys a positive relationship with the target person, and the target person's compliance with the powerholder's wishes may last for a considerable time even in the absence of the powerholder.

Legitimate power comes to the person who holds a social position in society that confers authority over others. The basis of legitimate power, or what can also be called *authority,* is found in societal positions or roles (i.e., physicians, professors, judges, police officers, etc.) wherein one person has certain rights over another's behavior. In our society, for instance, a police officer has authority, or legitimate power, over monitoring the driving habits of motorists. In most instances, according to French and Raven, the target person feels indifferent toward a person with legitimate power. Also, compliance with the wishes of one with legitimate power is usually quite complete. Legitimate power is one of the more complicated forms of power because it entails a knowledge of a society's social structures and the roles played out by its members in their different social structures.

Expert power is possessed by one who has superior knowledge or ability in a specific subject area. For example, most people will defer to an auto mechanic's decision about how to fix or maintain their cars because they consider the mechanic to be more knowledgeable than they are about a car's engine and its functioning. The target person of expert power generally feels somewhat different toward the person holding expert power and will, in most cases, comply with the powerholder's wishes in the long run.

A person who has access to some information that others may want or would find valuable has *informational power.* Informational power should not be confused with expert power. One need not be knowledgeable or skilled to have informational power, but simply be the possessor of some information that others think is important or valuable or information that others want. A major difference between informational power and the other five power bases is that informational power isn't based on the relationship between the powerholder and the target person. The essential feature of informational power is that one person holds information that others will be influenced by. The powerholder's personality and other attributes are of little importance. Thus the question of liking the powerholder holds little value for this power type.

Gender Differences in the Use of Various Power Bases

It is not surprising that people attribute different power bases to women and men. Traditionally, men have been viewed as having and using both reward and coercive power more than women have (Johnson, 1976, 1978). In fact, men have usually had greater access to various concrete rewards (e.g., money) and could therefore get others to comply with their wishes. On the other hand, women throughout the ages have had fewer concrete resources at their disposal with which to cause others to do their bidding.

For centuries, men have used coercive power—threats and punishment—to get their way. One of the most extreme examples of coercive power can be found in sexual victimization. We will discuss sexual victimization in a later section of this chapter.

Recall that a person with referent power is one who is liked or respected by others. Nearly everyone has admired someone in their lives, someone for whom they were willing to do almost anything. A distinctive feature of referent power is the absence of an aggressive element in the relationship between the powerholder (i.e., the one liked or respected) and the target person (i.e., the person who likes or respects the other). We might suggest that women would be more likely to use referent power than men would be because women are traditionally viewed as being more sensitive to others, more concerned with harmony in the group, and thought of as less aggressive than men. Indeed, Paula Johnson (1978) suggested that in general most people associate the use of referent power with women more than with men. However, men are taught early that they should not identify with women and that they should view women in negative ways (Doyle, 1995). Thus women's use of referent power with men may not be as pervasive as some may think.

The use of legitimate power depends on the powerholder having a socially sanctioned position or role that confers authority over others. In most societies men have an abundance of legitimate power because of their access to a variety of positions that sanction their authority over others, especially women and children. In a nuclear family lifestyle, for example, the mother has legitimate authority over the children, but the father still has ultimate authority over all family members, including the mother.

Men are often found in positions that bring with them an amount of expertise or ability and, therefore, expert power. Until the latter part of this century, most people felt little need for anything more than a basic education for girls and women, although many boys were sent to school to gain all the education and knowledge they could. Consequently, professional men in our society outnumber professional women in almost every high-status category (see chapter 8). In professions such as engineering and medicine, the disparity between women and men is especially obvious. Consequently, men are more apt to have more access to expert power than women are. Even when women do evidence expert power, they are more likely to be seen by others as less likable and less "feminine" than are men who use this form of power.

Somewhat related to the gender difference found in expert power is that found in informational power. Again, in most situations, men have greater access to information desired by others than women have. Thus we can say that men have greater informational power than women have. Overall, it appears that men are viewed as using a greater number of power bases than women are.

Strategies of Power Use

Although a general disparity exists with the numbers of power bases that women and men have, women still can influence others to comply with their wishes. Women are not powerless, but they do lack authority in many areas. The ways that women and men influence others to achieve their goals appear to differ. Johnson (1976) found that the power strategies used by women and men appear to fall along three separate dimensions: the directness a person uses to get others to comply, the resources a person uses, and the degree of competence a person shows in influencing others.

Direct vs. Indirect Power

When a person says, "Shut the door!" that person is using a *direct* form of power. When a person tries to influence another without that person being aware that s/he is being influenced, that would be an *indirect* form of power. For example, if I want you to shut the door, I may say, "Gee, it sure is cold in here," hoping that you will offer to close the door. *Manipulation* is another name for an indirect use of power. Generally speaking, those with little status or power and with few concrete resources are more apt to use an indirect power strategy to get others to comply with their wishes. Those with high status and many resources need not try to manipulate others to do their bidding; they can rely on the more direct form of power.

Thus men with their usually greater number of resources and their usually higher status are more likely to use more direct forms of gaining others' compliance. Many women, on the other hand, have little or no legitimate authority outside of the home; therefore, in most situations with others outside of their families, women must rely on more indirect forms of power.

Although the use of an indirect form of power may prove beneficial in the short run because one can influence another to comply with one's wishes, in the long run, it may prove disadvantageous. The secretary who relies on indirectly influencing the boss may never receive any credit for the ideas she or he so skillfully managed to get the boss to carry out. The boss ends up with the credit for all the changes that the secretary covertly initiated, leaving the secretary as the only one who knows who deserves the credit.

Personal vs. Concrete Resources

In every transaction wherein one person tries to influence another, there is some resource or resources that enter into the process. Johnson listed two main types of resources: *personal resources* such as friendship, affection, or approval, and *concrete resources* such as money, knowledge, or strength. In most instances, men have more concrete resources at their disposal than women do. Men often have more money and more education, which leads to greater expertise, and of course, the average man is usually physically stronger than the average woman. Men gain these advantages through their socialization. Women are more likely to have more personal resources, such as openness and friendliness toward others, by virtue of their socialization to be emotionally supportive toward others.

Having and using personal resources may be useful in getting people with whom you have a positive relationship to comply with your wishes. With personal resources, the relationship is central. With concrete resources, the relationship is less essential as a prime ingredient to assure that one gets one's way. A person with money need not be liked nor friendly in order to have others do her or his bidding.

Competence vs. Helplessness

Regarding the issue of *competence versus helplessness* as a power strategy, few beliefs are as strong as the notion that men are more competent than women in most areas, except those traditionally identified as "feminine." Such a grandiose belief is not hard to explain given the fact that the masculine stereotype contains traits like independent, active, and dominant, which, taken together with other socially desirable masculine traits, add up to a successful and competent person by our society's definition (Broverman et al., 1972). The generalized belief that men are more competent than women is so pervasive that it ranges across all types of activities, from writing essays (Paludi & Strayer, 1985) to painting (Pheterson et al., 1971) to the belief in men's superior ability in numerous jobs and occupations (Betz, 1993). However, some research has found a recent shift in public sentiment about women's competence, suggesting that people are beginning to see women as being competent in some situations (Unger & Saundra, 1993). But most people—including children as young as seven years old—still hold on to the belief that men are more competent in general than women.

The belief that women are generally less competent than men is supported by the stereotype of women as being "the weaker sex." By this token, many men feel more inclined to assist a "helpless" woman than a "helpless" man (Piliavin & Unger, 1985; Pomazal & Clore, 1973). A major problem in using a helpless strategy to influence others is that in the long run the person using such a technique can suffer a loss of self-esteem. Furthermore, feigning helplessness can make one dependent on another, which can have serious consequences if the relationship between the helpless one and the helper dissolves. Overall, although women have been portrayed as more helpless than men, women have shown that this portrayal is far from accurate. Women are as competent in their personal and work lives as men are. We should note that researchers have found that when women do use what can be considered a "masculine" type of power, they are more likely to be seen as less likable and more hostile and aggressive than men who use this power type.

Romantic Relationships and Power

Until now we have discussed power and the differences found between women and men in a general way. What about power in romantic relationships?

Mayta Caldwell and Letitia Anne Peplau (1984) studied lesbian women who were in a romantic/sexual relationship. Ninety-seven percent of the women in this study (77 in all participated) believed that both partners should have equal power in a relationship. Sixty-one percent reported that they were enjoying an equal-power relationship.

Letitia Anne Peplau and colleagues (1976) also asked over 200 dating couples, "Who has more to say in your relationship?" Having the last word about which movie to go to or to have or not have sexual relations are just a few of the ways that power can be expressed in an intimate relationship. About half of the couples reported they had what can be called an *egalitarian relationship,* in which power is supposedly shared fairly equally between the partners. Most of the remaining couples noted that the man had the final say in the relationship. Those few couples where the woman reportedly was more powerful expressed the most dissatisfaction in the relationship compared to those couples who shared power or where the man had the most power.

In a review of the literature, this time with married couples, researchers found that where the wife had most of the power, there was also greater dissatisfaction expressed than in those egalitarian marriages or husband-dominant marriages (Gray-Little & Burks, 1983). One explanation for this finding is that wife-dominant marriages are at odds with cultural norms. In other words, the marriage pattern (husband-dominant) and the more egalitarian one both have cultural approval or social support, and thus couples living in either type would sense that their marital arrangement is accepted and approved by society. Chances are, then, that such couples would feel more positive about their relationships and report greater satisfaction. However, in a wife-dominant marriage, there is a lack of cultural approval, and the participants may feel less satisfied living in a relationship that others see as a departure from the norm. Consequently, the couple may be more apt to report dissatisfaction in their personal and marital lives.

The relative power of wives and husbands in African American families is more evenly divided than it is in white families (Harrison, 1977). Contrary to the notion of the black matriarchy, Harrison pointed out that African American women do not earn more than African American men, they don't favor daughters over sons, and they don't oppose their husbands' views directly (Landrine, 1995).

Jessie Bernard (1973) viewed marriage not as one institution but two—hers and his. She wrote:

> *A substantial body of research shores up Emile Durkheim's conclusion that the "regulations imposed on the woman by marriage are always more stringent. Thus she loses more and gains less from the institution." Considerable well-authenticated data show that there are actually two*

marriages in every marital union—his and hers—which do not always coincide. Thus, for example, when researchers ask husbands and wives identical questions about their marriages, they often get quite different replies even on fairly simple factual questions. Although in nonclinical populations roughly the same proportion of men and women say they are happy, by and large when husbands and wives are asked about specific items in their relationships, the wives' marriages look less happy than their husbands'. For as Durkheim found, marriage is not the same for women as for men; it is not nearly as good. (pp. 146–147)

Why is it that marriage is thought of as "not nearly as good" for women as for men? The answer lies, at least partially, in the unequal status and the power imbalance that marriage accords both partners. Historically, wives were thought of as little more than a husband's property (Scanzoni, 1972). We need to go back only about 100 years to find a time when a wife was not allowed to control property, even the property she inherited from her premarriage family. According to English common law, the husband had total control over his wife. For example, a husband controlled his wife's wages, had the last say in their children's education and religion, and even had the right to physically beat his wife if she displeased him (Paludi, 1997). Today we hear more about marriages that seem more like corporations in which one partner (husband) plays the role of chief executive, while the other (wife) acts like a junior partner. In a growing number of marriages, both women and men have full-time careers and both share in all decisions as equal partners. A marriage where there is relative equality between the spouses' rights and privileges is called an *egalitarian* marriage. The difference between these two modern-day types of marriage seems to be in the amount of power a wife has in the marriage.

Marital Power and Happiness

One of the more often reported studies of the so-called "new marriage relationships" was conducted in Detroit more than 30 years ago (Blood & Wolfe, 1960). Over 900 wives were questioned about who in their marriages had the final say in matters like "what job the husband should take," "what car to buy," "what doctor to call when someone in the family was sick," and "how much to spend on the weekly groceries." By and large, the study found that husbands generally made decisions about their jobs and about buying new cars, while wives decided on which doctors to call in cases of illness and how much to spend on the weekly groceries. In tabulating their results, Robert Blood and Donald Wolfe assumed that all decisions were relatively equal in importance; thus they noted that many of the families in their study appeared to have an egalitarian marriage. However, we could question the assumption that deciding to buy a new car is equivalent to deciding about how much to spend on groceries. Most people would have to say that these decisions are not equivalent, and families that distribute the decision-making process along these issues are anything but egalitarian.

In speaking of an egalitarian marriage, researchers are now more apt to define two types of egalitarian marriages: syncratic and autonomic (Gray-Little & Burks, 1983). The *syncratic* relation describes a marital pattern in which both the wife and the husband wield power and make decisions jointly in all areas. The *autonomic* pattern refers to an egalitarian relationship in which husband and wife each exercise power and control over separate areas. Thus we can see that even egalitarian marriages are not all identical.

Sexual Victimization

Incest, rape, battering, and sexual harassment—types of sexual victimization—illustrate how men have more power than women. In rape, men have more physical power that may be increased even more by a weapon. In incest and battering, men have more physical power and that is increased by the power inequalities in the relationship, e.g., father-daughter or husband-wife. In sexual harassment, the harasser is an individual who holds expert and informational power in an academic or work setting, e.g., grades, letters of recommendation, promotions, and raises. In this section we will discuss the psychological literature on sexual victimization as a form of *power over*. We will also address individual, institutional, and societal approaches to change.

Rape

Rape is an act of violence, an attempted or completed sexual assault instigated by one or more persons against another human being. Most states define rape as sexual assault in which a man uses his penis to vaginally penetrate a woman against her will by force or threat of force or when she is mentally or physically unable to give her consent. In many states, the definition also includes unwanted oral and anal intercourse. Some states have removed the sex-specific language to broaden the applicability of rape laws. The historical roots of rape run deep in the patriarchal tradition of men's violence toward women (Koss, 1993; Rozee, 1997). Rape, to be understood, must not be seen as a violent sexual act of a few mentally ill men, but rather a violent sexual act performed by many men and reinforced by the dominant patriarchal values coming to the fore in our culture. A few cultures may be less prone to violent sexual acts by men to women, but ours and most others are definitely "rape-prone" cultures (Rozee, 1993).

In this section we will first take up the issue of rape as an act of dominance (not sex) and of power (not pathology) that is ingrained in the masculine gender role. Next we will put the statistics of rape in perspective by trying to give some scope to the enormity of the act of rape in the everyday lives of many women and some men. And then, we will note the rising concern and some of the actions taken among feminists over the issue of rape as a social phenomenon of epidemic proportions and not merely an isolated criminal act affecting a few.

Rape and Power

Throughout most of this century, those who influenced what others thought about rape saw it as a "victim-precipitated phenomenon" (Albin, 1977). Sigmund Freud (1927), in his study of the female personality, theorized that women were more "masochistic" than men and that rape—either in fantasy or in fact—was the one sexual act wherein a woman acted out her masochism to the utmost. This theory, however, was soon dismissed by the psychiatric and psychological communities who began to speculate that rape was the result of a disordered or aberrant sexual impulse within a certain small group of men. Today, however, rape is seen as an act of power or dominance of one person over another. Recently, some social scientists have noted that rape is used by men to dominate other men inside and outside of prison.

The element of aggression that is so deeply embedded in the masculine gender role is present in rape. For many men, aggression is one of the major ways of proving their masculinity, especially among those men who feel some sense of powerlessness in their lives. The male-as-dominant or male-as-aggressor is a theme so central to many men's self-concept that it literally carries over into their sexual lives. Sex, in fact, may be the one area where the average man can still prove his masculinity when few other areas can be found for him to prove himself in control or the dominant one in a relationship. Diana Russell (1973) addressed this issue when she stated that rape is not the act of a disturbed man, but rather an act of an over-conforming man. She wrote:

> *Rape is not so much a deviant act as an over-conforming act. Rape may be understood as an extreme acting-out of qualities that are regarded as super masculine in this and many other societies: aggression, force, power, strength, toughness, dominance, competitiveness. To win, to be superior, to be successful, to conquer—all demonstrate masculinity to those who subscribe to common cultural notions of masculinity, i.e., the masculine mystique. And it would be surprising if these notions of masculinity did not find expression in men's sexual behavior. Indeed, sex may be the arena where these notions of masculinity are most intensely played out, particularly by men who feel powerless in the rest of their lives, and hence, whose masculinity is threatened by this sense of powerlessness.* (p. 1)

The connection between aggression and sexuality for many men can be seen when we examine the area of sexual arousal as stimulated by graphic scenes of rape. Initially, researchers found that convicted rapists were more sexually aroused by depictions of violent sexuality than were men who had not raped. Thus it was thought that rapists must have a very low threshold for sexual arousal, and that the least little provocation would set off a male rapist; that theory held that a woman who would assertively say "no" to sexual advances or even put up a fight was enough to trigger a rapist. In more recent studies, however, when men who had never raped were exposed to depictions of sexual assault, they reported a heightened sexual arousal from such scenes and an increase in their rape fantasies (Malamuth & Check, 1981). Furthermore, when nonrapist men were shown depictions of sexual assault, they reported the possibility that they would even consider using force themselves in their sexual relations. The research appears to suggest that most men (i.e., rapists and nonrapists) find violence a stimulant to heighten or arouse their sexual feelings. There is evidence that men in general find sexuality related at some level to an expression of aggression, and in turn aggression heightens their sexual fantasies or actual sexual behaviors.

In summary, we can say that sexual assault or rape is first and foremost an act of sexual violence that to some degree draws upon the sexual fantasies of the rapist; it is linked to the rapist's need to show superiority and dominance over another.

The Problem of Numbers

Rape is one of the most underreported of all serious crimes in the United States and in other countries as well. When we try to get a true picture of the enormity of its incidence, we find the issue complicated by the lack of reliable rape statistics. The crime of rape presents some uniquely confounding problems.

One problem we encounter is the simple fact that many, if not most, rape victims simply refuse to come forward and report to the authorities incidents of sexual violence. For many rape victims, a sense of shame or guilt or self-blame about their role in the rape assaults may be enough to prevent them from coming forward and pressing charges. Those who do press charges, however, are apt to meet with questions, accusations, and other degrading and humiliating experiences by authorities who are sworn to uphold the laws of society that make the rape of a person a serious felony.

Another problem is that when rape victims do press charges against their assailants, their life histories, especially sexual activities, are shared with the public. In many instances, the public seems willing to blame the victim for the assault rather than the rapist. The reason for such an attribution of guilt to the victim rather than to the assailant seems to lie in the fact that many people have a tendency to blame others for their misfortunes, as if the world we live in was and is a "just world" where bad things happen only to those who somehow bring on or somehow deserve the consequences of their acts (Koss, 1993). Consequently, a likely result of such a "just world" orientation is that more often than not, the defenders of rapists will try to show that the rape victims acted in such a manner as to infer their complicity in the sexual assaults or that they "had it coming" because of their actions.

While we have no absolute statistics for the total number of completed or attempted rapes committed annually in North America, we can estimate the probability of a woman being the victim of rape during her lifetime. A conservative estimate is that 20 to 30 percent of girls now 12 years old will suffer a violent sexual act in their lifetime (Johnson, 1980). The enormity of the incidence of rape becomes even more staggering when we note that untold numbers of children under 12 years old are often the victims of sexual assault (Finkelhor & Dziuba-Leatherman, 1994). Adolescent and young adult women are in a high-risk range. The risk of rape is so high for African American women that elderly African American women are just as likely to be raped as young white women.

All women are threatened by rape; all women are vulnerable (Koss, 1993). Fear of rape restricts women's behavior.

> *I have never been free of the fear of rape. From a very early age, I, like most women, have thought of rape as part of my natural environment— something to be feared and prayed against like fire or lightning.* (Griffin, 1979, p. 3)

Date Rape

Mary Koss headed the *Ms.* national research project on acquaintance rape that was discussed in Robin Warshaw's (1988) book, *I Never Called It Rape.* Koss surveyed 32 college campuses in the United States. She reported that one in four women surveyed (a total of 1,387 were raped) were victims of rape or attempted rape, 84 percent of women who had been raped knew their attacker, and 57 percent of the rapes happened on dates. Koss further reported that 1 in 12 of the men students she surveyed had committed acts that met the legal definitions of rape or attempted rape. Approximately 75 percent of the men and 55 percent of the women involved in acquaintance rapes had been taking drugs, including drinking alcohol, before the rape.

This study found that women did not identify what had happened to them as rape when it took place between dating partners, when they had consented to sexual intimacy with this man on previous occasions, and when minimal violence was involved. One woman reported the following:

> *I didn't tell anyone. In fact, I wouldn't even admit it to myself until about four months later when the guilt and fear that had been eating at me became too much to hide and I came very close to a complete nervous breakdown. I tried to kill myself, but fortunately I chickened out at the last minute.*
>
> *There's no way to describe what was going on inside me. I was losing control and I'd never been so terrified and helpless in my life. I felt as if my whole world had been kicked out from under me and I had been left to drift all alone in the darkness. I had horrible nightmares in which I relived the rape and others which were even worse. I was terrified of being with people and terrified of being alone. I couldn't concentrate on anything and began failing several classes. Deciding what to wear in the morning was enough to make me panic and cry uncontrollably. I was convinced I was going crazy, and I'm still convinced I almost did.* (quoted in Warshaw, pp. 67–68)

Thirty percent of the women identified as rape victims in the *Ms.* study considered suicide after the rape, 31 percent sought psychotherapy, 22 percent took self-defense courses, and 82 percent said the experience had permanently changed them.

In the year prior to the research, 2,971 college men reported that they had committed 187 rapes, 157 attempted rapes, 327 episodes of sexual coercion, and 854 incidents of unwanted sexual contact. Eighty-four percent of the men who committed rape did not label their behavior as rape.

Rape As a Social Concern

Due to the concern over women's rights heralded by the reemergent women's movement, sexual assaults and their debilitating consequences for the victims have become one of the more pressing central issues of the last several decades. Consequently, many social scientists have turned their attention toward understanding the dynamics of rapists and their motives, the institutional and cultural factors promoting rape, and of course, the various factors affecting the assault on rape victims and their reactions.

To combat the growing number of rapes, more and more people are beginning to think in terms of prevention and not only of ways to deal with the debilitating aftermath of sexual assault. Many different ways have been suggested to stop the growing wave of sexual assaults in our society.

Two such preventive approaches are commonly suggested: first, a "restrictive approach," which focuses on women changing their lifestyles (e.g., not going out alone or not talking to strangers), and second, an "assertive approach" that suggests that women learn martial arts in order to fight back if assaulted. Both of these approaches, however, have some drawbacks. The restrictive approach, asking women to change their pattern of living, is an affront to women. Do we ask merchants to stop keeping money in their cash registers to prevent robberies? Why then should women change, for example, their dress or their social habits? The assertive approach has one possible value: the demise of the myth of the "defenseless woman" (Connell & Wilsen, 1974). However, one problem with this approach is that many times in order to coerce a victim, a rapist uses a deadly weapon, which nullifies any preventive action or force a victim may take to ward off an assailant.

Along with teaching young children and women to skillfully defend themselves, it seems that a broader based attack against sexual assaults should be taken against the social and institutional factors that promote sexual violence in our society. Two additional areas should be addressed if we are to see a reduction and, hopefully, an elimination in sexual assaults in our society. First, we need to examine the masculine gender role with its prescriptive aggressive element, especially aggression against women. Aggression and violence are still seen by many as an integral part of the masculine gender role (Doyle, 1995). One way to reduce sexual assault in our society would be to redefine the masculine gender role, incorporating nonaggressive or nonviolent elements rather than aggressiveness.

Many men on college campuses have established men's programs that conduct sexual victimization awareness education. For example, in Madison, Wisconsin, the organization Men Stopping Rape offers community educational programs about rape. This organization provides education for college students as well as high school and middle school children. At Cornell University men provide sexual victimization programs. They are "peer educators" on acquaintance rape and gender role socialization in the program, "How to Be a Better Lover." This program is sponsored by Cornell's health education unit.

Another controversial change that would reduce the number of sexual assaults is an attack on violence-oriented pornography and the multimillion-dollar business that supports it. The pornography industry has mainly directed its sales to men. Although some erotic material does not focus on violent sexual aggression, a large proportion of the male-oriented pornography sold in stores across our country portrays women as the victims of physical and sexual assault (Dworkin, 1981).

Researchers Neil Malamuth and Edward Donnerstein (1982) found that exposure to violent pornography generally increases sexual arousal as well as negative attitudes toward women and favorable attitudes toward sexual assault. Thus one possible way to reduce the sexual violence in our society against women would be to eliminate such material. Those who oppose such a plan immediately bring up the issue of a person's First Amendment rights, which guarantee freedom of speech. Such opposition, however, misinterprets the Constitution and its intent.

If our society is to change the problem of unequal power between women and men, we need to challenge many of our behaviors, our attitudes, and our social institutions that continue to cast women in an inferior role. Until that day, the problem of inequality between women and men is everyone's concern.

Incest

Judith Herman (1981) reported the following:

> *A fifteen-year-old girl appeared in the outpatient clinic, asking for tranquilizers. She had a history of addiction to alcohol and barbiturates, had been hospitalized several times for detoxification, and had had a number of unsuccessful placements in various residential treatment programs for adolescents. She revealed that from the age of eight she had been involved in a sexual relationship with her father which included fellatio and mutual masturbation. She ran away from home at age twelve, when her father attempted intercourse, and had essentially lived on the street since then. She expressed the hope, which seemed quite unrealistic, that her mother would divorce her father and allow her to come home.* (p. 8)

Research on child sexual abuse has indicated that at least 20 percent of women have been a victim of incest some time in their lives, 12 percent before the age of 14 years, 16 percent before the age of 18 years. These percentages translate into the sexual molestation of 100,000 children each year. In addition, most of the abuse is perpetrated by a family member or by an individual known to the family. Girls are more likely to be abused within the family; boys (although abuse of boys is more rare) are more likely to be abused by a non-family member (Courtois, 1988). About 10 percent of boys have experienced incest. The perpetrators of incestuous abuse are predominantly men (Courtois, 1988). Child sexual abuse involves coercion and misrepresentation of the relationship and abuse by individuals who should be protecting children—relatives, neighbors, and family friends (Finkelhor & Dziuba-Leatherman, 1994). As Christine Courtois stated:

> *The child is manipulated by the unequal power in the relationship, that is, by the relationship with the perpetrator on whom she is dependent. The child is further coerced by the perpetrator's strong desire to keep the activity a secret, which has the purpose of minimizing intervention and allowing repetition.* (p. 6)

If the child does disclose information about the incestuous relationship, she is typically met with adult disbelief and rationalization of the perpetrator's behavior (Courtois, 1988). Most children do not tell.

Lundberg-Love (1997) suggests that incest survivors are at risk for a number of psychological problems several years subsequent to their abuse. Feelings of isolation, stigmatization, and alienation have been reported. In addition, difficulties in the area of self-esteem, social functioning, and sexuality have been observed (Lundberg-Love, 1997). Women incest victims report fear, depression, anxiety, mistrust, increased worry regarding the safety of others, and difficulties in interpersonal relationships.

A common belief is that incest occurs more often in families of working-class background, of ethnic minorities, and in rural families. However, these beliefs have not been substantiated by research. In addition, the percentage of incest victims is comparable across all ethnic groups studied, with the exception of Asian women, who are at a lower risk (Landrine, 1995).

Children who are victims of sexual abuse suffer aftereffects, in many cases serious enough to warrant therapy in adulthood (Lundberg-Love, 1997). Consciousness-raising groups (see chapter 10) have been valuable for women and men who experienced incest.

Child Abductions and Missing Children

Children who are abducted by strangers or family members are often at risk for sexual abuse (Tedisco & Paludi, 1996). Myths about the motives of the abductor have clouded and complicated perceptions about the crime of child abduction. People want to cling to the illusion that abductors are insane, bizarre, or psychotic and therefore easily identifiable. Exceptions to these myths are quite difficult for some to accept. People do not want to believe that a "normal" person could abduct children or adolescents, especially their own daughters and sons. People expect child abductors to be sinister individuals who hang around school playgrounds, waiting to lure children with candy.

The illusion that there is a "typical" abductor who can be identified by his blatant mistreatment of children or adolescents is an oversimplification of a complex issue. While it may be difficult to accept that abductions are perpetrated by individuals who are familiar to us, who have family lives similar to ours, and who appear to be caring and sensitive individuals, that is indeed a reality.

The feature of apparent normalcy helps us to understand why children may go with a noncustodial parent. Children often believe they can easily identify an abductor. Children are taught to respect adults, especially adults' authority, and to only talk to people who "look nice." Children's faith in their own judgment about other people can be shattered; often survivors report that they don't know who to trust anymore. They question what is normal and who can be trusted long into their adult years. Indeed, the abductor's apparent normalcy may lead an adolescent or young adult to question his or her own perceptions of the abuse. Did it happen this way or did he or she imagine that this nice woman or man was so violent? This may be fueled by contact with an abductor who acts as if nothing has happened. This deception is further enhanced by the fact that the abductor may believe s/he has done nothing wrong and has the best interest of the child at heart.

Children and adolescents quite frequently experience a split reality: other people in their environment tell them continuously how lucky they are to have such a wonderful parent. They themselves may come to reframe the victimization, perhaps blaming themselves, perhaps believing that all children have similar experiences. Children are driven into regression, alienation, powerlessness, shame, embarrassment, humiliation, self-blame, and self-hate.

Thus the psychological impact of being abducted by a parent and living with this individual is stressful for children. Children experience fear, grief over the loss of the other parent, confusion about divorce and their role in it, guilt for not calling the other parent, and hatred for their parents.

Physical abuse and psychological abuse as well as incestuous relationships between the noncustodial parent and the child may occur. Children are thus further manipulated into silence—about the abduction and then about the sexual abuse. The child is thus manipulated by the unequal power in the relationship. The parent's desire to keep the activity a secret has the purpose of minimizing intervention and allowing repetition.

Research also suggests that few abductors are motivated by sexual needs. Abductors state that sexual satisfaction is absent in their abuse of children. If any sexual satisfaction does occur, it is in conjunction with the humiliation of the child and is inseparable from psychological needs.

The abductor's primary motivation is the feeling of power, one that is rooted in dominance and humiliation of others who are less powerful. One prime ingredient is the element of aggression that is deeply embedded in the masculine gender role in North American culture.

For men who abduct and sexually abuse children, aggression is one of the major ways of proving their masculinity, especially among those men who feel some sense of powerlessness in their lives. Abductors are skilled at manipulating children. They use seduction techniques, competition, peer pressure, motivation techniques, and threats to get children to comply with their requests to flee their home or school, or to engage in sex, steal, abuse drugs, or participate in prostitution or pornography. Part of the manipulation process involves lowering the inhibitions of children.

If children do disclose information about the incestuous relationship, they are typically met with disbelief and rationalization of the abductor's behavior. *Thus, most children do not tell.*

Research does suggest that 90 percent of parents who abduct their own children are emotionally unstable or abusive, and approximately half have criminal records. Children often live under cruel circumstances, almost paralleling the life of a fugitive, with frequent changes of residences and names.

However, many people deny children's responses to abductions along the domains of school outcomes and psychological and somatic outcomes. Children and adolescents may not label their experiences as abduction or abuse if their parent is the perpetrator, despite the fact the experiences meet the legal definition of this form of victimization. Consequently they may not label their stress-related responses as being caused or exacerbated by the abduction and subsequent abuse. Their responses are attributed by their abductor or others to other events in their life—biological and/or social. However, research has documented the high cost of abductions and abuse to children (Tedisco & Paludi, 1996).

Research has suggested that unlike physical abuse and neglect of children, where the evidence is apparent, psychological problems are subtle and may not surface for some years. Young children and adolescents who have been abducted may not be able to verbalize the impact of the abuse on them until much later in their lives. Victims of abduction initially believe that the victimization will stop. When the abductor's behavior escalates, the victim begins to feel powerless. Subsequent to the abductor's continuing behavior, victims feel trapped. A sense of learned helplessness sets in; children begin to believe that no matter what they do, the victimization will not cease. Once children recognize that they were legitimate victims who were not to blame for their abduction and abuse, anxiety often shifts to anger.

Most children experience an immediate postvictimization generalized distress response characterized as a state of psychological shock: repeated reexperiencing of the trauma by intrusive waking images or dreams, depression, and emotional numbing. Furthermore, research has suggested that abducted children who are found and returned to their families often remain psychologically tied to their abductors and continue to show psychological impairment.

The age of the child must be considered as an important factor in the nature and severity of injuries resulting from abductions. For example, small children are more vulnerable to death and serious harm as a result of inflicted blows. Older children and adolescents are at greater risk of contacting sexual abuse-related HIV infection, since older children suffer more penetrative sexual abuse.

Battered Women

Even with increased publicity about domestic violence or battering, most violence in interpersonal relationships remains a secret (Butts Stahly, 1996). Attesting to the privatization of family violence, the first book to examine family violence was entitled *Scream Quietly or the Neighbors Will Hear* (Pizzey, 1974). Still, the public is becoming more aware of the seriousness and magnitude of domestic violence, due in large measure to the efforts of the women's movement.

In the past decade or so, several researchers have turned their attention to reaching a fuller understanding of the issues and dynamics surrounding domestic violence (Browne, 1993; Butts Stahly, 1996). In this section we will first take up the question of the magnitude and degree of battered women. Next we will look at several different views about the probable causes for this violence. Then we will examine battered women in terms of institutional forms that support power inequities between women and men.

The Growing Phenomenon of Battering

Battering is neither a rare nor a recent phenomenon (Frieze, 1997; Graham & Rawlings, 1997). History is filled with episodes of family and marital violence. In the Old Testament a husband could have his wife put to death for her unfaithfulness and his children beaten or even killed for breaking the injunction to "honor thy father and mother" (Steinmetz, 1978). Through the centuries, attitudes toward domestic violence suggest a type of benign acceptance rather than disgust. This is due in large part to our society's patriarchal social order, which regards men as absolute rulers in their homes.

The women's movement has focused public attention on the plight of battered women and has forced the public to become aware of the magnitude of family violence. But how prevalent is domestic violence in relationships? This question is difficult to answer because of the usually private nature of its commission and the hesitancy on the part of many victims to seek outside help. For many people, domestic violence is a taboo topic and not readily admitted to. And yet, we have some evidence of the magnitude of the problem with estimates of families that harbor violence in their midst. For example, in studies of couples seeking divorces, physical abuse is often cited as reason for divorce or a frequent complaint lodged by women during the divorce proceedings. However, marriages that end in divorce do not truly represent the "average" marriage, and we should be careful about our interpretation of such findings.

Police records of family disputes involving physical violence are not the answer, either, simply because the majority of violent episodes among family members are thought to go unreported. Nevertheless, in nearly 85 percent of the cases in which a woman is killed by her husband or lover, the police had previously been called to stop domestic violence (Graham & Rawlings, 1997).

In a national sample of over 2,000 families, Murray Straus, Richard Gelles, and Suzanne Steinmetz (1980) found that one out of every six couples engage in at least one violent act each year. These authors note that over the course of a marriage, 25 percent of all couples will likely experience marital violence. Overall, we can conclude that "the American family and the American home are perhaps as or more violent than any other American institution or setting (with the exception of the military, and only then in time of war)" (Straus et al., 1980, p. 4).

Although a precise figure cannot be derived from police records, divorce cases, or even the extrapolations from national surveys, we can conclude that millions of families each year are embroiled in domestic crises that end up with women physically injured. Domestic violence warrants our serious attention and should be labeled as one of the most serious social problems today.

Tracking Down the Elusive Causes of Battering

"How could he have done that to her?" is a frequent question when people hear about an incident of battering. Many people are puzzled by violence between people who supposedly love and care for each other. If we are to stop battering, researchers must continue to search for its causes.

Initially, researchers believed that psychologically disordered individuals were chiefly responsible for domestic violence. After countless psychological studies, however, most researchers today can find no evidence to warrant the belief that family violence is caused by disordered thinking or that perpetrators of battering are any more likely to exhibit psychological disorders than is any other segment of society. Thus we need to look for other possible causes to explain this victimization.

In looking for the causes of battering, we should not lose sight of the fact that America is a violence-prone society, one with an ambivalent view of the role that violence plays in our lives (Doyle, 1995). On the one hand, Americans decry the violence found in many of America's urban settings, and on the other, many relish watching violent television programs, films, and sporting events.

Battered women may stay in a violent relationship because they believe the situation is inescapable or is part of their lot in life. They typically feel helpless about changing their lives and fear that any action they take will contribute to more violence. These fears are justified (Butts Stahly, 1996).

Battered women modify their own behavior so as to minimize the violence. However, these attempts may be met with further attacks (Walker, 1991). Whatever the woman does can be thought of as provocative by the man and thus can cause him to react in a violent way.

Women have been thought to be culpable in their own violence; this implies that violence is more likely to occur in those situations where wives outshine their husbands in some presumably important way. Thus to gain back a measure of self-respect, these husbands must batter their resourceful wives.

The problem with this perspective is that women, as a rule, do not have more resources than men have in income, education, or nearly any other valued resource imaginable that would account for the significant number of battered women. In families where wives do earn higher salaries than their husbands, there is no evidence that family violence is any greater than in families where the husbands earn more than the wives.

Instead of looking at battering from the viewpoint of the individual, we might be well served to look at it from the view of the imbalance of power that is normally found between women and men. Our society and its many institutions are decidedly sexist and misogynous. Although much of the recent literature on battering reflects a sincere wish to change the pattern of violence against women, many of the notions expressed continue to reinforce the belief that somehow women are to blame for the violence.

Men who batter women are likely to have witnessed their fathers beat their mothers. They are also more likely to abuse their children. Batterers are likely to be unemployed. However, batterers are no more likely to come from lower socioeconomic classes than wealthier ones.

A realistic view of battering can be found in the imbalance in power and the idea that men have a right to dominate women in nearly every social situation. Domestic violence is actually a symptom of a social system wherein men believe that their will is law, and that belief is supported by the social structures. To eliminate domestic violence, we should not simply concentrate on the individual—either the battered or the batterer—but rather on the social, political, and economic forces that perpetuate the bias against women. When men no longer believe they have the right to control women's lives, and when they stop thinking in terms of aggression as part of their masculine mandate, we will see a reduction of domestic violence.

Sexual Harassment

Sexual harassment in schools, colleges, and the workplace is a major barrier to individuals' professional development and a traumatic force that disrupts and damages their personal lives (Levy & Paludi, 1997; Paludi, 1996; Lott & Reilly, 1996). We will discuss sexual harassment in more detail in chapter 8. In this chapter we will discuss definitions of sexual harassment, its incidence, and explanatory models.

Incidence of Sexual Harassment

Individuals, mostly women, experience sexual harassment in many forms—from sexist remarks and covert physical contact (patting, brushing against their bodies) to blatant propositions and sexual assaults. Researchers have developed five categories to encompass the range of sexual harassment (Fitzgerald et al., 1988): gender harassment, seductive behavior, sexual bribery, sexual coercion, and sexual imposition. These levels of sexual harassment correlate with legal definitions of sexual harassment.

Gender harassment consists of generalized sexist remarks and behavior not designed to elicit sexual cooperation but rather to convey insulting, degrading, or sexist attitudes about women. *Seductive behavior* is unwanted, inappropriate, and offensive sexual advances. *Sexual bribery* is the solicitation of sexual activity or other sex-linked behavior by threat of punishment. *Sexual coercion* is the coercion of sexual activity or other sex-linked behavior by threat of punishment. And, *sexual imposition* includes gross sexual imposition, assault, and rape.

Incidence of Sexual Harassment: Workplace

Sexual harassment is similar to other forms of sexual victimization such as rape, incest, and battering in which various factors combine to produce underreporting and underestimates. Several major and smaller-scale studies do suggest that sexual harassment in the workplace is widespread. It is estimated that one out of every two women will be harassed at some point in their career.

The United States Merit Systems Protection Board addressed sexual harassment in the federal workplace and suggested that 42% of all women employees reported being sexually harassed (Merit Systems, 1981). Merit Systems reported that many incidents occurred repeatedly, were of long duration, and had a sizable practical impact, costing the government an estimated minimum of $189 million over the two years covered by the research project.

Results also indicated that 33 percent of the women reported receiving unwanted sexual remarks, 28 percent reported suggestive looks, and 26 percent reported being deliberately touched. These behaviors were classified in the study as "less severe" types of sexual harassment. When "more severe" forms of sexual harassment were addressed, 15 percent of the women reported experiencing pressure for dates, 9 percent reported being directly pressured for sexual favors, and 9 percent had received unwanted letters and telephone calls. One percent of the sample had experienced actual or attempted rape or assault. Merit Systems repeated its study of workplace sexual harassment in 1987 and reported identical results to 1981 findings.

Research by Barbara Gutek (1985) with women in the civilian workplace reports similar findings as well—that approximately half the female workforce experiences sexual harassment. Based on telephone interviews generated through random digit dialing procedures, Gutek's results suggested that 53 percent of women had reported one incident they believed was sexual harassment during their working lives, including degrading, insulting comments (15 percent), sexual touching (24 percent), socializing expected as part of the job requirement (11 percent), and expected sexual activity (8 percent).

Occupational Group Differences

There have been some studies reported in the literature that suggest that group differences in sexual harassment are common. For example, Louise Fitzgerald and colleagues (1988) found that women who were employed in a university setting (e.g., faculty, staff, and administrators) were more likely to experience sexual harassment than were women students in the same institution. Yael Gold (1987) reported that her sample of blue-collar tradeswomen experienced significantly higher levels of all forms of sexual harassment (e.g., gender harassment, seductive behavior, sexual bribery, sexual coercion, and sexual assault) than did either white-collar professional women or "pink-collar" clerical workers.

Nancy Baker (1989) studied a sample of 100 women employed in either traditional or nontraditional occupations, where traditionality was defined by the sex distribution in the work group. Baker also divided the traditional group into pink- and blue-collar workers. The pink-collar group included women who were secretaries and clerical workers. The blue-collar group included women who were industrial workers. Baker reported that high levels of sexual harassment are associated with having low numbers of women in the work group. For example, machinists reported significantly high frequencies of all levels of sexual harassment, whereas the traditional blue-collar workers reported very low levels. Clerical workers reported experiences that were more similar to those of the traditional blue-collar laborers than the nontraditional blue-collar workers. Baker also reported that women in the pink-collar and traditional blue-collar groups encountered just as many men as the machinists during the workday, but were treated differently. Thus these results suggest that as women approach numerical parity in various segments of the workforce, sexual harassment may decline.

This perspective has also been raised by Gutek (1985) who argued that sexual harassment is more likely to occur in occupations in which "sex-role spillover" has occurred. Gutek's model suggests that when occupations are dominated by one sex or the other, the sex role of the dominant sex influences (e.g., "spills over") the work role expectations for that job. Thus, sexual harassment can be viewed as a side effect of organizing society around gender stereotypes, an issue to which we now turn.

Incidence of Sexual Harassment: Schools and Colleges

Research has suggested that similar to employees, most students do not label their experiences as sexual behavior despite the fact the behavior they have experienced meets the legal definition of either quid pro quo or hostile environment harassment. The American Association of University Women (1993) studied 1,632 students in grades 8 through 11 from 79 schools across the United States. Students were asked: "During your whole school life, how often, if at all, has anyone (this includes students, teachers, other school employees, or anyone else) done the following things to you **when you did not want them to**?"

Made sexual comments, jokes, gestures, or looks.
Showed, gave, or left you sexual pictures, photographs, illustrations, messages, or notes.
Wrote sexual messages/graffiti about you on bathroom walls, in locker rooms, etc.
Spread sexual rumors about you.

Said you were gay or lesbian.
Spied on you as you dressed or showered at school.
Flashed or "mooned" you.
Touched, grabbed, or pinched you in a sexual way.
Pulled at your clothing in a sexual way.
Intentionally brushed against you in a sexual way.
Pulled your clothing off or down.
Blocked your way or cornered you in a sexual way.
Forced you to kiss him/her.
Forced you to do something sexual, other than kissing.

Results suggested that four out of five students (81%) reported that they have been the target of some form of sexual harassment during their school lives. With respect to gender comparisons, 85% of girls and 76% of boys surveyed reported they have experienced unwelcome sexual behavior that interferes with their ability to concentrate at school and with their personal lives. The AAUW study also analyzed for race comparisons. African American boys (81%) were more likely to have experienced sexual harassment than white boys (75%) and Latinos (69%). For girls, 87% of whites reported having experienced behaviors that constitute sexual harassment, compared with 84% of African American girls and 82% of Latinas.

The AAUW study also suggested that adolescents' experiences with sexual harassment are most likely to occur in the middle school/junior high school years of sixth to ninth grade. The behaviors reported by students, in rank order from most experienced to least experienced, are:

Sexual comments, jokes, gestures, or looks
Touched, grabbed, or pinched in a sexual way
Intentionally brushed against in a sexual way
Flashed or "mooned"
Had spread sexual rumors about them
Had clothing pulled at in a sexual way
Shown, given, or left sexual pictures, photographs, illustrations, messages, or
  notes
Had their way blocked or cornered in a sexual way
Had sexual messages/graffiti written about them on bathroom walls, in
  locker rooms, etc.
Forced to kiss someone
Called gay or lesbian
Had clothing pulled off or down
Forced to do something sexual, other than kissing
Spied on as they dressed or showered at school

Students reported that they experience these behaviors while in the classroom or in the hallways as they are going to class. The majority of harassment in schools is student-to-student. However, 25% of harassed girls and 10% of boys reported they were harassed by teachers or other school employees.

With respect to the incidence of sexual harassment of college/university students, Paludi (1996) reported that 30 percent of undergraduate women suffer sexual harassment from at least one of their instructors during their four years of college. When definitions of sexual harassment include sexist remarks and other forms of "gender harassment," the incidence rate in undergraduate populations nears 70 percent.

Nancy Bailey and Margaret Richards (1985) reported that of 246 women graduate students in their sample, 13 percent indicated they had been sexually harassed, 21 percent had not enrolled in a course to avoid such behavior, and 16 percent indicated they had been directly assaulted. Meg Bond (1988) reported that 75 percent of the 229 women who responded to her survey experienced jokes with sexual themes during their graduate training, 69 percent were subjected to sexist comments demeaning to women, and 58 percent of the women reported experiencing sexist remarks about their clothing, body, or sexual activities.

Fitzgerald and colleagues (1988) investigated approximately 2,000 women at two major state universities. Half of the women respondents reported experiencing some form of sexually harassing behavior. The majority of these women reported experiencing sexist comments by faculty; the next largest category of sexual harassing behavior was seductive behavior, including being invited for drinks and a backrub by faculty members, being brushed up against by their professors, and having their professors show up uninvited to their hotel rooms during out-of-town academic conferences or conventions.

Research by Michele Paludi, Darlene DeFour, and Rosemarie Roberts (1996) suggests that the incidence of academic sexual harassment of ethnic minority women students is even greater than that reported with white women. Ethnic minority women are more vulnerable to receiving sexual attention from professors. Ethnic minority women are subject to stereotypes about sex, viewed as mysterious, and less sure of themselves in their careers. Thus, although all students are vulnerable to some degree, male teachers and faculty tend to select those who are most vulnerable and needy (DeFour, 1990).

For certain student groups, the incidence of sexual harassment appears to be higher than others. For example:

Girls and women of color, especially those with "token" status

Graduate students, whose future careers are often determined by their association with a particular faculty member

Students in small colleges or small academic departments, where the number of faculty available to students is quite small

Girl and women students in male-populated fields, e.g., engineering

Students who are economically disadvantaged and work part-time or full-time while attending classes

Lesbian women, who may be harassed as part of homophobia

Physically or emotionally disabled students

Women students who work in dormitories as resident assistants

Girls and women who have been sexually abused

Inexperienced, unassertive, socially isolated girls and women, who may
  appear more vulnerable and appealing to those who would intimidate or
  entice them into an exploitive relationship

Explanatory Models of Sexual Harassment

Sexual harassment occurs, in most instances, when individuals exploit a position of power granted to them by their roles in an institutional structure. This is as true for the workplace as it is for the classroom. The major impasse to a general acknowledgment that sexual harassment is a devastating force continues to be the widespread belief that this is a matter of personal relations outside the control of the institution and unrelated to its own powers and prerogatives.

The idea that sexual harassment is an inherently personal rather than an institutional matter is a variation on the explanatory framework called the *natural/biological model* by Sandra Tangri and colleagues (1982). They have identified three explanatory models that individuals typically use to account for sexual harassment. The natural/biological model interprets sexual harassment as a consequence of natural sexual interactions between people, either attributing a stronger sex drive to men than to women or describing sexual harassment as part of the "game" between women and men. This model does not account for the stress reactions suffered by victims of sexual harassment. It is as fallacious as a racist theory that attributes the victimization of minorities to a "natural" prerogative or capacity of a superior race or to the "inevitable" workings of social forces.

The *sociocultural model* posits sexual harassment as only one manifestation of the much larger patriarchal system in which men are the dominant group. Therefore, harassment is an example of men asserting their personal power based on sex. According to this model, sex would be a better predictor of both recipient and initiator status than would organizational position. Thus, women should be much more likely to be victims of sexual harassment, especially when they are in male-populated college majors or careers.

This model gives a much more accurate account of sexual harassment since the overwhelming majority of victims are women and the overwhelming majority of harassers are men (90 to 95 percent in each case; Fitzgerald et al., 1988). Yet it can have the unfortunate effect of leaving women feeling nearly as powerless as the natural/biological model does. If sexual harassment is so ingrained in our whole culture, how can the individual withstand such a systemic force?

The *organizational model* asserts that sexual harassment results from opportunities presented by relations of power and authority that derive from the hierarchical structure of organizations. Thus, sexual harassment is an issue of organizational power. Since work (and academic) organizations are defined by vertical stratification and asymmetrical relations between supervisors and subordinates, teachers and students, individuals can use the power of their position to extort sexual gratification from their subordinates.

Organizational power is pervasively abused, victimizing literally tens of millions of women in the workplace, schools, colleges, and universities, *because* sexual inequality and victimization are endemic to our patriarchal culture. Just as the frequency of rape in warfare is a consequence of general cultural values licensed by the extreme "organizational structure" of war, so the frequency of sexual harassment is a consequence of these same values empowered by the routine structures of work and education (Paludi & Barickman, 1997).

Why Men Harass

The stereotype that there is a "typical" harasser who can be identified by his blatant mistreatment of women is an oversimplification of a complex issue. This stereotype also contributes to the misunderstanding of sexual harassment, women remaining silent about their victimization, and employers not taking women's accounts seriously. Harassers are found in all types of occupations, at all organizational levels, among business and professional individuals, and among college professors. Men who sexually harass have not been distinguishable from their colleagues who don't harass with respect to age, marital status, faculty rank, occupation, or academic discipline. Men who harass have a tendency to do this repeatedly to many women. And, men who harass hold attitudes toward women that are traditional, not egalitarian (Zalk, 1996).

For example, John Pryor (1987) noted that sexual harassment bears a conceptual similarity to rape. He developed a series of hypothetical scenarios of situations that provided opportunities for sexual harassment if the man so chose. Instructions asked men to imagine themselves in the roles of the men and to consider what they would do in each situation. They were further instructed to imagine that whatever their chosen course of action, no negative consequences would result from their choices. Men's scores on the likelihood of engaging in sexual harassment were related to gender role stereotyping and negatively related to feminist attitudes and that component of empathy having to do with the ability to take the standpoint of the other.

Thus, this research suggests that the man who is likely to initiate severe sexually harassing behavior appears to be one who emphasizes male social and sexual dominance and who demonstrates insensitivity to other individuals' perspectives. Men are also significantly more likely than women to agree with the following statements, taken from Paludi's (1995) "attitudes toward victim blame and victim responsibility" survey:

Women often claim sexual harassment to protect their reputations.
Many women claim sexual harassment if they have consented to sexual
    relations but have changed their minds afterwards.
Sexually experienced women are not really damaged by sexual harassment.
It would do some women good to be sexually harassed.

Women put themselves in situations in which they are likely to be sexually harassed because they have an unconscious wish to be harassed.

In most cases when a woman is sexually harassed, she deserved it.

Paludi (1996) has focused on men's attitudes toward other men, competition, and power in trying to understand why men harass. Many of the men with whom Paludi has discussed sexual harassment often act out of extreme competitiveness and concern with ego or out of fear of losing their positions of power. They don't want to appear weak or less masculine in the eyes of other men, so they engage in rating women's bodies, pinching women, making implied or overt threats, or spying on women. Women are the game to impress other men. When men are being encouraged to be obsessionally competitive and concerned with dominance, it is likely that they will eventually use violent means to achieve dominance. They are also likely to be abusive verbally and intimidating in their body language. Deindividuation is quite common among male office workers who may numerically rate women as they walk by in the halls or in the classroom. These men discontinue self-evaluation and adopt group norms and attitudes. Under these circumstances, group members behave more aggressively than they would as individuals.

Furthermore, men are less likely than women to define sexual harassment as including jokes, teasing remarks of a sexual nature, and unwanted suggestive looks or gestures. In addition, women are more likely than men to disapprove of romantic relationships between faculty and students and between managers and employees. Male faculty and employees typically view sexual harassment as a personal, not an organizational, issue. Men are also significantly more likely than women to agree with the following statements: "An attractive woman has to expect sexual advances and learn how to handle them." "It is only natural for a man to make sexual advances to a woman he finds attractive." And, "people who receive annoying sexual attention usually have provoked it." Finally, faculty men are more likely than women to believe individuals can handle unwanted sexual attention on their own without involving the college or university. Male faculty thus may perceive sexual harassment as an issue that does not merit the attention of the institution.

Women are much more likely than men to assign a central role to the college or workplace for preventing and dealing with all levels of sexual harassment. Since the research indicates that men attribute more responsibility to women victims of sexual harassment, men would also be likely to minimize the potential responsibility of organization officials.

We need to think of sexual harassment as being not the act of a disturbed man, but rather an act of an over-conforming man. In other words, sexual harassment, similar to rape, incest, and battering, may be understood as an extreme acting-out of qualities that are regarded as super masculine in this culture: aggression, power, dominance, and force. Thus men who harass are not pathological but individuals who exhibit behaviors characteristic of the masculine gender role in American culture (Paludi, 1993).

Related to this are the research findings that suggest that individuals who harass typically do not label their behavior as sexual harassment despite the fact they report they frequently engage in behaviors that fit the legal definition of sexual harassment. They deny the inherent power differential between themselves and their students or employees as well as the psychological power conferred by this differential that is as salient as the power derived from evaluation. The behavior that legally constitutes harassment is just that, despite what the professor's or employer's intentions may be. It is the woman's reaction to the behavior that is the critical variable.

The structure of the academy and workplace interacts with psychological dynamics to increase women's vulnerability to all forms of sexual harassment. For example, professors' greatest power lies in the capacity to enhance or diminish students' self-esteem. This power can motivate students to learn course material or convince them to give up. The tone and content of the student-professor interaction is especially important. Is the student encouraged or put down? Do the faculty members use their knowledge to let students know how "stupid" they are or to challenge their thinking? As Sue Zalk, Michele Paludi, and Judy Dederich (1991) point out, this is REAL POWER!

Because of power structures within the workplace and the academic setting as well as deeply embedded cultural biases, women are overwhelmingly the targets of sexual harassment. It is important to consider sexual harassment as a pattern of abuse. Identification of sexual harassment as a "woman's issue" rather than as a pervasive pattern of abuse that contaminates a whole community only creates another impediment to its identification and elimination.

Can/do women harass men? Research suggests the following summary comments (Paludi, 1996):

1. Women are highly unlikely to date or initiate sexual relationships with their male students or employees. Most of their interaction with students, for example, involves mentoring or friendship behaviors, most of which involve women students.
2. A small number of men in the workplace setting believe they have been sexually harassed by women. The behaviors many of these men label as sexual harassment, however, do not fit the legal definition of either quid pro quo or hostile environment sexual harassment.

   Men are more likely than women to interpret a particular behavior as sexual. For example, in research by Gutek (1985) men were likely to label a business lunch as a "date" if it is with a woman manager. Friendliness on the part of a woman is often interpreted by a man as a sexual gesture. This tendency to misattribute women's motives was apparent in the research of Fitzgerald and others with faculty men. For example, one professor reported that he knew a student was interested in having sex with him because of "the way she sat" and the fact that she made an appointment to see him shortly before the end of the working day. This tendency to sexualize their experiences makes it difficult to interpret men's reports of seductive advances.

3. The great majority of men report that they are flattered by women's advances, whereas women report feeling annoyed, insulted, and threatened.
4. It is rare for a woman to hold the organizational power and sociocultural power that would allow her to reward a man for sexual cooperation or punish him for withholding it, even if gender role prescriptions did not ensure that she was extremely unlikely to demand sexual favors in the first place. In research with faculty women and men where women held the same power as their male colleagues, none of the faculty women interviewed became sexually involved with their students. However, one in four of the men did.

Thus, although it is theoretically possible for women to harass men, in practice it is a rare event. This is due to both the women's relative lack of formal power and the socialization that stigmatizes the sexually assertive woman.

A Call to Action

In this chapter we have summarized the research that deals with violence against girls and women. Throughout this chapter lies a common thread: that legislation is needed to deal with violence against women. Legislators need the guidance and support of their constituents in this regard. A very powerful tool for constituents to use to convey their opinion, support, or opposition to bills dealing with violence against women is lobbying. Lobbyists are individuals or groups of individuals who provide members of state senates and assemblies with information that might otherwise not be available to them. The goals of lobbying—in person or in writing—are to inform and to persuade. Lobbying efforts have been successful in establishing federal and state laws. We must all work in our respective state legislatures if we are to make significant change.

U.S. Senator Joseph Biden (Delaware) described his attempt to address violence against women through federal legislation (1993):

> . . . *America as a nation has for too long failed to grasp either the scope or the seriousness of violence against women. . . . We live in a nation that has three times as many animal shelters as battered women's shelters. We live in a nation where crimes against women are still perceived as anything but crime—as a family problem, as a private matter, as "sexual miscommunication. . . ." I introduced the Violence Against Women Act in 1990 and have held hearings on this issue. The legislation's overarching aim is to telescope our vision, highlighting past obstacles, flushing out improper stereotypes, and recognizing the problem for what it is: a national tragedy played out every day in the lives of millions of American women at home, in the workplace, and on the street.* (pp. 1059, 1060)

The Violence Against Women Act identified by Senator Biden is addressing victimization from four main perspectives: rectifying imbalances, assisting survivors, providing education, and requiring equal treatment. Thus, the act creates new laws against rape and battering. It authorizes funds for service providers to give survivors of rape and battering resources they need and provides training for judges, police, prosecutors, and victim advocates about issues involved with women who are victims of sexual violence. In addition, it emphasizes that violence based on sex "assaults an ideal of equality shared by the entire nation" (Biden, 1993, p. 1060).

Sexual violence against women is a manifestation of power and domination of one person over another. Each of the types of sexual victimization reviewed in this chapter illustrates how men have more power than women. In rape, men have more physical power that may be increased by a weapon. In battering and incest, men have more physical power that is increased by the power inequities in the relationship (e.g., husband-wife; father-daughter). In sexual harassment, the teacher or employer who harasses holds authority over career decisions in an academic or work setting (e.g., grades, letters of recommendation, performance appraisals).

Legislation such as the Violence Against Women Act will elevate the status of women as well as reduce the social acceptability of abuse directed against them (Goodman et al., 1993). We must all work together in stopping violence against women as a way of life. And, we must work on redefining masculinity to not include sexual violence. Research has suggested that sexually aggressive men are more likely than nonaggressors to rate themselves as traditional on measures of masculinity (Goodman et al., 1993). Miedzian's observation is worth revisiting:

> *American boys must be protected from a culture of violence that exploits their worst tendencies by reinforcing and amplifying the atavistic values of the masculine mystique. Our country was not created so that future generations could maximize profit at any cost. It was created with humanistic, egalitarian, altruistic goals. We must put our enormous resources and talents to the task of creating a children's culture that is consistent with these goals.* (p. 298)

Summary

Interpersonal power involves the ability to achieve one's own goals by influencing others. In general, men tend to have a larger number of power bases—reward, coercive, expert, legitimate, and informational—than women have; women have greater referent power. Several differences have been found in how women and men influence others in terms of power strategies.

As a rule, men perceive themselves as having greater control over their lives than women do. This difference is borne out by finding men displaying an internal locus of control, whereas women are more likely to show an external locus of control pattern. Power is also an integral feature of intimate relations. Studies generally find men holding more power in intimate relations than women hold.

Sexual victimization—rape, incest, battering, and sexual harassment—are manifestations of power and domination of one person over another.

Suggested Readings

American Association of University Women (1993). *Hostile hallways.* Washington, DC: AAUW.

Butts Stahly, G. (1996). Battered women: Why don't they just leave? In J. Chrisler, C. Golden, & P. Rozee (Eds.), *Lectures on the psychology of women.* New York: McGraw-Hill.

Funk, R. E. (1993). *Stopping rape: A challenge for men.* Philadelphia: New Society Publishers.

Levy, A., & Paludi, M. (1997). *Workplace sexual harassment.* Englewood Cliffs, NJ: Prentice Hall.

Rozee, P. (1993). Forbidden or forgiven: Rape in cross-cultural perspective. *Psychology of Women Quarterly, 17,* 499–514.

Tedisco, J., & Paludi, M. (1996). *Missing children: A psychological approach to understanding the causes and consequences of stranger and non-stranger abduction of children.* Albany: State University of New York Press.

Resources on Sexual Victimization

What to Do If You Are Sexually Harassed

1. Don't blame yourself. It's not your fault.
2. Write down the description of the sexually harassing behavior. Include: date, times, circumstances, people present, how you felt.
3. Talk with someone you trust about the incident—a family member, friend, or advisor.
4. Don't hurry into a decision.
5. After thinking through the options available to you and deciding to seek resolution through the school or workplace, contact the individual who has been designated to handle sexual harassment complaints. Read through the policy statement and procedures. Know your rights and responsibilities. Be sure the procedures are confidential.
6. Consider participating in a support group.
7. Be good to yourself! Dealing with sexual harassment is emotionally and physically exhausting. Rest, eat well, exercise, get medical check-ups, and spend time with friends and family.

What Men Should Do about Rape (adapted from Warshaw,1988, pp. 161–164)

1. Never force a woman to have sex.
2. Don't pressure a woman to have sex.
3. Stay sober.
4. Don't buy the myth that a drunken woman "deserves" to be raped.
5. Do not "join in" if a friend invites you to participate in sexual behavior.
6. Do not confuse "scoring" with having a successful social encounter.
7. Don't assume that you know what a woman wants and vice versa.
8. "No" means "no."
9. Speak up if you feel you're getting a double message from a woman.
10. Communicate with women.
11. Communicate with other men.

What Women Should Do about Rape (adapted from Warshaw, 1988, pp. 161–164)

1. You have the right to set sexual limits and to communicate those limits.
2. Be assertive.
3. Stay sober.
4. Find out about a new date.
5. Remain in control.
6. Take care of yourself.
7. Trust your feelings.

For Friends of Rape Victims

1. Believe her.
2. Listen to her.
3. Comfort her.
4. Reinforce that rape was not her fault.
5. Provide protection (e.g., a place to sleep).
6. Suggest calling a rape crisis center.
7. Encourage her to preserve evidence.
8. Treat her medical needs.
9. Help her to organize her thoughts, but let her make decisions about how to proceed.
10. If you are her lover, with her approval, use appropriate touching and language to reestablish her feelings of worth.
11. Help her get psychological and legal help.
12. Be available.
13. Learn about rape-trauma syndrome.
14. Get therapeutic support for yourself.

What to Do If You Are Raped

1. Believe in yourself! The rape was not your fault.
2. Report the crime. Tell someone you trust—your roommate, parent, friend, professor.
3. Get medical attention immediately.
4. Decide whether you want to report the rape to college officials and to the police.
5. Give yourself lots of time to recover. If you have to, take some time off from classes and/or work.
6. Seek therapeutic support at your campus counseling center or local rape crisis center.
7. When you are ready, share your experiences with other women.

What to Do If You Have Been a Victim of Incest

1. Trust yourself. And believe that the abuse was not your fault.
2. You were not seductive; you did not initiate it. You cannot be held responsible for behavior that occurred when you were a child.
3. Report the abuse. Tell someone you trust—your roommate, friend, professor, counselor, or clergy.
4. Decide whether you want to report the incest to your relatives. If you do, get support for this—perhaps ask for an advocate to come with you.
5. Give yourself lots of time to recover. If you have to, take some time off from classes and/or work.
6. Seek therapeutic support at your campus counseling center or local rape crisis center.

If You Are Battered

1. Do not blame yourself for the beatings.
2. Get medical attention immediately.
3. Consider telling a friend or family member who can be trusted.
4. Decide whether you want to report the battering to the police.
5. Decide whether you want to go to a shelter.

If Someone You Know Tells You She Has Been Battered

1. Listen to her talk about the violence.
2. Let her know her feelings are valid.
3. Let her cry if she wants.
4. Don't give her advice.
5. When she calms down, try to figure out what she wants from you and offer information regarding:
   hotline any time of day or night
   legal counsel/advocacy
   group counseling

individual counseling
shelter
6. Help locate services nearest her.
7. Work with her to determine what she can do right now to make her life
   more what she wants.

Organizations Dealing with Sexual Violence against Women

Hotlines

National Child Safety Council	1-800-222-1464
National Runaway Hotline	1-800-621-4000
Runaway Hotline	1-800-231-6946
Women in Crisis	1-800-992-1101
Rape and Victim Assistance Center	1-800-422-3204
Domestic Assault Hotline	1-800-828-2023
National Center for Missing Children	1-800-843-5678

Organizations

Family Violence Research and Treatment Program
    1310 Clinic Drive
    Tyler, TX 75701
Women Against Pornography
    358 W. 47th St.
    New York, NY 10036
Stop Sexual Abuse of Children
    Chicago Public Education Project
    American Friends Service Committee
    407 Dearborn St.
    Chicago, IL 60605
Alliance Against Sexual Coercion
    P.O. Box 1
    Cambridge, MA 02139
Sexual Assault Recovery through Awareness and Hope
    P.O. Box 20353
    Bradenton, FL 34203
Survivors of Incest Anonymous
    P.O. Box 21817
    Baltimore, MD 21222
People Against Sexual Abuse
    26 Court Street, Suite 315
    Brooklyn, NY 11242

National Clearinghouse for the Defense of Battered Women
 125 South 9th St.
 Philadelphia, PA 19107

Women Against Rape
 Women's Action Collective
 P.O. Box 02084
 Columbus, OH 43202

National Center for the Prevention and Control of Rape
 National Institute of Mental Health
 5600 Fishers Lane
 Rockville, MD 20857

9 to 5
 YWCA
 140 Clarendon St.
 Boston, MA 02139

Equal Employment Opportunity Commission
 2401 E Street, NW
 Washington, DC 20506

National Coalition Against Domestic Violence
 P.O. Box 34103
 Washington, DC 20043

National Organization for Victim Assistance
 1757 Park Rd. NW
 Washington, DC 20010

National Woman Abuse Prevention Project
 1112 16th St., NW
 Washington, DC 20036

Child Find
 24 Main St.
 P.O. Box 277
 New Paltz, NY 12561

7

Communicating Verbally and Nonverbally

If women speak and hear a language of connection and intimacy, while men speak and hear a language of status and independence, then communication between men and women can be like cross-cultural communication, prey to a clash of conversational styles. Instead of different dialects, it has been said they speak different genderlects.

Deborah Tannen

What's Your Opinion?

Do you smile when the issue doesn't require a smile or laugh? Why or why not?

Do you rely on nonverbal cues when talking with friends? What kinds of nonverbal cues do you use (e.g., smiling, eye contact, touching, body posture, physical distance)?

Professors use various means of encouraging student participation in class discussion (e.g., using eye contact, calling on students, responding to student comments and questions). Indicate how your professors exhibit these behavior patterns in encouraging student participation in your classes.

How often do you use the following in your speech: well, y'know, kinda, sorta, I guess?

Are you prone to gesturing while speaking?

Do you believe great care should be taken in the selection of words?

Why do you believe people avoid eye contact while speaking to another: shame? guilt? respect?

Human communication—with its words and gestures—has helped create a division between women and men. At one moment our communications smooth relations between the sexes, and the next they create an imbalance or asymmetry that shows in no uncertain terms the difference in power between women and men. Although language is essential for human interaction, it remains one of the most powerful forces buttressing the age-old inequalities between the sexes and has helped to keep women and men separate and unequal.

In this chapter we will examine language and its role in the way women and men relate. We will look at how language generally favors men while disparaging women. We will also describe some of the ways women and men use language differently. And finally, we will focus on nonverbal communication to see how women and men communicate subtle gender differences with respect to dominance and status.

Communication Strategies

Language allows us to express our deepest feelings and our loftiest thoughts. With language, two people can become more intimate or can separate forever. Language is not, however, sex-neutral. Language divides, separates, and differentiates women from men.

John Gray (1996) is a noted facilitator of seminars for women and men to improve their communication skills and hence their relationship. He believes that women and men do not know how to communicate with each other because they do not know how to interpret each other's words. Gray provides this common pattern to illustrate this point (pp. 46–48):

She Says	**He Says**
She says: How was your day?	He says: Fine.
She means: Let's talk, I'm interested in your day, and I hope you are interested in mine.	*He means: I am giving you a short answer because I need some time alone.*
She says: How did your meeting go with your new client?	He says: It was OK.
She means: I will keep asking you questions so you know I really care and I am interested in your day. I hope you will be interested in my day. I have a lot to say.	*He means: I am trying to be polite and not reject you, but would you stop bothering me with more questions?*
She says: I can tell something is wrong. What is it?	He says nothing and walks away.
She means: I know something is wrong, and if you don't talk, it will get worse. You need to talk!	*He means: I don't want to get mad at you, so I am just walking away. After a while I will be back, and I will not be mad at you for annoying me.*

Women frequently talk to share sympathy and community. Language is thus a tool used to get closer to someone, to become intimate with another, to provide support for a friend. Women are socialized from early childhood to use language in this way and to listen attentively when others speak so as to nurture them. Men, on the other hand, have not typically been socialized in the same way with respect to using language. Talking is goal-oriented for men; it is used to help solve problems, not delve into emotions. Women talk to share their feelings without focusing on solving the problems that cause them.

Thus, misunderstandings arise from the mixed messages and crossed signals: Men believe they are helping a woman with her problems by suggesting how to solve them; women feel their talking needs are not met.

Do women and men talk differently? To many people's way of thinking, the answer is yes. Many would argue that speech patterns and topics can be divided into feminine and masculine speech.

If women have less power than men in most situations, we should not be surprised to find that women's speech patterns are often filled with words that weaken their messages. A person with power may speak directly, make commands, state a direct request, and avoid excessive words. In nearly every instance, this describes the verbal or communication strategies of men. Interviewer Phil Donahue once stated:

> *I've always felt a little anxious about the possibility of a program at night with a male audience. The problem as I perceive it—and this is a generalization—is that men tend to give you a speech, whereas women will ask a question and then listen for the answer and make another contribution to the dialogue. In countless situations I have a male in my audience stand up and say in effect, "I don't know what you're arguing about; here's the answer to this thing." And then proceed to give a mini-speech.* (quoted in Steinem, 1986, p. 207)

Let's highlight four different communication strategies to see some common differences in how women and men speak and the effects these different strategies have on the perception of the speaker's power.

Tag Questions

A *tag question* is partly a statement and partly a question. For example, suppose one of us were to say, "Christine Todd Whitman would be a fine presidential candidate, wouldn't she?" Here we have a statement, "Christine Todd Whitman would be a fine presidential candidate," and a tag question, "wouldn't she?" When someone tags a question onto a statement, we might infer that they are just being polite by asking for our opinion on the subject addressed in the statement. And many times, a tag question does just that: It shows a degree of politeness and consideration for another's idea on the subject of the initial statement. On the other hand, the tag question at the end of a statement may make the statement seem weaker, less assertive, and less commanding. For example, if a friend of yours were to say, "I think arms control would be good for world peace, don't you?" Here you may think that your friend is somewhat less sure of how to attain world peace because s/he appears to be asking for your approval of the statement by asking "don't you?" If your friend believed strongly enough in her or his idea about world peace, s/he probably would not need to ask for your support or approval.

Thus in some situations, tag questions may be seen as showing that the people who use them are unsure or even afraid to assert their own opinions or to stand up for their own ideas in the face of possible rejection. One woman analyzed her own use of tag questions in the following way.

> *I often say to my boyfriend, "That's a pretty good album, isn't it?" I sup-pose I put it that way because I don't want to put my tastes on the line and commit myself like I would if I announced, "That's a good album." Then he could contradict me and say, "No, I don't think the arrange-ments are good." By tailing a question to my statement, I don't come on so strong and I'm putting part of the judgment on his shoulders. Since I don't stick my neck out, I don't lose much. In fact, if he violently dislikes the album I can always say, "Oh, I didn't think so anyway. That's why I asked."* (quoted in Eakins & Eakins, 1978, p. 41)

Although there is very little empirical research on the use of tag questions in mixed-sex relationships, Robin Lakoff (1973) suggested that women are more likely to use them when discussing their personal feelings. For exam-ple, "I don't feel like going to the movies tonight, do you?" is the kind of tag question that Lakoff suggests is more common in women's speech than in men's. If Lakoff's hypothesis is correct, and there has been some supportive research for it (Crosby et al., 1982), we may infer that women's greater tenta-tiveness in strongly expressing her opinions or beliefs may be partially the result of the power difference between women and men.

Qualifiers

A *qualifier* is a word or words that blunt or soften a statement. Take, for ex-ample, the direct statement, "This psychology class is boring!" No question about it, the person who makes such a statement is putting forth his or her idea in no uncertain terms. But what of the statement, "Well, ah, I think this class is boring," or "I may be wrong about it, but I think this class is boring." What we have in these last two statements are watered-down statements about the class. In the first we hear "Well, ah," and the statement about the psychology class. Using such qualifiers reveals tentativeness and uncertainty. Even more tentative is the second statement, which has a disclaimer preced-ing the statement: "I may be wrong about it but. . . ."

Lengthening of Requests

As we all know, you can make a request of someone in several different ways. A drill instructor may simply say, "Attention!" Another person may say, "Will you please pay attention?" Which one of these two requests seems to be more direct, more forceful, and more in command? Of course, the one-word request, "Attention!" does the job in the most direct and powerful way. Adding more words—"will you please pay"—reduces the impact of the request. Women tend to use longer requests in their speech than men do.

Fillers

Fillers are those words or phrases like *you know, ah, uhm, let me see, well, and oh.* Again, little research has been done on fillers, but according to the research that is available, women are more apt to use fillers in their conversations than men are. Women use fewer fillers in female-female conversations than in female-male conversations. This may suggest that women are more comfortable in conversing with other women than with men.

Deborah Tannen (1994) argued that women's speech must not be taken as obvious evidence of some intrapsychic states, such as lack of self-confidence or insecurity. On the contrary, according to Tannen:

> *It is simply that, considering the many influences on conversational style, individuals have a wide range of ways of getting things done and expressing their emotional states. Personality characteristics such as insecurity cannot be linked to ways of speaking in an automatic, self-evident way.* (p. 86)

Nancy Henley (1995a) shares Tannen's sentiment, especially when one considers the research on the interface of ethnicity and gender in language. Henley noted that a great deal of the research on gender and language is founded on the belief of white upper middle class women's and men's experiences.

Thus, language is influenced by the social context. Research by Nichols (1983) suggests that African American women use innovative speech, thus not supporting the claim of universal female linguistic conservatism. Henley (1995a) interpreted this finding as evidence that Lakoff's ideas were based on the division of labor within the white middle class and thus can not be generalized to other races and ethnic groups.

In the courses that one of your textbook authors (Paludi) teaches, she asks students to complete an exercise in which they are asked to do the following:

1. Read a newspaper or magazine article and discuss the direct and indirect messages about women and men.
2. Reverse the pronouns and reread the article with the modifications.
3. Compare and contrast the messages about women and men before and after the modifications.

Students have reported being surprised at the differences in meaning and symbolism in popularly written articles. Most students have reported that their "modified" article "doesn't make sense" or "sounds silly."

Examples of the "modified" statements include the following:

> *I like to work in my herb garden by day and bathe in herb sachets (made from my garden) by night, while my wife makes one of her gourmet dinners.*

Does this statement sound odd to you? Why? What if you read the same sentence before the modifications?

I like to work in my herb garden by day and bathe in herb sachets (made from my garden) by night, while my husband makes one of his gourmet dinners.

Do you now believe this sentence "make sense?" Why? Does it fit with your gender schemas? Do you no longer have cognitive dissonance when reading this sentence? Do you believe women talk differently than men?

Talking about Ourselves

Talking about oneself may be extremely pleasing and even healthy (Jourard, 1964), but social scientists have found that women and men differ in the amount of personal information they share with others as well as with whom they share this information.

Sidney Jourard suggested the term *self-disclosure* to indicate when people share personal or intimate information about themselves with others. Jourard, along with several colleagues, found that men usually disclosed less about their personal feelings than women did (Jourard, 1971). Sociologist Mirra Komarovsky (1964) found that male blue-collar workers, for example, had special difficulty in disclosing personal information about themselves and were also uncomfortable in listening to others' self-disclosures. Komarovsky (1976) later studied male college students and found them to be more self-disclosing than her blue-collar sample, but the college students still limited their self-disclosures primarily to women friends and mothers and not to other men.

The pattern of men's resistance to self-disclosure has been found in laboratory studies as well (Gerdes et al., 1981). It is interesting that women, who generally exhibit more self-disclosing information to a wider range of people than men do, report that they like others who self-disclose to them, whereas men do not (Petty & Mirels, 1981). Thus there seems to be some empirical evidence to support the constant request of many women that the men in their lives open up more and share their feelings with them.

Women, so the research suggests, would actually like the self-disclosing man more than one who keeps everything to himself. Men, however, appear to be somewhat uncomfortable when another discloses too much. Among many men, especially those who hold traditional attitudes about gender roles, the act of disclosing personal material is interpreted as a sign of weakness, and men shun any sign of weakness for fear of appearing effeminate (Lombardo & Lavine, 1981). Even though men talk more than women, they talk less about those intimate and personal matters that for reasons unknown they believe better left unsaid. However, men may exceed women in disclosing personal information in opposite-sex relationships in order to control the development of the relationships (Derlega et al., 1984). Some men, it seems, use self-disclosure as a strategy to influence the way women feel about them.

While men may
talk more than
women, their
conversations tend
to be less self-
disclosing.

© Rhoda Sidney/Photo Edit

Nancy Collins and Lynn Carol Miller (1994) concluded from their meta-analysis on research on self-disclosure that individuals who engage in intimate disclosures tend to be liked more than people who disclose at lower levels and people disclose more to those whom they initially like than to those they dislike. Other researchers (Pegalis et al., 1994) report similar findings.

Silence

Few stereotypes are as pervasive about men and women in our culture as those that portray women engaged in endless chatter while men sit by in painful silence. Contrary to popular belief, the fact is that men, not women, talk more. In study after study, the evidence is rather conclusive: Men are the more talkative members of the human species, and women are typically silenced.

In one of the earliest studies of husbands and wives and their communication patterns, Fred Strodtbeck (1951) found that husbands out-talked their wives and not vice versa. Using both married and unmarried couples, other researchers found similar evidence that showed that men are more "gabby" than women (Hilpert et al., 1975). In one of the most frequently cited studies of verbal output, Marjorie Swacker (1975) asked women and men to tape-record their impressions of different paintings. The participants were told to take as much time as they needed to describe the paintings they saw.

Women talked for an average of just over 3 minutes; men talked for an average of over 13 minutes. In fact, three of the men in Swacker's study talked on until the 30-minute tape ran out. When researchers Barbara Eakins and Gene Eakins (1978) tape-recorded a college faculty meeting, they also found the men surpassing the women for verbal output. Not every study, however, has found men more talkative than women. Some have found that women talk as much (Piliavin & Martin, 1978). However, even when women do get a chance to get a word in edgewise, they are more apt to be interrupted by men than vice versa, attesting to the power difference between women and men in general (Zimmerman & West, 1975). Again, the rules of conversation allow the powerful person to interrupt the powerless person, as we see between mothers and children, the one conversational relation where women are seen in a more powerful position (West & Zimmerman, 1977).

Typically women are silenced intellectually and creatively. Lakoff (1973) represented this silencing on the front cover of her book: a picture of a woman with a Band-Aid over her mouth. Esther Rothblum and Ellen Cole (1986) represented this silencing in their edited book, *Another Silenced Trauma,* about "Ruth," a Navy nurse in Vietnam in 1969 and 1970. As Laura Brown (1986), Ruth's therapist summarized: ". . . I had ample opportunity to observe the negative synergy of trauma and silence, abuse and secrecy, that would lead women to feel and act crazy, when in fact it was mainly the context in which they were forced to operate that was pathological" (p. 15).

Roberta Hall and Bernice Sandler (1982) represented women students' accounts of their being silenced:

> *What I find damaging and disheartening are the underlying attitudes . . . the surprise I see when a woman does well in an exam—the condescending smile when she doesn't.* (p. 6)
>
> *I have witnessed female students in two lower division courses treated as ornaments—as if they lacked any semblance of intellectual capacity—both occasions by male instructors.* (p. 6)
>
> *In classes, I experienced myself as a person to be taken lightly. In one seminar, I was never allowed to finish a sentence. There seemed to be a tacit understanding that I never had anything to say.* (p. 7)
>
> *She (a black female medical student) cited a small group learning situation in which the instructor never looked at her and responded only to the other people on either side of her.* (p. 12)

As we discussed in chapter 6, after they have experienced incest, battering, sexual harassment, or rape, women may also be silenced by law enforcement personnel, physicians, family, friends, and the legal system (Nugent, 1994; Paludi, 1997). Women may fear reporting their experiences for fear of retaliation, fear of being blamed for the victimization, and fear of not being believed. They thus remain silent about their victimization.

In general, women are not expected to make substantive verbal contributions in a mixed setting. This theme is quite prominent in literature. For example, D. H. Lawrence, in *Lady Chatterley's Lover* (1957), highlighted women's silence during men's dialogue:

> *Silence fell. The four men smoked. And Connie sat there and put another stitch in her sewing. . . . Yes, she sat there! She had to sit mum. She had to be quiet as a mouse, not to interfere with the immensely important speculations of these highly-mental gentlemen. But she had to be there. They didn't get on so well without her; their ideas didn't flow so freely.*

And, when Connie finally speaks:

> *"There are nice women in the world," said Connie, lifting her head up and speaking at last. The men resented it . . . she should have pretended to hear nothing. They hated her admitting she had attended so closely to such talk.*

Ibsen's character *Hedda Gabler* (1957) also rejects domesticity and wants access to the public sphere of life. In one part of the play, "Hedda paces about the room, raises her arms and clenches her hands as though in desperation. She flings back the curtains of the glass door and stands gazing out" (Ibsen, 1957, p. 354). Michael Kaufman (1989) interpreted this scene as expressing ". . . a profound dislocation between Hedda's longing and aspirations for the world beyond the glass and the reduced reality of a back room existence; it conveys her ultimate resignation to her confinement as a tragic disjunction between her former condition as the general's daughter galloping free on horseback in a fine riding suit, and her present situation which she will . . . characterize . . . in the metaphor of an endless train ride, stopping only briefly at stations on the line, occasionally breaking the monotony" (pp. 35–36).

Chaucer also noted, through the Wife of Bath in *The Canterbury Tales,* that women do not comment on men in anything like the manner that men had written of women. Elizabeth Segal (1988) has noted that most books for adolescent girls written in the century after the Civil War (e.g., Phelps' *Gypsy Breynton,* Alcott's *Little Women,* Coolidge's *What Kay Did*) focused on silencing assertive, independent, creative girls ("tomboys"). The silencing typically took the form of illness, including being bedridden throughout the adolescent years, which denied the girl her "dream of doing something grand" (p. 13) and instead taught the heroine through pain the value of self-sacrifice. These books taught adolescent girls that the "best daughter" was the invalid daughter, dedicating herself to her family.

Although ethnic minority girls and women are rare in children's and adolescents' literature, they are presented in very stereotypic ways. Characters represented in stories are intended to expose children to new vistas and allow them to share vicariously experiences of other children. For girls, however, they may also receive through stereotyped characters confirmation of societal assumptions that girls do not take risks, accomplish exciting feats, or leave the security of their homes and the protection of men (Reid & Paludi, 1993). The absence of girls and women in literature conveys a message that they are not important enough to be represented (chapter 4).

Consider the following song, popularized in the movie, *The Little Mermaid*. Girls are given a great deal of information about how girls' silence is prized by boys.

> *You'll have your looks, your pretty face*
> *And don't underestimate the importance of body language*
> *The men up there don't like a lot of blabber*
> *They think a girl who gossips is a bore*
> *Yes on land it's much preferred for ladies not to say a word*
> *And after all, dear, what is idle prattle for?*
> *Come on they're not all that impressed with conversation*
> *True gentlemen avoid it when they can*
> *But they dote and swoon and fawn on a lady who's withdrawn*
> *It's she who holds her tongue who gets her man*

A cultural interpretation of silence is important. One of your textbook authors (Paludi) frequently spends class time asking students to comment on the issues we are discussing, a technique she labels as "data collecting out loud." Some students initially are uncomfortable with sharing their views, especially if their views are different from research findings. And, some students are uncomfortable with being asked to challenge the professor's statements.

Takie Sugiyama Libra (1987) noted that one of the basic values in Japanese culture is *omoiyari* or empathy. Because of omoiyari, individuals don't have to state an opinion explicitly; people should be able to understand or sense other's meaning intuitively. Libra also found a related value, *enryo*, which refers to the self-restraint required to avoid disagreeing with opinions held by the majority.

Libra noted that, in direct contrast to American values that makes directness ideal, Japanese hold in esteem individuals who communicate indirectly, subtly, nonverbally, and implicitly. These speakers trust their listeners' empathy to complete the meaning.

While Americans may dismiss these conversational habits, Tannen (1994) reminds us that "the success of Japanese businesses makes it impossible to continue to maintain that there is anything inherently inefficient about such conversational rituals" (p. 97).

Theresa LaFromboise and her colleagues (1995) noted that American Indian women maintain a respect for the power of words. American Indian women are socialized to use words positively (to inform, think, reconcile with others) as well as negatively (to insult or threaten). Many also use disclaimers to their humbleness and limitations prior to expressing an opinion.

Nonverbal Communication

In some areas women and men differ in their verbal patterns. It should not, therefore, come as a surprise to find that men and women also differ in some of their nonverbal communications as well. In this section, we will first look at the research evidence that women and men differ in the way in which and the frequency with which they express their emotions. We shall note also that women are generally better at expressing or sending nonverbal messages and receiving and decoding others' nonverbal messages. Then we will look at several specific areas of nonverbal patterns where women and men differ, namely eye contact, touch, and body posture. As we will see, the areas of nonverbal communication provide yet another fascinating study of how women and men differ with respect to communication styles (Henley, 1995a).

Emotions and Gender

Most men can remember their boyhood days when one of the worst insults one could hurl at another little boy was to call him a "crybaby." Little boys aren't supposed to cry, aren't supposed to show fears, aren't supposed to act like "little girls," of course (Doyle, 1995). For most, the lessons of childhood seem to take root. In everyday life, one isn't shocked to see a woman cry when she feels pain or anger or is upset. But what do we see when men are upset or in pain? Most men will not cry; that would be "feminine." Men are more apt to show anger rather than tears when they get upset. Men who cry or show some sign of hurt and pain are apt to be branded as weak or effeminate. This is further illustration of the devaluation of what is considered feminine in this culture.

There is no concrete evidence that women and men experience different emotions, but there is considerable experiential evidence in all of our lives to suggest that women and men differ, more often than not, in how they express their emotions and what emotions they feel free enough to express in public (Henley, 1995a).

Senders and Receivers

Have you ever known a person who seemed to know what you were feeling even before you mentioned a word? A person who seemed to know your feelings and possibly made you a bit uncomfortable with such insight into your personal life? Chances are that person was a woman, and you may have said that she possessed something many people call "feminine intuition." There is growing evidence that women are more adept in some aspects of nonverbal communications than men. In fact, women seem more able to express their emotions or feelings nonverbally than men. *Encoding* is the term used to refer to this ability. Also, there is evidence that women are more proficient at evaluating or judging others' nonverbal messages, or what is referred to as *decoding*.

But how can we explain women's purported better skills in such matters? As we noted in a previous chapter, the gender role stereotypes for women and men differ in several areas that are related to nonverbal skills. The masculine stereotype contains elements such as instrumentality and control; the feminine stereotype involves elements such as expressivity, supportiveness, and interpersonal sensitivity (Deaux & Kite, 1993). Because these gender-role related stereotypic differences have become part of our cultural norms, there is a strong possibility that parents and other significant socializing agents encourage girls and boys differentially with respect to these traits' expressions. For example, little girls may be reinforced to be more emotionally expressive than little boys are. In fact, there is some evidence showing that differential parental treatment may affect a child's nonverbal ability (Henley, 1995). Thus girls' and women's upbringing may influence them to develop a slightly better ability in certain nonverbal skills.

While there has been some consistency of findings, we should note that most researchers have focused on white middle-class families (Reid & Paludi, 1993). There is some evidence that parental responses may vary considerably based on both ethnicity and social class. For example, black preschool girls are typically expected by their parents to be more mature and responsible than are white girls. Little empirical data exists on gender role expectations for other ethnic groups. However, anecdotal information suggests that Asian American and Hispanic American parents expect their daughters to be even more submissive and dependent than white American parents.

The idea that early socialization of children plays a role in women's generally more skillful use and interpretation of nonverbal cues has received some empirical support. In a series of studies conducted by psychologist Miron Zuckerman and several colleagues (1981, 1982), women or men who score high on so-called "feminine traits" are better at sending nonverbal messages than men or women who score high on so-called "masculine traits." Specifically, these researchers found that femininity scores positively correlated with one's ability at sending both auditory and facial cues. We must keep in mind that these results did not find all women better at sending nonverbal messages, only those who scored high in feminine traits (i.e., androgynous and feminine women and androgynous and feminine men). Men who are sensitive and emotionally expressive are just as good at sending nonverbal messages as sensitive and emotionally expressive women are. In yet another study, men who scored androgynous were found to be more expressive of their feelings than those men who scored very high only in masculine traits. These studies indicate that women don't possess a sixth sense by virtue of their biological sex, but rather because of upbringing that encourages certain traits.

The evidence is fairly clear that women in general or women and men with feminine traits appear better at sending nonverbal messages, but the research is somewhat ambiguous about which sex has the edge in interpreting nonverbal messages.

Eye Contact

When two people look at each other, there can be several messages that can be inferred from such nonverbal behavior. If the "eyes are the mirror of the soul" as one adage suggests, then we might expect that *eye contact* can be a very powerful nonverbal message. When researchers videotaped women and men in conversations and then timed the amount of eye contact between the participants, the results are fairly straightforward. Women generally show more social eye contact than men, meaning that in conversations between same-sex and opposite-sex pairs, women will look at the other more than men will (Aiello, 1972; Mehrabian, 1971). Eye contact may be linked to a person's expression of affection or just wanting to develop a relationship with another. According to the research, women tend to show greater eye contact and display longer gazes at others than men do (Russo, 1975). Wayne Podrouzek and David Furrow (1988) found these gender differences in children as young as two and four years of age!

Althea Smith (1983) and Uwe Gielen (1979) observed race and sex interactions in eye contact: Black women look less often than do white women dyads; black women leaned synchronously more often than white female and black male dyads. In addition, white adults look at each other more frequently than blacks. Interracial female dyads and white male dyads reflect the highest degree of mutual trust and liking, while interracial male and male-female dyads express the least.

Another form of eye contact can imply aggression and is usually known as *staring*. Most women tend to look away when they notice they are the target of someone else's stare. The reason for such avoidance may be linked to the idea that staring is often interpreted as an aggressive or even sexual nonverbal message.

Touch

Touching another person has been thought to be one of the most powerful means of suggesting status or dominance in a dyad. For example, most people would find it acceptable for a manager to touch the shoulder of a subordinate, but for a subordinate to touch the shoulder of a manager is another situation altogether. Touching another is one way to express power or dominance over another (Henley, 1973, 1977). In general, men or those with more power and dominance in most situations are more apt to touch a woman and not vice versa.

Touching may be interpreted to mean power, but it also may have an affectional or sexual connotation to it. Thus if a woman touches the arm or shoulder of a man, it may be interpreted as being sexual. But women are supposed to know that, when a male manager puts a hand on the shoulder of his female secretary, it is nothing more than a simple friendly gesture. Or is it?

Although the research on touching is rather scanty, two studies stand out. In the first, both women and men librarians either touched or did not touch those to whom they gave a library card. Those people who were touched by the librarian had more positive opinions of the library and the librarian than those who were not touched during the transaction (Fisher et al., 1976). It seems that in a public situation, another's touch can be interpreted in a positive and friendly way. This would suggest that touching is a most important way of forming friendships and one that most people find desirable. In another study, this one conducted by Carie Forden (1981), students watched a videotape of a man and woman conversing. One group of students saw a woman touch a man on the shoulder; another group saw a man touch a woman on the shoulder. Forden found that when the students saw a woman touch a man, she was thought quite dominant, and a man who was touched was seen as passive. Forden concluded that touching does carry a dominance message and that touching seems more appropriate for men to do than for women.

Body Position and Posture

Researchers have systematically catalogued how body positions and posture (which are as revealing as verbal cues) convey different messages about relationships. Consequently, we are learning some rather interesting differences in the ways women and men position their bodies and what these positions mean in terms of a person's status and dominance. For example, men are more likely to occupy or control more *personal space* around their bodies than women occupy. From this specific nonverbal message, we can infer that men are more dominant and have a higher status than women. The rationale here is that the person who controls more physical space is more powerful and more dominant and has a higher status than the person who controls less space.

With respect to body position, men tend to sit in a more relaxed way than women. In general, women tend to display a more restricted body posture than men, who seem to have a wider range of possible body positions. Traditionally, little girls are encouraged to sit in "ladylike" ways. Specifically, women are taught to sit with their legs close together or crossed at the ankles and their hands placed on their lap. Men, on the other hand, are more apt to sit with their legs crossed by putting the ankle of one leg over the knee of the other leg or sitting with the legs apart. The man's body posture usually appears more relaxed than the woman's. These generalized postures and their nearly universal association with either men or women can be seen even when a drawing is "sexless" and even by young children.

Most of our information pertaining to body posture and gender differences is of the anecdotal type rather than from controlled studies. Many people have had, for instance, personal experiences in which they were reprimanded for standing or sitting in ways not deemed appropriate for their sex. Two such examples can serve to make this point:

When I was a kid I was sitting on the sofa reading and my legs were crossed, right knee draped over left. My father said, "You're sitting like a girl!" and demonstrated the right way. He placed his left ankle on his right knee so that his thighs were separated at the immodest masculine angle. For a couple years after that I thought men were supposed to cross legs left over right, while women crossed them right over left. Or was it

*the other way? I could never remember which. So rather than make a
mistake and do it like a girl, I preferred not to cross my legs at all.*

And another man recounted:

*I was out by the mailboxes talking with my next-door neighbor, a foot-
ball coach, whom I respected enormously. We were standing there talking. I had my hands on my hips. He said jokingly that I was standing in
a woman's way, with my thumbs forward. I was 27 years old and I had
never really thought about the best way to stand with my arms akimbo.
But now, whenever I find myself standing with thumbs forward I feel an
effeminate flash, even when I'm alone, and I quickly turn my hands
around the other way.* (both quotes taken from Wagenvoord & Bailey,
1978, p. 44)

Valuing Women's Communication Styles

Tannen's (1990) research has echoed Gray's advice: for many women, conversation is a "language of rapport: a way of establishing connections and
negotiating relationships. . . . For most men, talk is primarily a means to preserve independence and negotiate and maintain status in a hierarchical social
order." (p. 77)

Women may be somewhat more likely to use tag questions, qualifiers,
longer requests, and fillers. Some individuals may argue that women would
be best to adopt a "masculine" style in order to achieve more prominence
and credibility. That criticism of women's speech patterns may be a way of
dismissing women without dealing with the content of what women are saying (Steinem, 1986). Researchers have noted that women who adopt a masculine style are perceived as "aggressive" and may be rejected outright (Hall
& Sandler, 1982). Instead of asking women to conform to the "male as normative" in verbal communication, we suggest viewing "women's speech" as
valuable in fostering a more cooperative, less competitive atmosphere in the
classroom and workplace environment as well as in friendships and romantic
relationships. Tag questions invite the listener to contribute to the conversation. Several nonverbal communication strategies typically exhibited by
women (e.g., maintaining eye contact) encourage individuals to participate in
the conversation.

Mary Ritchie Key (1975a) called for androgynous communication that
would be concerned with "quality of life rather than power" (p. 147). She
concluded:

*In the days when an androgynous language is spoken, women will be
freed from the repression that has resulted in hesitant language or silence.
Men will be freed to creativity when they can permit themselves sensitivity
and intuition. Men will profit from passiveness when it implies an empti-
ness and receptiveness that is able to receive a new thought—a creation—
an idea born in its time—an invention that will produce.* (p. 147)

And, according to Tannen (1990):

Understanding the other's ways of talking is a giant leap across the communication gap between women and men and a giant step toward opening lines of communication. (p. 298)

Communicating about Women and Men

Linguistic Sexism

One of your textbook authors (Doyle) once overheard a couple having a rather heated conversation at a nearby table in a restaurant. The man was asking the woman why she was so insistent on being addressed as "Ms." at the office rather than as "Miss." The woman took pains to explain that she didn't like having a title that defined her in terms of her relationship or lack of relationship with a man, and that the distinction did not amount to a trivial matter.

What's in a word, anyway? Why the concern over what you call or don't call a person as long as it isn't abusive or obscene?

Words are important! Words are some of the most powerful and richly endowed creations of the human spirit. Surely, everyone recalls Edward Bulwer-Lytton's famous statement that "the pen is mightier than the sword." Lytton's statement is no mere rhetoric, not when we consider how powerful language is and the ways that powerful people use language. Those who have power know this fact well. For as historian Sheila Rowbotham (1973) pointed out, language "is carefully guarded by the superior people because it is one of the means through which they conserve their supremacy" (p. 32). Words are extremely important. Words give definition and meaning to reality. How we see the world and the things in it are to a great extent structured by the types and numbers of words we use.

Our world is populated by both women and men, and yet the English language not only favors men, but affords men greater power over women. Men, by their control of language, can name, and by naming they make valid their existence. Again, Rowbotham (1973) stated the case for language being a potent vehicle of men's power: "Language conveys a certain power. It is one of the instruments of domination. . . . The language of theory—removed language—only expresses a reality experienced by the oppressors. It speaks only for their world, for their point of view" (p. 32). Consequently, men exert an even greater degree of power over women because of language. Boys are socialized to believe they have valuable information to impart. To make the point that our language and the way we speak it contains sexist elements, we will discuss a special form of sexism known as *linguistic sexism* or the fact that sexist ideology is perpetuated and reinforced through the content of a language (Nilsen et al., 1977). Linguistic sexism in the English language takes one of three distinct forms: how the English language ignores women, how it defines women, and how it deprecates women.

Ignoring Women

Although girls and women make up almost 52 percent of the human race, they are systematically left out in our daily speech. In fact, when we talk about our species as a whole, we talk about "man" or "mankind" and not "woman" or "womankind." However, since girls and women are the majority, it would be perfectly logical to use "womankind" rather than "mankind" as the generic word meaning human race. Furthermore, we are taught that when we read the word "he," it supposedly is a pronoun robust enough to include girls and women as well as boys and men in its definition. The English language takes what psychologist Wendy Martyna (1980) termed a "he/man" approach.

> The "he/man" approach to language involves the use of male terms to refer both specifically to males and generically to human beings (A Man for All Seasons *is specific:* "No man is an island" *is generic). The he/man approach has received most attention in current debates on sexist language, not only because of its ubiquity but also because of its status as one of the least subtle of sexist forms. In linguistic terms, some have characterized the male as an unmarked, the female as a marked, category. The unmarked category represents both maleness and femaleness, while the marked represents femaleness only. Thus the male in Lionel Tiger's* Men in Groups *excludes the female in Phyllis Chesler's* Women and Madness, *while the male in Thomas Paine's* Rights of Man *is supposed to encompass the female of Mary Wollstonecraft's* Vindication of the Rights of Woman. (p. 483)

But the "he/man" generics don't always live up to their name. When generic pronouns (e.g., he, his, him) are used in spoken or printed forms, more often than not, the listener or reader conjures up a picture of a male, not an image of both a male and a female (Cole et al., 1983; Key, 1975a; Stericker, 1981). For example, what comes to your mind when you read, "Every student in the classroom did his best on the exam"? Does your mind really conjure up a scene of women and men all working feverishly away on a test? Or, do you unconsciously imagine a room full of boys at some all-male prep school bent over their desks with pencils in hand staring at their test papers? In several studies investigating the impact of the generic pronoun "he" in textbooks, it was found that most of the antecedents in the texts referred to men, and not to both men and women (Bertilson et al., 1982). In yet another study, students who searched for potential illustrations for a book were more likely to select all-male photographs when the chapter titles were "Industrial Man," or "Social Man," rather than "Industrial Life" or "Society" (Schneider & Hacker, 1973).

Janet Hyde (1984) reported that children do not know that "he" is supposed to refer to girls and women. When first grade students were asked to make up a story about the average student in a school, only 12 percent who read the pronoun "he" in the instructions told a story about a girl/woman. When the pronoun was given as "they," 18 percent told a story about a girl/woman. When the pronoun was "he" or "she," 42 percent of the children's stories contained references to girls and/or women.

The use of the generic pronouns can, in fact, misrepresent reality. An example of such linguistic doublethink is provided by sociologist Joan Huber (1976) when she noted that in one sociology text she found the statement: "The more education an individual attains, the better his occupation is likely to be, and the more money he is likely to earn." The use of the generic pronouns in this statement (i.e., "his" and "he") is misleading. In fact, this statement mostly holds true only for men. Briere and Lanktree (1983) found that students who saw the generic masculine version rate a career in psychology as less attractive for women than do students who see sex-neutral versions.

Watching our words may seem like a small concession and one requiring little effort. Rather than "mankind," why not "humanity," "human beings," or just plain "people"? Rather than something being described as "manmade," why not "artificial," or "synthetic"? As we have already noted, words are powerful symbols, and ignoring over half the human race is unrealistic of the world we live in (Burr et al., 1972; Fillmer & Haswell, 1977). For too long, women have existed as the "other" in a second-class position, and language has contributed greatly to this perception (de Beauvoir, 1952). In 1848 in Seneca Falls, New York, nineteenth-century American feminists wrote the "Declaration of Sentiments" in which they made clear how they understood that the generic "man" of the Declaration of Independence obscured the rights of women:

> *We hold these truths to be self-evident: that all men and women are created equal. . . . The history of mankind is a history of repeated injuries and usurpations on the part of man toward woman, having in direct object the establishment of an absolute tyranny over her. . . . He has endeavored, in every way he could, to destroy her confidence in her own powers, to lessen her self-respect, and to make her willing to lead a dependent and abject life.*

Hall and Sandler (1982) suggested that a learning environment that ignores women contributes to a "chilly climate" for women students:

> *A chilling classroom climate puts women students at a significant educational disadvantage. Overtly disparaging remarks about women, as well as more subtle differential behaviors, can have a critical and lasting effect. When they occur frequently—especially when they involve "gatekeepers" who act as advisors, or serve as chairs of departments— such behaviors can have a profound negative impact on women's academic and career development by . . . discouraging classroom participation. . . . Instead of sharpening their intellectual abilities, women may begin to believe and act as though . . . their presence in a given class, department, program or institution is at best peripheral, or at worst an unwelcome intrusion; their capacity for full intellectual development and professional success is limited; their academic and career goals are not matters for serious attention or concern. (p. 3)*

Hall and Sandler reported that certain groups of women students are likely to receive the "chilly" treatment in the classroom: women in traditionally male-populated majors, ethnic minority women (because of the interface of ethnicity and sex), and reentry women students (because of their age and part-time status).

Languages that have no distinction of female and male for the third-person pronoun (e.g., Aztec, Chinese, Finnish, Hungarian) do not have the problem the English language does when describing an unspecified referent. However, there are ways the generic masculine terms may be eliminated in the English language. The American Psychological Association's publication manual (1983) provides guidelines for nonsexist language (see chapter 1).

Casey Miller and Kate Swift (1988), in their book *The Handbook of Nonsexist Writing*, offer a brief thesaurus. For example:

Want to Avoid?	*Try*
Businessman	Businessperson
Career Girl	Business Woman
Chairman, Chairwoman	Chair, Head, President, Leader, Moderator, Coordinator
Coed	Student
Forefathers	Ancestors
Housewife, Househusband	Homemaker
Man-made	Handmade, Synthetic, Fabricated, Constructed
Man-to-Man	One-to-One, Person-to-Person
Saleswoman, Salesgirl	Salesclerk
Seamstress	Tailor
Waiter, Waitress	Server

Defining Women

How many times have you heard a woman referred to as "Bill's wife/daughter/widow"? Defining women in terms of her relationship to a man is one of those commonly accepted customs that most people rarely question. And yet more and more women today are keeping their birth names after marriage. But in the first place, why should a woman give up her surname once she marries, outside of keeping up with the ancient patriarchal tradition of the woman being seen as yet another possession or property of her husband?

Margaret Intons-Peterson and Jill Crawford (1985) found that among faculty and students, surnames convey an important sense of identity to women just as they do to men. They also found that decisions about marital-surname choice are influenced by societal beliefs, even when these beliefs have no legal basis. Men, more than women, and married men, more than single men, thought that children should take their fathers' surnames. Women were more willing than men to consider nontraditional surname styles.

What does a change in name signify? If a name is part of one's identity, then changing one's names implies (if not requires) that the person change or lose some aspect of her or his identity to some degree. When a woman marries and takes on her husband's name, she loses a powerful symbolic tie to her past identity: her name. Leo Kanowitz (1969) viewed the change in a woman's name upon marriage as thus:

> *The probable effects of this unilateral name change upon the relations between the sexes, though subtle in character, are profound. In a very real sense, the loss of a woman's surname represents the destruction of an important part of her personality and its submersion in that of her husband. . . . This name change is consistent with the characterization of coverture as "the old common-law fiction that the husband and wife are one . . . which has worked out in reality to mean that the one is the husband."* (p. 41)

Men, of course, do not change their names, and thus they continue to have a degree of continuity with their premarriage identity. By taking her husband's name, the married woman to a large extent changes her self-identity as well as her social status. She now becomes, to many people's way of thinking, "Mrs. James Smith," dropping even her given first name in the process. For all those who think this is "romantic" or simply "no big deal," ask them if changing the groom's name to that of the bride's would be an acceptable practice. Chances are that most would think the groom changing his name to that of the bride's would be different somehow. Different, yes, but it would also indicate that he was no longer considered the first in the relationship, the one whose name the couple takes as their identity. But isn't that what happens to most married women? They become subsumed under their husbands, and their name change signifies as much. As we have said, a person's name is part of her or his very identity. And tradition in this culture holds that a woman's identity must be submerged into that of her husband's. In Spanish-speaking countries, however, a woman retains her own name after marriage, adding her husband's surname after her own. Dutch women do not change their name upon marriage (Bailey, 1954).

Women who choose to use "Miss" or "Mrs." are perceived as lower in instrumental characteristics, such as competence and leadership. They are perceived to be stronger in expressive traits and are judged more likable than a woman who chooses to use "Ms." (Dion & Cota, 1991; Dion & Schuller, 1990).

Deprecating Women

Throughout history women have been deprecated and abused by the pronouncements of men. Listen to just a small sampling of some of the deprecations of women.

> *There is a good principle which created order, light, and man, and an evil principle which created chaos, darkness, and woman.*
>
>   **Pythagoras**

The five worst infirmities that afflict the female are indocility, discontent, slander, jealousy, and silliness. . . . Such is the stupidity of woman's character, that it is incumbent upon her, in every particular, to distrust herself and to obey her husband.

Confucian Marriage Manual

Most women have no character at all.

Alexander Pope

My secretary is a lovable slave.

Morris Ernest

Women are to be talked to as below men and above children.

Lord Chesterfield

The list could go on and on, but these few samples should give a fair example of the kinds of words used in conjunction with the female. Words such as "evil," "chaos," "darkness," "stupidity," and "slave" are anything but flattering. Even when we examine some parallel terms, we find a less than subtle deprecation of the female, for example, "mister-mistress" or "bachelor-spinster." When we note the numbers of words indicative of sexual promiscuity, we find well over 200 such words to describe a sexually active woman (e.g., prostitute, harlot, courtesan, concubine, tramp, etc.), but we only find just over 20 words to describe lustful men (satyr, dirty old man, etc.) (Stanley, 1977). Lakoff (1973) offered sociolinguistic arguments to support her contention that "gentleman" and "lady" are connotatively dissimilar. Lerner (1976) suggested that the linguistic choice of lady, woman, or girl is indicative of an unconscious attitude toward women, with "lady" implying propriety and "girl" implying immaturity.

We find women deprecated even when people are asked to judge the merit of some production (e.g., a painting or piece of writing). People perceive the quality or value of an object as less if the author or creator is a woman. For example, researchers have found that an article or painting bearing a woman's name is generally seen as being of lesser merit than the *identical* piece bearing a man's signature (Paludi & Bauer, 1979; Paludi & Strayer, 1985; Pheterson et al., 1971). Also, such supposedly innocuous female euphemisms as "girl" or "gal" have been found to cause people to look unfavorably at the woman being described (Dayhoff, 1983; Lipton & Hershaft, 1984). This pro-male evaluation bias is also present when men and women are asked to evaluate an academic article with no name given or with initials or a sexually ambiguous name attached (Paludi & Strayer, 1985)! In this study, 87 percent of the participants (300 college students) attributed an article on politics to a man and 96 percent attributed an article on the psychology of women to a woman. Explanations provided by students for their decisions centered around traditional gender role stereotypes, e.g., "men are associated with business, economics, and politics," "the author seems to have insight into women's feelings," or "the author is male because the style is abrupt."

Several women authors, including George Eliot, Emily Bronte, and George Sand did not indicate their sex on the title page of their work and used a masculine pseudonym. Jane Austen published her first novel as the work of "A Lady," suggesting perhaps that her readers needed to be alerted to a feminine voice, the voice of a maiden who desires to please. And, Susan Brown-miller (1984) wrote:

> *Caution is what marked the writing style of women. . . . I understand the tendency to play it safe when one feels grateful to be allowed to play at all. . . . A . . . woman might have given up thought of publication altogether, to pour her passion into her diary where she could express her emotions as freely as she wished, and never face up to the unfeminine task of pounding her thoughts into hard-edged shape. The hope, of course, would always remain that one day a reader would discover her soul.* (p. 126)

Discrimination in the form of evaluation bias is observed when the target person is a member of an ethnic minority group (Romero & Garza, 1986). Jean Hughes and Bernice Sandler (1988) noted that because of myths and stereotypes that portray women of color as sexually active, erotic, and exotic, these women are subjected to harassing comments because of their sex and their ethnicity. As Robert Moore (1988) suggested:

> *Three of the dictionary definitions of white are "fairness of complexion, purity, innocence." These definitions affect the standard of beauty in our culture, in which whiteness represents the norm. "Blondes have more fun" and "Wouldn't you really rather be a blonde?" are sexist in their attitudes toward women generally, but are racist white standards when applied to the third world women. A 1971 Mademoiselle advertisement pictured a curly-headed, ivory-skinned woman over the caption, "When you go blonde go all the way," and asked: "Isn't this how, in the back of your mind, you always wanted to look? All wide-eyed and silky blonde down to there, and innocent?" Whatever the advertising people meant by this particular woman's innocence, one must remember that "innocent" is one of the definitions of the word white. This standard of beauty when preached to all women is racist. The statement "Isn't this how, in the back of your mind, you always wanted to look?" either ignores third world women or assumes they long to be white.* (pp. 271–272)

Irving Allen (1984) studied terms that refer specifically to women of different ethnic groups and concluded that derogatory names for women of ethnic groups display the strains of traditional masculine gender roles and aggression. The words stereotype physical differences among women (e.g., hair texture, shape of eyes) and also make derogatory sexual allusions, using animal and food metaphors (e.g., fortune cookie, hot chocolate, hot tamale).

Thus many of the words used to describe women are highly negative and deprecatory. When young girls read and hear these terms, what must they learn from such invectives? In the final analysis, girls and women are victimized by verbal deprecation that forces many to think little of themselves and their own abilities (see chapter 8).

It seems clear that the English language treats women in less than an equitable fashion. And yet this should come as no surprise when we note that language, like most other features of our society, is but one ". . . symbolic system closely tied to a patriarchal social structure" (Kramer et al., 1978). Men—white men—have played the largest role in creating language, and their views of women have been translated far more faithfully than many may wish to acknowledge. We live in a sexist and patriarchal society, and our language portrays these ideologies well. Learning to watch our language is a cliche most of us were taught as children. If avoiding offensive language is something we value, why then can we not watch our language even more closely, lest it offend over half of the human race?

Summary

Language is one of the most powerful features of culture. The English language has a strong undercurrent of linguistic sexism, exemplified by the ways women are ignored, defined, and deprecated in our language.

Several differences are found in the verbal output of women and men. For example, men generally talk more than women, but men disclose less about their personal lives than women do. Also, some slight differences have been speculated about in the use of certain verbal patterns; women are found to use more tag questions, qualifiers, longer requests, and fillers.

When it comes to communication's nonverbal features, several differences between women and men are found in terms of emotional expressions, sending and receiving nonverbal messages, eye contact, touching, body positions, and postures.

Suggested Readings

Crawford, M. (1995). *Talking difference: On gender and language*. London: Sage.

Espin, O. (1995). "Race," racism and sexuality in the life narratives of immigrant women. *Feminism and Psychology, 5*, 223–238.

Henley, N. (1995a). Ethnicity and gender issues in language. In H. Landrine (Ed.), *Bringing cultural diversity to feminist psychology: Theory, research, and practice*. Washington, DC: American Psychological Association.

Henley, N. (1995b). Body politics revisited: What do we know today? In P. Kalbfleisch & M. Cody (Eds.), *Gender, power, and communication in human relationships*. Hillsdale, NJ: Lawrence Erlbaum Associates, Inc.

Education and Work

An African proverb says it takes the whole village to educate a child: grandparents and parents, teachers and school administrators, law-makers and civic leaders. When all these citizens from our American village join forces, they can transform our educational institutions into the most powerful levers for equity, places where girls are valued as much as boys, daughters are cherished as fully as sons, and tomorrow's women are prepared to be full partners in all activities of the next century and beyond.

Myra Sadker and David Sadker

What's Your Opinion?

How do you define success?

How do you feel about the possibility of achieving these goals? About not achieving them?

What blocks in yourself and in the world will you have to overcome in order to achieve these goals?

Have you ever been in a situation where you were about to succeed at something and wondered if it was worth it or became afraid of the success or something it might produce?

In this chapter we will look at both the educational system and the work-place to examine the importance of gender role stereotypes in determining how individuals are treated by these social institutions.

The Educational System and Gender

Abilities such as reading, writing, and arithmetic are essential skills that people need to deal adequately with the demands of everyday life. For the most part, school is where we learn these basic skills. However, that's not all we learn in school. Socially approved values, attitudes, and beliefs are as much a part of the school's curriculum as are reading and writing. The so-called "hidden curriculum" of our educational system stresses such socially desirable traits as orderliness, conformity, respect for authority, competency, and discipline, all of which are thought necessary for students whether they become office assistants, nurses, physicians, or salespersons.

All too often, though, the goals of education are translated very differently, leaving lasting effects for girls and women and boys and men (Betz, 1993). Even among first- and second-graders, we find evidence of gender bias in the kinds of jobs children think about in terms of their future employment (Reid & Paludi, 1993). For example, third- and fifth-grade girls most frequently chose the occupations of nurse, teacher, and stewardess, while boys chose policeman, truck driver, pilot, and architect (MacKay & Miller, 1982). These responses are provided in more recent years (Betz, 1993). Nancy Betz (1993) reported that highly feminine stereotyped activities among third- through seventh-graders included knitting, sewing, selling perfume, and being a secretary. Highly masculine stereotyped activities included being a soldier, TV service person, and plumber. Once set, children's range of occupations is difficult to change.

A stereotyped view of the world reinforces many of the common gender role stereotypes and is a factor in prompting young boys' interest in more than twice as many occupations as young girls'. Consequently, when young girls reach high school, they tend to restrict their occupational aspirations. Many girls focus on jobs that bring less status and less money than the jobs that boys think about. The charge of sexism, or the view that girls and women and/or their activities are less important than boys and men and/or their activities, has been leveled at the educational system (Sadker & Sadker, 1994).

How do we account for the wide disparity between girls' and boys' occupational goals? There are many socializing forces in school that shape the outcome of a student's life. Recall that in chapter 5 we discussed the effects that teachers can have on shaping gender role behaviors along traditional lines. However, teachers contribute to only part of the sexism we find in the educational system.

Many school systems literally direct girls and boys into different courses by a differential "tracking system," whereby girls are taught to think in terms of becoming mothers, nurses, and secretaries while boys are taught to think about becoming physicians and engineers (Sadker & Sadker, 1994). We need to examine the educational system's academic programs and hiring practices as examples of some of the ways in which the educational system treats girls and women and boys and men differently.

Myra Sadker and David Sadker (1994) offer the following "snapshots" of an elementary school classroom:

Snapshot #1	*Tim answers a question.*
Snapshot #2	*The teacher reprimands Alex.*
Snapshot #3	*Judy and Alice sit with hands raised while Brad answers a question.*
Snapshot #4	*Sally answers a question.*
Snapshot #5	*The teacher praises Marcus for skill in spelling.*

Snapshot #6	*The teacher helps Sam with a spelling mistake.*
Snapshot #7	*The teacher compliments Alice on her neat paper.*
Snapshot #8	*Students are in lines for a spelling bee. Boys are on one side of the room and girls are on the other.* (p. 42)

Sadker and Sadker note that these snapshots suggest a gender message, that the classroom consists of two worlds: one of boys in action and the other of girls' inaction. Boys are more involved in all aspects of an elementary school classroom, from answering questions to being reprimanded. Girls are relatively invisible. Sadker and Sadker further illustrate the gender-related messages by sharing part of a discussion in a fifth grade class about presidents of the United States.

> *"Just a minute," the teacher admonishes. "There are too many of us here to all shout out at once. I want you to raise your hands, and then I'll call on you. If you shout out, I'll pick somebody else."*
>
> *Stephen calls out: I think Lincoln was the best president. He held the country together during the war.*
>
> *Teacher: A lot of historians would agree with you.*
>
> *Mike (seeing that nothing happened to Stephen, calls out): I don't. Lincoln was okay, but my Dad likes Reagan. He always said Reagan was a great president.*
>
> *David (calling out): Reagan? Are you kidding?*
>
> *Teacher: Who do you think our best president was, Dave?*
>
> *David: FDR. He saved us from the Depression.*
>
> *Max (calling out): I don't think it's right to pick one best president. There were a lot of good ones.*
>
> *Teacher: That's interesting.*
>
> *Kimberly (calling out): I don't think the presidents today are as good as the ones we used to have.*
>
> *Teacher: Okay, Kimberly. But you forgot the rule. You're supposed to raise your hand.* (pp. 42–43)

Programs

Sexism in our school systems has a long history. It was not until 1833 that the first woman was even allowed admission to an institution of higher learning, Oberlin College in Ohio. But even at Oberlin, a highly progressive and liberal institution for its day, women primarily learned the arts and home economics, which were "intended to prepare them for homemaking or teaching" (Deckard, 1983, p. 245). Nineteenth-century Oberlin College women students were discouraged from pursuing academic programs thought too strenuous for women; science and commerce were areas of study considered suitable "for men only" (Flexner, 1971). Besides their course work, these women were also required to engage in other nonacademic duties: "Washing the men's clothes, caring for their rooms, serving them at table, listening to their orations, but themselves remaining respectfully silent in public assemblages, the

Oberlin 'coeds' were being prepared for intelligent motherhood and a properly subservient wifehood" (Flexner, 1971, p. 30).

Today, college women no longer wash men's clothes or listen quietly to their orations as part of their educational experience at Oberlin College or any other college or university. Still, sexism in its more subtle forms can still be found in most modern-day schools, ranging from the early grades all the way up through the professional and graduate levels. For example, with the explosive development in computers and their related technology in the last several years, students today must have a grasp of basic mathematical principles and reasoning. And yet, remedial programs to assist students who have difficulty with these academic skills are sorely lacking in many school systems. This problem becomes a gender-oriented issue when we note that many girls are directed away from taking math and science courses and may be unprepared for the technology that awaits them. In contrast, remedial programs directed at helping students with reading difficulties—a problem more frequently encountered among boys than girls—have been set up in most school systems for years. On the surface, it seems that within our educational system, programs directed at eliminating academic deficiencies among boys are given a higher priority than programs that could assist girls.

Furthermore, there is growing concern that girls are losing out to boys in the important area of "hands-on" experience at computer terminals (Arch & Cummins, 1989). This, along with the lack of sex-specific remedial programs, can be taken as more than circumstantial evidence that sexism exists to some degree in many school systems.

Another area where sexism is present in educational programs is the practice of encouraging girls and boys to take different academic programs that lead to different skills, many of which are gender role stereotyped. Many programs taken in the junior high years funnel girls into traditionally feminine courses (e.g., home economics and typing) and encourage boys to take traditionally masculine courses (e.g., woodworking and shop). However, recent efforts by educators have attempted to change the sexism in these courses. One such educational system studied the effects of both girls and boys participating in courses that were once sex-segregated, and the results proved positive for both.

In spite of the fact that sexism is found in many schools and that girls and boys are covertly, if not overtly, treated differently by the educational system, women have many of the same academic goals as men have. Women want to learn academic skills that will better prepare them to be self-sufficient. As we have already noted, it was only within the last century and a half that women have been able to pursue a higher education. The number of women who pursue a college education has steadily grown over the years.

The events at Mills College in the spring of 1990 restimulated a great deal of discussion about the value of all women's colleges for women's career development, self-concept, and feminist identity development. Mills College, located in Oakland, Calif., has been an all-women's college for 138 years. In the spring of 1990, the Board of Trustees announced that declining enrollment and budget problems had left them no choice: men would be admitted as undergraduate students beginning in August, 1991 (men have been admitted as graduate students since the 1930s). Hundreds of women students at Mills College expressed concern over the Board of Trustees' decision. For example:

> *I felt like my best friend had died.*
> *It was like the earth fell out from our feet, and we were falling.*
> *We love men. But we want this place to ourselves.*
> *We'll do whatever it takes to reverse the decision.*
> *They can't run a school if they don't have any students.*
> *We have the power to close the college.*
> (Kunen, McNeil, & Waggoner, 1990, p. 63)

Women went on strike, demanded the resignation of Board of Trustees' President Warren Hellman, boycotted classes, and wore yellow arm bands, anklets, and bandanas to symbolize women's "hostage status." The protesters put up banners that proclaimed:

WE HAVE BEEN BETRAYED

A few weeks after their decision to admit men as undergraduate students at Mills College, the Board reversed its decision and accepted a plan proposed by alumni and faculty to increase the budget. Faculty members have agreed to teach an extra course a year and recruit more women students to Mills. Hellman, when announcing the new decision, exclaimed: "All of you have had a lot of banners for us all week. Here's one for you:"

MILLS. FOR WOMEN. AGAIN.

Sexual Harassment on Campus

One area that is receiving greater attention is sexual harassment of students by professors (Lott & Reilly, 1996; Paludi, 1996). Sexual harassment in U.S. colleges and universities is a major barrier to women's and men's vocational development and a traumatic force that disrupts their personal lives. As we discussed in chapter 5, the incidence of sexual harassment on college campuses is extremely high: nearly 70 percent of women and 10 percent of men are experiencing either quid pro quo or hostile environment sexual harassment from their professors.

The following behavior constitutes sexual harassment of college students: verbal harassment; subtle pressure for sexual activity; sexist remarks about a woman's clothing, competence, body, or sexual activities; unnecessary touching, patting, or pinching; leering or ogling at a woman's body; brushing against a woman's body; demanding sexual favors accompanied by implied or overt threats concerning one's grades or letters of recommendation; and physical assault.

Women students who have been harassed often change their entire educational program as a result. And, stress reactions—often severe—almost invariably follow sexual harassment, including depression, tension, anger and fear, insomnia, headaches, feelings of helplessness and embarrassment, and decreased motivation (Quina, 1996). Performance in course work suffers, and many women drop out of school altogether. Women have noted the following:

> *I was discussing my work in a public setting when a professor cut me off and asked if I had freckles all over my body.*
>
> *He (the teaching assistant) kept saying, don't worry about the grade, and you know we'll settle everything out of class.*
>
> *I see male colleagues and professors chum it up and hear all the talk about making the old boy network operate for women, so I thought nothing of accepting an invitation from a . . . professor to attend a gathering at his house. Other graduate students were present. . . . The professor made a fool out of himself pursuing me (it took me a while to catch on) and then blurted, "You know I want to sleep with you; I have a great deal of influence. Now, of course I don't want to force you into anything, but I'm sure you're going to be sensible about this." I fled.*
>
> *Playboy centerfolds were used as Anatomy teaching slides. . . . In slides, lectures, teaching aids and even our own student note service, we found that nurses were presented as sexy, bitchy, or bossy but never as professional health care workers. The financial officer made it clear that I could get the money I needed if I slept with him.* (U.S. Department of Education, Office for Civil Rights)

Research has also indicated that some groups of women tend to experience sexual harassment more often than others. On many campuses, ethnic minority women are victims of sexual harassment because of the stereotypes that portray women of color as sexually active, exotic, and erotic (DeFour, 1996). Physically challenged women experience a considerable amount of psychological victimization when reporting sexual harassment due to stereotypes about their sexuality. Lesbian women have been the victims of gender harassment. And, women students and faculty who support women's studies programs are often targeted for sexual harassment.

Research suggests that male professors' perceptions of what their behavior means are different from women's (Stites, 1996). Thus, there is often little disagreement with what has happened between women and men, but rather with what the behavior means. Men try to justify their behavior on the grounds that they are just friendly and trying to make women feel welcome or that they thought women would be flattered by the attention.

Male faculty have reported their attempts to initiate personal relationships with women students—dating and getting together for drinks (Stites, 1996). Louise Fitzgerald and colleagues (1988) reported that in their research with faculty men, 11 percent reported that they had attempted to stroke, caress, or touch women students. These faculty were not distinguishable from their colleagues who did not report these behaviors with respect to age, rank, or academic discipline. Most sexual harassers have somewhat of a "reputation" for harassment. Sexual harassment is clearly prohibited within the college/university system as a form of sexual discrimination, under Title IX of the 1972 Education Amendments (and for employees, Title VII of the 1964 Civil Rights Act). A key definition of sexual harassment has been issued by the Education Department's Office of Civil Rights (OCR):

> *Sexual harassment consists of verbal or physical conduct of a sexual nature, imposed on the basis of sex, by an employee or agent of a recipient of federal funds that denies, limits, provides different, or conditions the provision of aid, benefits, services, or treatment protected under Title IX.*

In addition, guidelines first issued by the Equal Employment Opportunity Commission (interpreting Title VII) and adopted in 1981 by the OCR further specify the range of sexual harassment covered by these statutes (see chapter 5). According to these guidelines, behavior constitutes sexual harassment when:

> *The person engaging in such behavior explicitly or implicitly makes your submission to it a term or condition of your employment or academic standing.*
> *The person engaging in such behavior makes decisions affecting your employment or academic life according to whether you accept or reject that behavior.*
> *The person's behavior is an attempt to interfere, or has the effect of interfering, with your work or academic performance, or creates an intimidating, hostile, or offensive working or learning environment.*

'Consensual Relationships'

Neither Title IX nor Title VII prohibit consensual sexual relationships; however, a number of institutions are developing policies on this matter. While consensual relationships may not always be unethical, they always cause problems. This happens, according to Bernice Sandler & Michele Paludi (1993) for the following reasons:

> *The situation involves one person exerting power over another.*
> *The seduction of a much younger individual is involved.*
> *Conflict of interest issues arise, e.g., How can a teacher fairly grade a student with whom they are having a sexual relationship?*
> *The potential for exploitation and abuse is high.*
> *The potential for retaliatory harassment is high when the sexual relationship ceases.*
> *Other individuals may be affected and claim favoritism.*

M. Cynara Stites (1996) noted that including consensual relationships as part of the definition of academic sexual harassment has been met with considerable resistance. A few campuses (e.g., University of Iowa, Harvard University, Temple University) prohibit sexual relationships between faculty and students over whom the professor has some authority (i.e., advising, supervising, grading, teaching). A few other campuses have "discouragement policies," in which "consensual relations" are not strictly prohibited but discouraged (e.g., University of Minnesota, University of Connecticut, New York University Law School, Massachusetts Institute of Technology).

The University of Virginia called for a total ban on all sexual relationships between faculty and students regardless of the professor's role vis-a-vis the student. However, the Faculty Senate approved a prohibition-only policy rather than the total ban policy. Thus, this campus prohibits sexual relations between faculty and student when the faculty has some organizational power over the student. The case can be made, however, that a faculty member does not have to be the student's professor in order for that faculty member to be powerful and potentially abuse that power over the student.

All faculty members have an ethical and professional responsibility to provide a learning environment that is respectful of students and fosters the academic performance and intellectual development of students. The fact that a student is defined as an adult by chronological age can in no way remove the obligation of a teacher or administrator to refrain from engaging in sexual harassment, and the student's adulthood is in no way a proxy for consenting to a relationship. The stories women tell about their "consensual relationships" do not parallel romances or typical stories about sexual affairs; instead, they resemble stories depicting patterns of manipulation and victimization, responses identical to those women who are sexually harassed in a nonconsensual relationship (Zalk, Paludi, & Dederich, 1991).

Is there such a thing as female student's informed consent in a sexual relationship with a male faculty member? In answering this question, Stites (1996) asks us to think about power relations in the school setting that are stratified by sex. The structure of educational institutions interacts with psychological dynamics to increase students' vulnerability to all forms of sexual harassment. Professors have the power to enhance or diminish students' self-esteem. This power can motivate students to learn course material or convince them to give up. The tone and content of the student-professor interaction is especially important. Is the student encouraged or put down? Do the teachers use their knowledge to let students know how "stupid" they are or to challenge their thinking?

To effectively deal with sexual harassment in schools and colleges/universities, the following components are recommended: (1) an effective policy statement; (2) an effective grievance procedure; and (3) education/training programs for all members of the educational institution (Paludi, 1996; Paludi & Barickman, 1997).

The Classroom Climate

In 1982 the Association of American Colleges published *The Classroom Climate: A Chilly One for Women?* This report noted that women on college campuses were being ignored in the classroom, had their term papers graded on appearance rather than on content (as their male peers' work was graded) and were assumed by faculty not to be totally invested in their careers but instead in fulfilling affiliative needs. In the years since the publication of this report, there have been efforts to improve this climate for college women, including faculty development seminars related to gender and teaching (see chapter 5), more integration of women's studies scholarship into the curriculum, and training programs for faculty on pedagogy. Those programs focus on the "how" of the classroom: seating arrangements, assignment of written work, and participation of all members of the class, not just a select few. Have these efforts been successful?

Kristen Lippert-Martin (1992) asked faculty and researchers concerned with the classroom climate the following questions:

> *How do you think the classroom climate for women has changed in the last ten years? Has it improved?*
>
> *Has women's studies played a role in changing the climate? How about curriculum integration projects?*
>
> *What are individuals—as opposed to institutions—able to do to make a difference for women students?*

Responses to these questions were obtained from Directors of Women's Studies Programs and administrators at the following campuses: University of Missouri-Columbia, University of Colorado, Lewis and Clark College, Hunter College, Old Dominion University, Temple University, Lesley College, and California State University-Fullerton. Some responses included:

> *I think there are pockets where (the climate has) changed.*
>
> *Increasingly, as more women—and especially feminists—are hired as faculty, there will be more of a sensitivity to women students and support for women students in the classroom. I think women's studies classes are kind of an oasis. . . . Lip service is given to diversity, both racial and gender, but in practice things haven't changed that much outside of these pockets.*
>
> *There has been some consciousness raised about the needs of learners other than majority culture learners (if such a learner exists in the first place).*
>
> *On the campuses where women have been able or encouraged to take women's studies classes, they are more aware. If they take these courses early, they will tend to be conscious of the climate and try to speak up more. From that point of view, there is much promise.*
>
> *These chilly climate issues are discussed predominantly in women's studies classes, and then women talk about them in their other classes. Women's studies programs have been a catalyst for change in that respect.* (pp. 2–3)

When asked whether these scholars believed there are fields in which women still feel closed out, all replied: yes, especially with respect to the sciences. Recent data (Monthly Forum on Women in Higher Education, 1996) suggest that since 1983, the number of women earning doctorates has risen by 50%; however, men continue to dominate doctoral level higher education. The doctorates earned by women still tend to be concentrated in the social sciences, humanities, and most especially in education. Men dominate the scientific disciplines and engineering. The forum also cited the following statistics:

> *In 1994, 78.4 percent of women who earned doctorates in the United States were U.S. citizens.*
>
> *The only major scientific field where women did not earn a Ph.D. was in nuclear chemistry.*
>
> *A little more than half of women earning Ph.D.'s are married.*
> *More than 60% of men are married.*
>
> *The median age of women doctoral recipients in 1994 was 35.9 years. For men, the median age was 33.2 years.*
>
> *For women, the median amount of time to complete their doctoral studies was 12 years after their undergraduate degree; for men the median age was 10 years.*

The forum also reported that more women than men planned on employment at an educational institution after earning their doctorate, suggesting gender-related issues in employment as well as education.

Few areas in education show the prevalence of sexism as much as the area of teacher employment. (Occupational roles in general will be discussed more fully in the next section.) Historically, the teaching profession enjoyed a position of high status and considerable respect in our country. During the eighteenth century and into the nineteenth century, teachers were considered pillars of their communities. At that time, teaching was almost totally an all-male profession. As women began entering the teaching profession in greater numbers (circa 1830–1850), they were restricted primarily to teaching the early grades, where the goal was not so much to educate children as to civilize them (Kaufman, 1984). As the years went by, women taught more than men. However, the position of principal—a position of greater status than that of teacher—in most grade schools remained male-populated.

During this century, the teaching profession became more dominated by women, especially among the primary grades. However, women teachers found their career paths blocked at higher levels of the educational system (Sadker & Sadker, 1994). At the college or university level, for example, it seems that men are preferred over women.

Work, the Workplace, and Gender

In this section we will discuss the areas where work, the workplace, and gender role stereotypes intersect. We will discuss the issues of women's participation in the labor force and their earnings. We will also examine work "ghettos" where we find certain jobs primarily occupied by women rather than by equal numbers of women and men. Next we will note some of the contributing factors that promote segregation in the work force, leaving women at a greater disadvantage than men in general, including pay inequity. The better we understand the problems that women, especially ethnic minority women, have in job-related areas, the sooner we can do something to end the pervasiveness of discrimination and segregation in the workplace.

Some Common Myths about Women, Gender Roles, and the Workplace

Several myths have evolved regarding the workplace and workers. These myths act as barriers to keep some groups out of certain jobs while favoring others. In this section we will detail three myths related to women and the workplace: the myths of pin money, home-bound women, and women's lack of achievement motivation.

Pin money is the euphemism for a small amount of money that a woman earned to be used for "little extras" for her family (or, more rarely, for herself). Pin money is considered nonessential money because it is the husband's salary that supposedly provides for the family financially. The idea of pin money devalued a woman's financial contribution to the family's economic well-being and soothed a husband's pride that rested to a large degree on the knowledge that his salary was the family's primary income.

With respect to all working women 16 years and older, we find different numbers of working women depending on their marital status. The single largest category of working women has been and still is the single woman. Approximately 40 percent of all separated, divorced, or widowed women are employed outside the home. Also we find that more than 50 percent of all married women whose husbands were present in the home are employed. Even women with children are entering the paid labor force in ever increasing numbers. "The working woman then is not a variation from the norm, she *is* the norm" (Hyde, 1985, p. 169).

American attitudes toward working women have changed as well. For example, in 1978, nearly 75 percent of all Americans approved of women working outside of the home even if their husbands' salaries were sufficient for the family. Not only have more men become more accepting of women working outside of the home, but women have come to resist the idea that they should give up their jobs even during their children's early years. Married women with families are becoming a major part of the work force for the same reason that men work: financial needs. Furthermore, during any crisis—war or poverty, for example—women do the same work as men in addition to being mothers and wives.

One of the consistent findings regarding employment, sex, and ethnicity issues is that in comparison to white women, African American women have been expected to work outside the home for all of their adult lives (Landrine, 1995). The labor force participation rate of African American women has traditionally been greater than that of white women. Furthermore, African American women are more likely than white women to be heads of households.

However, African American women are more disadvantaged in the labor force than are white women; they face "double jeopardy" because of their participating in a culture that has valued neither women nor minorities (Beale, 1970).

For example, African American women earn less money than women or men of any ethnic group. Black women earn substantially less than do black men (Betz, 1993). Similar to white women, African American women work mainly in low-paying, stereotypic "feminine" jobs, such as domestic and service jobs.

Hortensia Amaro (1988), Gloria Romero and colleagues (Romero et al., 1988), and Angela Ginorio and colleagues (Ginorio et al., 1995) indicated that Latinas also suffer the disadvantages of "double jeopardy" in the workplace. Further, Ginorio and colleagues (1995) pointed out that the Latina/Latino cultural patterns are built around a *machismo* norm that puts little emphasis on education for women while promoting frequent childbearing. These cultural beliefs prevent women from entering the labor force and may contribute to stress at home for those women who are employed. Ginorio and colleagues (1995) point out that while Latinos have higher labor force participation than in white and African American men, Latinas have the lowest labor force participation.

Maria Root (1995) suggested that Asian American women typically have been socialized to avoid male-populated careers where the emphasis is on independence, competitiveness, and activism. Deborah Woo (1992) noted the gap between striving and achieving for Asian American women. As she stated: "For Asian American women education seems to serve less as an opportunity for upward mobility than as protection against jobs as service or assembly workers, or as machine operatives—male areas where foreign-born Asian women are far more likely to find themselves" (p. 180).

Root also notes that there is diversity of employment within Asian America by group. For example, Filipina women are employed at a higher rate than men because of their high educational levels, whereas Vietnamese women are employed at the lowest rate because of lack of skills relevant to employment opportunities in the United States. Root also reminds us that with respect to immigrant Asian women, many who have earned degrees and received specialized training cannot transfer their credentials to the United States. The impact of this on women's self-esteem and self-concept is enormous.

The last myth, that of the nonachievement-oriented woman, is probably the most difficult one to dislodge from many people's minds. The doggedness with which this myth hangs on is due, at least in part, to the popularity of the "fear of success" construct (Horner, 1968; Paludi, 1984).

In 1964, Matina Horner asked college women to write a story based on the following opening sentence: "At the end of first term finals, Anne finds herself at the top of her medical school class." She asked college men to write a story based on a similar opening sentence: "After first term finals,

John finds himself at the top of his medical school class." Based on the responses received from a majority of women in the study, Horner concluded that women had a fear of success. They believed that success would lead to unpleasant consequences, including unpopularity and a loss of femininity.

The popular media promoted the idea that women feared success whereas men did not, and many people felt they had "scientific" justification for thinking that women lacked the motivation to become successful in the business or professional world. The problems with this research, however, and the many studies that followed it seem almost endless: a lack of replication of the findings, a confounding of "fear of success" with "fear of failure," and other methodological problems (Paludi, 1984).

More support has been obtained for Jean Lipman-Blumen's theory concerning direct and relational achieving styles (Lipman-Blumen et al., 1983). *Direct achieving styles* are used by people who confront achievement tasks directly; a direct achiever may enjoy winning over competitors or may enjoy the thrill of accomplishment. *Relational achieving styles* are used by people who seek success through their relationships with others—for example, working in collaboration with other people. Women show wide variability in the kinds of achieving style they prefer.

The politically motivated response to research on fear of success masked a more general phenomenon implicit in it: role conflict. The conflict surrounding achievement strivings arises from attempts to implement values, goals, and aspirations that appear to be mutually exclusive or at least in conflict with one another. Fear of success may be thought of as a conscious solution to a realistic role conflict of women's reluctance to violate important social norms where these violations would be costly (Paludi & Fankell-Hauser, 1986). Men may be more conforming to the stereotypic core elements of the masculine role in this culture that socializes them to appear self-confident, worry free, and fearless in achievement situations.

The idea that women work only for pin money is more myth than fact. Women work to survive and support their families. The idea that nearly all women spend their adult years at home waiting for their husbands to come in after a hard day's labor is clearly more myth than fact (and illustrates heterosexism as well). The notion that women spend their days baking cookies for their children while their husbands are at work may be a stereotype of women as presented on television in the 1950s, but it surely doesn't reflect life on the other side of the television screen.

Finally, the notion that women fear success and will subvert their own progress is, like the other notions, myth. If given opportunities, women will perform as well as men in the labor force. After the more than 25 years that women's motivation or commitment to work has been questioned, the institutional and social barriers are much greater than any possible "fear" that some women may have at succeeding in the workplace.

A Fair Day's Pay

Salaries not only provide for one's needs, they are also a tangible means to show someone her or his worth in the job market. As we noted before, increasing numbers of women are employed today, more than ever before, and a large proportion of these women are solely responsible for their families financially. When it comes to the salaries these women earn, one fact stands out. As a group, women earn significantly less than men. In fact, the problem has gotten worse rather than better in the last 25 years or so. When we consider the interface of race and sex, we note that women of color earn substantially less than white women, who earn less than men. To highlight the wage disparity, we should note that the average working woman must work at least eight and a half days to earn as much as the average working man earns in five!

Even when we compare employed women with employed men who have comparable educational status and occupational credentials and who have pursued their careers full time throughout most of their working years, we still find great disparity between the women's and men's incomes (Betz, 1993). When job category, education, and experience are taken into account, there still is a wide disparity between the salaries of women and men, suggesting that women suffer from a very costly form of discrimination. Part of this salary disparity is due to the cultural belief that men should earn more than women because men supposedly are the primary "breadwinners" of the family.

A major assumption in any discussion of comparable worth is that the value or worth of various jobs can be quantified in some objective fashion. Social scientists, especially those involved in industrial organizations, have been working on the development of valid and reliable measures for evaluating jobs and their component factors since the 1930s and 1940s. And yet not all experts in job evaluation agree on the means of evaluation. The type of measurement for such evaluation, as well as the findings, can be disputed as being biased.

The real opposition to evaluating different job categories in terms of comparable worth seems to come from certain government agencies and corporations that stand to lose literally billions of dollars if comparable worth standards are applied to the hundreds of jobs that traditionally have paid less than other jobs. Many people argue that rectifying the problem of salary inequities between women and men should be required by new laws, court orders, or complicated formulas that compare the worth of one job to another. They argue that allowing the marketplace to determine the worth or value of someone's work is still the best way to solve the problem of wage disparity. The issue of the comparable worth of traditionally women-populated jobs as opposed to traditionally men-populated jobs is growing. The vast number of women who work in the secretarial pools and on the hospital wards are certainly underpaid for the work demanded of them. Many have sole financial responsibility for their families. If the marketplace rules the day, the age-old discriminatory practices against women will continue.

Work Ghettos

Setting aside for the moment the question of equivalent jobs and unequal salaries for women and men, one of the major reasons that women receive, on the average, only 60 cents for every dollar earned by men is that for the most part women hold very different kinds of jobs than men hold (Betz, 1993). When we look at various job categories, one striking fact that stands out is the proportion of jobs that have a disproportionate number of either women or men in them. It is as if there existed *work ghettos* in the labor market. The occupations that are categorized as "women's work" (e.g., secretaries, child-care workers, and librarians) usually carry with them extremely low salary ranges, low prestige and status, and little chance for advancement or promotion. Some occupations that have historically been male-populated (e.g., the legal profession) have attracted more women in the last several decades. Some professions that once were mostly male-populated have in fact become nearly female-populated professions, as the real estate field demonstrates.

In insurance companies, women and men may process policy applications. The men are typically called "underwriters" while the women are referred to as "raters." By labeling identical work differently for women and men, insurance companies can justify paying women less than men (Hunter College Women's Studies Collective, 1983).

How do we account, then, for the work ghettos that we find so prevalent in the business sectors? And why do the jobs that women generally occupy pay so much less than those that men occupy? To answer these and other related gender-work questions, we need to explore the issue of job segregation.

Job Segregation

Job segregation still exists to a large extent for women (Mednick & Thomas, 1993). Some jobs are *de facto* segregated simply because women make up nearly the entire work force. Occupations such as secretary-stenographer, household worker, waitress, elementary schoolteacher, and bookkeeper are nearly totally female-populated occupations. These five occupations account for almost 25 percent of all working women. Thus these five occupations represent a kind of occupational ghetto for women and are sometimes referred to as the "pink-collar" ghetto. Compounding the problem of job segregation is the fact that the jobs populated by women generally have lower pay scales than those populated by men.

One explanation for employed women's lower pay is the economic principle of "supply and demand" brought on by job segregation (Blau, 1975). Generally speaking, there are more trained women workers (i.e., large supply) than there are jobs available (i.e., low demand), especially in segregated occupations. Economist Barbara Bergmann (1974) was one of the first to use the term *overcrowding* to explain the relationship between job segregation and lower wages.

Studies have found a basis for Bergmann's notion of overcrowding as affecting women's salaries. Evelyn Glen and Roslyn Feldberg (1977) found that during the last century, clerical work was primarily a male-populated occupation that brought men relatively high status and good wages. However, during this century, women became the dominant group in clerical work, and the status accruing from such work has fallen, as have the wages relative to male-populated jobs that require similar skills.

Causes of Job Segregation

Job segregation appears to be one of the dominant causes for women's lower wages in the work force. But what factors normally contribute to women being segregated in so few jobs? We will consider three different explanations: the belief that a woman's biology prevents her from competing in the work force for high-paying jobs, the socialization of young girls to avoid higher status positions, and, last, the various social or institutional forces that build barriers to prevent women from entering high-paying and high-status positions.

Anatomy Is Occupational Destiny

When women are kept out of occupations for reasons of their biology, it is usually because of discrimination and not because women are actually restricted by their physical makeup. In the last several years, even in occupations historically male-populated (e.g., in coal mines and in heavy construction), women have shown they can do the work as well as men.

Socializing Women out of the Marketplace

Girls and boys are socialized differently. As a result, boys and girls learn to become more comfortable with certain types of jobs. For example, many fathers will work with their sons on the family cars, which may give young boys a basic knowledge of the workings of combustible engines. These young boys may grow up to be auto mechanics, race car drivers, or even car salespeople. Young girls washing the dishes and doing the laundry may grow up to be household workers or maids. The difference in pay between an auto mechanic and a household worker is considerable.

Socialization may even influence the attitudes women and men have toward work and the possibility of rewards and success contingent on work. Joan Crowley, along with several of her colleagues (1973), reported on the differences between the attitudes of women and men as a possible factor contributing to women's lower wages. These researchers found men more concerned about their promotions, whereas women were more concerned about a job's social aspects and the number of hours demanded by the job. From this we might suspect that women are less ambitious than men and that this may be partially to blame for women's lower pay. However, Rosabeth Kanter (1984) and others (e.g., Betz, 1993; Mednick & Thomas, 1993) suggest that women are no less ambitious or motivated for success than men are, but many women may "give up" because they realize that they are in "dead-end" jobs.

Personality characteristics are another aspect where socialization may play a role in the future jobs that women and men hold. We have noted that the stereotypic view of masculinity is one of instrumentality, independence, assertiveness, and emotional constraint (Deaux & Kite, 1993). Such characteristics lend themselves to success in the business world. On the other hand, the belief in women's purported greater emotionality, supportiveness, and concern for social cohesiveness may not be as helpful in the marketplace, especially in jobs that demand independent action and confidence in one's own ability.

However, although socialization probably plays a role in job segregation, we should not focus only on this feature to explain the difference found between women and men in their occupations and the resultant disparities. Institutional barriers play a role in job segregation as well.

Social and Institutional Barriers

Women are highly visible and distinct from men, and more often than not the characteristics and traits commonly associated with women are viewed as less desirable than those attributed to men. Even those jobs customarily thought of as "women's work" are thought of by many as less worthwhile or desirable than jobs associated with men.

While it is not likely that most men will be blatantly antifemale in their attitudes toward women, many men still demonstrate antifeminine sentiment in innumerable ways (Doyle, 1995). The area of job segregation is but one of the more formidable ways of discriminating against females; there are also several social and institutional outlets for such discrimination.

Prejudice. One thing that prevents women from gaining a foothold in the male-dominant job market is simple and blatant prejudice against women. Some men simply cannot accept women entering a "man's working world." Or when women do, there is a conscious attempt to belittle them and their work in comparison to men's. Even for those women who have made it in a male-populated profession, the insidious nature of prejudice against women remains a constant threat.

Research suggests that men are less likely to hold liberal views than women about women's roles and degree of career commitment (Betz, 1993). Women may receive less professional support from men than women colleagues. Indifference in the workplace may undermine women's commitment to their professional careers and contribute to self-fulfilling prophecies about not being competent enough to succeed in male-populated careers.

Related to these attitudes is the differential evaluation of individuals on the basis of sex. Paludi and Strayer (1985), for example, reported than men are rated higher than equivalent women in performing certain tasks and job qualifications. Similarly, women receive lower recognition and economic rewards for their work than men, and lower prestige, knowledge, and expertise are attributed to them as well. Widely accepted stereotypes depict men, but not women, as having the requisite skills and characteristics for managerial and leadership positions (Paludi, 1992). These stereotypes persist even though gender differences are not found in leadership ability or job performance.

Thus, because women are expected to conform to the gender role stereotypes, they may be negatively evaluated when they don't. Research has indicated that this attributional prejudice against women's performance is found in children as young as eight years old (McNeer et al., 1984). Girls' and women's successes are attributed to luck rather than skill (Deaux & Kite, 1993). Because male teachers and employers attribute women's successes to luck, women's levels of aspiration remain low. Therefore, many women never establish any occupational life plan or prepare themselves for a career. People may be more likely to give promotions to employees whose success has been attributed to ability. If men are more likely than women to have their success explained in terms of ability, then they may be more likely than women to receive promotions.

Maria de la Luz Reyes and John Halcon (1988) pointed out the interface between racism and sexism in attitudes about competency. For example, ethnic minority workers are plagued with the stereotype that they are tokens and have been hired without professional experience, credentials, and qualifications. In addition, many organizations operate under the "one-minority-per-pot" syndrome: De la Luz Reyes and Halcon concluded that in academia:

> *We believe that implicit in this practice is a deep-seated belief that minorities are not as qualified as non-minorities. This conviction stems from an unspoken fear that the presence of more than one minority . . . in a mainstream, traditional department might reduce the department's . . . reputation. . . . Typically, consideration of minority candidates occurs only when there is pressure applied to diversify. . . . The limitation on minority hiring that is part of the "one-minority-per-pot" syndrome has the effect of restricting the career goals and aspirations of Hispanics and other minority faculty.* (pp. 305–306)

Gatekeepers. Another way that job segregation is perpetuated is by the presence of gatekeepers, especially in high-status professions such as law, medicine, and engineering. A gatekeeper is one who keeps women out of various careers or limits their advancement. Graduate school professors who believe that women have no place in their particular profession can be especially powerful gatekeepers (LaFrance, 1988). Gatekeepers often don't see themselves as prejudiced against women *per se*. They rationalize that their resistance to women in the profession is based on "facts." To their way of thinking, a woman can never be as serious about a career as a man; even if women do enter the field, they'll leave once they start their families.

Lack of informal groups. Women who have acquired sufficient training, education, and experience and who have attained a career may still experience a subtle form of discrimination. As most successful men in a profession will agree, "who you know" is often more important than "what you know." Men have had their careers immeasurably helped by the aid of a mentor, a sponsor, or some other person who knows where there is a job opening or who even has a possible solution to a job-related problem. The men's professional network, or what is sometimes referred to as the "old boys' club," has helped many men advance their careers. But for women it is very different. The lack of informal groups for many women professionals can be very debilitating to their careers (Forisha, 1981). As Judith Lorber (1984) commented:

> *Those who are excluded from informal work groups are at a disadvantage in filling the true requirements of their jobs, since important aspects of the work experience are not shared with them. Additionally, they are not sponsored for promotion and, should they gain a formal position of power, they discover it is extremely difficult to find loyal subordinates or exert their authority. Therefore, they rarely rise to truly high levels of power and prestige within their work organizations. As a result, they have fewer resources to offer their colleagues, which further perpetuates their exclusion from the colleague peer group.* (p. 371)

Of course, many men might say that being shunned by professional colleagues should not dissuade a truly talented and highly motivated person; if a woman wants to "play with the big boys," she had better be prepared to take up the challenge of possibly having to "go it alone." Most highly successful men, however, did not "go it alone." The idea of the successful loner is quite unrealistic given the interpersonal nature of most professions today (White, 1975).

Jo Freeman (1975) discussed the "null educational environment" that neither discourages nor encourages women, but rather ignores them.

> *An academic situation that neither encourages nor discourages students of either sex is inherently discriminatory against women because it fails to take into account the differentiating external environments from which women and men students come from.* (p. 221)

Betz (1993) concluded:

> *The critical aspect of this concept for educators, counselors, parents, etc., is that if we are not actively supporting and encouraging women we are, in effect, leaving them at the mercy of gender role and occupational stereotypes.* (p. 646)

Relative to the topic of informal groups has been a decade-long focus on mentoring and its benefits to women's careers. Arguments in favor of mentors (preferably women) for women have stressed the importance of women's identification with female models, the importance of the information provided by the mentor's behavior, and the positive incentive through illustrative success. Women have been advised to find a woman mentor and to be one to other women. This appeal is most likely a response to the suggestion that women do not receive as much mentoring as do men. Explanations for this assertion have concerned the paucity of women who are in positions of power to serve as mentors.

Attention has been devoted to developmental issues in the mentor-protege relationship for women (Haring-Hidore & Paludi, 1989). One developmental consideration relates to reentry of women's experiences with mentors. This focus is a direct result of the increasing number of women who are returning to college or work or beginning college or work for the first time when they are in middle and older adulthood.

For example, two transitions commonly experienced by older women include transforming one's role from housekeeper to college student or worker. These transitions generally occur at a later point in women's adulthood, whereas men (and perhaps younger women) tend to experience a more traditional route of transitions, e.g., high school to college to graduate school to career.

Because the transitional phases are different for women, women tend to have additional and/or different needs from a mentoring relationship. For example, older women seek a mentor who will assist them in planning their futures so that they are successful. Marilyn Haring-Hidore and Michele Paludi (1989) observed that male mentors may not want to invest time in older women because of their perception that these women are less dedicated to their career and have a shortened career life span. Thus, the different transitions for older women may negatively affect their mentoring opportunities because they seem out of step with well-known career transitions for younger individuals. A newly divorced 45-year-old woman who is making a transition from housekeeping to her first college class does not resemble either an 18-year-old who enters college immediately after completing high school or a 45-year-old man whose career transition most likely is from mid- to upper-level management and requires additional course work. As a consequence of the timing of her transition, such a woman probably has fewer prospects of finding a mentor to invest in her and her career.

Older women may thus be isolated from collegial contacts and consequently may receive less encouragement for their successes and/or be avoided by their male mentors. In addition, the more older women get the mentoring they need in certain educational and vocational pursuits, the more they will be perceived as needing the mentoring they get (LaFrance, 1988). Their achievements may thus be explained by external attributions—getting assistance—rather than internal attributions—ability and effort. Thus, in mentoring relationships for older women, it may be difficult for a woman to achieve colleague status due to the interface of sexism and ageism.

Sexual Harassment

The events surrounding Anita Hill's testimony to the Judiciary Committee hearings for the confirmation of Clarence Thomas to the Supreme Court in October 1991 continued to raise public awareness around issues of sexual harassment. Experts in sexual harassment frequently were asked the following questions during the confirmation hearings:

Professor Anita Hill speaking at the Senate Judiciary confirmation hearings, October, 1991.

© 1993 David Burnett/ Contact Press Images

"She wasn't physically assaulted so she couldn't have been sexually harassed, right?"

"Men who harass are pathological. Clarence Thomas did not look like a crazy man. He couldn't have harassed Anita Hill, right?"

"Why did she wait so long to talk about her experiences? Why didn't she report it 10 years ago?"

These questions reflect the need for information about the definition of sexual harassment, the extent it exists in the workplace (as well as the classroom), the impact of sexual harassment on individuals, and psychological profiles of sexual harassers. Let's address each of these questions and discuss the myths versus realities that exist in this area.

"She wasn't physically assaulted so she couldn't have been sexually harassed, right?"

As we pointed out in our discussion of academic sexual harassment and in chapter 6, most sexual harassment is far more pervasive and less obvious than physical assault. Propositions or threats demanding sexual activity in exchange for favors (such as a raise or promotion) and unwelcome physical gestures like brushing up against the person, squeezing, and pinching are all forms of sexual harassment. So are threats of physical assault, subtle pressure for sexual interactions, sexist comments, and sending lewd cartoons, cards, presents, or letters.

Sexual harassment does not fall within the range of personal private relationships. It happens when a person with power abuses that power to intimidate, coerce, or humiliate someone because of her or his sex. It is a breach of trust that normally exists among members of an organization. Sexual harassment does create confusion because the boundary between professional roles and personal relationships is blurred. The harasser introduces a sexual element into what should be a collegial situation.

There is a distinct difference between sexual harassment and voluntary sexual relationships. The difference is the element of coercion (real or implied), threat (real or implied), and/or unwanted attention. Sexual harassment is unwelcome. It can be an action that occurs only once, or it may be repeated. In voluntary sexual relationships individuals can exercise freedom of choice in deciding whether to establish a close, intimate relationship. This freedom of choice is absent in sexual harassment.

Thus, physical assault is not a required element of sexual harassment. In fact, most individuals who experience sexual harassment never endure any physical touching throughout the duration of the victimization.

> *"Men who harass are pathological. Clarence Thomas did not look like a crazy man. He couldn't have harassed Anita Hill, right?"*

Louise Fitzgerald and Lauren Weitzman (1990) reported that the assumption that there is a "typical" harasser is a serious oversimplification of a complex issue and contributes to the misunderstanding of this issue. Harassers are found in all types of occupations, at all organizational levels, among business and professional individuals, including college professors. Research has also suggested that individuals who harass typically do not label their behavior as sexual harassment despite the fact that they report that they frequently engage in behaviors that fit the legal definition of sexual harassment. They deny the inherent power differential between themselves and their students or employees as well as the psychological power conferred by this differential that is as salient as the power derived from evaluation.

The behavior that legally constitutes harassment is just that, despite what the professor's or employer's intentions may be (Levy & Paludi, 1997). It is the power differential and/or the woman's reaction to the behavior that are the critical variables.

We may think of sexual harassment as being not the act of a disturbed man, but rather an act of an over-conforming man. In other words, sexual harassment, similar to rape, incest, and battering, may be understood as an extreme acting-out of qualities that are regarded as super masculine: aggression, power, dominance, force. Thus, men who harass are not pathological but individuals who exhibit behaviors characteristic of the masculine gender role in American culture.

> *"Why did she wait so long to talk about her experiences. Why didn't she report it 10 years ago?"*
>
> *"Why did Anita Hill continue a cordial relationship with Clarence Thomas if he was really doing what she described?"*
>
> *"I don't think she got harmed in any way—she looks like she's successful—so what's the big deal anyway?"*

Women's performance on the job suffers, and many women change their career goals altogether. Stress reactions invariably follow sexual harassment, including depression, tension, anger and fear, insomnia, headaches, feelings of helplessness and embarrassment, and decreased motivation. For ethnic minority women who have been sexually harassed, economic vulnerability is paramount. For example, they are dependent on financial aid to fund their education; they have loans more often than research or teaching assistantships. Women feel powerless, not in control, afraid, not flattered, by sexual harassment. Their emotional and physical well-being resembles victims of other sexual abuses, i.e., rape, incest, and battering. Their behavior does not resemble "courtship behaviors" (Paludi & Barickman, 1997).

Furthermore, like victims of rape who go to court, sexual harassment victims frequently experience a second victimization when they attempt to deal with the situation through legal and/or institutional means. Stereotypes about sexual harassment and women's victimization blame women for the harassment. These stereotypes center around the myths that sexual harassment is a form of seduction, that women secretly want to be sexually harassed, and that women do not tell the truth.

Individual responses to workplace sexual harassment vary, of course, as a function of the victim's personal style, the severity of the harassment, and the availability of the social support after the harassment. Sadly, sexual harassment is often treated as a minor problem or as a joke. Hearing the actual responses of those who have been sexually harassed dispels this assumption.

Nancy Betz and Louise Fitzgerald (1987) reported that sexual harassment dates back to the time women first entered the marketplace. In 1908, *Harper's Bazaar* published a series of women's stories documenting sexual harassment. Women carried knives to work to protect themselves from sexual harassment in their workplace, a broom factory. Betz and Fitzgerald (1987) suggested that like women at the turn of the century, more women today are refused employment, fired, or forced to quit work as the result of sexual harassment than for any other single cause. The incidence of sexual harassment of employed women parallels the incidence for women students.

The most pervasive form of sexual harassment for employed women is gender harassment, the intimidating, hostile environment, including peer harassment (hostility, anger, and violence from male peers and employers). In a 1986 decision, *Meritor Savings Bank v. Vinson,* the Supreme Court unanimously affirmed that "sexual harassment claims are not limited simply to those for which the complainant is subjected to an offensive, discriminatory work environment ('hostile environment sexual harassment')."

The consequences of sexual harassment for women workers include physical and emotional difficulties, negative feelings about work, and poor job performance (Levy & Paludi, 1997). We encourage you to reread the discussion of sexual harassment in chapter 6, in which a power analysis of this form of victimization is discussed.

Conflict between Roles

Most men who are highly successful feel little conflict between their work role and their family role. Having a mate who takes care of the pressing problems of raising the children and tending to the everyday chores of running a household can be a blessing that most busy men who are scrambling up the career ladder often forget. One of the problems married professional women with children have is that they cannot devote full time to their careers during that period when full-time involvement may be essential for later advancement (Betz, 1993).

When one considers the scope of the different forms of discrimination against women, added to the socialization that prevents many young women from venturing into "male-only" occupations, it is a wonder that the number of women who succeed in business or professional careers is as large as it is. Women must cope with their socialization, which for many gave them little encouragement to seek achievement in nonfeminine pursuits. Women who did pursue professional careers have had to contend with male prejudice, gatekeepers who wittingly or unwittingly made their pursuits more difficult, the lack of informal groups where peer contacts could prove helpful, sexual harassment, and, finally, the struggle between their responsibilities to families and the demands of their careers.

Redefining Achievement: Valuing What Is Female and Feminine

Betz (1993) pointed out that among men, the relationship of intellect to obtained educational and occupational level holds well. However, among women, this relationship breaks down in adolescence and young adulthood. While girls perform better academically than boys at all educational levels, and while girls' school progress is superior to boys', girls' and women's abilities are underutilized.

This underutilization results from our culture's value-laden definition of achievement. The areas that are considered successful usually have a masculine bias. Success may be represented by achievement at a prestigious occupation, academic excellence, and other accomplishments that are associated with masculine values. Consequently, accomplishments that are associated with traditionally feminine values receive little or no attention. Women manage a household and children, and yet this accomplishment is rarely studied in the topic of achievement motivation and work. We need to redefine achievement and achievement-related issues in a way that does not keep women's lives and realities invisible.

The focus on one educational and vocational pattern—characterized by full-time, uninterrupted work—may shut women out of many careers. Institutions do not take into account that most women have children and grandchildren for whom they are primarily responsible, and thus women need to or want to take time out from full-time careers to raise children, go to school, and/or work part-time.

Traditional educational and occupational policies reflect the separation of work and family life and the societal expectation that mothers remain at home to care for their children. Thus a general incompatibility exists between the school and the workplace and family demands as well as the relative lack of provisions to ease women's integration of these roles. These conditions may be expected to produce greater potential stress and conflict among student and employed mothers, who hold the primary responsibility for child rearing and child care. Many universities and businesses have adopted family-oriented policies such as job sharing, flexible work hours, or employer-sponsored day care as an employee benefit. These organizations have found positive ramifications for the schools and businesses as well as for parents, including lower absenteeism, higher morale, positive publicity, lower rate of turnover, child care hours that conform to work hours, and access to quality infant and toddler day care (DeCenzo & Robbins, 1996).

As Veronica Nieva and Barbara Gutek (1982) stated in their conclusion to their book, *Women and Work:* "Virtually every institution in society must change to achieve equity at work" (p. 136).

Summary

Formal education is essential for providing girls and boys with the skills to become fully participating members of society. Traditionally, the educational system has favored boys and men over girls and women. Although a serious attempt is under way to remedy sexism in education, signs of sexism persist in various academic programs and in employment opportunities at the university or college level.

The workplace not only provides a means of making a living; it also gives the employed a sense of identity and self-worth. Several myths have evolved over the years about women workers. The ideas that women work only for extra pin money and that they lack the motivation to succeed in the workplace have been shown to be false. Women find discrimination to be common in the workplace. For example, the average woman worker earns only 60 cents compared to the average man worker's dollar. Also, a large proportion of women are forced into certain job categories, creating a type of low-paying and low-status job ghetto. Several social barriers—prejudice against women workers, the presence of gatekeepers, lack of informal groups, sexual harassment, and conflict between women's work roles and mother roles—continue to keep women in low-paying and low-status jobs.

The issue of comparable worth promises to be one of the most controversial social concerns for this decade. Businesses and the federal government appear to be blocking moves to implement equalizing salaries on the basis of a person's contributions rather than setting salaries according to job titles.

Studies have found that when jobs have similar duties and responsibilities but unequal pay, the higher-paying jobs are more likely to be held by men, while the lower-paying jobs employ more women.

Suggested Readings

Betz, N. (1993). Women's career development. In F. L. Denmark & M. Paludi (Eds.), *The psychology of women: A handbook of issues and theories.* Westport, CT: Greenwood Press.

Cheng, C. (Ed.). (1996). *Masculinities in organizations.* Thousand Oaks, CA: Sage.

Thomas, V., & Miles, S. (1995). Psychology of Black women: Past, present, and future. In H. Landrine (Ed.), *Bringing cultural diversity to feminist psychology: Theory, research, and practice.* Washington, DC: American Psychological Association.

Williams, C. (Ed.). (1993). *Doing "women's work": Men in nontraditional occupations.* Thousand Oaks, CA: Sage.

Religion and Politics

We must enable, nurture and encourage women to take part in the decision-making of the Catholic church. Women must continue to have a very visible role.

Fr. John Provost

By the close of the decade, women could have constituted an immensely powerful voting bloc—if only women's rights and other progressive leaders had mobilized their vast numbers. But in the 1980s, the backlash in the Capitol kept this historic political opportunity for women in check with a steady strafing of ostracism, hostility, and ridicule.

Susan Faludi

The religious need of the human mind remains alive, never more so.

Charlotte Perkins Gilman

What's Your Opinion?

How do you believe the Judeo-Christian tradition has affected our thinking about femininity and masculinity?

What do you think about Jesus Christ's message and actions that women are the equal of men in learning?

What barriers do you see preventing women's full political participation?

Do you believe in the "gender gap" in politics?

Few social institutions have as much influence on women and men as do religion and politics, even for those individuals who do not practice a religion or vote in elections. In this chapter, we will begin by examining the institution of religion. We will note how the Judeo-Christian tradition has affected our thinking about femininity and masculinity, with special attention to how religion has defined and treated women. Next, we will focus on politics. Here again, we will concentrate on how women, who only a little over 60 years ago won the right to vote, are now being seen as one of the most powerful voting blocs in our political system.

Religions and Gender Roles

Religion both advocates a status quo view of gender roles and provides support for society's patriarchal views of gender differences, thus endorsing various forms of gender discrimination (Neal, 1979; Ruether, 1974a). Susan Setta (1989) stated:

> *Religions provide symbols that appear real and that organize the individual's universe; therefore, they are powerful. The view that God's law prohibits passage of the ERA, for example, is self-validating. Those who hold this belief think no one should question what to them is obviously the inviolate will of God; all definitive statements on women have already been made.* (p. 84)

In this section, we will begin by examining the ways that women are presented in the Hebrew Bible (or what Christians refer to as the Old Testament). We then will move our discussion to the issue of early Christianity and examine how the liberating words and deeds of Jesus Christ soon faded into a misogynous treatment of women. And finally, we will examine some of the recent theological and social forces that are striving for full participation of women in church rituals and leadership positions.

Women in the Old Testament

A study of the Hebrew Bible is made especially difficult by the fact that it was written by several different authors during a period of time that spanned well over 1,000 years (approximately 1200 to 300 B.C.E.). Yet, some generalizations can be made. The most important fact is that the authors of the Hebrew Bible did not see the exposition of women's roles as a major feature of their writings. The Hebrew Bible was, first and foremost, a collection of books written about and for men. In the words of Scripture scholar, Phyllis Bird (1974), the Hebrew Bible was a "man's book":

> *For most of us the image of woman in the Old Testament is the image of Eve, augmented perhaps by a handful of Bible-story "heroines," or villainesses, as the case may be (Sarah, Deborah, Ruth, Esther, Jezebel, Delilah). Some may also perceive in the background the indistinct shapes of a host of unnamed mothers, who, silent and unacknowledged, bear all the endless genealogies of males. But it is the named women, by and large, the exceptional women, who supply the primary images for the usual portrait of the Old Testament woman. These few great women together with the first woman (curiously incompatible figures in most interpretations) fill the void that looms when we consider the image of woman in the Old Testament. For the Old Testament is a man's "book," where women appear for the most part simply as adjuncts of men, significant only in the context of men's activities.* (p. 41)

Within the Hebrew Bible then, we read of women being placed in positions of honor and respect right alongside men; in other places, we read of women being used in degrading and dehumanizing ways. For example:

I brought you up from the land of Egypt, and redeemed you from the house of bondage; and I sent before you Moses, Aaron, and Miriam. (Micah 6:4)

Everyone who curses his father or his mother shall be put to death. (Leviticus 20:9)

So God created man in his own image, in the image of God he created him; male and female he created them. (Genesis 1:27)

The men of the city, base fellows, beset the house about, beating on the door; and they said to the old man, the master of the house, "Bring out the man who came into your house, that we may know him." And the man, the master of the house, went out to them and said to them, "No, my brethren, do not act so wickedly . . . here are my virgin daughter and his concubine; let me bring them out now. Ravish them and do with them what seems good to you; but against this man do not do so vile a thing." (Judges 19:22–24)

If a woman conceives and bears a male child, then she shall be unclean seven days. . . . But if she bears a female child, then she shall be unclean two weeks. (Leviticus 12:2,5)

To better understand women's position in the Hebrew Bible, we need first discuss the controversy surrounding the two accounts of creation and then move on to a discussion of women's roles in the Hebrew Bible (Pagels, 1988).

The Creation Stories

Much of the controversy over women's status in the Hebrew Bible stems from the two views of creation as described in Genesis. In Genesis 1:27, we read: "And God created man to his own image; to the image of God he created him. Male and female he created them." Yet, in Genesis 2:22, we read: "And the Lord God built the rib which he took from Adam into a woman; and brought her to Adam."

Some contemporary writers have noted that the account of woman being made from Adam's rib and created second implies a degree of inferiority and subordination of women's status with respect to men's. Some authors have used this version to justify the idea of a husband's dominance over his wife (Sapp, 1977). Others, however, have noted a different interpretation of this passage (Swidler, 1976; Terrien, 1976), pointing out that being created second need not imply woman's inferior status:

In the early myth, woman is created as help and succor to man's loneliness. Far from denoting the idea of service in a subordinated position, the word "help" ('ezer) is generally applied to God, who is par excellence the succor of those in need and in despair. Woman is not a mere tool of physiological or psychological delight. She fulfills a function of creative complementariness. Without her, man is created incomplete. It is the woman who brings man to completion. Woman is presented as the completion of man's creation. She is not a secondary being inferior to man because, as some exegetes have thought in the past, she is created after him and out of him. The order of creation goes from the imperfect to the perfect. Woman constitutes the crowning of creation. (Terrien, 1976, p. 18)

Although we could debate the interpretations given to either one of the creation stories, the fact remains that in chapter 3 of Genesis, Eve is tempted by the serpent and is described as being chiefly responsible for women's and men's expulsion from paradise. God curses Eve because of her act and foretells her sufferings and her subjugation to man: "Unto the woman he said, I will greatly multiply thy sorrow and thy conception; in sorrow thou shalt bring forth children; and thy desire shall be to thy husband, and he shall rule over thee" (Genesis 3:16). Unfortunately, many people have used Genesis with its stories of creation and expulsion to support a misogynous view of woman.

The Two Periods in Jewish History

Setting aside the debate over the meaning of the two versions of creation, what can we make of the different views of women in various parts of the Hebrew Bible? One possible explanation lies in the extreme social changes that took place for the Jewish people during the sixth century B.C.E. Prior to the fall of Jerusalem (587 B.C.E.), Jewish women held a relatively high status within the Jewish community. Women were viewed in a rather positive fashion, as can be seen in the portrayal of them and the feminine presence in the *Song of Songs,* for example. During this period, women were primarily extolled for their wifely and motherly virtues. The dutiful and resourceful wife became the ideal for all Jewish women to emulate (Proverbs 31:10–31).

The Jewish woman was to make her home her life's center and her family her focus of attention. Granted, there were the few exceptional matriarchal women (e.g., Sarah, Rachel, and Rebeccah) mentioned in different places in the Hebrew Bible, but it is highly unlikely that these few and their extraordinary deeds were typical of the women of pre-exile Israel. In fact, the women of Israel during the pre-exile period were not treated as well as nor did they attain the status of many of their women contemporaries in other lands. For example, a wife in Egypt was often the head of the family, with the rights and obligations that such a position entailed. And in Babylon, a wife could acquire property and be party to contractual agreements. Yet, the status of the women of Israel was higher than other women in the region, such as those living in Assyria. During the pre-exile period, we can say that Jewish women's roles were sometimes valued less and sometimes valued more than were women's roles in other areas. But, given what is said of Jewish women in books written before the fall of Jerusalem, it does not seem warranted to suggest that Jewish women of this period were generally despised.

After the fall of Jerusalem (587 B.C.E.) and the rise and rigidification of Jewish laws, however, Jewish women's status fell. During these years, there was a change in how the Jewish nation viewed women in general. The Jewish nation became concerned with an awareness of sin and ritual cleanliness. The prophet Ezekiel spoke of sex and sexuality in terms of ritual uncleanness, not in terms of love. Ritual uncleanness became associated with physical contact with corpses, foreigners, and women.

In summary, we can say that the Hebrew Bible portrays a masculine and patriarchal world where women, before the fall of Jerusalem, are valued in their roles as dutiful wives and concerned mothers. After Jerusalem's fall, women are seen as the embodiment of sin and evil.

Women in the New Testament

The religious rituals of Judaism, the culture of the Hellenized Roman world, and of course, the teachings of Jesus Christ played a role in Christianity's early development. Jesus' views about women and his interactions with them showed that he broke with established Jewish traditions regarding women's place in society (Ketter, 1952). Jesus may have been what people today would call the first feminist (Swidler, 1971).

Yet, the early Christian church soon fell into a misogynous pattern, and many people have pointed to St. Paul's writings as being the basis for the antifemale approach taken by Christianity ever since that time. In this section we will concentrate first on Jesus and note how he redefined women's roles; we will then discuss the writings of St. Paul to see just how he dealt with the question of women's place in the early church.

Jesus Redefines Women's Roles

The exclusion of women from all but domestic duties was by Jesus' time a well-established norm within Jewish society. Women did, however, fare much better in Roman society, with many attaining a classical education and some even reaching positions of influence. In the pagan religions of the day, women held a prominent place and served as vestal virgins in many cults. In fact, many pagan religions were organized around women goddesses such as Isis and Astarte. But such was not the case in Judaism, which was organized around the monotheistic male figure Jahweh. By Jesus' time, Jewish women were seen strictly as obedient servants to their menfolk, and their primary duties were confined to the home. Yet, Jesus brought forth an entirely different view of femininity, one which caused much consternation among the Pharisees and his disciples, who evidenced the prevalent antifemale Jewish sentiment of the day. No account so graphically points to Jesus' radically different view of woman's place than does his encounter with the two sisters Mary and Martha.

In the course of their journey he came to a village, and a woman named Martha welcomed him into her house. She had a sister called

Mary, who sat down at the Lord's feet and listened to him speaking. Now Martha who was distracted with all the serving said, "Lord, do you not care that my sister is leaving me to do the serving all by myself? Please tell her to help me." But the Lord answered: "Martha, Martha," he said, "you worry and fret about so many things, and yet few are needed, indeed only one. It is Mary who has chosen the better part; it is not to be taken from her." (Luke 10:38–42)

It is this passage above all others in the New Testament that points out the extent to which Jesus chose to break with tradition over women's place in society. In this encounter, Jesus established a view of woman heretofore unacceptable in Jewish society. In describing this passage, Scripture scholar Constance Parvey (1974) noted:

The inclusion of this story about Jesus, unique to Luke's gospel, is the keystone of the changed status of women that it reflects. While previously the learning of Scriptures was limited to men, now it is opened to women. The story of Mary and Martha enabled women to choose. Mary departed from her ascribed role and was commended by Jesus for so doing. This meant that other women were encouraged to choose this new alternative: to be allowed, as were the young men, to learn the Scriptures at the feet of a rabbi. (p. 141)

Jesus' message and his actions are clear with respect to women: They are the equal of men in that most important aspect of Jewish life, that of learning. Women are to learn the message of the New Gospel and spread it just as Jesus commanded of men. The men around Jesus were not as accepting of women as he was. Let's now discuss one of the most influential followers of Jesus and one who many believe set the stage for the later antifemale sentiment and attitudes that swept the early Christian church: St. Paul.

St. Paul's Teachings about Women

The basis for many people's thinking that Paul was responsible for much of the antifemale sentiment in the early Christian church stems, for the most part, from his dealings with and preachings to the Christian congregation located in Corinth. At Corinth, Paul found tension and divisiveness among the Christian congregation, and much of it was attributed to the members who had been influenced by gnostic teachings. Speculation has it that many of these "troublesome" members spoke out and openly prophesized in the worship services, causing a rift in the congregation (Parvey, 1974). Jewish tradition specifically prescribed that women were to be silent and segregated in religious services, and at Corinth many women were acting in non-Jewish ways. Thus, Paul, probably frustrated by the errant ways of some of the congregation, took it upon himself to admonish the congregation:

Any man who prays or prophesies with his head covered dishonors his head, but any woman who prays or prophesies with her head unveiled dishonors her head—it is the same as if her head were shaven. (1 Corinthians 11:4–5)

   As in all the churches of the saints, the women should keep silence in the churches. For they are not permitted to speak, but should be subordinate, as even the law says. (1 Corinthians 14:34–35)

Rather than viewing those words as an attack against the women members of the Corinthian congregation, we may consider that Paul was rebuking the congregation's members—women and men—for their disorderly and indecent conduct in religious services. In the second quote, Paul forbids women to speak in the service, suggesting that he is following Jewish tradition, but later on he states: "So, my brethren, earnestly desire to prophesy, and do not forbid speaking in tongues; but all things should be done decently and in order" (1 Corinthians 14:39–40). There is no mention here that women should remain silent and restrained as many would think an antifemale stance would dictate.

   Yet, if we accept that Paul may not have been as misogynous as many believe him to have been (see Bristow, 1988; Rosenblatt & Witherup, 1996), how then can we account for all those who have pointed to his writings as the basis for the later church's antifemale practices and sentiments? Parvey (1974) argued:

> *The subordinated role of women in the Christian tradition is not so much a problem caused by Paul as it is a problem of how the Christian tradition has since chosen to interpret Paul. By using his dicta against women as a justification for maintaining the status quo, the Church has overlooked the new theology of men and women in Christ that was envisioned, and neglected these uniquely new theological formulations of 1 Cor. 11:11–12 and Gal. 3:28. With this neglect it lost its meaning for the continual transformation of itself from the old to the new creation.* (p. 137)

Women in the Early Church

During Christianity's first century, it seemed that women were drawn to the teachings of Jesus more than men were. We infer this because women are mentioned so prominently by the early commentators. Yet, because of the Jewish custom of the day, men's, not women's, activities should have received most of the attention of the early Christian writers. Thus, women must surely have played a larger role in the growth of the new church than many present-day Christians may think. Women are frequently mentioned in the Acts of the Apostles (e.g., Acts 13:50, 17:4, 12); for example, the woman called Lydia who lived in the town of Thyatira and was a dealer in purple dye (Acts 16:14–15). It is recorded that after she was converted by Paul, Lydia's entire household was baptized.

   Also, a number of women who are mentioned in Acts broke with Judaic tradition and behaved in characteristically nontraditional feminine ways. In fact, we read about several who chose the way of Mary and not of Martha by studying the Scriptures alongside men. Many wives joined their husbands to spread the Good News and became active in the public ministry. One of the more prominent husband-and-wife teams was Aquila and Priscilla, who worked with Paul (Acts 18:18, 26; 1 Corinthians 16:19). If we wish to have further proof of just how influential women were to the early Christian church, we need only note the miraculous account surrounding the death of the woman called Tabitha. Parvey (1974) believed Tabitha to have been one of the most important of all among the early Christians, namely, a disciple. She wrote:

> *There were also other women with special status, including one who was referred to as a "disciple"—a Jewish woman of independent means, a seamstress living in the Jewish city of Joppa, who was called Tabitha (also referred to as Dorcas) (Acts 9:36–43). Tabitha was evidently well known and admired for her charitable work, her fine craftsmanship as a seamstress and her graceful manner (Tabitha means "gazelle"). Like Paul and Barnabas, she was never named with "the Twelve." Unlike them, her designation as "disciple" has been minimized by the Church. Contrary to popular belief, there is no agreement in the New Testament itself as to how many disciples there actually were, or who they were. The term can imply one who is merely a follower, or it may refer to one who is under the instruction of a specific rabbi or teacher and part of a small elite group of his adherents. Whatever the specific significance of the title "disciple" as applied to Tabitha, she was felt to be so valuable to the Christian community in Joppa that many widows wept at her death and Peter rushed to her side from a neighboring town to raise her from the dead—the first such miracle performed by an apostle. To be recorded as raised from the dead, and to be the focus of the first such miracle by a fellow disciple, she must have been considered indispensable to the congregation. Her exact status remains unknown, but that she was much more than merely one of the many followers is clear from the story about her.* (pp. 144–145)

Yet, the early Christian community, with its concern over the immediacy of the Lord's return, soon gave way to the struggle between different versions and interpretations of the Scriptures. As we mentioned above, the influence of gnosticism proved most troublesome to many of the early church leaders. Probably one of the more serious rifts in the early church was over the image of God as female or male or both (Pagels, 1976). In fact, many of the early "heretical" gospels, for example, the Gospel of Thomas and the Secret Book of John, which were not accepted as "orthodox," mention a female presence in reference to the Deity. Many of the early Christians influenced by the gnostic traditions offered prayers that included both a female and a male presence. "From Thee, Father, and through Thee, Mother, the two immortal names, Parents of the divine being, and thou, dweller in heaven, mankind of the mighty name" (quoted in Pagels, 1976, p. 294).

As Setta (1989) argued, the masculine bias inherent in religious scholarship omitted women and the feminine from religion despite the fact that women have played prominent roles in the founding and practicing of religions from the ancient times to the present.

In earliest Christianity women were attracted to groups called Mary cults. Women were allowed full participation in such cults and worshiped Mary as God. Mary cults, such as the Marianites and Collyridians, began as early as the second century and continue to some extent into the present. In part, they developed in response to the absence of the feminine and female in the expression of Christianity. (p. 86)

The Early Church Fathers and Women

The growing conflict between Christian and gnostic teachings led many of the early church fathers to focus on the question of the natures of women and men. By the third and fourth centuries, the common Christian view of woman's nature was that she was not made in the image of God. Woman was incarnate evil and the cause of man's downfall. Woman could only be complete when she was united with a man in marriage. Augustine, one of the most influential of the early church fathers, noted:

How then did the apostle tell us that the man is the image of God and therefore he is forbidden to cover his head, but that the woman is not so, and therefore she is commanded to cover hers? Unless forsooth according to that which I have said already, when I was treating of the nature of the human mind, that the woman, together with her own husband, is the image of God, so that the whole substance may be one image, but when she is referred to separately in her quality as a helpmeet, which regards the woman alone, then she is not the image of God, but, as regards the man alone, he is the image of God as fully and completely as when the woman too is joined with him in one. (quoted in Ruether, 1974b, p. 156)

Tertullian, a church father of the second century, laid the blame for the fall of humankind entirely on the shoulders of Eve and all of her daughters. It was woman and woman alone who was to blame for sin and evil. Tertullian felt no compunction in preaching his antifemale beliefs, thus setting the stage for others to follow in one long litany of misogynous sentiment.

You are the Devil's gateway. You are the unsealer of that forbidden tree. You are the first deserter of the divine Law. You are she who persuaded him whom the Devil was not valiant enough to attack. You destroyed so easily God's image, man. On account of your desert, that is death, even the Son of God had to die. (quoted in Ruether, 1974b, p. 157)

By the fourth century B.C.E., misogyny already had become a staple feature of church doctrine. The liberating teachings of Jesus toward women were replaced by a patriarchal church structure that raised men to the level of the near-divine, while casting women in the role of adulteress and sin incarnate. However, during the fourth through tenth centuries, many women became involved to a large degree in the growing monastic movement. Some women even attained the position of abbess, which suggests that even though a patriarchal spirit was becoming entrenched in the church, some women still achieved high status within its hierarchal structures (McLaughlin, 1974).

Medieval and Reformational Times and Women

Over the centuries, Christian tradition and teachings became more and more misogynous. Thomas Aquinas stated that woman is a misbegotten man (McLaughlin, 1974; Winslow, 1976). According to Thomas, woman's inferiority to man is justified by the Genesis account of creation—the one relating that Eve was created after Adam and out of his rib. Eleanor McLaughlin (1974), a scholar in medieval history, interpreted Thomas's view of women's subordinate nature in the following manner:

> *Finally, as the Church takes her origin from Christ, so sacramentally it is proper that woman be formed of man. Her creation from the side rather than his head is a reminder that she is not to be despised. The subordination and inferiority of Eve—and therefore of all womankind—to the male are thus established before the Fall in the order of God's original creation: first, by reason of the primacy of Adam's creation, who was not only first in time and the founder of the human race but also the material source of the first woman; and second, by reason of finality, for Adam displays the peculiar end and essence of human nature, intellectual activity, whereas Eve's finality is purely auxiliary and summed up in her bodily, generative function.* (pp. 217–218)

One of the problems faced in the medieval church was the proliferation of women's convents. As their numbers grew, so did resentment toward religious women. By the end of the thirteenth century, the resentment toward religious women had grown to such proportions that men sought to justify their efforts to prevent women from joining the monastic life. The extent of misogynist sentiment toward church nuns can be seen in the following late-thirteenth-century church statement:

> *The iniquity of women surpasses all iniquities which are in the world, and that there is no wrath greater than the wrath of a woman, that the poisons of vipers and dragons are healthier and less harmful for men than familiarity with women . . . wanting to provide our descendants with things necessary for the well-being of their souls as well as their bodies, we shall receive under no condition any more sisters for the increase of our perdition, but rather we shall avoid accepting them as if poisonous beasts.* (quoted in McLaughlin, 1974, pp. 242–243)

Martin Luther protested not only the exclusion of God's people from religious ritual, but the church's stance on human sexuality and, indirectly, on the degradation of femininity. Rather than seeing celibacy as the perfect state, Luther championed marriage as the chosen state for the blessed. Luther, along with the other Protestant patriarchs like Knox and Calvin, believed that the institution of marriage was sacred but preached that women should remain submissive to men in all matters (Douglass, 1974); submission to her husband was paramount in the Reformation's view of marriage (Boyd, 1990). Even if a wife was mistreated and abused, she was to bear her sufferings in patience and silence, ever prayerful that her husband would desist from his brutalities by observing her example of humility and resignation (see chapter 7). When a woman sought counsel from John Calvin, for example, with the complaint of her husband's abuse, Calvin replied:

> *We have a special sympathy for poor women who are evilly and roughly treated by their husbands, because of the roughness and cruelty of the tyranny and captivity which is their lot. We do not find ourselves permitted by the Word of God, however, to advise a woman to leave her husband, except by force of necessity; and we do not understand this force to be operative when a husband behaves roughly and uses threats to his wife, nor even when he beats her, but when there is imminent peril to her life, whether from persecution by the husband or by his conspiring with the enemies of the truth, or from some other source . . . we exhort her . . . to bear with patience the cross which God has seen fit to place upon her; and meanwhile not to deviate from the duty which she has before God to please her husband, but to be faithful whatever happens.* (quoted in Douglass, 1974, pp. 300–301)

John Knox countered this trend with the opinion that women's nature was: "weak, fraile, impacient, feble, and foolishe; and experience hath declared them to be inconstant, variable, cruell, and lacking the spirit of counsel and regiment" (quoted in Douglass, 1974, p. 301).

The Reformationists' views on the nature of women seem to have been every bit as misogynous as their Roman predecessors. However, not all the Reformed churches held such antifemale beliefs. The sixteenth-century Anabaptists, for example, placed many women in high positions of authority within the church structure (Williams, 1978).

Thus, we see that in the formative centuries of Christianity, up until just a few centuries ago, women's status changed. Women went from a position of importance in early Christianity to a position of vilification during the patristic period, and finally to a position of some status accorded women as wives and mothers during the Reformation period. Overall though, women's treatment by religion has been one of extreme misogyny. George Albee (1984) summed up the treatment of women by religion over the centuries as follows:

> *In the name of religion, five hundred thousand women were burned alive as witches over the centuries. The world's major religions have perpetuated the most terrible barbarisms on women, as well as other forms of inequality and exploitation.* (p. 83)

Women and Religion Today

One of the controversial aspects of the nineteenth-century feminist movement was the debate over the inherent sexist treatment of women by established patriarchal religions. To draw attention to the inequities and injustices suffered by women, Elizabeth Cady Stanton, along with 23 scholars, wrote *The Woman's Bible* in two parts at the end of the last century.

Others have pushed the issues surrounding religion and women's roles in the church. Today, the question of ordination seems to be one of the most pressing theological concerns for many Christian denominations (Christ & Plaskow, 1979; Swidler & Swidler, 1977). In the last several years, some churches, including the United Methodist and Episcopalian congregations, have ordained women as ministers and as priests. In the Episcopal church, fewer than 800 women worldwide have been ordained. The question of women's ordination, however, has split the Episcopal church's hierarchy. For instance, the former Archbishop of Canterbury, the Most Reverend Robert Runcie, was opposed to any further women's ordinations because he thought it would damage the possibility of religious rapprochement with the Roman Catholic church. Among Jews, only a handful of women have taken up the Mary role by becoming rabbis in their own right. All of the women rabbis—fewer than 100—have come from the Reform group; among Orthodox and Conservative Jewish synagogues, no woman has ever achieved the position of rabbi. In the Roman Catholic church, the question of women's ordination remains one of the most contentious issues (Elizondo & Greenacher, 1980; Gardiner, 1976; Ruether, 1974a).

The possibility that the Roman Catholic church will ordain women to the priesthood seems very distant at present, given the stance against such a change taken by the recent popes. However, as more women venture into this male-dominated profession, research into their backgrounds and motivations will provide important insights into the role of women as ministers (Steward et al., 1983).

In addition to theological issues, other issues of importance to women are also becoming concerns for many theological scholars, issues such as abortion and relationships between women and men in general (Ruether & Bianchi, 1976; Russell, 1974; Schaef, 1981). The controversy over Sonia Johnson's stand on the Equal Rights Amendment is a case in point. Johnson, a Mormon, openly supported the ERA and was censured by the Mormon church for her position (Weathers & Lord, 1979). Research has shown that religious denominations that are more traditional in their theological teachings (e.g., the Baptist and Mormon churches) are more likely to discriminate against women's achievements in the workplace and support traditional roles for women (Rhodes, 1983).

In Presbyterian and Episcopal churches as well as in the United Church of Christ, women and men celebrate God as mother. As Setta (1989) concluded:

Rev. Pauli Murray. First Black woman ordained an Episcopal Priest, 1977.

AP/Wide World Photo.

This new image of women restores moral power and, in turn, removes any restrictions society places on women because of their moral inferiority. God's law, then, cannot forbid the Equal Rights Amendment because the Bible does not distinguish between the ethical capabilities of men and women. Thus, female imagery of the Divine empowers women both within their religious traditions and in the world at large. (p. 97)

In summary, we can conclude that religion, which is one of the more powerful social institutions, has looked generally upon women as the "other" or as a second-class participant in religious ritual. The exception to this pattern of discrimination against women may be found in the dissident religious-healing cults where many women have gained considerable power and influence (Finkler, 1981).

We see the Reverend Mary Schron, an Episcopal priest, celebrating a Eucharist service. Such scenes would have been impossible up until a few years ago. Although the number of women clergy is small, many believe that women clergy will become commonplace in the future.

AP/Wide World Photos.

Women, Men, and Religions Revisited

In this chapter we have discussed the Judeo-Christian tradition and its impact on gender, especially images of women. Other religious images of women should be noted. While we are all familiar with Mary, the mother of Jesus Christ, we may not be familiar with Kuan-Yin, a Buddhist Goddess of Mercy. Kuan-Yin became a goddess after earthly tragedies prevented her from becoming a wife and mother. Both images of virgin goddesses allow us to keep our negative views of female sexuality and power.

Islamic religions present a social order that depends on caste differences because of an individual's sex. Thus, men worship in the mosque; women must be veiled from head to toe so that no part of her body is exposed as she leaves her home to go outside. This behavior of leaving the home to enter the public sphere, by the way, is discouraged in traditional Islam.

Muslim societies have not considered women and men as equal, especially in the context of marriage. However, one gets a very different view of women and men by reading the Qur'an, which in Muslim religion is the Book of Revelation believed by Muslims to be the Word of God. One passage from the Qur'an is as follows:

For Muslim men and women,
For believing men and women,

For devout men and women,
For true men and women,
For men and women who are
Patient and constant, for men
And women who humble themselves,
For men and women who give
In Charity, for men and women
Who fast (and deny themselves),
For men and women who
Engage much in God's praise,
For them has God prepared
Forgiveness and great reward.
(Surah 23; Al-Ahzab 35; The Holy Qur'an, 1116–17)

The Qur'an makes it clear that women and men are equal in the sight of God and that they are members and protectors of each other. Thus, according to Riffat Hassan (1994):

> . . . *the Qur'an does not create a hierarchy in which men are placed above women (as they are by many formulators of the Christian tradition), nor does it pit men against women in an adversary relationship. They are created as equal creatures of a universal, just, and merciful God whose pleasure it is that they live—in harmony and in righteousness—together* (pp. 53–54)

Muslim societies have rejected the Qur'an discussion of equality between the sexes because they believe women are inferior in creation; Muslims believe a woman was made from a crooked rib of a man (Hassan, 1994).

Negative views of women are also promoted in other religions. For example, the yin and yang in Chinese religion refers to the following: the yin is the feminine side and represents darkness and evil; the yang, the masculine side, represents goodness and light. In the Hindu religion, a woman is defined in terms of her husband, as we discussed in chapter 5. Consequently, an unmarried woman or a widow is not portrayed as having an identity.

Also in the Hindu religion, the goddess Kali is portrayed as a dark monster with a blood-stained tongue, face, and breasts as well as crossed eyes and fanged teeth. Kali is seen as destructive to the world unless she submits to her husband, who in turn helps her to harness her energy, and she thus does good deeds. Lina Gupta (1994) described Kali in the following way:

> *The myth of Kali offers a story of a woman in a plight. She is the personified wrath of all women in all cultures. . . . Kali's anger is an expression of a deep, long-buried emotion, a character trait that symbolizes deep emotional response to her situations and surroundings. She is not simply malevolent. Her "terrifying howls" are also a demand for equality where femininity is equated with meekness and subservience, since such anger is the only language that can be heard.* (p. 31)

The following are passages from Manu Samhita (Laws of Manu) that explain the basic rules of conduct for Hindu women, including dependency:

> *Let the [husband] employ his [wife] in the collection and expenditure of his wealth, in keeping [everything] clean, in [the fulfillment] of religious duties, in the preparation of his food, and in looking after the household utensils.* (Manu, 329)
>
> *She who drinks spirituous liquor or is of bad conduct, rebellious, diseased, mischievous, or wasteful, may at any time be superseded by another wife.* (Manu, 341)
>
> *Her father protects [her] in childhood; her husband protects [her] in youth; and her sons protect [her] in old age; a woman is never fit for independence.* (Manu, 328)

We must also recognize that spirituality movements have blossomed in which ancient goddesses are rediscovered or reinvented and thus the female nature of the divine is celebrated (Culpepper, 1994; Eller, 1993).

In many races, spirituality is central to individuals' lives. For example, American Indian women of the Cahuilla tribe reflect an understanding shared by Navajo and Sioux holy women and men that spiritual and emotional health cannot be made distinct (Benally, 1992). However, Western psychology has typically not dealt with spirituality. The lack of attention to this issue has been recently noted by Theresa LaFromboise and her colleagues (1995). They interpret the lack of attention to understanding spirituality to an "historic hostility toward things spiritual in general and a suspicion of clients who are highly religious" (p. 213). LaFromboise and colleagues call for more attention to be paid to the importance of spirituality in individuals' lives and for a valuing of a diversity of forms of religious expressions.

Politics and Gender

In this section, we will concentrate on politics and see how women, for the most part, have been systematically denied access to political power. We will begin by reviewing the history of women in political movements, ranging from women's involvement in the Revolutionary War up to the current debate over the impact of women's preferences in political matters, known as the *gender gap*. Next we will discuss some of the important barriers erected to hinder women's full participation in politics.

Women in Politics

In American politics, men have made decisions and passed laws that to a great extent took little notice of or had little concern for women's lives and realities. However, women's presence has been felt at various times in the early political arenas.

The Revolutionary Period and Women's Involvement

As the early patriots' resistance toward England's control of the colonies grew, colonial women became increasingly involved in the resistance movement. A good example of women's involvement is that colonial women banded together to form the Daughters of Liberty (Kerber, 1980). The Daughters of Liberty met in public to spin cloth and to encourage other women to make their own cloth, thus ending America's dependence on imported English cloth (Deckard, 1983). The public statements and actions of the Daughters of Liberty served as an example to encourage others to stand up against English domination.

Colonial women not only made their own cloth as a patriotic and political gesture against England's interference; they also "lobbied" against the consumption of tea. Women from all over the colonies met in small groups to pledge an end to the use of English tea. One way that many colonial women used to discourage tea drinking was the trading of recipes for tea substitutes, such as coffee. One of the better-known colonial protest groups came from North Carolina and became known as the Edenton Ladies Tea Party. Women met not to discuss tea, but rather to discuss various ways they could break England's grip over the colonies (Norton, 1980).

After war finally broke out, many colonial men spent long periods away from their homes. Consequently, their wives took over the duties of running the homes and farms. Before the war, what was expected of women and men was usually defined in traditional terms: Women were to keep the home and children, while men were to tend to the "outdoor affairs," the traditional public sphere/private sphere split. The war placed a great strain on family relations because of the long separations of married couples, and it also began to erode the traditional separation of gender-role related activities.

At the war's outbreak, Abigail Adam's "raised consciousness" of the inferior status of colonial women prompted her to speak out about the injustice perpetrated on women. She desired that the "revolution against tyranny" would lead to a new social and political order where the rights of all free people—women as well as men—would be guaranteed. In the early spring of 1776, she wrote to her husband of her concerns:

> *In the new codes of laws which I suppose it will be necessary for you to make I desire you would remember the ladies, and be more generous and favorable to them than your ancestors. Do not put such unlimited power into the hands of husbands. Remember all men would be tyrants if they could. If particular care and attention is not paid to the ladies we are determined to foment a rebellion, and will not hold ourselves bound by any laws in which we have no voice, or representation.* (quoted in Bartlett, 1980, p. 392)

After the war, Americans had a new definition of what was appropriate for women's roles. Never again could people assert with such assuredness that a woman could not handle the day-to-day tasks of running a farm or the many other duties of keeping a house without the assistance of a man. The question of women's rights, however, did not start a "rebellion" as promised in Abigail Adams's letter to her husband some years earlier.

Ironically, when the New Jersey state constitution was drawn up in 1776, it loosely defined the category of voter to include "all free inhabitants" who met specific property qualifications. Thus, for some years, property-holding single women and widows had the right to vote in New Jersey's elections. However, in 1807 the state legislature saw fit to rescind the woman's vote. The reason given by the all-men assembly was that they feared that women were too easily manipulated.

Thus the Revolutionary War set the stage for a new definition of the gender roles in America. After the war, it was abundantly clear that the situation warranted it. Although few dramatic changes with respect to gender roles occurred in the everyday lives of those of the new republic, the grip of popular wisdom on what constituted women's behavior was broken, and in the not-too-distant future, women were to once again champion their cause in the political arena.

The Rise of Feminism

Although we will examine the history of the feminist movement in greater detail in chapter 11, we need to point out here that beginning in the 1830s and 1840s, many women participated in politics. The path leading to women's political involvement came by way of religion. Around the early 1800s, a religious movement called the *Second Great Awakening* began. The religious fervor of this movement was based on an emotional outpouring of one's belief, rather than on a serious study of doctrine. The religious experience known as *conversion* came about through an emotional release prompted by the group's support. Revivals were noted for their "loud ejaculations of prayer, . . . some struck with terror, . . . others, trembling, weeping and crying out . . . fainting and swooning away, . . . others surrounding them with melodious songs, or fervent prayers for their happy resurrection, in the love of Christ" (quoted in Norton et al., 1982, p. 186).

The religious fervor of the Second Great Awakening found special favor among women (Cott, 1975; Douglas, 1977; Welter, 1974). Women, who were thought more emotional than men by conventional wisdom, dominated the religious services. In the name of salvation, they began to speak out in public and to organize among themselves. Consequently, women learned valuable techniques that would serve them well later on in their struggle for their own rights. Before these women took up the issue of women's rights, however, many turned their attention to the crusade to end slavery. Large numbers of women publicly supported the antislavery cause and advocated an end to the misery and injustice suffered by black people. Two of the more outspoken female abolitionists were Angeline Grimke and Sarah Grimke. The Grimke sisters traveled extensively, speaking against slavery. When they met severe criticism because they "dared" speak before mixed groups of women and men, the Grimke sisters noted that the criticism was not, for the most part, directed at their abolitionist message, but rather at what many considered their impudence—women who were so reckless as to speak out in public before men. The idea that women should be silent and subordinate before men left these two crusaders angered at the unfair treatment accorded to women. In 1838, Sarah Grimke wrote a powerful tract that was included in the now famous *Letters on the Condition of Women and the Equality of the Sexes* that called specifically for women's rights (Lerner, 1975).

A turning point in women's political involvement with respect to their own rights came in 1840 when the World Anti-Slavery Convention met in London. Abolitionists from around the British empire and the United States met to support a worldwide ban on slavery. Among the convention's participants were some of the most active and well-known women abolitionists of the day: Lydia Maria Child, Maria Weston Chapman, Lucretia Mott, and others. When women delegates sought seating in the main auditorium, they were refused. The convention ruled that it would be unseemly for such "delicate" women to sit with men; therefore, women were relegated to sit "behind a bar and curtain, where they could observe the proceedings without being viewed by the participants" (Wagner, 1984, p. 35). Consequently, many of the women in attendance returned to the United States determined that women needed to fight for their own cause.

Thus, the battle for women's rights began when women abolitionists found themselves attacked by friend and foe alike for the cause of antislavery. In 1848, the first convention to deal specifically with the women's issue was held in Seneca Falls, New York. Over the next 70 years, women fought ceaselessly to win their American right to vote. The battle took many forms, and women soon learned that a simple appeal for justice was not sufficient to sway others' opinions of the righteousness of their cause. American feminists took lessons from their English sisters and used unconventional tactics such as public marches and open protests to get their message—the injustices suffered by women at the hands of men—across to the public (Hurwitz, 1978).

Women did not win the vote until 1920 with the passage of the Nineteenth Amendment to the Constitution, but there were some small gains during the previous decades of struggle. For example, in 1869 the state of Wyoming granted women the right to vote. However, Wyoming did not accord women their right as citizens for any but the most selfish of reasons. Specifically, Wyoming in the 1860s was in dire need of women, and those in charge of state politics thought suffrage would attract more women to their state (Deckard, 1983; Flexner, 1971). Although the years from 1850 to 1920 found feminist-oriented women concentrating on winning the vote, many women got directly involved with other political and social issues, ranging from unionism to socialism (Buhle, 1980; Dye, 1980).

During the years spanning the decades from 1830 to 1920, women had learned much about how politics worked. From those early years when women stood up at religious revivals and publicly proclaimed their conversions, to some 60 years later when they organized, marched, picketed, and attacked the male-dominated institutions in order to win a better life for all women, women found that the game of politics could be played by women as well as by men (Kraditor, 1971).

The decades after the passage of the Nineteenth Amendment found the feminist movement without a cause. With so much energy expended on the single issue of vote, after the battle was won, many within the suffrage movement lost interest in continuing the fight for other women's issues. The promise of many of the early feminist pioneers that politics would become more humane and responsive to the country's well-being by including women's votes proved rather baseless (Scharf, 1980; Ware, 1981).

During the immediate years following passage of the suffrage amendment, some women found themselves in high political positions. Some even attained the governor's seat of their respective states. Women like Miriam "Ma" Ferguson of Texas (elected in 1924 and 1932), Nellie Taylor Ross of Wyoming (elected in 1925), and Lurleen Wallace of Alabama (elected in 1966) all served as their states' highest elected political officials. These women's accomplishments may be seen as somewhat muted when we note that Ferguson served because of the popularity of her husband, who was impeached as governor of Texas, Ross served out the unexpired term of her dead husband, and Wallace served because Alabama's state constitution prohibited her husband from seeking reelection. Thus, each of these three women came to the office of governor through marriage.

It was 1974 when Ella Grasso of Connecticut finally won a governor's seat on her own merit without first being married to a governor. Soon after, other women won governor seats, including Dixie Lee Ray, Martha Layne Collins, Madeleine Kunin, Christine Todd Whitman, and Ann Richards.

Additional examples also attest to women's emergence into the political sphere. In 1981, Sandra Day O'Connor became the first woman Supreme Court justice. Ironically, O'Connor, who graduated in the top 10 percent of her law class at Stanford University in the early 1950s, could not find a position in any of the law firms in San Francisco or Los Angeles after graduation because of the long-standing tradition of not hiring women. She was, however, offered a job as a legal secretary. In 1993 Ruth Bader Ginsburg became the second woman to be seated on the Supreme Court.

Other women who have gained power in the political arena include Kim Campbell, the first female prime minister of Canada; Betsy McCaughy Ross, Lieutenant Governor of New York; Congressperson Patricia Schroeder; U.S. Senator Carol Moseley Braun; and U.S. Senator Olympia Snowe.

The reemergence of the women's movement in the 1960s focused many women's attention on politics. In the past several years, in fact, we have heard about the emergent political clout of women in terms of the gender gap. Let us now take a look at this political phenomenon and see to just what extent women are changing the rules of the political game.

The Gender Gap

Soon after the 1980 elections, political analysts quickly pointed out the emergence of what has become known as the *gender gap*. At the heart of the gender gap phenomenon is the fact that since the early 1980s, women have in increasing numbers registered as Democrats rather than as Republicans. Furthermore, women were found more critical of former President Reagan's policies than men were.

Specifically, in a May 1982, *New York Times*/CBS Poll, 55 percent of the women surveyed identified themselves with the Democratic party and only 34 percent with the Republican party. The same poll found that 49 percent of the men who were questioned identified themselves as Democrats and 37 percent as Republicans (Lynn, 1984). Regarding policy issues, women, more so than men, took a more critical view of Reagan's job performance. Only 41 percent of all women approved of Reagan's presidential performance, while 50 percent of all men approved (Lynn, 1984). Women's more pronounced dissatisfaction over Reagan and their disenchantment with the Republican party, coupled with the fact that women under age 45 tend to vote more regularly than do similar-aged men, suggested a possible problem for the Republican party and a potential boon for the Democratic party in future elections.

However, finding women differing from men on various political issues is not something that just sprung up in the 1980s. Women's disenchantment with the Republican party may be a new phenomenon, but American women's political views have differed from men's for some years. Ever since the 1950s, as a matter of fact, larger numbers of women than men have registered their displeasure over such issues as political corruption, the Vietnam War, military expansionism, and the misuse of the environment (Baxter & Lansing, 1980; Lynn, 1975; Melich, 1995; Rossi, 1982, 1983).

The political future of the major political parties and their candidates appears to be in the hands of women if women will vote in the numbers they represent. Beginning with the 1984 elections and continuing with those to come, women will have the numbers to decide who will govern and who will not.

The gender gap, however, did not carry the Democratic party to victory in 1984 as many predicted. Although more women voted than men as expected (53 percent versus 47 percent, respectively) a majority of women voted for Reagan rather than Mondale (57 percent versus 42 percent, respectively) (*The New York Times*/CBS Poll, 1984). Why women did not support the Mondale-Ferraro ticket in greater numbers is an open question. Speculating on women's support for Reagan, Ann Lewis, political director of the Democratic National Committee, noted that women are affected by an expanding economy every bit as much as are men and that it appears a majority of voting women supported the status quo and were influenced by pocketbook issues rather than any so-called women's issues (*The New York Times*, 1984). All that can be said for the moment is that we will have to wait for future elections to see if the gender gap proves as potent a political force as many have thought.

A recent report from the National Women's Political Caucus (Kalis, 1996), which detailed the 1990, 1992, and 1994 elections, suggests that Republicans won't attract a significant number of women voters simply by producing more women candidates. According to Kalis:

> *In nearly every race, a majority of women preferred the Democratic candidate, regardless. . . . For example, given a choice between two men, more women voted Democratic, with average gender gaps of 5.4 percentage points in the 89 Senate races and 4.8 points in the 76 gubernatorial races. Women leaned ever further toward the Democrats when the candidate was female; the gap increased by slightly more than three points in both cases. When the Republican was a woman, the tendency for women to vote Democratic shrank but did not disappear. . . . In the three election years studied, there were 17 contests pitting a male Democrat against a female Republican. In only four of those races did a majority of women vote Republican, and in three of those cases the Republican was an incumbent . . . , a known quantity running for a new office . . . , or both.*

Political Barriers and Women Politicians

Several surveys of Americans' willingness to vote for a qualified woman presidential candidate have found that approximately eight out of every ten women and men would do so. Yet, the question is not so much whether Americans will vote for women, but rather, whether there will be sufficient numbers of qualified women candidates for public office. If female gender is not a liability in seeking public office (Lynn, 1984), then why are there so few qualified women in the political process?

The answer lies in the simple fact that historically women have found significantly more social and institutional barriers preventing them from seeking public office than men have. In this section we will note some of the more common and significant barriers preventing women from moving into the political arena in larger numbers.

Socialization and Political-Oriented Traits

We have noted in previous discussions that women and men are socialized toward different goals (see chapter 8). Politics is generally not seen as a career goal for most women (nor for most men, for that matter). Could there be certain personality traits that men, more so than women, are socialized to exhibit that would increase men's chances of entering politics? One such trait that seems a likely candidate for a gender difference is ambition.

Jeane Kirkpatrick (1976) in her classic study of the 1972 participants in the national political conventions noted that, "in both parties, in all candidate groups, and in all age cohorts women had significantly lower levels of

Senator Nancy Kassebaum
© John Nordell/The Image Works

Senator Olympia Snowe
REUTERS/CORBIS-BETTMANN

Governor Christine Todd Whitman
© Stephen Jaffe/The Image Works

Senator Diane Feinstein
© Stephen Jaffe/The Image Works

Congressperson Susan Molinari
© Stephen Jaffe/The Image Works

Senator Carol Mosley-Braun
AP/WIDE WORLD PHOTOS

ambition for public office than men" (p. 411). Other researchers have noted a similar gender difference with respect to women and men politicians (Farah, 1976; Jennings & Farah, 1978). To put up with the demands of running for political office requires that the candidate truly wants to be victorious. In other words, a political candidate must be ambitious and desirous of victory if s/he is to win political office nowadays. In contrast, other more recent research has not found any evidence that women politicians, as a group, are less ambitious than men politicians (Merritt, 1982).

One critical difference, however, has been found between women and men politicians. As a group, women tend to be more public-minded or public-spirited in their approach to political involvement than men are. Men appear more self-serving in their style and approach to politics (Kirkpatrick, 1974; Lynn & Flora, 1977; Merritt, 1982). Finding women more public-minded than men may have far-reaching consequences for the future of our political system. We might suspect that just on an intuitive basis, the public-minded politician may be a more conscientious politician, putting the good of all before self-serving and narrow-minded interest groups' needs.

Structural Barriers to Women Politicians

Most politicians come from groups like the business community and certain professions like law. Geraldine Ferraro, for example, went to law school at night while she was a school teacher and earned a law degree. Consequently, she obtained a position in a large city prosecutor's office, a position that is often a springboard into politics. Thus part of the reason that so few women political candidates have emerged is the limited numbers of women found in what can be described as "political pools" (Welch, 1978). As more women enter the business world and various politically oriented professions (e.g., law), we should see the numbers of women political candidates increase.

Another barrier that prevents women from entering politics is the "gatekeeper" phenomenon. As we discussed in the employment section (chapter 8), gatekeepers are individuals who have the position and power to keep certain groups out of their professions. Over the years, political party leaders, the *de facto* gatekeepers of the political arena, have prevented many well-qualified women from entering politics (Keohane, 1981). On the other hand, a powerful gatekeeper can help launch a political newcomer. Such was the case when House Speaker Thomas O'Neill helped persuade Walter Mondale to choose Geraldine Ferraro as his vice-presidential running mate in 1984.

Still another barrier facing many young women who may be interested in politics is the lack of women politicians as role models and mentors. The limited number of women, especially married women with families, who have successfully blended a political career with family life may prove a handicap for prospective women candidates. As the lives of political women like Geraldine Ferraro, Dianne Feinstein, Elizabeth Holtzman, Lindy Boggs, Juanita Kreps, Nancy Kassebaum, Elaine Noble, Elizabeth Dole, and Rose Bird become better known, and as people become aware of how these and other women have woven politics and family life together, it is hoped that more women will step forward and throw their hats into the political ring.

Situational Barriers to Women Politicians

The motherhood role is still one of the most important elements of women's identity. Naomi Lynn and Cornelia Flora (1977) found that motherhood was an especially difficult barrier preventing many women from pursuing political office. The odd hours and constant demands on time that are required of the politician create special problems, especially for women with children.

Another problem faced by many women is their relationships with their husbands. One's spouse can either help or hinder one's progress in pursuit of

one's goals. The media's concern over Geraldine Ferraro's husband's (John Zaccaro) finances proved just this point. At times during the early months of the 1984 campaign, Ferraro's campaign took a backseat to questions of her husband's business dealings. One irate columnist wrote: "Most married women who will run for office in the future will have husbands involved in a business or a profession, a government job or another political office. Will the husband's work and his other interests forever dominate and take precedence over a female candidate's own background and qualifications?" (Kassell, 1984). The answer was definitely yes in Ferraro's unsuccessful bid for political office.

There are no valid reasons that women cannot enter politics. Nor are there any reasons that once they have entered the political arena, women cannot pursue a prolonged career of service to their community and their country, a career that is every bit as distinguished as any man's. The problem is, however, that prescriptive gender roles, various structural barriers, and some potent situational barriers all conspire to keep the numbers of dedicated political women low.

For example, in 1995, the 104th Congress abolished the bipartisan Congressional Caucus on Women's Issues along with the Congressional Black and Hispanic Caucuses. These caucuses provided essential policy analysis regarding the impact of public policy proposals on women, African Americans, and Hispanics, respectively. They also provided a strong voice of advocacy for women and men on workplace, education, and health issues.

A 1996 *Ladies Home Journal* poll reported that the majority of the 1,002 women polled are unhappy about politics, but are not ready to give up on government:

> *Women's frustration, the survey shows, stems from their belief that government can and should play a more active role in helping families. . . . What women want, the poll results suggest, is a government that is more responsive to their concerns.* (Weir, 1996, p. 5)

As many of these barriers weaken and give way, it is hoped that more women and individuals of color will move into the political ranks, where their presence may make a discernible difference in the quality of our lives. We need an electorate that is representative of the nation.

Summary

Our views of how women and men should relate have been shaped to a large degree by the Hebrew and Christian Bibles. Generally speaking, early Judaic traditions glorified women in their wifely and motherly roles. However, this view was changed around the fifth century B.C.E., after which women were portrayed as unclean and were to be kept separate from men.

The teachings and behavior of Jesus Christ added a new dimension to women's roles by supporting their involvement with learning. The writings of Paul were used by many later Christian leaders to support their antifemale stance. Although the leaders of the Reformation took a more positive view of marriage, they still supported a strict interpretation of women's subordination to men, especially in marriage. Today, controversy continues about women's place in religious matters, and more women than ever before are pushing for total equality in religious matters.

Politics has usually been a men-only pursuit. However, women have been involved in various political actions since colonial revolutionary times. During the nineteenth century, women played a significant role in the abolitionist movement, which ultimately led women to work for their own suffrage.

Today, women are a powerful force in politics as the recent attention to the gender gap shows. Still, many structural and situational barriers exist to keep women from running for political office.

Suggested Readings

Boyd, S. B. (1995). *The men we long to be: Beyond domination to a new Christian understanding of manhood*. San Francisco: Harper.

Cooey, P., Eakin, W., & McDaniel, J. (1994). *After patriarchy: Feminist transformations of the world religions*. Maryknoll, NY: Orbis Books.

Melich, T. (1995). *The Republican war against women*. New York: Bantam.

Nelson, J. B. (1988). *The intimate connection: Male sexuality, masculine spirituality*. Philadelphia: Westminister Press.

Neuman, N. (1996). *A voice of our own: Leading American women celebrate the right to vote*. New York: Jossey Bass.

Paloutzian, R. (1996). *Invitation to the psychology of religion*. Needham Heights, MA: Allyn & Bacon.

Health and Gender

10

Since clinicians and researchers, as well as their patients and subjects, adhere to a masculine standard of mental health; women, by definition, are viewed as psychiatrically impaired simply because they are women.

Phyllis Chesler

Feminist analyses of women's health reaffirm that "the personal is political." Often what might initially be viewed as biologically impersonal and objective is embedded in a social and political context. Thus, whether an Egyptian woman carries the burden of schistosomiasis, or an Indian woman suffers pesticide poisoning, or a homeless New York woman contracts HIV infection is shaped not only by access to medical care, but also by sociocultural factors.

Carol Travis

Today, in countries with Westernized medical systems, gender . . . strongly affects health and longevity not through physiological factors but through different work and family responsibilities, risk-taking, health and illness behavior, and marital and economic status. Women tend to have more illnesses and to see physicians more often because of the stresses of routinized jobs, child care, care of elderly parents, and the "double day" of work and housework. Men are more prone to chronic and life-threatening diseases, such as heart attacks, but tend to be healthier mentally and physically if they are married than married women are.

Judith Lorber

What's Your Opinion?

How would you describe a mentally healthy adult man? a mentally healthy adult woman?

Why do you think more women than men are diagnosed with a mental disorder?

How do you explain the research finding that married women report more depression than single women and that single men report more depression than married men?

Are you living a healthy lifestyle?

What do you like and dislike about your physique? Do you believe you are engaging in unhealthy practices in order to achieve the "ideal" physique? What is an "ideal" physique?

In general, people seem apprehensive, anxious, and emotionally upset when a society's status quo is challenged or disrupted. In the past decade or so, many women and men have experienced considerable personal strain because society's traditional gender roles have been challenged from many sides. Consequently, we need to discuss the issues of mental health and mental illness as they relate to gender role stereotypes and gender role expectations. We must also discuss physical health, including diseases commonly related to the sex of an individual, such as breast diseases for women and prostate cancer for men.

In this chapter we will begin our discussion of gender and health by examining differences in the incidence of women and men who are diagnosed and treated for various mental illnesses. Then we will discuss the charge that therapy is biased against women. We will focus our attention on nonsexist and feminist therapies.

We will then discuss physical health concerns, including gender comparisons in mortality and morbidity rates, eating disorders, and prostate cancer.

Mental Health

Sex Ratios and Mental Illness

The research on mental illness suggests that women are diagnosed and treated for mental illness at a much higher rate than men (Chesler, 1972; Dohrenwend & Dohrenwend, 1976; Rohrbaugh, 1979). However, the finding that more women than men are diagnosed and treated for mental and emotional problems must be viewed cautiously. As a matter of record, from the turn of the century until the early 1960s, men outnumbered women in mental health treatment facilities (Al-Issa, 1982; Cleary, 1987; Schowalter, 1985).

Why, then, has the trend reversed so that more women than men are now diagnosed and treated for various mental disorders? Several explanations have been suggested. One possibility is that women are not more mentally ill than men, but simply more likely to exhibit behaviors that others are apt to label as mental illness. Many women, for example, have been taught that they should be emotional, while most men have been taught the opposite (see chapter 3). A person who is emotionally expressive may be perceived as disturbed or troubled. If women are encouraged to express their emotions, and they express feelings of sorrow or sadness, for example, some individuals may quickly come to the conclusion that women are more readily predisposed to emotional disorders. Men, on the other hand, are taught from their early years to suppress their emotional expressions. According to this perspective, then, it

is little wonder that women may be seen as displaying more emotional problems than men simply because women have been taught to express themselves in this way. The difference in the rates of mental illness could be related to the possibility that men disguise or will not admit their emotional
problems, whereas women freely discuss them.

A second explanation for the gender difference in the diagnosis of mental
illness concerns women's unequal social position and greater discrimination.
Many women are more likely to experience certain trauma-producing events
(e.g., incest, sexual harassment, rape, and marital abuse) to a greater degree
than men (Paludi, 1997). The abuse many women experience may precipi-
tate their emotional problems. Furthermore, many employed mothers not
only have to deal with discrimination in their workplaces but also must contend with the workload of housekeeping and child-rearing. Many women
find themselves doing "double duty" in the workplace and at home, which
can cause some to experience greater personal strain than their husbands
(Russo & Greene, 1993).

Women who are single heads of households are at high risk for stress.
The interface of gender, ethnicity, and race is particularly salient here. For
example, among Hispanics, Puerto Ricans have had the highest proportion of
families headed by women (44 percent), followed by Central/South Americans (21.9 percent), Mexican Americans (18.6 percent), and Cubans (16 percent) (Amaro & Russo, 1987).

Deborah Belle (1984) noted the impact of ethnicity and low income on
women's depressive symptomatology. In one study, Belle and her colleagues
found that their sample of 42 urban low-income mothers had personally experienced 37 violent events and witnessed 35 stressful events to family and
friends during the preceding two years. Brown (1995) suggested that inadequate housing, dangerous neighborhoods, and financial concerns are more
serious stressors than acute crises.

Theresa LaFromboise and her colleagues (1995) pointed out that adolescent American Indian girls are a particularly vulnerable population. They are
six times more likely to be sexually abused than are American Indian boys,
more prone to depression than boys and more likely to be suicidal. Furthermore, the incidence of female alcohol abuse is high. In fact, the death rate of
Indian women from chronic liver disease and cirrhosis exceeds the rate of Indian, African American, Hispanic, Asian, and white men. LaFromboise and
colleagues offer this interpretation of those findings:

> *The impact of the welfare culture and the . . . losses can be identified at
> the individual level by feelings of victimization attributable to racism
> and stereotyping, value conflicts, or confusion, isolation, and oppres-
> sion. Unresolved grief overlosses and effects of ongoing cultural genocide
> are often presented by clients in the form of chronic cycles of crisis and
> depression.* (p. 201)

Some categories of women are more likely to be diagnosed and treated for
mental illnesses. For example, married women have a higher rate of mental

illness than married men, but single men have a higher rate of mental illness than single women. Jeanne Marecek (1978) explained this difference by noting that many married women experience a loss of status and autonomy as well as difficulties associated with being a mother, all of which can create severe stress and lead to emotional problems. Jessie Bernard (1975) suggested that women in general are taught from childhood to be more dependent on others. Consequently, many women have a large part of their self-identities tied to their ability to successfully establish intimate relationships. If for some reason the intimate relationship ends, a woman may experience emotional problems as a consequence of thinking herself a failure as a woman.

Men, on the other hand, are not as likely to define themselves in terms of their relationships with others. If relational problems develop, men may blame others rather than themselves for the relational breakups.

Another possible explanation for women's greater incidence of mental illness was proposed by Phyllis Chesler (1972). Chesler suggested that women in our society are in a "double bind" situation when it comes to their mental health. According to Chesler, women can be labeled as emotionally disturbed for either overconforming or underconforming to feminine gender role stereotypes. In other words, a woman who is overdependent, too emotional, and less rational is overconforming to the traditional feminine gender role stereotype. On the other hand, a woman who is independent, puts her career ahead of family interests, doesn't express emotions, and acts in a worldly and self-confident manner is one who is underconforming to feminine gender role stereotypes. In either case, the woman may be thought disturbed.

Support for this position also comes from a reanalysis of Sigmund Freud's "Case of Dora." In 1905, Freud published a paper entitled "Fragment of an Analysis of a Case of Hysteria." This "case of hysteria" is better known in psychology as the Case of Dora. Dora was an 18-year-old woman whose real name was Ida Bauer. She was brought to see Freud by her father, a former patient of Freud's. Her parents were concerned about a letter she had written them in which she said "goodbye," with the implied intention of committing suicide. Dora also had a "nervous" cough, a history of fainting spells, headaches, and depression which all dated back to her childhood. Her "most troubling symptom" was "a complete loss of voice."

Freud diagnosed these symptoms as a "typical case of hysteria"; his goal was to explain to Dora the sexual meanings of her symptoms, since he believed the cause of those symptoms lay in the repressed content of her early sexuality. Freud believed that hysteria resulted from masturbatory fantasies, lesbian fantasies, and incestuous desires for one's father. Dora's family included her parents and a brother.

In the family context, her brother took their mother's side; Dora was aligned with her father. Freud described Dora as an attractive, "sharp-sighted" girl whose father had taken great pride in the "early growth of her intelligence." Freud wrote that Dora's "critical powers" and her "intellectual precocity" were from her father, since he perceived her mother to be "an uncultivated woman" who "was occupied all day long in cleaning the house with its furniture and utensils."

Dora's father was having an affair with Frau K., wife of a family friend, Herr K. Herr K. had attempted to seduce Dora (the first time when she was 14 years old), and she felt that "she had been handed over to Herr K." by her father in exchange for his complicity in the adultery. Dora believed that her father "handed her over" to Freud because he feared she would discuss the affair. Her father hired Freud hoping for someone to "bring her to reason."

Freud believed Dora's account of why her father had brought her to see him: ". . . I came to the conclusion that Dora's story must correspond to the facts in every respect" (Freud, 1976, p. 46). He believed that Dora's father and Herr K. conspired against Dora: "[E]ach of the two men avoided drawing any conclusions from the other's behavior which would have been awkward for his own plans" (p. 35). However, Freud published the case (even though it was incomplete) because he thought it demonstrated the sexual origin of hysteria. As Elaine Schowalter (1985) commented:

> *In his case history of Dora, if not in the actual treatment, Freud is deter-*
> *mined to have the last word—he even has a postscript—in constructing*
> *his own "intelligible, consistent, and unbroken" account of her hysteria.*
> *He asserts his intellectual superiority to this bright but rebellious young*
> *woman. He uses his text to demonstrate his power to bring a woman to*
> *reason, and to bring reason to the mysteries of woman.* (p. 160)

Schowalter's passage suggests there is an alternative analysis of this case: Ida's perspective. What was it like for Ida to be a young woman in Vienna at the turn of the century? To have been seduced by a trusted family friend when she was a young adolescent? Ida believed—correctly—that she was caught in a web of deceit and betrayal. She believed she was caught in a double bind, and this again was true. The situation with her father, Freud, and Herr K.—all individuals in whom she placed a great deal of trust—was ample cause for depression and suicidal ideas. As Juanita Williams (1983) commented: Freud might have said to [Ida], "You are right and they are wrong" (p. 42). He did not, however, and she continued to have the pattern of symptoms throughout her adult life.

For Helene Cixous, a French feminist theorist, the case of Dora describes the silencing of women who question the patriarchical assumptions: "Silence: silence is the mark of hysteria. The great hysterics have lost speech . . . their tongues are cut off and what talks isn't heard because it's the body that talks and man doesn't hear the body" (1976, p. 49).

Schowalter (1985) recognized that women's hysteria fits in well with patriarchy:

> *Hysteria is tolerated because in fact it has no power to effect cultural*
> *change; it is much safer for the patriarchal order to encourage and allow*
> *discontented women to express their wrongs through psychosomatic ill-*
> *ness than to have them agitating for economic and legal rights.* (p. 161)

Marcie Kaplan (1983a, 1983b) claimed that the various categories of mental illnesses listed in the American Psychiatric Association's (1980) *Diagnostic and Statistical Manual of Mental Disorders* (DSM-III), the manual used by mental health professionals to categorize the various symptoms associated with mental illnesses, contains "masculine-biased assumptions about what behaviors are healthy and what behaviors are crazy" (1983a, p. 788). The basis for Kaplan's argument is that the same behavior that is thought of as indicative of emotional disturbance in a woman goes unnoticed or is not thought of as indicative of mental illness if seen in a man. The categories for different emotional and mental problems are thus arbitrarily defined by the psychiatric establishment to the detriment of women. A man, Kaplan asserts, would not be thought emotionally disturbed if he put career ahead of family, was unable to express his emotions, and felt little concern over others' feelings. This man is acting in ways expected of most men. But women who act according to their social expectations can be thought of as disturbed. It seems, then, that simply being too "feminine" or not "feminine" enough is grounds for being considered disturbed (Chesler, 1972).

Not surprisingly, those who helped in the development of the DSM-III believe that Kaplan overstated her case by charging male bias in the diagnostic categories (Williams & Spitzer, 1983). These authors asserted that "strenuous efforts were made to avoid the introduction of male-biased assumptions" (p. 797). However, given our society's attitudes toward women and the underlying sexist ideology that permeates our social institutions, women and men may still be looked at very differently when they behave in ways that don't fit their prescribed gender roles. In questioning the potential male bias of DSM-III's categories, Marjorie McC. Dachowski (1984) noted that,

> We are more likely to label women who cannot adapt as sick and men who cannot adapt as criminal, but in fact both groups are out of step with our social system and are being pressured, one way or another, to make significant behavioral changes if they wish to be a functioning part of our society. (p. 703)

More recently, feminist psychologists and psychiatrists have challenged diagnoses proposed for the DSM-III-R (American Psychiatric Association, 1987): paraphilic rapism, self-defeating personality disorder, and late luteal phase dysphoric disorder (the new psychiatric label for premenstrual syndrome) (Kupers, 1995; Sparks, 1985). Leonore Tiefer (1990) has also noted that diagnoses of sexual dysfunction need to be redefined since current definitions of sexual functioning are based in an implicit model of men's sexual gratification.

Some of the earlier concerns over gender bias appear to have been addressed in DSM-IV (American Psychiatric Association, 1994). Psychiatrist Terry Kupers (1995) notes as much when he writes:

> The DSM-IV is definitely an improvement over previous editions. There is more participation by women in the work groups; homosexuality has

been deleted from the list of disorders as has DSM-III's Ego-Dystonic Homosexuality; the proposal to add Self-Defeating Personality has been defeated; and there are sections on racial and ethnic differences. . . . (p. 76)

No simple answer explains why more women than men are now diagnosed and treated for mental illnesses. As we can see, the area of mental health and mental illness is fraught with several problems, not the least of which is the question of whether women and society's expectations of them can ever be judged without the influence of antifemale bias (Busfield, 1996). As Jeanne Marecek and Rachel Hare-Mustin (1991, p. 525) noted:

Beyond the battles won and lost regarding specific diagnostic categories, the deeper issue is the political meaning of diagnosis. Diagnostic categories provide the language that therapists speak, and thus, the very framework for their judgments and actions. . . . To what extent are diagnoses a means of social control, ensuring conformity to the interests of those in power, and denying the connection between social inequities and psychological distress?

Gender Comparisons in Mental Illnesses

Several emotional disorders are more likely to be found among women than among men. For example, depression, agoraphobia, and eating disorders are just a few of the disorders more commonly found among women than men (Russo, 1993). On the other hand, antisocial personality, intermittent explosive disorder, substance abuse disorders, paraphilias, and paranoid personality disorders are more frequently found among men than women (Kupers, 1995). The exact reasons for these gender differences are unknown. However, when we examine several of the emotional disorders more commonly found either among women or men, we discover an interesting feature. In many of the so-called "female disorders" (e.g., depression, anxieties, and eating disorders), the woman's negative feelings, anxiety, or personal conflict are directed "inward" against her self. In general, women exhibit behaviors that are self-critical, self-deprecating, and self-destructive. As for the so-called "male disorders" (e.g., antisocial personality and intermittent explosive disorder), men's conflict is more likely to be directed "outward" against others rather than inward. Men are more likely to strike out at others rather than harm themselves.

In this section we will look at two types of emotional problems in which there is an obvious gender difference. We will first examine depression, which is more frequently found among women. Then we will focus on the antisocial personality disorder, which is found more frequently among men.

Depression

Nearly everyone at one time or another has had a bout with the "blues." But a sizable portion of the population, with estimates ranging from 15 to 25 percent, at some time in their lives will suffer from extreme sadness and despair that is serious enough to interfere with their work, social, and family lives.

Clinical depression is usually signaled by two prominent symptoms: dysphoria and loss of interest. *Dysphoria* refers to a state of extreme sadness and worry and feelings of hopelessness. Also, depressed persons usually show little interest in activities that once gave them pleasure and happiness.

Evidence suggests that younger and older women are more likely than men to experience serious bouts of depression (Russo, 1993) and to be diagnosed as depressive both in psychiatric centers and in the community at large. Angela Ginorio and her colleagues (1995) reported a high risk of depression among Latinas, especially because of race discrimination and the conflicts between cultural expectations and achievement as minorities. In addition, Theresa LaFromboise and her colleagues (1995) cited depression as a major clinical problem of American Indian women. Married, divorced, or separated women exhibit more depressive symptoms than men of the same marital status (Wu & DeMaris, 1996). Single men and widowers, however, show more signs of depression than single women or widows. Generally, estimates suggest that depression occurs about twice as often in women as in men (Russo, 1993).

Several different theories have been suggested to account for the greater incidence of depression among women than among men. One general view is that women are no more likely to experience depression than men are but are more likely to admit to depressive symptoms. Others suggest that because women suffer greater discrimination and a relative lack of power in society compared to men, the consequence is "legal and economic helplessness, dependency on others, chronically low self-esteem, low aspirations, and ultimately, clinical depression" (Weissman & Klerman, 1977, p. 106). Another view suggests that women are more susceptible to depression by virtue of the learned helplessness that is acquired through the socialization process (Russo, 1993) and the acceptance of feminine gender role expectations (Silverstein et al., 1995). Still others believe that because women are socialized to be less assertive, they are less likely to obtain as many rewards from their environment as men, and this may cause in some women a tendency toward depression (Katz et al., 1993). As Phyllis Katz and her colleagues (1993, p. 268) commented:

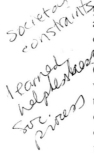

> *The devaluation of this central orientation of women may well put them at risk for depression, since an integral part of their identity is often degraded. If their self-esteem is indeed based on relatedness and yet this aspect of self is labeled and responded to in negative ways by society, it follows that females would feel quite negatively about themselves.*

Antisocial Personality: Violence Directed toward Women and Men
Although we have noted that women are more likely than men to be diagnosed as mentally ill, the rate of mental illness among young boys is greater than among young girls. One of the problems more frequently found among young boys and men is that of *antisocial personality* (Rosenfield, 1980). The

antisocial personality is signaled by a lack of ethical or moral development and by behavior that is contrary to socially acceptable guidelines. The terms *sociopathic personality* and *psychopathic personality* are other designations frequently used to refer to this disorder. More men fit this description than women, with estimates suggesting that the ratio is approximately three to one.

Men with an antisocial personality lack a sense of personal ethics. Also, they don't appear to feel any guilt or anxiety about hurting others' feelings. Quite often, they act impulsively and do not stop to think how their actions may affect others. They frequently display a general disregard for authority. Antisocial personalities also have difficulty establishing good interpersonal relationships (Carson et al., 1988).

One contributing factor to this illness may be the social expectations placed on boys and men. For example, our society encourages boys more than girls to become aggressive, competitive, and success-driven, to win at all costs if need be (Doyle, 1995). Such an orientation may lead to the development of features associated with antisocial personality characteristics in the early adult years. Young boys are also encouraged to hide their feelings, especially their tender feelings of love and concern for others, which, if taken to the extreme, can become fertile ground for acting in what may be considered as antisocial ways (Doyle, 1995).

This socialization of boys and men has been linked to men's violence against women in the form of incest, rape, battering, and sexual harassment (see chapter 6). Conclusions drawn across multiple studies suggest that women are victimized more often than men, that large numbers of women are affected, and that men are the perpetrators more than women (Paludi, 1997). When boys and men are abused, the abuse is often in conjunction with a girl or woman victim.

Thirty percent of all women are battered at least once in their adult lives. Wife-to-husband violence is usually in self-defense (Browne, 1994). Incidence of sexual harassment among undergraduate women ranges between 30 percent and 70 percent each year. The incidence is even higher for women in graduate school and in the workforce (Paludi, 1996). The incidence of rape is higher among women than men (Koss, 1993). Between 8 percent and 15 percent of college women disclosed they were raped, and at least one-third of battered women have been raped by the batterer.

Timothy Beneke (1982) asked men to view rape (and we could extend this to other forms of victimization) as their problem, too, because it is men who rape and who collectively have the power to stop rape. Robin Warshaw (1988) argued that "to harness that power, many men will have to rethink their beliefs about women and sex and change their behaviors" (p. 161). Warshaw offered the following guidelines (adapted from rape awareness advocates) to help men achieve this goal (pp. 161–164):

1. Never force a woman to have sex.
2. Don't pressure a woman to have sex.
3. Stay sober.
4. Don't buy the myth that a drunken woman "deserves" to be raped.

5. Do not "join in" if a friend invites you to participate in sexual behavior.
6. Do not confuse "scoring" with having a successful social encounter.
7. Don't assume that you know what a woman wants and vice versa.
8. "No" means "no."
9. Speak up if you feel you're getting a double message from a woman.
10. Communicate with women.
11. Communicate with other men.

Men have more physical and economic power than women. And, women are left feeling more powerless after they have been victimized. Women may not regain power by reporting such acts of violence because the police and legal procedures (typically male-populated and stereotyped in their views of women) are humiliating. Thus, acts of violence encourage women to remain silent and invisible. This is especially true of ethnic minority women and economically poor women. Paludi (1997) reported that ethnic minority women, older women, physically challenged women, and lesbian women are singled out more often than others.

Violent movies, music videos, and publications that depict women as being victimized are harmful (Cowan, 1995; Johnson et al., 1995). "They, too, promote a perception of women as outsiders, as objects that exist for men to exploit, manipulate, and harm" (Hughes & Sandler, 1988, p. 7). For example, in one music video, "All She Wants to Do Is Dance," an ethnic minority woman is depicted as hedonistic and sexual while a revolution is going on. Men in the video step on her image in a mirror (Basow, 1986).

Therapy: The Concern over Sex Bias

Earlier we noted that researchers believe women are ill-served because of the masculine bias of the psychiatric categories of mental illnesses. In this section we will examine the charge that psychotherapy needs to be demasculinized.

Most of us may believe that therapy is an effective way of helping a mentally distressed person. And yet, for well over a decade, several feminist-oriented social scientists have voiced severe criticism of traditional therapy and have sounded a warning that therapy may be hazardous to women's mental and emotional well-being (Brown, 1995). Concern over the possible "dangers" inherent in therapists' and counselors' treatment of women, to a great extent, grew out of the findings of the now classic study conducted by Inge Broverman and colleagues (1970).

These researchers asked a group of 79 mental health practitioners (33 women and 46 men) to describe the traits that characterized a mature, healthy, and socially competent adult woman, adult man, or an adult whose sex was not specified. They were asked to check off a series of descriptive bipolar characteristics that best described each person. The descriptive categories contained bipolar items such as those listed below:

Very subjective   Very objective
Very submissive   Very dominant

Not at all ambitious	Very ambitious
Very passive	Very active
Feelings easily hurt	Feelings not easily hurt

Broverman and her colleagues found considerable agreement in the way the clinicians described the characteristics of adult men and adults in general (e.g., very direct, very logical, can make decisions easily, never cries), which differed from the characteristics assigned to adult women (e.g., very excitable in minor crises, easily influenced, less adventurous, less independent, very illogical, very sneaky). Second, there was considerable agreement among the women and men in the way they described the different persons. Overall, Broverman found that the clinicians in her study had a "double standard" for mental health. In other words, the criteria of mental health these clinicians applied to an adult was also applied to an adult man but not to an adult woman. Broverman noted that "the general standard of health is actually applied only to men, while healthy women are perceived as significantly less healthy by adult standards" (p. 5).

Soon after Broverman's study, Chesler published her indictment against the predominantly male professions of psychiatry and clinical psychology in her book *Women and Madness* (1972). Chesler charged the mental health profession with a conspiracy against women, carried out mainly by the male psychiatric and psychological establishments. She wrote:

> *The ethic of mental health is masculine in our culture. This double standard of sexual mental health, which exists side by side with a single and masculine standard of human mental health, is enforced by both society and clinicians. Although the limited "ego resources," and unlimited "dependence," and fearfulness of most women is pitied, disliked, and "diagnosed," by society and its agent-clinicians, any other kind of behavior is unacceptable in women!* (p. 69)

Other researchers and therapists provided support for the existence of a double standard of mental health wherein the standards set for women differed greatly from those set for men. Career and vocational counselors also were found to evidence gender bias toward women's career aspirations (Betz, 1993). The culprit behind the double standard for mental health and career opportunities seems to be society's prevalent sexist ideology.

As Broverman's and Chesler's work became better known, some evidence indicated that the problem of sexism, or sex bias, lessened somewhat among the helping professions. In her review of 10 studies of counselors' and therapists' attitudes toward women, Julia Sherman (1980) found that, for the most part, clinicians hadn't changed much over the decade since Broverman's classic study. However, she did find that women were less biased than men. Women, more than men, may participate in new courses dealing with women and therapy during their graduate training where discussions of sex bias in psychotherapy are held. In support of this explanation, Sherman and her colleagues (1978) found that therapists lack preparation and information about women in general and were generally uninformed about research on the psychology of women, especially in the areas of sexuality, pregnancy, and menopause. Sherman noted that older therapists and those with a Freudian orientation were more likely to be biased against women than were younger and non-Freudian-oriented therapists.

In contrast, several researchers found little evidence for sex bias in therapy (Billingsley, 1977; Johnson, 1978). Other reviewers stressed that a clinical judgment was rarely based solely on a client's sex label (Davidson & Abramowitz, 1980; Smith, 1980). Moreover, Mary Smith (1980) reviewed over 30 published and nonpublished (doctoral dissertations) studies of sex bias in therapy and found "no evidence for the existence of counselor sex bias when the research results are taken as a whole" (p. 404). Smith also reported that there was greater bias found in earlier studies than in the later ones, suggesting that professionals apparently had become more aware of and/or sensitive to the issue of sex bias over the decade. The studies published in professional journals were more likely to report sex bias than nonpublished studies (see chapter 1 for a discussion of publication bias).

How are we to interpret the conflicting data over whether or not therapy is bad for women? On the one hand, several studies point out the presence of a double standard that, if applied, can be considered harmful to women. On the other hand, considerable research suggests that sex bias is minimal or not as pervasive as some may think. The solution to the dilemma of whether sex bias exists in therapy may be settled if we note a methodological difference among many of the studies involved. A large portion of the studies finding a lack of sex bias among therapists are analogue studies (e.g., Lopez et al., 1993). *Analogue studies* are those in which a therapist is presented with a "contrived" situation where the patient's sex is the independent variable in the study. For example, a therapist may be presented with a written case study—involving either a woman or man as the client—and asked to make a clinical judgment based on the material in the case. The important feature to keep in mind is that reading an analogue study is not the same as sitting across from a client in a "real" therapy session. The analogue is a substitute for the real thing and, many argue, a poor substitute for the study of potential therapist bias.

When *naturalistic data* of what transpires in actual therapy sessions are examined or when records from real therapy sessions between clients and therapists are analyzed, there appears to be substantial evidence for therapist bias against women. For example, women are seen for longer periods of time in therapy and given stronger prescriptive medications than men are (Travis, 1993). In addition, there are biases in the types of questions therapists ask women and men. Thus the conflicting results may be due to the type of studies examined. Analogue studies provide little evidence of sex bias, but in naturalistic studies, sex bias appears to be a real problem. In summarizing the issue, Rachel Hare-Mustin (1983) concludes that:

> *Clinical analogues have failed to produce impressive evidence of sex bias, whereas naturalistic studies have produced supporting data. It*

may be that analogue studies have become too transparent and subject to responses in the socially desirable direction. More sophisticated research designs are needed to deal with the complex factors in evaluating therapy. (p. 595)

We should also note that traditional psychotherapy has been heterosexist in its practice (as well as in theory and research). In theories of psychological development, a heterosexual sexual orientation is viewed as normative; lesbian, gay, and bisexual orientations are viewed as deviant and changeworthy (Brown, 1996). Consequently, lesbian women, gay men, and bisexual individuals have been ignored, deprecated, and considered mentally ill. It is only recently, with alternative therapies, that lesbian, gay, and bisexual lifestyles have been affirmed. It is also important to acknowledge issues of cultural sensitivity of psychotherapists (Brown, 1996; LaFromboise et al., 1995).

Finally, we must point out that the Ethical Principles of Psychologists of the American Psychological Association are clear about specifying that sexual relations with clients are unethical. Based on self-reports, more than 5 percent of male therapists reported having sex with women clients. Research has indicated that power needs motivate the therapists to engage in this unethical conduct (Bouhoutsos, 1984). Approximately half of the complaints to state licensing boards against psychologists concern sexual misconduct in therapy. Seven states have criminalized such behavior (Youngstrom, 1990).

Graduate training programs in clinical and counseling psychology must teach students to be more sensitive to and aware of sex, ethnicity, and class and to become aware of their own hidden gender role biases (Porter, 1995).

Nontraditional Therapies

A person who is distressed or emotionally distraught with her or his life may turn to a therapist for help. A key issue is what goals the therapist may have in mind to best help the client. For instance, should a therapist help clients adjust to their life situations by gaining insight into why they feel the way they do? Or should a therapist encourage and assist clients to break free of what they perceive to be constrictions or limitations in their lives? We have a quandary of sorts in defining the goals of therapy: should therapy focus on change or adjustment? The man who feels his work is meaningless and becomes upset or depressed with his life or the woman who feels overdependent on others and wishes she could be more independent may both seek professional help. But what kind of help do they need? And what are the goals a therapist may bring into the therapy sessions? Should the woman be helped to adjust to her dependency and learn to accept others' support? Should the man be encouraged to "tough it out" at work because it is only a few more years until retirement? Do these two people need intensive therapy to help them adjust to the status quo called for by their traditional gender role stereotypes and roles? Or should both be helped to break free from the restrictions of their past conditioning, to take charge of their own lives, and to seek personal fulfillment by examining other options and choices that may be contrary to their past experiences (Brown, 1995)? Concern over the question of how best to deal with women's and men's unique problems as related to gender roles has led the helping professions to an intense study of both sexes.

Several feminists have noted that traditional therapies are political in nature because they serve the needs of society's dominant group and do little more than support society's status quo. Thus, several nontraditional approaches to counseling and therapy have been instituted in the past several years to help both women and men find alternatives and options that are free of outmoded and potentially harmful gender stereotypes and roles. Let's examine two nontraditional therapies that are used to help people break free of traditional gender role stereotypes and roles: consciousness-raising groups and feminist therapies. These therapies avoid language that labels one sex as more socially desirable or more valuable than the other. They recognize prevailing societal forces that differentially reinforce women and men for gender-role related behaviors that ignore or punish ethnicity and lifestyle choices.

Consciousness-Raising Groups

Several feminists maintain that consciousness-raising (CR) groups are a powerful alternative or adjunct to traditional therapies (Brodsky, 1977; Reed & Garvin, 1983; Wong, 1978). CR groups differ from other more traditional forms of therapy. Usually, in a CR group, several people meet in a group member's home. Also, CR groups usually are leaderless, or the members take turns being responsible for facilitating the session. This assures that no single member can take over and monopolize the discussion or act as an authority figure within the group. Normally, the main focus for the CR group centers on the group members' feelings and self-perceptions.

Some theorists (e.g., Reid et al., 1995) maintain that many of the personal problems that women experience are a direct result of their socialization process. For example, girls and women are taught at an early age to belittle their achievements and their value as human beings (see chapter 9). Rather than seeking help from male therapists, who may represent just another male authority ignoring the value of women, women meet in a CR group to define their experiences in terms of their own criteria. Thus for many women, the CR group becomes a form of resocialization.

In the past several years, some men have followed the lead of women and have formed all-male CR groups where men can deal with their feelings of what it means to be men in our society (Doyle, 1995). The benefits accruing to men of unstructured and leaderless CR groups are many. For example, men can learn how to deal with little or no structure in a group, which for many men is seen as an arena where they can show off for others. Personal issues, such as emotional constraints and concerns over expressing positive feelings toward other men and fear of homosexuality, are just a few of the issues which all-male CR groups can deal with.

Rape awareness programs, a form of the CR groups for men, have been established at several colleges and universities, including the College of Great

Falls in Montana, Cornell University, Princeton University, the University of Arizona, and the University of Florida at Gainesville. In Madison, Wisconsin, Men Stopping Rape has been active at the University of Wisconsin and now offers CR groups to high schools and middle schools.

Warshaw (1988, p. 167) offered several comments from men who have participated in these groups:

> *It's a tough topic and there are still a lot of people in the system who don't understand it or don't think we need it, they think we're wasting their time . . . but I know in my fraternity, the attitudes really have changed.*
>
> *. . . . it's difficult to get men to come to a discussion that's so threatening to them. I want other people to be aware that this sort of thing can happen and that it happens a lot more than most people ever imagine. . . . It just has to stop.*

Feminist Therapies

Many people think the terms *feminist therapy* and *nonsexist therapy* mean the same thing. However, some feminist therapists wish to differentiate between the two because each is based on different assumptions (Rawlings & Carter, 1977). *Feminist therapy* is usually based on a philosophical critique of society wherein women are seen as having less political and economic power than men have. Another assumption is that the bases for women's personal problems are social, not personal. A major goal of feminist therapies is for women to learn to strive for and acquire economic and psychological independence. Finally, feminist therapies accept the idea that society's definitions of gender roles and the opposing complements expected between women's and men's behaviors must end.

Nonsexist therapy means that the therapist has become aware of and has overcome, for the most part, her or his own sexist attitudes and values. For example, a nonsexist therapist would look at an independent woman or a dependent man as not necessarily demonstrating emotional or personal problems by acting in counterstereotypic ways. Another assumption that nonsexist therapists make is that marriage is not thought to be any better for women than for men. Both women and men are encouraged to act in androgynous ways rather than in stereotypic feminine or masculine ways. In summarizing the differences between these two alternative approaches to therapy, Marilyn Johnson (1980) noted:

> *The primary distinction between the nonsexist and feminist therapist is that the feminist incorporates feminist theory and practice into therapy and the nonsexist does not. Both believe in egalitarianism between the sexes; this belief springs from a humanistic philosophy among nonsexists and from feminist ideology in feminists. Proponents of each approach offer their own messages to the client. Nonsexist: Some of your problems arise from the way the world is. If you had been socialized differently, you would not have to work through these*

many issues. Feminist: Some of your problems arise from the way the world is. Remember that the power differential between women and men is an often ignored contributor to your problem. You can work to change your life and you will have the support of many others like yourself. (p. 366)

As we can see, there are certain basic differences between feminist therapies and nonsexist therapies. However, both take a "change-oriented" approach in assisting clients to work out the problems in their lives. Also, these two approaches take into account that women's and men's lives are not complementary and that both must have the freedom to work out their own definitions for healthy and fulfilling lifestyles.

Individual approaches to feminist psychology vary in terms of the importance they place in key issues (Russo & Green, 1993). However, three common concepts are: (1) recognition of the inequality of social and institutional power distributions, (2) integration of values into scientific study, and (3) responsibility to advocate for change. Guidelines that are endorsed by feminist therapists have been outlined by Judith Worell (1980):

1. Providing an egalitarian relationship with shared responsibility between counselor and client. The client is encouraged to trust her own judgment and to arrive at her own decisions. In contrast to many traditional counseling relationships, the client is never in a one-down position of having to accept counselor interpretations of her behavior or external prescriptions for appropriate living.

2. Employing a consciousness-raising approach. Women are helped to become aware of the societal restraints on their development and opportunities. Clients are helped to differentiate between the politics of the sexist social structure and those problems over which they have realistic personal control.

3. Helping women explore a sense of their personal power and how they can use it constructively in personal, business, and political relationships.

4. Helping women to get in touch with unexpressed anger in order to combat depression and to make choices about how to use their anger constructively.

5. Helping women to redefine themselves apart from their role relationships to men, children, and home; exploring women's fears about potential role changes that may alienate spouse and children, as well as co-workers and boss.

6. Encouraging women to nurture themselves as well as caring for others, thereby raising self-confidence and self-esteem.

7. Encouraging multiple skill development to increase women's competence and productivity. This may include assertiveness training, economic and career skills, and negotiation skills with important others who resist change (pp. 480–481).

Hannah Lerman and Natalie Porter (1990) offer the following as some guidelines for feminist therapists:

1. A feminist therapist increases her accessibility to and for a wide range of clients from her own and other identified groups through flexible delivery of services. When appropriate, the feminist therapist assists clients in accessing other services.
2. A feminist therapist is aware of the meaning and impact of her own ethnic and cultural background, gender, class, and sexual orientation, and actively attempts to become knowledgeable about alternatives from sources other than her clients. The therapist's goal is to uncover and respect cultural and experiential differences.
3. A feminist therapist evaluates her ongoing interactions with her clientele for any evidence of the therapist's biases or discriminatory attitudes and practice. The feminist therapist accepts responsibility for taking appropriate action to confront and change any interfering or oppressing biases she has.
4. A feminist therapist acknowledges the inherent power differentials between client and therapist and models effective use of personal power. In using the power differential to the benefit of the client, she does not take control of power which rightfully belongs to her client.
5. A feminist therapist discloses information to the client which facilitates the therapeutic process. The therapist is responsible for using self-disclosure with purpose and discretion in the interests of the client.

Thus feminist therapists believe that what has been called "mental illness" needs to be reconsidered. Lynne Bravo Rosewater (1984) suggested that therapists should not concentrate on diagnosis *per se*, but rather on the implication of the diagnosis. She concluded:

> *To treat the source of the problem, a policy change in the concept of our treatment modality is needed; it should look beyond the label given to a mental health problem to its consequence. If a woman is diagnosed as depressed, what assumptions underlie that label? Is it assumed that women are generally unhappy individuals? Is it assumed that depressed individuals are hopeless? Is the appropriate remedy psychotherapy or chemotherapy or shock treatments? . . . A feminist analysis of depression sees it as originating from women's role in society. . . . A feminist treatment of depression, therefore, centers on an examination of the environmental impact on the woman in treatment, historically and currently. Depression may be viewed as a coping skill . . . or as a healthy reaction to an unjust situation. . . . The role expectations for women in our society and whether a given role is right for any particular woman needs to be critically examined. Feminist therapy aids in the reevaluating and renegotiating of specific roles and the rules governing those roles.* (pp. 272–273)

Thus feminist therapists change the concept of treatment by the assumption that the behavior that is typically labeled as a disorder may be valuable. Rosewater (1984) and Jean Baker Miller (1976) suggest reassessing women's behavior so that the image of passive "feminine" behavior is viewed positively as having worth. In traditional therapy, the focus of the woman's treatment has been on what the woman has failed to do, e.g., the battered woman who has not left the batterer, the rape victim who has not reported the crime. However, a revisionist perspective would suggest we view these women in a different way, as showing strength, as coping with unjust situations, as being survivors, not victims.

One of the ethical guidelines for feminist therapists concerns respect for cultural differences among women. This respect includes an understanding of ethnic minority women clients who see the interface of gender, ethnicity, and sex in their lives rather than gender as the primary issue (Unger, 1995).

Physical Health

A great deal of attention has focused on the relationship between an individual's sex and health problems that develop throughout the life span. Women's and men's access to and utilization of health care (Travis, 1993) is another crucial issue. Noted sex comparisons exist in the area of health status. For example, men's greater vulnerability holds true from conception to old age, and the death rate for American men is higher than that for women in every decade of life. Women have an overall life span expectancy that surpasses men at every age regardless of race (Klonoff, Landrine, & Scott, 1995; Travis, 1993).

Approximately 33 percent more boys than girls die in their first year of life. An equal sex ratio does not occur until 18 years of age, when 100 men are alive for every 100 women. However, the ratio steadily decreases throughout adulthood: By age 87, one man is alive for every two women. The life expectancy for women in the United States is 78.2 years, for men 70.9 years. African American women live longer (73.8 years) than both African American men (64.8 years) and white men (71.4 years).

On the average, women have more physician visits than men and women are more likely to be admitted to hospitals and utilize more days of hospital care than men. Travis (1993) reported that approximately 9 million operations are performed on men each year and 17 million on women.

In adulthood, the mortality rates for men exceed those of women for most disorders, especially heart disease, malignancy, accidents, and chronic pulmonary disease (Strickland, 1988).

Lung cancer now surpasses breast cancer as the leading cause of death for women. This rise in lung cancer in women is directly related to the increase in women smoking cigarettes accounting for approximately 85 percent of lung cancer deaths. Following World War II, a significant number of women began smoking, until the prevalence of smoking among women reached its peak in the late 1960s and early 1970s. Today, adolescent and young adult women surpass men in acquiring this habit (Hanson, 1994). Magazine advertisements for cigarettes depict women as glamorous, sophisticated, young, liberated ("You've come a long way, baby!"), and they equate cigarette smoking with adult status and slimness ("Virginia Slims"). Adolescent women may be especially vulnerable to such advertisements in their search for an identity status.

Nicotine obtained through cigarette smoking is a powerful addicting agent. In addition to lung cancer, other diseases and deaths are related to cigarette smoking. For example, 30 percent of all heart disease deaths are attributed to cigarette smoking. In addition, compared to women who do not smoke, women who do smoke are more likely to have strokes and other serious cardiovascular disorders. Women who smoke and use oral contraceptives are 10 times more likely than nonsmoking women to suffer coronary heart disease. Cigarette smoking in women also is correlated with cancers of the urinary tract, larynx, oral cavity, esophagus, kidney, pancreas, and uterus. Women who smoke are likely to suffer from bronchitis, emphysema, chronic sinusitis, and severe hypertension.

Maternal health is adversely affected by cigarette smoking as well. During pregnancy, nicotine retards the rate of fetal growth and increases the likelihood of spontaneous abortion, low birth weight, fetal death, and neonatal death. Children of smoking mothers are found to have deficiencies in physical growth, intellectual development, and social-emotional development that are all independent of other risk factors. They are also at risk for respiratory disorders.

Breast cancer is the second leading cause of cancer deaths among women between 35 and 55 years old. Cancer of the prostate accounts for 10 percent of the malignancies that occur in men.

Breast self-examination for breast cancer is used by only a fraction of the women who might benefit from it, however. Research has also indicated that older women—who are at greater risk for breast cancer—are least likely to examine their breasts (Grady, 1988). The failure of women to use breast self-examination may result from women being discouraged from touching their bodies. This may be especially true for older women who were socialized in a cohort that discouraged any form of self-touching, including masturbation.

Statistics reveal that over 100,000 women each year in the United States are diagnosed with breast cancer; risk increases considerably with age. Although death rates from breast cancer are declining among women between the ages of 45 and 54, they are dramatically increasing for women over 55. The etiology of breast cancer is unknown; thus, early detection is important to reduce mortality (Travis, 1993).

Women's feelings about their breasts may be positive and negative. These feelings are reinforced by this culture's fixation on breasts, especially large breasts. Women's breasts are used in advertisements to sell cars, alcohol, and cigarettes.

The fact that women's breasts are varied (one woman's breast may even be different in size and shape from her other breast) contributes to women not having sufficient information about what is normal in appearance and what requires attention. Lack of information also contributes to women fearing that any changes in their breasts—which frequently accompany various stages of menstrual cycles and menopause—are serious. Most conditions that contribute to changes in women's breasts, however, are not cancer. They are benign conditions, such as fibrocystic condition or fibroadenomas.

Fibrocystic condition refers to the breast cells retaining fluid. Cysts often develop during ovulation and just prior to menstruation when hormone levels change. Lumps appear during these times and decrease or disappear within a day or two after menstruation begins. This condition affects some women at menarche and affects others during their young adult years; it disappears at menopause for the majority of women. Research has indicated that fibrocystic condition is not a causative factor in breast cancer (Grady, 1988).

Fibroadenomas are lumps that do not fluctuate with the menstrual cycle. These lumps most often appear in women's teens or twenties. They may interfere with circulation or distort the shape of the breast. When this occurs, they may be surgically removed. At menopause, fibroadenomas shrink, suggesting that they are a normal occurrence. There is no evidence to link fibroadenomas with breast cancer.

Mammograms help detect breast cancer in its early stages, revealing cancers as small as one-quarter-inch in diameter. The American Cancer Society recommends that women get a baseline (i.e., initial) mammogram between the ages of 35 and 40, get mammograms every one or two years from ages 40 to 49, and have annual exams after the age of 50. Some women may not want to get mammograms because they fear the radiation, but the radiation used in mammograms is very low and thus safe. Other women may not get mammograms because of the cost involved. Consequently, some health care facilities offer free or low-charge mammograms for preventive measures.

Gender Differences

In adulthood, women exceed men with Alzheimer's disease by two or three to one. In addition, women are more likely than men to be subject to chronic and disabling diseases, such as arthritis, rheumatism, hypertension, and diabetes.

The highest male-to-female death ratios occur for AIDS (approximately eight times more men than women), suicide (approximately four times more men), homicide (three times more men), accidents (twice as many men), and chronic liver diseases (twice as many men).

Medical professionals once believed that as women participated in more male-populated (considered "high stress") careers, they would increase their chances of heart disease. However, research has indicated that women in executive career positions do not show a higher incidence of heart disease than women not in these positions (Haynes & Feinleib, 1980). Heart disease is more likely to be found among women in clerical or low-status jobs where they have poor or no support systems. Role strain is increased for women in low-income jobs with many child care demands and no assistance with housekeeping. Illness and poor health are more likely to be found among individuals of lower socioeconomic status.

Research does point to the negative effects of socialization practices of boys and men. Anxiety associated with conforming to the masculine gender role, including the emphasis on competitiveness and achievement, may lead to the development of compensatory behaviors that are hazardous to men's health: exhibitions of violence, smoking, excessive consumption of alcohol, drug abuse, risk-taking behavior. African American men in particular are vulnerable to physical illnesses and death (Klonoff, Landrine, & Scott, 1995). They may have inadequate access to affordable health care and suffer the added stress of racism (Wade, 1996). Black males have higher rates of infant mortality, low birth weight, sickle cell anemia, nonfatal and fatal accidents, elevated blood pressure, and sexually transmitted diseases. Among black men, homicide is the leading cause of death (Wade, 1996).

Elizabeth Klonoff, Hope Landrine, and Judith Scott (1995) pointed out that across many cultures with different stressors men still die earlier and have a greater incidence of chromosomal abnormalities than do women (Matsumoto & Fletcher, 1996). A biological predisposition seems to interact with cultural factors to make men more physically vulnerable than women (Sherman et al., 1996). Research does suggest that female hormones may be protective (Rodin & Ickovics, 1990; Travis, 1993). Girls' and women's ability to withstand infection may be transmitted via the X chromosome, or their lower metabolic rate may contribute to their viability.

Klonoff and her colleagues (1995) also point out the need to continue to do research on the interface of sex and race in health psychology since this field has relatively ignored the problems of people of color in general and women of color in particular. As these authors argue:

> *Differences in beliefs, religion, foods, customs, traditional folk remedies, and so forth, all may have significant implications for research with minorities. When ethnicity is ignored, the potential role of these factors is therefore artificially obscured.* (p. 355)

Let us turn now to one major health concern facing many girls and women: eating disorders. Then we will consider a major health concern of men: prostate cancer.

Eating Disorders

Every society has its definition of what is beautiful or attractive. Social psychologist Karen Dion (Unger & Saundra, 1993) has identified that attractive or beautiful children and adults are thought of by others as more interesting, more exciting, and more sensitive than less attractive individuals.

Women have usually been more willing than men to harm themselves mentally and physically to achieve the elusive status of being beautiful (Jackson, 1992; Pipher, 1994). A major feature of what is thought of as beautiful in the Western world today is a thin body. If we believe many of the commercials on TV ("You can't pinch an inch"), thin is in and fat is out. With beauty so prized and rewarded in our society, it is little wonder that many women seem so concerned with keeping their bodies youthful and beautiful, and one way to do that is to keep thin. Consequently, some women are on a never-ending cycle of dieting, daily visits to health and fitness centers, and generally working for the "fashion model" look that borders on emaciation. For many women, especially younger women, the concern over weight and attractiveness is taken to extremes (Dyer & Tiggermann, 1996).

The racism and classism in this culture's standard of physical beauty is reinforced by the media; the fashion model look includes being white, tall, blond, and middle-class (Thompson, Sargent, & Kemper, 1996). Toni Morrison's *The Bluest Eye* (1970) describes the obsession of Pecola, a black adolescent girl, to be attractive according to white standards:

> *It had occurred to Pecola some time ago that if her eyes, those eyes that held the pictures, and knew the sights—if those eyes of hers were different, that is to say, beautiful, she herself would be different. Her teeth were good, and at least her nose was not big and flat like some of those who were thought so cute. If she looked different, beautiful, maybe . . . they'd say, "Why, look at pretty-eyed Pecola. We mustn't do bad things in front of those pretty eyes. . . ." Each night without fail, she prayed for blue eyes. . . . (p. 40)*

Many women in this culture report feeling dissatisfaction with their bodies. In fact, many girls and women of normal weight believe they are too fat (Pipher, 1994). More girls and women, especially adolescent young women, report that they are too fat, in comparison to boys and men. Boys tend to emphasize physical competence while girls are concerned with the social appeal of their appearance. Adolescent girls may perceive the normative physical developmental changes accompanying pubescence (including the redistribution of weight) as weight gain and a need to diet. Women only 20 or 30 pounds overweight experience substantial effects on their lives; men, on the other hand, have a considerably wider margin of error before anyone (including themselves) sees them as overweight.

Susan Wooley and Wayne Wooley (1980) observed this to be the case with television personalities. You may want to see if their results are still true today. How many women on popular television shows are even a few pounds overweight? How many of the men who are actors are overweight? Are there ethnic and age differences in your observations?

According to one college man:

> *That's the way all of us are. Even the shy, sweet ones. Like everyone else, we college men are products of our environment. . . . We're warped by the media. We're conditioned by Charlie's Angels, by Playboy Advisor and Penthouse Forum and the Sports Illustrated bathing suit issue, by all the impossibly smooth airbrushed centerfolds, by rock-n-roll lyrics*

Media's influence on girl's and women's acquisition of a gender role identity.

Bob Coyle Photo

and TV ads. . . . The only thing college men want is to sleep with beautiful college women. (*Nutshell* magazine, 1982, p. 44, cited in Hatfield & Sprecher, 1986, p. 105)

Susan Brownmiller (1984) argued that dieting has replaced corseting and foot binding as a way women conform to a masculine-biased view of ideal physical femininity. She concluded:

Appearance, not accomplishment, is the feminine demonstration of desirability and worth. In striving to approach a physical ideal, by corsetry in the old days or by a cottage-cheese-and-celery diet that begins tomorrow, one arms oneself to fight the competitive wars. Feminine armor is never metal or muscle, but, paradoxically, an exaggeration of physical vulnerability that is reassuring (unthreatening) to men. Because she is forced to concentrate on the minutiae of her body parts, a woman is never free of self-consciousness. She is never quite satisfied, and never secure, for desperate, unending absorption in the drive for a perfect appearance—call it feminine vanity—is the ultimate restriction on freedom of mind. (pp. 50–51)

Laura Brown (1987) contended that women's fear of fat, distortions of body image, and poor self-feeding are consequences of the conflict between adherence to the following male-biased rules governing women's behavior and wanting to be healthy: (1) small is beautiful, (2) weakness of body is valued, (3) women are forbidden to nurture themselves in a straightforward manner, (4) women are forbidden to act powerfully in overt ways, and (5) women are valued only when they adhere unfailingly to the first four rules. Brown has also reported that lesbian women are less likely to have eating disorders than women in general. She stated:

> *Lesbians are at risk from fat oppression in different ways than are heterosexual women. A lesbian's own internalized homophobia is likely to determine the degree to which she fat-oppresses herself. The more a lesbian has examined and worked through her internalized homophobia, the less at risk she is to be affected by the rules that govern fat oppression. . . . Once having successfully begun to challenge the rule against loving women in a patriarchal and misogynist context, a woman may be more likely not to impose other such rules on herself, for example, conventions about attractiveness, size, and strength.* (p. 299)

Two eating disorders exhibit women's extreme fear of being fat: anorexia nervosa and bulimia.

Anorexia Nervosa

Anorexia nervosa has taken on near epidemic proportions. Estimates suggest that approximately 1 percent of all women between the ages of 12 and 25—approximately 260,000 women—suffer from this severe eating disorder (Smith, 1996). The incidence of anorexia nervosa has been increasing since 1970.

The most likely age for anorexia nervosa is 12 to 18 years. Anorexia nervosa is regarded as a serious eating disorder because 15 percent of anorexics die (Smith, 1996). There is an increasing incidence of anorexia nervosa among black adolescent and young adult women (Jackson, Sullivan & Rostker, 1988). Anorexia nervosa generally is characterized by three common symptoms:

> *self-induced severe weight loss*
> *amenorrhea (i.e., cessation of menstrual periods)*
> *an intense fear of losing control over eating and becoming fat*

The anorexic is not one who goes through the "normal" ritual of dieting to lose a pound or two but one who voluntarily induces a dramatic loss of body weight (i.e., 25 percent of original body weight) that can damage body organs and threaten her life.

Although several psychosocial characteristics have been suggested as contributing to anorexia, such as a distorted body image and an extreme concern with pleasing others, there is no universally accepted theory about its onset (Smith, 1996).

With respect to body image disturbances in anorexia nervosa, investigators have reported that anorexics overestimate overall body size and the sizes of body parts to a significant extent than do nonanorexics (Travis, 1993). However, body-size overestimation is characteristic of girls and women in general.

Thus it is not the critical defining feature of anorexia. Often this eating disorder occurs in response to a new situation where women may be judged by masculine-biased standards, such as dating, entering college, or marriage (Smith, 1996). Our society's obsession with the fashion model look for women may lead some young women to develop an intense fear of gaining weight because they may associate gaining weight with rejection by others.

Florence Nightingale (1979) in *Cassandra* interpreted anorexic behavior as a form of female cultural protest:

> *To have no food for our heads, no food for our hearts, no food for our activity, is that nothing? If we have no food for the body, how do we cry out, how all the world hears of it, how all the newspapers talk of it, with a paragraph headed in great capital letters, DEATH FROM STARVATION! But suppose we were to put a paragraph in the 'Times,' Death of Thought from Starvation, or Death of Moral Activity from Starvation, how people would stare, how they would laugh and wonder! One would think we had no heads or hearts, by the indifference of the public towards them. Our bodies are the only things of consequence.* (pp. 41–42)

Women anorexics outnumber men, with estimates suggesting a 20 to 1 ratio (Smith, 1996). Research with anorexic men suggests that they resemble anorexic women in several ways, including family characteristics and factors that influence the outcome of their treatment (Travis, 1993).

Bulimia

Bulimia, or the "binge-purge" syndrome, has received considerable attention in the past several years (Smith, 1996). Bulimia is characterized by episodes of inconspicuous gross overeating ("food binges") that usually last for an hour or two. The food is usually high in calories, soft, and sweet. The food binge stops when the bulimic experiences severe abdominal pain, goes to sleep, is interrupted, or engages in self-induced purging (e.g., vomiting or using laxatives). Although the bulimic, like the anorexic, has an abnormal concern with becoming fat, the bulimic differs from the anorexic in several ways. Generally, a bulimic is only slightly underweight or even of normal weight. Also, amenorrhea is not a usual feature among bulimics.

Although both anorexics and bulimics have a morbid fear of becoming fat, the bulimic's weight fluctuates between weight loss and weight gain, whereas the anorexic loses weight to an extreme degree (Jackson, 1992). Bulimics admit more readily to their eating disorder than do anorexics.

The exact extent of bulimia is unknown, but authorities consider it a fairly common problem. Surveys of college populations have found a high incidence (13 percent to 67 percent) of undergraduate women engaging in bulimic behaviors. One of the reasons why a reliable estimate of the number of bulimics is difficult to make is that extreme secrecy surrounds the bulimic's behavior. The bulimic's food binges and vomiting usually occur in private. Adding to the problem is the bulimic's normal appearance in terms of body weight. Also, her eating habits in social situations appear quite normal.

Although many authorities believe only women engage in bulimic behaviors, others have found that some men (e.g., wrestlers needing to maintain weight) also exhibit this eating disorder (Jackson, 1992). Bulimia does lead to medical complications such as kidney and intestinal problems as well as dental problems (caused by the acid in the vomited food).

In the book, *Reviving Ophelia: Saving the Selves of Adolescent Girls,* author Mary Pipher states:

> *Bulimic young women have lost their true selves. In their eagerness to please, they have developed an addiction that destroys their central core. They have sold their souls in an attempt to have the perfect body. They have a long road back. . . . Anorexic young women tend to be popular with the opposite sex. They epitomize our cultural definitions of feminine: thin, passive, weak and eager to please. Oftentimes young women report that they are complimented on their appearance right up until they are admitted to hospitals for emergency feeding.* (pp. 170, 175)

The title of Pipher's book refers to the Ophelia character in *Hamlet*. As a girl Ophelia is happy and has freedom. At adolescence, this character loses her self. For example, when she falls in love with Hamlet, she lives only for his approval. Ophelia is torn apart by her efforts to please Hamlet and her father. Eventually Hamlet leaves her because of her obedience to her father. Ophelia reacts with grief, dresses in very heavy, elegant clothes, and drowns in a flower-strewn stream.

Adjusting to a masculine-biased definition of feminine physical beauty can be hazardous to women's health (Cash, Winstead, & Janda, 1986). Severe dieting can lead to death. Another danger is complying with a masculine-biased definition of an employed mother—one who combines career, lifestyle, and parenting all by herself, with no help from a mate or an employer. That burden is related to declines in physical health (McBride, 1990).

Prostate Cancer

In the summer of 1996, the National Prostate Cancer Coalition (NPCC) announced some startling statistics. Over 6 million men currently have some form of prostate cancer in the United States. Further, in 1996, a projected 317,000 new cases of prostate cancer would be diagnosed, and 41,000 men would die from prostate cancer (Oesterling, 1996). Prostate cancer is now the leading cancer threat and the second leading cause of cancer-related deaths in American men. As pointed out in a recent publication, "in blacks the statistics are even more sobering, with a higher incidence of disease, a higher likelihood of diagnosis at a more advanced stage of disease, and a lower rate of survival after adjustment for disease stage than among whites" (Morgan et al., 1996, p. 304). The disturbing fact is that African American men suffer a higher incidence of prostate cancer than any population in the world. Granted, these statistics are alarming, but they take on tragic proportions when we consider that prostate cancer is relatively easy to diagnose and treat if action is taken early. To understand this serious male health concern, let's examine the physiology of the prostate, some common symptoms associated with a noncancerous prostate condition (i.e., benign prostatic hyperplasia, or BPH), and two diagnostic tests available to men for the early detection of prostate cancer.

The sex gland called the prostate is located just below the bladder and in front of the rectum's inner wall. The prostate surrounds the urethra (the tube that carries urine from the bladder) and during sexual arousal secretes fluids that help transport sperm during ejaculation. For a man's first 40 to 50 years, the prostate poses few problems. However, beginning in middle age for reasons not yet clearly understood, a man's prostate experiences a "growth spurt" that often leads to a condition known as *benign prostatic hyperplasia* (BPH), a noncancerous enlargement of the prostate.

Although slow in developing, many middle-aged or older men know all too well the symptoms associated with BPH. The most common symptoms are a hesitancy to begin urination, a decrease in the force and stream while urinating, and the need to get up two to three times a night to urinate, a condition called *nocturia*. Are the symptoms associated with BPH common? The best estimates suggest that nearly 60 percent of men over 60 years and more than 95 percent of men in their eighties have one or more symptoms of BPH (Cunningham, 1990).

If men had to worry only about a decline in their force and stream while urinating and the inconvenience of frequent nightly trips to the bathroom, we could end our discussion here. However, an enlarged prostate is especially vulnerable to cancerous growth. How then can middle-aged men prevent the lethal consequences often associated with untreated prostate cancer?

The two most common and readily assessible diagnostic tests to screen for prostate cancer are the digital rectal exam (DRE) and the prostate-specific antigen (PSA) blood test. Regarding the value of the latter test, Joseph Oesterling (1996) notes that "the measurement of prostate-specific antigen (PSA) in serum is *the most useful tool available today for the diagnosis of early, curable adenocarcinoma of the prostate* (p. 345; italics added). Although many men may object to the slight discomforts associated with a rectal exam and having their blood drawn, these two tests taken together can be one of the most effective ways for middle-aged men (especially those with family histories of cancer and African American men) to detect the possibility of cancer. If a man's physician detects an enlarged and hard prostate and the PSA is above normal limits, the next step would be to biopsy prostate tissue to check for cancerous cells. Detecting the cancer before it moves outside of the prostate gland is the key to successful treatment of prostate cancer.

If prostate cancer is found, surgery to remove the prostate is a common treatment. One reason many men avoid consulting their physician (or their urologist) with a potential prostate problem is the notion that prostate surgery leaves a man impotent. However, today's surgical techniques avoid disturbing the nerve bundles that run along either side of the prostate and control a man's ability to have an erection.

The best advise we can provide here is that all middle-aged men (beginning in the early forties for those with family histories of cancer and African American men, beginning in the early fifties for all others) should include prostate examinations (DRE and PSA) as part of their yearly routine medical checkup.

Summary

Much attention has been given to the fact that women are more likely than men to be diagnosed as suffering from mental illnesses. Gender differences do appear among some psychological disorders. For example, women are more likely to exhibit certain eating disorders, such as anorexia nervosa and bulimia, and depression. A personality pattern known as antisocial personality is more commonly found among men.

A growing concern among many mental health professionals is the presence of sex bias in therapy. Researchers have contended that the mental health profession holds a double standard of mental health that penalizes women for acting in "nonfeminine" ways as well as in "feminine" ways. To eliminate the constricting effects of gender roles, several new approaches to therapy have recently been introduced, including consciousness-raising groups and feminist therapies.

Sex comparisons exist in health status and individuals' access to and utilization of health care. Physical health is a social as well as biomedical phenomenon.

Suggested Readings

Busfield, J. (1996). *Men, women, and madness: Understanding gender and mental disorders*. New York: New York University Press.

Klonoff, E., Landrine, H., & Scott, J. (1995). Double jeopardy: Ethnicity and gender in health research. In H. Landrine (Ed.), *Bringing cultural diversity to feminist psychology: Theory, research, and practice*. Washington, DC: American Psychological Association.

Russo, N. F., & Green, B. (1993). Women and mental health. In F. Denmark & M. Paludi (Eds.), *Psychology of women: A handbook of issues and theories*. Westport, CT: Greenwood Press.

Sabo, D., & Gordon, D. (Eds.). (1995). *Men's health and illness: Gender, power, and the body*. Thousand Oaks, CA: Sage.

White, E. (Ed.) (1994). *The black women's health book*. Seattle: Seal Press.

PART THREE

Future

11

Social Movements
and Gender

As we face a new century, American men remain bewildered by the sea of changes in our culture, besieged by the forces of reform, and bereft by the emotional impoverishment of our lives. For straight white middle-class men a virtual siege mentality has set in. The frontier is gone and competition in the global marketplace is keener than ever. The current era, in which middle-class incomes seem to slip downward (in purchasing power) for the first time since World War II, makes pinning one's proof of manhood on the capacity to succeed as a breadwinner and provider increasingly perilous. The Self-Made Man, that model of manhood we have inherited as the only marker of our success as men, leads more than ever before to chronic anxiety and insecurity.

Michael Kimmel

I myself have never been able to find out precisely what feminism is: I only know that people call me a feminist whenever I express sentiments that differentiate me from a doormat.

Rebecca West

What's Your Opinion?

Do you believe the goals outlined in the late 1960s and early 1970s by the women's movement still speak to current college men and women?

What goals would you identify for a new men's movement?

How are issues of race and class addressed in social movements dealing with rethinking femininity and masculinity?

"Nothing endures but change" wrote Heraclitus. And yet change is often resisted. Over the centuries, social movements have provided a powerful impetus for social change. Although the American Revolution, the suffrage movement, the civil rights marches of the 1960s, and the antinuclear movement show wide differences in their approaches and goals, they all share several features: "a commotion, a stirring among the people, an unrest, a collective attempt to reach a visualized goal" (Herberle, 1951, p. 6). Thus a *social movement* is a group of people organized and led to some extent to promote or resist social change. Society's definitions of feminine and masculine gender role expectations have also changed throughout history. Today, gender roles are once again being challenged by certain social movements, and there is growing evidence that these social movements will continue into the near future.

In this chapter we will concentrate on the social movements that have pushed and are still pushing for new definitions of society's gender roles. First we will examine the social conditions that have created the women's movement. We will trace the roots of the modern-day women's movement back to the early strivings for economic independence in the last Middle Ages by the women who challenged many powerful patriarchal social structures. We will continue by exploring the rise of feminism in the nineteenth century, and we will end by discussing the reemergence of the women's movement of the 1970s and 1980s. Next we will focus on men who are calling for changes in masculine gender role expectations. Finally, we will offer suggestions for future social policy applications of sex and gender.

Individuals don't change in a vacuum; rather, the social forces that surround them either prompt change or restrain it. Although individuals affect the times in which they live, the social forces that arise from various social institutions play a decisive role in creating the situations wherein individuals may choose to act.

The Women's Movement

Many people believe that what is presently called *the women's movement* is a rather recent social phenomenon. In fact, the history of the present-day women's movement extends back several centuries. However, Myra Sadker and David Sadker (1994) note that most textbooks now used in history classes devote only 2 to 3 percent of their content to women and the women's movement.

Whenever there has been an upheaval in society and in its social institutions, we are apt to find the prevalent gender roles challenged and, to some extent, modified or changed. We will concentrate here on three separate periods in history, each of which has had an effect on women's and men's lives and realities: the late Middle Ages (from the eleventh century to the fifteenth century), the latter half of the nineteenth century, and from the mid-1960s to the present. In each of these periods we find significant changes in the social structures of society; therefore, it is not surprising that the traditional gender roles have been challenged and changed during each of these periods.

Feminism in the Late Middle Ages

During medieval times, images of women were limited to that of child bearer or sexual seductress. A common picture of the medieval woman is that of an unschooled and illiterate person whose life was totally dominated by men. During her early years a young woman was ruled by her father and brothers; after marriage she was ruled by her husband in all secular matters. In all spiritual affairs the church's clergy ruled over a woman. In medieval drama, women were merely shadowy figures in the background while men were on center stage.

Scholars have begun to challenge the nearly universal view that men dominated women in the Middle Ages. For example, some women, like Hildegard von Bingen (1098–1179) and Isotta Nogarola (1418–1466), gained considerable prestige and status for their scholarly works (Flanagan, 1989). Less visible but just as important were the women "ambassadors of culture" who owned books, for they "substantially influenced the development of lay piety and vernacular literature in the later Middle Ages" (Bell, 1982, p. 743). Other women also broke the tradition of women's total dependency on and subservience to men. Some women chose to live in all-female religious or secular communities. Those who joined women's religious groups, however, usually found themselves under the rule of existing men's religious communities (McLaughlin, 1974; Schulenberg, 1989). We will focus our attention on the women who joined secular communities where domination by men was remarkably absent. Although not constituting a majority, the medieval women who charted a new lifestyle—either of scholarship or without men—laid the pattern that other women would follow several centuries later.

The Beguines

During the medieval era the Roman Catholic church found itself under increasing attack from heretical groups. Groups such as the Albigensians and Waldensians openly attacked the church and the institution of marriage, which the church had sacramentalized. The Albigensians believed marriage to be an abomination: "physical marriage has always been a mortal sin, and that in the future life no one will be punished more severely because of adultery or incest than for legitimate matrimony" (Herlihy, 1973, p. 134). The Waldensians believed that both women and men should seek spiritual perfection in the single life. These antichurch groups attracted many women who despised the "lecherous" ways of the church's clergy. Furthermore, many families supported their daughters joining these groups for an education, something they would not have gotten from the church (Herlihy, 1973).

Many Orthodox Catholic women who wished to join a religious convent were actually prevented from doing so by the church. Although some religious orders welcomed women, the majority did not and declared that they had justification for excluding women aspirants. Thus large numbers of women during this period led a single life. Their choice was a result of many factors: the popularity of heretical groups with their prohibitions against marriage, the clergy who would not allow women into the religious life, and the fact that there were more marriageable women than men in the population (Guttentag & Secord, 1983).

Many single women joined communities known as the Beguines. During the twelfth century in Northern Europe, the Beguine movement attracted mainly unmarried and widowed women (McConnell, 1969; Neel, 1989). Unlike the unmarried women who entered religious convents, the Beguines did not take vows of chastity or practice an ascetic lifestyle. The Beguines did not have a single founder or rule of life, unlike the norm for the religious communities of women. The Beguine communities supported themselves through various occupations that could be practiced within their local communities. The church took a rather dim view of the Beguine communities and decreed them to be an "abominable sect of women."

By the fourteenth century, many unmarried women, either individually or in groups such as the Beguines, sought nontraditional means of self-support. One means of self-support was to enter the various trades or guilds that represented different occupations. Initially, entrance into a guild was strictly forbidden to all women. Over a period of time, however, women found their way into the labor force in such occupations as weaving and sewing. Finally, near the end of the Middle Ages, some guilds were comprised of all women; the members of these guilds became widely accepted by their communities as skilled craftspersons (Guttentag & Secord, 1983).

Although a majority of women of the latter Middle Ages did not enter the Beguines or other female secular groups or solely provide for their economic sustenance outside of marriage, a small but decidedly independent number did. What is most important about the Beguines and other independent women during this period is that these women broke away from tradition and lived on their own without the supervision and support of men. Today's women's movement can be thought of as a continuation of the efforts of these medieval women who challenged and changed the traditional male-defined gender role expectations of women.

The Women's Movement in the Nineteenth Century and Early Twentieth Century

The nineteenth century found social change the rule in England and in the United States. In the United States there was no single American lifestyle during the nineteenth century. During this period, at least three different areas in the United States could be delineated as having distinct lifestyles: the established industrial New England states, the antebellum agrarian South, and the frontier stretching westward from the Ohio Valley. The conditions of life for women were vastly different in each of these geographical areas. One thing most nineteenth-century women had in common, however, was their experience of hard and ceaseless work.

In the New England states, women found themselves involved in the daily routines of working to help support their families. Large numbers found work in the textile factories of New England. Those not working in textile mills helped support themselves and their families by weaving and sewing in their homes. The change in the meaning of the term "spinster" helps show

how the textile industry affected women's lives. Originally the term simply meant a female spinner. But eventually the term came to mean an unmarried woman (Cott, 1977).

The South has been romanticized as the portion of the United States where women were placed on pedestals, and men were the epitome of gentlemanly ways. In fact, women of the antebellum South were not strangers to work. Historian Anne Scott (1970) described the daily life of a Southern woman as one of work from sunrise to sunset:

> *No matter how large or wealthy the establishment, the mistress was expected to understand not only the skills of spinning, weaving, and sewing, but also gardening, care of poultry, care of the sick, and all aspects of food preparation from the sowing of seed to the appearance of the final product on the table. Fine ladies thought nothing of supervising hog butchering on the first cold days in fall, or of drying fruits and vegetables for the winter. They made their own yeast, lard, and soap, set their own hens, and were expected to be able to make with equal skill a rough dress for a slave or a ball gown for themselves. It was customary for the mistress to rise at five or six, and to be in the kitchen when the cook arrived to "overlook" all the arrangements for the day. A Virginia gentleman's bland assertion that "a considerable portion of her life must be spent in the nursery and the sickroom" was a simple description of reality. (p. 31)*

Slave women were essential to the economy of the antebellum South. Black women who did not work in the fields were domestic servants. Slave women were also valued for their fertility. The image of slave women held by slave masters was one of sex object, in contrast to the "virtuous" Southern woman. This image was one means by which Southern society justified rape.

Most slave women did not have opportunities that permitted their escape. Most of the runaway slaves were young men (Sterling, 1988). Because slave women had children at an early age they were less likely to attempt escape. Women did resist slavery by poisoning their masters, sabotaging work, and feeding runaway slaves. Through their religion, song, and storytelling, they passed on black culture to the children. As Dorothy Sterling (1988) noted:

> *Slave narratives testify to the strength slave women exhibited in resisting the degradation of slavery, in maintaining their fervent belief that they had a right to be free, and in sustaining the hope for freedom in their children. Their persistent belief in their own humanity undercut the most basic principle of slavery—that blacks were less than human. (p. xxv)*

Frontier women worked in fields and woods. The lack of even the most common amenities proved to be one of the harsher realities of life. To tame the land and make a home, women's work was every bit as essential as men's work.

Before the nineteenth century, few voices were raised to protest women's subordinate role and inferior status. One exception was Mary Wollstonecraft,

Mary
Wollstonecraft,
photograph
of etching.

Sophia Smith Collection,
Smith College

who wrote a powerful treatise, *A Vindication of the Rights of Women* (1792), which called for an end to women's "slavish obedience" to men. Although Wollstonecraft's book set the stage for a women's movement to develop, most women resisted because they believed that such a movement was opposed to all that was "natural."

The women's movement of today actually has its roots in the early anti-slavery or abolition movement that began in the early part of the nineteenth century. Sarah Grimke and Angeline Grimke, the daughters of a

Box 11-1

> ### *Mary Wollstonecraft*
> ### *Excerpt from:* A Vindication of the Rights of Women *(1833)*
>
> To account for, and excuse the tyranny of man, many ingenious arguments have been brought forward to prove, that the two sexes, in the acquirement of virtue, ought to aim at attaining a very different character: or, to speak explicitly, women are not allowed to have sufficient strength of mind to acquire what really deserves the name of virtue. . . . Strengthen the female mind by enlarging it, and there will be an end to blind obedience; but, as blind obedience is ever sought for by power, tyrants and sensualists are in the right when they endeavour to keep women in the dark, because the former only want slaves, and the latter a play-thing. The sensualist, indeed, has been the most dangerous of tyrants, and women have been duped by their lovers, as princes by their ministers, whilst dreaming that they reigned over them. . . .

South Carolina slaveholder, were two notable female abolitionists who also became involved with the "women's issue" during their fight against slavery. Sarah Grimke blamed men for women's subjugation, a point of view not readily admitted to by most individuals of that period. In 1837 she wrote:

> *All history attests that man has subjugated woman to his will, used her as a means to promote his selfish gratification, to minister to his sensual pleasure, to be instrumental in promoting his comfort; but never has he desired to elevate her to that rank she was created to fill. He has done all he could to debase and enslave her mind; and now he looks triumphantly on the ruin he has wrought, and says, the being he thus deeply injured is his inferior. . . . But I ask no favors for my sex. . . . All I ask of our brethren is, that they will take their feet from off our necks and permit us to stand upright on that ground which God designed us to occupy.* (quoted in Hole & Levine, 1984, p. 534)

Surprisingly, the majority of men abolitionists, although they championed the freedom and rights of the slave, did not support women's rights. The women abolitionists were looked upon by men only as willing workers for the cause of antislavery, willing workers in the sense of handing out leaflets and ministering to men. Even the most dedicated women abolitionists were not allowed to occupy official positions within the abolitionist movement.

The demeaning second-class status of women abolitionists became obvious in 1840 at the World Anti-Slavery Convention held in London. Women delegates were prohibited from engaging in any of the proceedings and relegated to sit in the galleries away from the official events. Experiencing this discrimination firsthand, Lucretia Mott and Elizabeth Cady Stanton vowed to press for women's rights as well as an end to slavery when they returned to the United States. Consequently, the first Women's Rights Convention was held in Seneca Falls, N.Y., on July 19 and 20, 1848. The Seneca Falls Convention is generally regarded as the birth of the modern-day women's movement.

Box 11-2

Excerpt from: The First Women's Rights Convention
Seneca Falls, New York
July 19–20, 1848

When, in the course of human events, it becomes necessary for one portion of the family of man to assume among the people of the earth a position different from that which they have hitherto occupied, but one to which the laws of nature and of nature's God entitle them, a decent respect to the opinions of mankind requires that they should declare the causes that impel them to such a course.

We hold these truths to be self-evident: that all men and women are created equal; that they are endowed by their Creator with certain inalienable rights; that among these are life, liberty, and the pursuit of happiness; that to secure these rights governments are instituted, deriving their just powers from the governed.

The history of mankind is a history of repeated injuries and usurpations on the part of man toward woman, having in direct object the establishment of an absolute tyranny over her. To prove this, let facts be submitted to a candid world.

He has never permitted her to exercise her inalienable right in the elective franchise.

He has taken from her all right in property, even to the wages she earns.

He has denied her the facilities for obtaining a thorough education, all colleges being closed against her.

He has endeavored, in every way that he could, to destroy her confidence in her own powers, to lessen her self-respect, and to make her willing to lead a dependent and abject life.

Resolutions Adopted

That woman is man's equal—was intended so by the Creator, and the highest good of the race demands that she should be recognized as such.

That the same amount of virtue, delicacy, and refinement of behavior that is required of woman in the social state, should also be required of man, and the same transgressions should be visited with equal severity on both man and woman.

The only resolution at the Seneca Falls Convention that was not passed by unanimous agreement was the one dealing with women's suffrage. However, two years later at a women's convention held in Salem, Ohio, the question of women's suffrage was a prominent issue, and for the first time, men were prohibited from participating in the convention's activities. The fact that men were barred from participation signaled a new fervor among the new feminists' consciousness.

The Salem Convention had one peculiar characteristic. It was officered by women; not a man was allowed to sit on the platform, to speak, or vote. Never did men so suffer. They implored just to say a word; but no;

*the President was inflexible—no man should be heard. If one meekly
arose to make a suggestion he was at once ruled out of order. For the
first time in the world's history, men learned how it felt to sit in silence
when questions in which they were interested were under discussion.*
(quoted in Hole & Levine, 1984, p. 537)

One of the most moving stories of this period is the exchange between a
group of antifeminist clergymen and an ex-slave by the name of Sojourner
Truth. The incident occurred at the second National Woman's Suffrage Convention, held in Akron, Ohio, in 1852, when a group of clergymen took the
floor and spoke at length about women's "inferior nature" and their "proper
place in God's plan." They went on and on about women's delicate nature
and their need for men's benevolent protection. No longer able to tolerate
these men's harangues, Sojourner Truth took the floor and recounted her
days as a slave. She told how she had suffered physical privations and
watched helplessly as her children were sold to other plantation owners. And
when it came to the issue of women's fragile and delicate nature, Sojourner
Truth held up her strong arms and said:

*"I have plowed and planted and gathered into barns, and no man
could head me! And ain't I a woman?"* (quoted in Brawley, 1921)

Her epochal statement, "And ain't I a woman?" stands as a testament to all
women who have been exploited, mistreated, and abused by insensitive, un-
caring, and powerful individuals.

The Turbulent Years (1865–1920)

During the Civil War years, the women's movement receded into the background of social concerns. Most of the women who worked for women's
rights during the 1850s believed that once the war ended, the rights of both
blacks and women would be assured. However, after the Civil War, the abolitionist movement and women's movement parted company. The abolitionist
and women's rights alliance that had worked for decades to win a measure
of human dignity for blacks was soon shattered because the newly won freedom was to be for the black man only, not for the white woman and not for
the black woman. Sadly, many of the white male abolitionists were merely
interested in putting an end to slavery for business reasons. With slavery
abolished, these men saw no need for women's emancipation. Thus, after
years of being linked to the cause for black freedom, the women's movement finally came into its own (DuBois, 1978).

The newly formed women's movement that began in the late 1860s was to
witness several turbulent decades, during which women from many different
organizations fought the battle for women's suffrage from many different perspectives. During the latter half of the nineteenth century and during the
early twentieth century, the women's movement included many groups with
many different ideologies and strategies.

Sojourner Truth
seated with
Knitting. Entered
according to Act of
Congress in the
year 1864, but
S. T., in the clerk's
office of the U.S.
District for Eastern
District of
Michigan.

Sophia Smith Collection,
Smith College

In 1869 Elizabeth Cady Stanton and Susan B. Anthony formed the militant National Woman Suffrage Association (NWSA), which worked for women's suffrage, lobbied against the exploitation of women, and sought better working conditions for women. Also in 1869 the American Woman Suffrage Association (AWSA) was founded; the AWSA was more moderate and restricted its efforts solely to winning women's right to vote. Thus, almost immediately the women's movement had two organizations with very different views of what needed to be accomplished and how to accomplish those goals.

The fight for federal suffrage began almost immediately after the war's end. An amendment for women's suffrage was introduced in Congress in 1868 and every year thereafter. Wyoming was the first territory to grant women's suffrage, thanks to the work of Esther Morris. (However, Wyoming legislators' support of women's suffrage was motivated less by their concern for women's rights than by their desire to encourage Eastern women to move west and reverse the chronic shortage of women in the territory.) When Wyoming sought statehood in 1889, many Southern men who were members of Congress fought its admission because of its passage of women's suffrage. When confronted by the powerful Southern block, a Wyoming delegate telegraphed the legislature back home and asked if they wished to repeal women's suffrage. The reply from Wyoming was succinct and defiant: "We will remain out of the Union a hundred years rather than come in without the women" (quoted in Deckard, 1983, p. 262). Wyoming won statehood in 1890.

In the same year, the national and American organizations merged to become the National American Woman Suffrage Association (NAWSA). Since its inception in 1869, the national organization had grown more conservative and focused primarily on the suffrage issue, setting aside its original concerns for better working conditions and an end to female exploitation by industry. The new organization consisted mainly of middle- and upper-class women who worked for women's suffrage. NAWSA's antiblack sentiment was as much a ploy to curry favor with Southern men in Congress as it was an indication of just how much the women's movement had changed in less than 30 years from the time when it was in the forefront for the struggle for black rights. However, the men in Congress were never persuaded to support women's suffrage.

The number of employed women steadily grew during this period: 4 million in 1890 to 5.3 million in 1900 to 7.4 million in 1910. In 1900, the International Ladies Garment Workers Union formed to rectify the countless injustices so widespread in the textile and garment industries. The National Women's Trade Union League was formed in 1903. The first task on their agenda was to lobby Congress to study the intolerable working conditions of most working women. For the most part, women union members were suspicious of the women who fought only for women's suffrage. In the eyes of many union women, suffrage had become a middle-class and elitist women's issue.

Another social force making its contribution to women's rights was the Socialist party, which went on record at its 1901 convention to support "equal civil and political rights for men and women" (Buhle, 1971). In 1904, a

Woman's National Socialist Union was formed. Josephine Kaneko founded the newspaper *Socialist Woman* in 1907; this newspaper advocated socialism and women's rights. In the main, however, socialist men expected their wives to remain in the background and fight for socialist goals rather than women's rights, believing that "women, like blacks, needed no special demands or special organizations but should just join the party; the victory of socialism would solve all problems" (quoted in Deckard, 1983, p. 270).

Harriet Blatch founded the Women's Political Union in 1907. By 1914, certain factions within NAWSA became committed to more militant actions and were expelled from the organization. These women joined forces with the Women's Political Union, and the Women's party was born. The Women's party was militant in its women's rights activities and pacifistic with respect to the United States' entry into World War I. Among women who fought for women's suffrage during the years leading up to the war, another serious split developed between those in favor of war (NAWSA) and those opposed to war (the Women's party).

After the war's end, there was considerable public sentiment in support of women's suffrage. Many women had worked tirelessly in the war movement. Finally, in May and June of 1919, both houses of Congress passed the Nineteenth Amendment giving women the right to vote. The next step was to gain the necessary two-thirds ratification from the states. By the summer of 1920, 35 states had ratified the Nineteenth Amendment, but one more state was needed. The South was committed to fight against its passage, so the only state left to gain the needed two-thirds was the border state of Tennessee. In August, Tennessee was flooded with both proponents and opponents of the amendment. The amendment passed by only two votes, but those two were enough to make the Nineteenth Amendment part of the U.S. Constitution. The day was August 26, 1920, and the Nineteenth Amendment was part of the Constitution. To achieve this goal, Carrie Chapman Catt, NAWSA's president, calculated that it took:

> . . . *fifty-two years of pauseless campaign . . . fifty-six campaigns of referenda to male voters; 480 campaigns to get Legislatures to submit suffrage amendments to votes; 47 campaigns to get State constitutional conventions to write woman suffrage into state constitutions; 277 campaigns to get State party conventions to include woman suffrage planks; 30 campaigns to get presidential party conventions to adopt woman suffrage planks in party platforms, and 19 campaigns with 19 successive Congresses.* (quoted in Hole & Levine, 1984, p. 541)

Millions of women from vastly different backgrounds and ideologies worked together and separately to gain for all women a measure of the human dignity and respect that had been denied them for centuries. Not only did these women gain the right to vote, they won a sense of accomplishment and achievement in winning a battle against the centuries-old sexist doctrines that had prevented women from exercising their rights as citizens of the United States.

Women's suffrage
demonstration,
New York City,
May 16, 1912.
Library of Congress

The Modern-Day Women's Movement

Once women had gained the right to vote, many expected that they would
turn out *en masse* at the polls. However, it is estimated that only 43 percent
of all eligible women voted in the fall of 1920 (Gruberg, 1968). Even so, most
men politicians were ready to accommodate women. Both the Republican
and Democratic parties included most of the organized women's demands in
their party platforms in 1920 (Chafe, 1972; Lemons, 1973). A number of bills
passed Congress in the early 1920s, all of which had the support of various
women's groups. For example, there were bills to fund programs to help
teach mothers to better care for their babies, to regulate meat inspection, to
standardize and equalize women's and men's citizenship requirements, and
to extend the civil service's merit system to include women (Deckard, 1983).
In 1923 and every year thereafter, the Equal Rights Amendment was introduced into Congress. It finally passed in 1972.

But the liberal forces of the women's movement soon weakened and were
replaced by a nationwide surge of conservatism. According to Barbara
Deckard (1983), several factors contributed to this untimely end to what was
expected to be a new era for women and for the political system as a whole:

*The conservative swing in the country reflected the economic upswing in
the 1920s . . . and the fact that a large, native-born industrial labor
movement was still nascent and weak. The women's confused response
to the all-out attack on them was also conditioned by the narrow, legal-
istic ideology of the suffragists that propagandized suffrage as the single
goal—neglecting basic social and economic equality. As a result, the*

Pamphlet
identifying reasons
women wanted the
vote.
CULVER PICTURES

THE WOMEN
of Washington Want
THE BALLOT
WHY?

Because Those who obey laws should have something to say as to their making.

Because Those who pay taxes to support government should be represented in government.

Because Those who have the homes in charge should be able to aid in the law-making which protects and relates in any way to children and the home.

Because It is the most womanly, economical, and efficient way of influencing public affairs.

Because Government is a question of the people, for the people, and should be by the people, not by men alone.

Because It has been eminently successful wherever tried, both in the United States and in foreign countries.

Because Women themselves want it. There are 6,000,000 club women and 6,000,000 working women in the United States who are asking for the ballot.

Because It is the only method of government that is moral and just.

*women's liberation movement disappeared almost completely after 1923
and, for other reasons as well, remained dormant for 40 years (from
about 1923 to 1963).* (p. 286)

During World War II women entered the workforce in numbers never before seen (Summerfield, 1980). However, the war years saw little progress in terms of women's issues and women's rights. After the war, industries fired women in order to give their jobs to the returning soldiers. Four million women were fired between 1945 and 1947. The country fell back into the sexist pattern of insisting that women remain in the private sphere and men remain in the public sphere.

The Reemergent Women's Movement

Three events occurred in the early 1960s that revitalized the women's movement. First, in December 1961, President John F. Kennedy, at the urging of Esther Peterson, then director of the U.S. Women's Bureau, appointed a commission to examine the status of women in America. Subsequently, commissions on the status of women were formed in all 50 states. Second, Betty Friedan's *The Feminine Mystique* (1963) articulated the problems many women were facing in their everyday lives because of sexism. And third, Congressperson Howard W. Smith (D–Va.) miscalculated on a crucial vote in Congress. Smith, an arch-conservative and chairperson of the powerful

House Rules Committee, planned to scuttle a civil rights bill that was to be voted on in 1964. Opposing the bill because it would prohibit job discrimination against black men and fearing that many liberal congresspersons would vote for it, Smith decided to sabotage the bill by adding an amendment. Smith's amendment included "sex" as another category. He reasoned that with the inclusion of sex, the bill would be so radical that moderates and even a few liberals would vote against it. But, to Smith's astonishment, the bill—and the amendment—passed. Thus, when the 1964 Civil Rights Act was passed, it prohibited employers, labor unions, and employment agencies from discriminating on the basis of race, color, religion, national origin, and sex.

However, the Civil Rights Act of 1964 was only as good as the enforcement behind it. Although the Equal Employment Opportunity Commission (EEOC) was responsible for the enforcement of such laws, the Commission seemed more concerned about protecting the rights of black men than about protecting women's rights. In June 1966, several women met with Friedan while attending the Third National Conference of the President's Commission on the Status of Women. From this informal meeting the National Organization for Women (NOW) was born. In October, a press conference was called announcing the existence of NOW and presenting its goal: "To take action to bring women into full participation in the mainstream of American society now, exercising all the privileges and responsibilities thereof in truly equal partnership with men" (quoted in Deckard, 1983, p. 324).

As the newly reemergent women's movement gained momentum, it soon became evident that it actually had two distinct branches, both of which had very different orientations, memberships, and organizational approaches.

One approach began with the founding of NOW. Over the years, NOW grew into an organization comprised of a national governing board and well over 800 local chapters. The membership has been primarily middle-class, white, college-educated women who initiated legal suits, lobbied, staged boycotts, and used other traditional strategies to achieve social change.

At the second national NOW conference, held in November 1967, a women's Bill of Rights was drawn up. Looking back now, the demands set forth in this document may not be thought of as extreme or radical. Bear in mind, though, that the year was 1967 and the women's movement was neither a household word nor a powerful social force. The public's attention was focused more on the growing Vietnam conflict, and few considered women's plight as second-class citizens. At the top of the list of demands was the call for an Equal Rights Amendment to the Constitution. The delegates further demanded that the federal government should place greater emphasis on enforcing the 1964 Civil Rights Law that banned discrimination against women in employment. Other demands dealt with instituting maternity leave as a benefit in the employment sector, an increase in child-care facilities, equal opportunities in both the educational and employment sectors, and finally, a choice for women about their bodies, especially in terms of reproduction.

Two of the demands proved too radical for some members in attendance, namely the Equal Rights Amendment and the abortion proposal. The women from the United Auto Workers argued against the call for an Equal Rights Amendment because their union officials opposed such an amendment. Many others argued against the abortion proposal, saying it was not an issue of women's rights. However, NOW continued to grow and become one of the more visible organizations championing women's rights during the 1970s.

Other feminists' organizations were also founded during this time that more or less focused on very specific goals. For example, the Women's Equity Action League (WEAL) was formed for the purpose of securing less gender-stereotypic legislation. The National Women's Political Caucus (NWPC) was formed to promote women seeking political office. The infrastructure governing NOW and other professional women's organizations was rather formal, with elected officers, boards of directors, by-laws, and a national membership.

A second group of the women's movement was a less structured and, some would say, more radical branch, advocating changes in women's lives. During the late 1960s, thousands of women began to see that many of the social movements of that time (e.g., the student movement and the anti-Vietnam movement) relegated women to little more than "manning typewriters and mimeograph machines, bringing coffee, and serving as 'chicks' to be 'balled' for sport and relaxation" (Sherif, 1976, p. 375). Angered by such patronizing attitudes and behaviors, many women began to develop their own women's movement. In detailing the meteoric rise of this radical branch of the women's movement, Jo Freeman (1984) wrote:

> *This expansion was more amoebic than organized, because the younger branch of the movement prides itself on its lack of organization. Eschewing structure and damning leadership, it has carried the concept of "everyone doing her own thing" almost to its logical extreme. The thousands of sister chapters around the country are virtually independent of each other, linked only by journals, newsletters, and cross-country travelers. Some cities have a coordinating committee that tries to maintain communication among local groups and to channel newcomers into appropriate ones, but none of these committees has any power over the activities, let alone the ideas, of any of the groups it serves. One result of this style is a very broadly based, creative movement, to which individuals can relate as they desire, with no concern for orthodoxy or doctrine.* (p. 545)

This branch of the women's movement has encouraged several groups that have all added their own distinctive ideologies and approaches to women's issues: the New York Radical Women, the Redstockings, the Stanton-Anthony Brigade, and the Feminist. One result of this approach to women's liberation was the consciousness-raising group, a resocializing technique whereby women met in small groups to exchange thoughts and share feelings about what it meant to be women in a sexist society.

Both approaches agreed on the passage of the Equal Rights Amendment (ERA). The proposition stated:

Section 1. Equality of rights under the law shall not be denied or abridged by the United States or by any State on account of sex.

Section 2. The Congress shall have the power to enforce, by appropriate legislation, the provisions of this article.

Section 3. This amendment shall take effect two years after the date of ratification. (SJ RES 10)

The ERA passed its legal ratification period on June 30, 1982, and failed to gain an additional three states to secure a total of 38 states for ratification. The reasons for the defeat of ERA are complex, but some possible factors are the skillful anti-ERA campaigns run by such groups as STOPERA, the Moral Majority, and other conservative groups (Dworkin, 1983; Eisenstein, 1982). Also, some people just didn't know what the ERA stated, which led to all kinds of misconceptions about the amendment (Jacobson, 1983). President Ronald Reagan's opposition to ERA certainly did not help. His opposition broke the presidential tradition that was set by his six predecessors, who had all supported ERA's passage.

The campaigns against ERA in various state legislatures were earmarked by half-truths and deceptive issues conjured up to play on people's fears— unisex bathrooms, women soldiers, and the end of a heterosexual orientation in favor of a lesbian slant. All of these false issues and others kept many Americans in a state of confusion and helped to defeat a constitutional amendment that would have made it illegal to discriminate against a person on the basis of her or his sex.

Even with the defeat of ERA, the women's movement is not dead. In the last several years women have made considerable progress in their struggle for full equality in several social sectors. There is a flourishing women's movement in several European countries, including Germany (Altbach, 1984; Harrigan, 1982; Janssen-Jurreit, 1982) and France (Burke, 1978; Kaufman-McCall, 1983; Stewart, 1980).

During the 1980s, some people suggested that the women's movement had peaked or served its purpose and was once again moving toward its demise. In March 1984, *Ms.* magazine commissioned Louis Harris and Associates to poll a national sample of women and men to examine several issues crucial to women in the 1980s, such as the gender gap and gender equality in the workplace. Regarding the results, Gloria Steinem (1984) reported:

Perhaps more important for the future than any other single result of this Harris poll, a full 57 percent of American women nationwide now believe that the Women's Movement "has just begun." Only 24 percent believe it "has peaked and will be less important in the future"; 13 percent believe it "has now reached its full size and impact"; and 6 percent are "not sure." (p. 54)

Thus a majority of the women of the United States believe that the women's movement is "alive and well." The women's movement has been the single most influential social movement in the past several decades.

The role of lesbian women in the women's movement was addressed in 1955 by Del Martin and Phyllis Lyon, who founded the Daughters of Bilitis (DOB). The DOB was the first public organization devoted to the needs of lesbians and to promoting an accurate image of the lesbian in society. Two years later, Barbara Gittings founded the New York City chapter of the DOB. Gittings was also instrumental in starting the publication *The Ladder,* which during its years in print (1956–1972) was to become one of the most visible manifestations of lesbian liberation.

During the late 1960s many lesbians joined the women's movement. Most, however, did not discuss their sexual orientation. One who did was Rita Mae Brown, who had joined NOW in 1969 and refused to keep her sexual orientation a secret. In 1970, after considerable pressure, Brown resigned from NOW, stating: "Lesbianism is the one word which gives the New York N.O.W. Executive Committee a collective heart attack" (quoted in Abbott & Love, 1973, p. 112). After leaving NOW, Brown and others formed the group Radicalesbians.

The women's movement struggled with the question of lesbians and their double oppression, first as women and second as lesbians. In September 1971 at the national convention of NOW, a strongly worded resolution was passed by the membership. The resolution openly admitted that NOW had treated its lesbian members rather shamefully during its formative years. Although potential members were never questioned about their sexual orientation, NOW did admit that its lesbian members had been an embarrassment to the organization and that the group had treated them as if they were "stepsisters" in the movement. The resolution noted how NOW had accepted its lesbian members' contributions of financial support and work but assiduously avoided taking any public stance on lesbian issues or providing any support when lesbians and their relationships were denounced in public. The resolution made it clear that NOW would from that time onward give its full support to all women, regardless of their sexual orientation. Moreover, NOW acknowledged that specific lesbian issues and demands were to be considered an integral part of the women's movement in general.

The role of women of color in the women's movement has been a matter of debate during the last decade (Landrine, 1995; Reid, 1984). Beale (1970) introduced the term "double jeopardy" to describe the situation of African American women (and we can extend this to all minority women), who deal with the interface of racism and sexism in relationships, education, and the workplace. As Pamela Reid (1984) suggested:

Since the rise of Black and other ethnic equity groups together with the feminist movement, "double bind" may also accurately reflect the dilemma in which minority women now find themselves. Black women are in the position where, too often, they must decide between their dual identities as Blacks and women. Sometimes, a decision representing loy-alty to one identity results in rejection by the other group members, hence a double bind. (p. 247)

Women of color do feel that it should be feasible to work for an end to racism and sexism (DeFour, 1990). They have typically not participated in the women's movement, however, because of the social inequalities between the groups. Zellman (1978) noted that feminist organizations have been characteristically middle-class while many women of color are of working-class background. As Deckard (1983) discussed:

Many black and Chicano women were repelled by the racial and class composition of the women's movement. Especially during the early years, they felt that they had little in common with movement women and that the movement did not attack problems of central concern to them. In class and color, movement women looked too much like "Miss Ann," the employer and oppressor of the black woman domestic. Even when militant Third World Women became aware that they were play-ing the traditional subservient feminine role in black or Chicano libera-tion groups, racial or ethnic loyalty often kept them from public revolt. (p. 343–344)

The cooperation of women's groups and civil rights groups has eased the position of many women of color (Landrine, 1995).

Let's now consider the social movements involving issues of concern to men and analyze the men's movement of the 1970s and 1980s.

The Men's Movement

Why is a men's movement needed? Surely, men don't need liberation in the same way that women do. Or do they? Few people deny that men have the advantage when it comes to many elements that women have been working so fervently for during the past hundred years or more. What can men gain from a men's movement? In fact, hasn't nearly every movement over the centuries—political, religious, military, and economic—been a men's movement of sorts in that at least some men have benefited?

As the term *men's movement* is used here, we mean the very recent social movement that has called attention to the limiting features of the masculine gender role and the social institutions that have supported sexist ideology. Men are affected by certain psychological and emotional constraints as women are (Brannon, 1982). Many authors have noted, for example, that some features of the masculine gender role are rather damaging for men in general (Brod, 1989; Doyle, 1995).

The prescriptive norms of the masculine gender role have changed over the centuries, with various social institutions upholding different norms for men (Pleck & Pleck, 1980; Rotundo, 1993). But overall, we can suggest that the masculine gender role has stressed dominance and power over the environment. It is these aspects of the masculine gender role that are being challenged by some individuals.

The Early Years and the Women's Movement

Most of the men who formed the present-day men's movements came to a heightened awareness of their gender role expectations and limitations by way of the women's movement. Many of these men had previously been involved in other liberal causes and social movements, such as the civil rights movement, the student movement, and the anti-war movement, that rocked the United States during the 1960s. The move from concern over Vietnam or free speech on campus to an awareness of gender-related issues was, for most of these men, influenced by personal relationships with women who brought women's issues to the men's attention. Sociologist Jon Snodgrass (1977), whose relationship with a woman forced him to question some of his sexist attitudes and beliefs, wrote about such a transition:

> *My full introduction to the women's movement came through a personal relationship. . . . I met and fell in love with a woman who was being politicized by women's liberation. As our relationship developed, I began to receive repeated criticism for being sexist. At first I responded, as part of the male backlash, with anger and denial. In time, however, I began to recognize the validity of the accusation, and eventually even to acknowledge the sexism in my denial of the accusation. . . . One evening, my lover challenged the male supremacist remarks of a television commentator. I defended the commentator and we argued. I denied that I was being sexist and I denied that my refusal to admit being wrong in an intellectual argument with a woman was also associated with my masculinity. Subsequently, I realized that I had supported the commentator simply because he was a man and not because I believed he was correct. Threatened by the challenge to my male dominance, I had identified with him against the person I loved because he and I were genitally males. Thus I dimly recognized patriarchal bonding and faintly perceived my own misogyny.* (p. 7)

These initial challenges to some men's sexist beliefs and the entrenched patriarchal values in their lives led small groups of men around the country to form consciousness-raising groups, modeled after the women's groups. Many of these early men's CR groups focused on some of the problems men encountered in trying to fulfill masculine gender role expectations. Still other groups of men met to discuss the issue of sexism and its social supports that had oppressed women for centuries. Then in 1974, a small group organized the first Men and Masculinity Conference, which was held in Knoxville, Tenn. Since then there has been a national conference nearly every year. The focus of these conferences is the overriding issue that men in our society are cut off from their full potential as human beings and that many of the masculine gender role's prescriptions harm women and men.

During the late 1970s and into the 1980s, those interested in pursuing the issues of gender roles in society became divided into a number of factions (Clatterbaugh, 1990). The two most strident wings of the men's movement were the men's rights and the antisexist groups. During the late 1970s and early 1980s, many men began to organize "men's rights" and "fathers' rights" groups. The focus of the men's rights groups has been primarily on changing the laws they feel discriminate against men in their roles as husbands and fathers, such as divorce laws, child custody laws, and visitation rights. Most of these men support the ERA.

The second wing of the men's movement is much more socially and politically conscious and more concerned with ending the patriarchal social structures that have oppressed and discriminated against women, people of color, lesbians, and gay men. For this group, the men's rights wing of the men's movement is elitist (i.e., white, middle-class, and college-educated) and covertly, if not overtly, antifeminist. In fact, many of those involved with this group disavow totally the title of men's movement, seeing in it further evidence of the not-so-subtle antiwoman bias.

For these men, the questions of unfair divorce settlements, child custody cases, and the like are a ruse used by some men who favor perpetuating their own dominant status in society. It seems that the two factions of the men's movement have little in common except that they support another bid for the ERA.

Sensing the growing division among the two factions of the men's movement, many women and men have made a concerted effort in recent years to form national organizations that could address the personal concerns for men caught up in these changing times and confront head-on the oppression caused by the sexist ideology that permeates our social structures. One such national organization had its roots in the early 1980s when a group met in New York and announced the formation of the National Organization for Men (NOM).

In his opening remarks, Robert Brannon (1982), the National Council chairperson for NOM, noted the goals and some of the history behind NOM. He stated:

> *This afternoon marks the first public appearance of a new national organization. It is one composed primarily of American men, and devoted to a wide range of issues and actions which especially affect the lives of men in this society.*
>
> *We wish to make clear also that together with our concern for the lives and welfare of men, we are committed to changing other injustices which have since ancient times been associated with a human being's sex. We are committed to full equality and justice for women, and with equal conviction, to full equality and acceptance of those who have been stigmatized because of their sexual preference. We believe, in fact, that all of these issues are far more closely connected than most human beings have recognized in the past.*

> *There have been other, previous groups of men who were concerned about one or another of the many special problems and issues of men. There are today organizations of women who demand equal treatment, and organizations of gay men and lesbian women who are asking for the simple justice of being treated fairly and equally. Although less well-known, there have also been groups of men in the past who fought valiantly for the rights of women, and there have been heterosexual men who worked for an end to prejudice against gays. But the record will show that there has never before been an organized national movement of men with the breadth of concern, and the determination to bring about social change, as the one that we are launching today.* (p. 5)

In April 1984, the governing council of NOM (after a vote of the membership) changed its name to the National Organization for Changing Men (NOCM). The abrupt organizational name change resulted, at least partly, from the action of Sidney Siller, a New York lawyer and outspoken critic of the women's movement. Siller selected the name National Organization for Men to identify his newly formed group, which contends that men have suffered unduly because of the actions of feminist women. Thus to clearly differentiate themselves from Siller's group, the membership of NOM voted to become the National Organization for Changing Men (NOCM). In 1990, by another vote of the membership, NOCM changed its name again, this time to the National Organization for Men Against Sexism (NOMAS).

The men's movement consists of numerous men's rights groups across the country and antisexist groups, like NOMAS; however, these groups have not succeeded in coalescing. Further, the men's movement has been unsuccessful in its attempts to attract large numbers of women and men to its cause. In fact, the membership of NOMAS has remained around 450 over the years. We will have to wait to see how successful NOMAS and other national groups are in achieving their goals. Alan Gross, Ronald Smith, and Barbara Wallston (1983) gave a less than enthusiastic analysis of the men's movement and its impact on the social and psychological conditions that caused its members to seek change. They wrote:

> *Theoretically at least, the fledgling U.S. men's movement has easy access to money, organizational skills, and other resources traditionally controlled by males, yet in the past decade it has failed to cohere and prosper as a nationally influential movement. In contrast with its frequent comparison, modern feminism, it has not succeeded in significantly altering the fabric of society, in suggesting new legislation, or even in providing an alternative avenue for the personal frustrations of millions of American men. Nonetheless, the men's movement, largely through men's groups, men's conferences, and a few shoestring publications, has directly and indirectly influenced the lives of several thousand men. The men's movement is certainly not a case study of success. . . .*

If there is to be a real and significant change in men's lives, it probably will not come from anything approaching a bona fide organized social movement rallying for a change in the masculine gender role. Rather, change is more likely to come from the grassroots where men from every walk of life and educational background begin to change their own attitudes, behavior, and beliefs, which affect not only their own lives but the lives of others around them. Are most men ready to take this step toward their own liberation from their restrictive gender role and an end to the patriarchal systems that favor men over women? Some are, but more are not.

Before any significant change can come about in the system that oppresses women in so many ways and oppresses men mainly in psychological ways, social institutions must change and legislation must be passed that will cause a majority of men to evaluate their gender role and decide that self-change is both necessary and beneficial.

In October 1995, thousands of African American men were in Washington, D.C., attending the Million Man March, a march devoted to convincing African American men to look at the importance of themselves and their relationships to mates and children and to network with other African American men. Shuron Morton, a college student participating in one of your textbook author's (Paludi) classes on the psychology of gender, attended this Million Man March. He offered the following account of his experiences:

> . . . *there was a great sense of security and brotherhood in the air. All brothers from all walks of life were here, together, to support one another, and most importantly, to establish a new beginning. A beginning in which we would set all of our wrong doings aside and behind us and try to start with a clean slate. . . . There was a type of spiritual essence that came over me. The theme of the Million Man March was a challenge for us black men to make a spiritual atonement for our past indecisions in order to move our lives in a more positive direction.*

To the Future: Changing Perspectives on Gender

Throughout our discussions we have noted that the study of gender has been a study of "differences" between girls and boys, women and men. Eleanor Maccoby and Carol Nagy Jacklin (1974) challenged this longstanding tradition of emphasis on gender differences by alerting us to *well-established gender differences* (i.e., verbal ability, mathematical ability, visual-spatial ability, and aggression), *unfounded gender differences* (e.g., suggestibility, self-esteem, cognition, analytic skills, achievement motivation), and *unresolved gender differences* (e.g., tactile sensitivity, fear and anxiety, competitiveness, compliance).

Maccoby and Jacklin's review suggested that continued emphasis on gender differences prevents us from seeing gender similarities while encouraging us to exaggerate those differences we do find.

The Million Man
March.

© Daniel Sheehan/The
Image Works.

The need, therefore, is to redefine the constructs typically used in studies of gender. For example, an ethic of care needs to be considered an alternative moral theory, not as a complement to justice theories of moral reasoning (Tronto, 1987). Rejecting social programs as inappropriate to one's needs must be included in coping strategies for dealing with victimization, not viewed as an act of relinquishing control or helplessness (Koss, 1993). Work needs to be redefined to include child care, housekeeping, and volunteer services (Paludi & Fankell-Hauser, 1986). And, power needs to be considered as a "capacity" rather than a "thing" word (Hartsock, 1983). As Flax (1987) suggested, a feminist utopia would be characterized by (1) equal sharing and valuing by women and men of all socially useful work, (2) redistribution of all socially necessary work, (3) dissolution of the division between private and public work, and (4) equitable rewards for all those who participate in doing work of benefit to society. We need to redefine these constructs so we do not keep women's lives and realities invisible.

We are thus suggesting that gender be conceptualized as a system of social relations. To fully comprehend gender, we need to develop a perspective of the dialectics of ethnicity, sex, gender role, class, age, and sexual orientation. The meaning of gender is constantly altered by social context (Unger, 1989). For example, what have appeared to be gender differences in interpersonal behavior and achievement may be better described as differences due to power and status (Kahn & Gaeddert, 1985). Conceptualizing gender in terms of status suggests we look to the institutional or structural factors to explain women's and men's behavior rather than within the individual. As Arnold Kahn and William Gaeddert (1985) concluded:

> *In our society, men and women do have different status, and it is the status of women that must be improved if sex differences are to disappear, and this will not be accomplished by changing perceptions or making women act more like men.* (p. 141)

Rhoda Unger (1995) recently argued:

> *We need to move away from sex and gender as our only major explanatory tool.*
>
> *We need to operationalize what feminist psychologists mean by social construction and not view it simply as everything that biology is not.*
>
> *We need to interrogate both ourselves and our discipline in terms of the biases with which we examine the world.*
>
> *We need to explore the empiricist feminist dilemma of how to be social constructionist and still use "data." This process includes the obvious technique of redefining what we mean by data as well as deconstructing our customary categories of analysis.*
>
> *We need to begin to develop a "moral" basis for feminist psychology and its concern with diversity. To do so, we will need to move beyond our laboratory context, where issues of poverty and power are irrelevant. We will also need to leave our comfortable surroundings for much less*

pleasant realities so that we can better understand healthy coping in dire circumstances.

We may have to recognize that some dilemmas are not absolutely resolvable and that "solutions" need to be constantly redefined. Certainty is possible only in a homogeneous and unchanging world.

We should not let our preoccupation with scholarship that asks what is really true stop us from doing activist, challenging feminist psychology. (pp. 427–428)

This is an exciting time to be studying the psychology of sex and gender. We encourage you to continue to think critically about this discipline as well as others, to value cultural experiences, and to integrate your knowledge of research and theories with life.

Suggested Readings

Bohan, J. (1993). Regarding gender: Essentialism, constructionism, and feminist psychology. *Psychology of Women Quarterly, 17,* 5–21.

Doyle, J. A. (1995). *The male experience* (3rd ed.). Dubuque, IA: Brown & Benchmark.

Kimmel, M. (1996). *Manhood in America: A cultural history.* New York: Free Press.

Landrine, H. (1995). Cultural diversity, contextualism, and feminist psychology. In H. Landrine (Ed.), *Bringing cultural diversity to feminist psychology: Theory, research, and practice.* Washington, DC: American Psychological Association.

Unger, R. (1995). Cultural diversity and the future of feminist psychology. In H. Landrine (Ed.), *Bringing cultural diversity to feminist psychology: Theory, research, and practice.* Washington, DC: American Psychological Association.

References

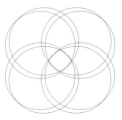

Abbott, S., & Love, B. (1973). *Sappho was a right-on woman*. New York: Stein & Day.

Abu-Lughod, R. (1983). *A community of secrets: The separate world of Bedouin women*. Paper presented at the Conference on Communities of Women, sponsored by Aiello, J. Signs, Stanford University. (1972). A test of equilibrium theory: Visual interaction in relation to orientation, distance, and sex of interactants. *Psychonomic Science, 27,* 335–336.

Albee, G. (1984). Reply to Lantz. *American Psychologist, 39,* 82–84.

Albin, R. (1977). Psychological studies of rape. *Signs, 3,* 423–435.

Aiello, J. (1972). A test of equilibrium theory: Visual interaction in relation to orientation, distance, and sex of interactants. *Psychonomic Science, 27,* 335–336.

Al-Issa, I. (1982). Gender and adult psychopathology. In I. Al-Issa (Ed.), *Gender and psychopathology*. New York: Academic Press.

Allen, I. (1984). Male sex roles and epithets for ethnic women in American slang. *Sex Roles, 11,* 43–50.

Altbach, E. (1984). The new German women's movement. *Signs, 9,* 454–469.

Amaro, H. (1988). Women in the Mexican American community: Religion, culture, and reproductive attitudes and experiences. *Journal of Community Psychology, 16,* 6–20.

Amaro, H., & Russo, N. F. (1987). Hispanic women and mental health: An overview of contemporary issues in research and practice. *Psychology of Women Quarterly, 11,* 393–407.

American Association of University Women (1993). *Hostile hallways*. Washington, DC: APUW.

American Psychiatric Association (1994). *Diagnostic and statistical manual of mental disorders* (4th ed.). Washington, DC: APA.

American Psychological Association. (1983). *Publication manual*. Washington, DC: APA.

Antill, J. K., Goodnow, J., Russell, G., & Cotton, S. (1996). The influence of parents and family context on children's involvement in household tasks. *Sex Roles, 34,* 215–236.

Arch, E. C., & Cummins, D. E. (1989). Structured and unstructured exposure to computers: Sex differences in attitude and use among college students. *Sex Roles, 20,* 245–254.

Ashmore, R., & DelBoca, F. (1981). Conceptual approaches to stereotypes and stereotyping. In D. Hamilton, (Ed.), *Cognitive processes in stereotyping and intergroup behavior.* Hillsdale, NJ: Erlbaum.

Association of American Colleges. (1982). *The classroom climate: A chilly one for women?* Washington, DC: Project on the Status and Education of Women.

Baenninger, M., & Newcombe, N. (1989). The role of experience in spatial test performance: A meta-analysis. *Sex Roles, 20,* 327–344.

Bailey, N., & Richards, M. (1985). *Sexual harassment in graduate training programs in psychology.* Paper presented at the American Psychological Association, Los Angeles.

Bailey, R. F. (1954). Dutch systems in family naming: New York–New Jersey. *Genealogical Publications of the National Genealogical Society,* no. 12

Baker, N. (1989). *Sexual harassment and job satisfaction in traditional and nontraditional industrial occupations.* Unpublished doctoral dissertation, California School of Professional Psychology, Los Angeles.

Baker, S., & Ehrhardt, A. (1978). Prenatal androgen, intelligence, and cognitive sex differences. In R. Friedman et al., (Eds.), *Sex differences in behavior.* Huntington, NY: Krieger Publishing.

Bandura, A. (1969). *Principles of behavior modification.* New York: Holt, Rinehart & Winston.

Bartlett, J. (1980). *Familiar quotations* (15th ed.). Boston: Little, Brown.

Bar-Yosef, R., & Lieblich, A. (1983). Comments on Brandow's "Ideology, myth, and reality: Sex equality in Israel." *Sex Roles, 9,* 419–426.

Basow, S. (1986). *Gender role stereotypes: Traditions and alternatives.* Monterey, CA: Brooks/Cole.

Basow, S. (1992). *Sex role stereotypes: Traditions and alternatives* (2nd ed.). Monterey, CA: Brooks/Cole.

Baude, A. (1979). Public policy and changing family patterns in Sweden, 1930–1977. In J. Lipman-Blumen & J. Bernard (Eds.), *Sex roles and social policy.* Newbury Park, CA: Sage.

Baxter, S., & Lansing, M. (1980). *Women and politics.* Ann Arbor: University of Michigan Press.

Beale, F. (1970). Double jeopardy: To be black and female. In T. Cade (Ed.), *The black woman: An anthology.* New York: New American Library.

Beck, L., & Keddie, N. (Eds.). (1978). *Women in the Muslim world.* Cambridge, MA: Harvard University Press.

Bell, S. (1982). Medieval women book owners: Arbiters of lay piety and ambassadors of culture. *Signs, 7,* 742–768.

Belle, D. (1984). Inequality and mental health: Low income and minority women. In L. Walker (Ed.), *Women and mental health policy.* Newbury Park, CA: Sage.

Bem, S. L. (1974). The measurement of psychological androgyny. *Journal of Consulting and Clinical Psychology, 42,* 155–162.

Bem, S. L. (1977). On the utility of alternative procedures for assessing psychological androgyny. *Journal of Personality and Social Psychology, 31,* 634–643.

Bem, S. L. (1981). Gender schema theory: A cognitive account of sex typing. *Psychological Review, 88,* 354–364.

Bem, S. L. (1983). Gender schema theory and its implications for child development: Raising gender-schematic children in a gender-schematic society. *Signs, 8,* 598–616.

Bem, S. L. (1993). *The lenses of gender: Transforming the debate on sexual inequality.* New Haven, CT: Yale University Press.

Benally, H. J. (1992). Spiritual knowledge for a secular society: Traditional Navajo spirituality offers lessons for the nation. *Tribal College: Journal of American Indian Higher Education, 3,* 19–22.

Beneke, T. (1982). *Men on rape.* New York: St. Martin's Press.

Bentzen, F. (1963). Sex ratios in learning and behavior disorders. *American Journal of Orthopsychiatry, 33,* 9–98.

Bergmann, B. (1974). Occupational segregation, wages and profits when employers discriminate by race and sex. *Eastern Economic Journal, 1,* 103–110.

Bernard, J. (1973). *The future of marriage.* New York: Bantam Books.

Bernard, J. (1975). *Women, wives, and mothers.* Chicago: Aldine.

Bernard, J. (1988). The inferiority curriculum. *Psychology of Women Quarterly, 12,* 261–268.

Bertilson, H., Springer, K., & Fierke, K. (1982). Underrepresentation of female referents as pronouns: Examples and pictures in introductory college textbooks. *Psychological Reports, 51,* 923–931.

Berzins, J., Welling, M., & Wetter, R. (1975). *The PRF Andro scale user's manual.* Unpublished manual, University of Kentucky.

Betz, N. (1993). Women's career development. In F. Denmark & M. Paludi (Eds.), *Psychology of women: A handbook of issues and theories.* Westport, CT: Greenwood Press.

Betz, N., & Fitzgerald, L. F. (1987). *The career psychology of women.* New York: Academic Press.

Beyene, Y. (1986). Cultural significance and physiological manifestations of menopause: A biocultural analysis. *Culture, Medicine and Psychiatry, 10,* 47–71.

Biden, J. (1993). Violence against women: The Congressional response. *American Psychologist, 48,* 1059–1061.

Billingsley, D. (1977). Sex bias in psychotherapy: An examination of the effects of client sex, client pathology, and therapist sex on treatment planning. *Journal of Consulting and Clinical Psychology, 45,* 250–256.

Bird, P. (1974). Images of women in the Old Testament. In R. Ruether (Ed.), *Religion and sexism.* New York: Simon & Schuster.

Blackwood, E. (1984). Sexuality and gender in certain Native American tribes: The case of cross-gender females. *Signs, 10,* 27–42.

Blau, F. (1975). Women in the labor force. In J. Freeman (Ed.), *Women.* Palo Alto, CA: Mayfield.

Block, J. (1976). Issues, problems, and pitfalls in assessing sex differences: A critical review of the psychology of sex differences. *Merrill-Palmer Quarterly, 22,* 283–308.

Blood, R., & Wolfe, D. (1960). *Husbands and wives*. New York: Free Press.

Blumberg, R. (1976). Kibbutz women: From the fields of revolution to the laundries of discontent. In L. Iglitzin & R. Ross (Eds.), *Women in the world*. Santa Barbara, CA: ABC Clio.

Blumberg, R. (1978). *Stratification: Socioeconomic and sexual inequality*. Dubuque, IA: Brown & Benchmark.

Bouhoutsos, J. (1984). Sexual intimacy between psychotherapists and clients: Policy implications for the future. In L. Walker (Ed.), *Women and mental health policy*. Newbury Park, CA: Sage.

Boyd, S. B. (1990). Domination as punishment *Men's Studies Review, 7* (2), 1, 4–9.

Brandow, S. (1980). Ideology, myth, and reality: Sex equality in Israel. *Sex Roles, 6,* 403–419.

Brannon, R. (1976). The male sex role: Our culture's blueprint of manhood, and what it's done for us lately. In D. David & R. Brannon, (Eds.), *The forty-nine percent majority*. Reading, MA: Addison-Wesley.

Brannon, R. (1982, October). The men's movement. *Ms.,* p. 42.

Brawley, B. (1921). *A social history of the American Negro*. New York: Macmillan.

Briefer, K. (1987, March). *Beyond sexism: Heterosexist bias in feminist psychology*. Paper presented at the Association for Women in Psychology, Denver.

Briere, J., & Lanktree, C. (1983). Sex-role related effects of sex bias in language. *Sex Roles, 9,* 625–632.

Brinn, J., Kraemer, K., Warm, J. S., & Paludi, M. A. (1984). Sex role preferences in four age groups. *Sex Roles, 11,* 901–910.

Bristow, J. T. (1988). *What Paul really said about women*. New York: Harper Collins.

Brittain, A. W. (1996, July 19). The credibility of sociobiology. *The Chronicle of Higher Education,* B3. [Letters to the Editor].

Brod, H. (1989, May). *Men's studies as feminism*. Paper presented at the Second Biennial Meeting of the Midwestern Society for Feminist Studies, Muncie, IN.

Brodsky, A. (1977). Countertransference issues and the woman therapist: Sex and the student therapist. *The Clinical Psychologist, 30,* 12–14.

Broverman, I., Broverman, D., Clarkson, F., Rosenkrantz, P., & Vogel, S. (1970). Sex-role stereotypes and clinical judgments of mental health. *Journal of Consulting and Clinical Psychology, 34,* 1–7.

Broverman, I., Vogel, S., Broverman, D., Clarkson, F., & Rosenkrantz, P. (1972). Sex-role stereotypes: A current appraisal. *Journal of Social Issues, 28,* 59–78.

Brown, D. (1956a). *The IT Scale for Children*. Missoula, MN: Psychological Test Specialists.

Brown, D. (1956b). Sex role preference in young children. *Psychological Monographs, 70,* whole no. 421.

Brown, D. (1957). Masculinity-femininity development in children. *Journal of Consulting Psychology, 21,* 197–202.

Brown, L. (1986). From alienation to connection: Feminist therapy with post-traumatic stress disorder. In E. Rothblum & E. Cole (Eds.), *Another silenced trauma.* New York: Haworth.

Brown L. (1987). Lesbians, weight, and eating: New analyses and perspectives. In Boston Lesbian Psychologies Collective (Ed.), *Lesbian psychologies: Explorations and challenges.* Urbana: University of Illinois Press.

Brown, L. (1995). Cultural diversity in feminist therapy. In H. Landrine (Ed.), *Bringing cultural diversity to feminist psychology: Theory, research, and practice.* Washington, DC: American Psychological Association.

Browne, A. (1993). Violence against women by male partners: Prevalence, outcomes, and policy implications. *American Psychologist, 48,* 1077–1087.

Brownmiller, S. (1984). *Femininity.* New York: Fawcett Columbine.

Buhle, M. (1980). *Women and American socialism, 1870–1920.* Urbana: University of Illinois Press.

Burger, J., & Solano, C. (1994). Changes in desire for control over time: Gender differences in a ten-year longitudinal study. *Sex Roles, 31,* 465–472.

Burke, C. (1978). Report from Paris: Women's writing and the women's movement. *Signs, 3,* 843–855.

Burr, E., Dunn, S., & Farquhar, N. (1972). Women and the language of inequality. *Social Education, 36,* 841–845.

Busfield, J. (1996). *Men, women, and madness: Understanding gender and mental disorders.* New York: New York University Press.

Butts Stahly, G. (1996). Battered women: Why don't they just leave? In J. Chrisler, C. Golden, & P. Rozee (Eds.), *Lectures on the psychology of women.* New York: McGraw-Hill.

Caldwell, M. A., & Peplau, L. A. (1984). The balance of power in lesbian relationships. *Sex Roles, 10,* 587–599.

Callender, C., & Kochems, L. (1983). The North American berdache. *Current Anthropology, 24,* 443–470.

Campbell, P. B. (1988). *Rethinking research: Challenges for new and not so new researchers.* Washington, DC: U.S. Department of Education.

Cantor, M., & Pingree, S. (1983). *The soap opera.* Newbury Park, CA: Sage.

Carlsson, M. (1977). Equality between men and women in Sweden. In *Women and men: Changing roles, relationships, and perceptions.* New York: Praeger.

Carson, R., Butcher, J., & Coleman, J. (1988). *Abnormal psychology and modern life.* Glenview, IL: Scott, Foresman.

Cash, T., Winstead, B., and Janda, L. (1986, April). The great American shape-up. *Psychology Today,* pp. 30–37.

Chafe, W. (1972). *The American woman.* New York: Oxford University Press.

Chesler, P. (1972). *Women and madness.* New York: Avon.

Chia, R. C., Moore, J., Lam, K., Chuang, C., & Cheng, B. (1994). Cultural differences in gender role attitudes between Chinese and American students. *Sex Roles, 31,* 23–30.

Chodorow, N. (1977). Considerations on "A bio-social perspective on parenting." *Berkeley Journal of Sociology, 22,* 179–198.

Chodorow, N. (1978). *The reproduction of mothering: Psychoanalysis and the sociology of gender.* Berkeley: University of California Press.

Christ, C., & Plaskow, J. (1979). *Womanspirit rising.* New York: Harper & Row.

Cixous, H. (1976). *Portrait de Dora.* Paris: Editions des femmes.

Clatterbaugh, K. (1990). *Contemporary perspectives on masculinity.* Boulder, CO: Westview Press.

Cleary, P. (1987). Gender differences in stress-related disorders. In R. Barnett, L. Biener & G. Baruch (Eds.), *Gender and stress.* New York: Free Press.

Cole, C., Hill, F., & Dayley, L. (1983). Do masculine pronouns used generically lead to thoughts of men? *Sex Roles, 9,* 737–750.

Collins, N., & Miller, L. (1994). Self-disclosure and liking: A meta-analytic review. *Psychological Bulletin, 11,* 457–475.

Coltrane, S., & Allan, K. (1994). "New" fathers and old stereotypes: Representations of masculinity in 1980s television advertising. *Masculinities, 2,* 43–66.

Connell, N., & Wilsen, C. (Eds.). (1974). *Rape.* New York: New American Library.

Constantinople, A. (1973). Masculinity-femininity: An exception to a famous dictum? *Psychological Bulletin, 80,* 389–407.

Constantinople, A. (1979). Sex role acquisition: In search of the elephant. *Sex Roles, 5,* 121–133.

Cook, A. S., Fritz, J. J., McCormack, B. L., & Visperas, C. (1985). Early gender differences in the functional usage of language. *Sex Roles, 12,* 909–915.

Cott, N. (1975). Young women in the Second Great Awakening in New England. *Feminist Studies, 3,* 15–29.

Courtois, C. (1988). *Healing the incest wound.* New York: Norton.

Cowan, G. (1995). Black and white (and Blue): Ethnicity and pornography. In H. Landrine (Ed.), *Bringing cultural diversity to feminist psychology: Theory, research, and practice.* Washington, DC: American Psychological Association.

Craddick, R. A. (1963). The self-image in the Draw-A-Person Test and self-portrait drawings. *Journal of Projective Techniques, 27,* 288–291.

Crews, D. (1987). Functional associations in behavioral endocrinology. In J. Reinsch et al. (Eds.), *Masculinity/femininity: Basic perspectives.* New York: Oxford University Press.

Croll, E. (1981a). Women in rural production and reproduction in the Soviet Union, China, Cuba, and Tanzania: Socialist development experiences. *Signs, 7,* 361–374.

Croll, E. (1981b). Women in rural production and reproduction in the Soviet Union, China, and Tanzania: Case studies. *Signs, 7,* 375–399.

Crosby, F., Jose, P., & Wong-McCarthy, W. (1982). Gender, androgyny, and conversational assertiveness. In C. Mayo & N. Henley (Eds.), *Gender and nonverbal behavior.* New York: Springer-Verlag.

Crowley, J., Levitan, T., & Quinn, R. (1973, March). Seven deadly half-truths about women. *Psychology Today,* pp. 94–96.

Culpepper, E. (1994). The spiritual, political journey of a feminist freethinker. In P. Cooey, W. Eakin, & J. McDaniel (Eds.), *After patriarchy: Feminist transformations of the world religions.* Maryknoll, NY: Orbis.

Cunningham, C. (1990). *The prostate problem.* New York: Pinnacle Books.

Curtin, K. (1975). *Women in China.* New York: Pathfinder.

Dachowski, M. (1984). DSM-III: Sexism or societal reality? *American Psychologist, 39,* 702–703.

Dahlberg, F. (Ed.). (1981). *Woman the gatherer.* New Haven, CT: Yale University Press.

Dahlstrom, E. (Ed.). (1971). *The changing roles of men and women.* Boston: Beacon Press.

Dalton, K. (1964). *The premenstrual syndrome.* Springfield, IL: Thomas.

Dalton, K. (1980). Cyclical criminal acts in premenstrual syndrome. *Lancet, 2,* 1070–1071.

Daniloff, N. (1982, June 28). For Russian women, worst of both worlds. *U.S. News & World Report,* pp. 53–54.

Darwin, C. (1859/1967). *On the origin of the species.* New York: Atheneum.

Davidson, C., & Abramowitz, S. (1980). Sex bias in clinical judgment: Later empirical returns. *Psychology of Women Quarterly, 4,* 377–395.

Dayhoff, S. (1983). Sexist language and person perception: Evaluation of candidates from newspaper articles. *Sex Roles, 9,* 527–539.

Deaux, K., & Kite, M. (1993). Gender stereotypes. In F. L. Denmark & M. A. Paludi (Eds.), *Handbook on the psychology of women.*Westport, CT: Greenwood Press.

Deaux, K., & Lewis, L. (1984). Structure of gender stereotypes: Interrelationships among components and gender label. *Journal of Personality and Social Psychology, 32,* 629–636.

de Beauvoir, S. (1952). *The second sex.* New York: Random House.

DeCenzo, D., & Robbins, S. (1996). *Human resource management.* New York: Wiley.

Deckard, B. (1983). *The women's movement.* (3rd ed.). New York: Harper & Row.

DeFour, D. C. (1988). *Racism and sexism in sexual harassment.* Paper presented at the International Congress on Victimology, Tuscany, Italy.

DeFour, D. C. (1990). The interface of racism and sexism in sexual harassment. In M. A. Paludi (Ed.), *Ivory power: Sexual harassment on campus.* Albany: State University of New York Press.

DeFour, D. C. (1996). The interface of racism and sexism on college campuses. In M. Paludi (Ed.), *Sexual harassment on college campuses: Abusing the ivory power.* Albany: State University of New York Press.

DeFour, D. C., & Hirsch, B. J. (1990). The adaptation of black graduate students: A social networks approach. *American Journal of Community Psychology, 18,* 489–505.

DeFour, D. C., & Paludi, M. A. (1988). *Integrating the scholarship on women of color and ethnicity in the psychology of women course.* Workshop presented at the Association for Women in Psychology Conference, Bethesda, MD.

de la Luz Reyes, M., & Halcon, J. (1988). Racism in academia: The old wolf revisited. *Harvard Education Review, 58,* 299–314.

Delaney, J., Lupton, M., & Toth, E. (1988). *The curse: A cultural history of menstruation.* Champaign: University of Illinois Press.

Denmark, F. L. (1994). Engendering psychology. *American Psychologist, 49,* 329–334.

Denmark, F. L., Russo, N. F., Frieze, I. H., & Sechzur, J. (1988). Guidelines for avoiding sexism in psychological research: A report of the Ad Hoc Committee on nonsexist research. *American Psychologist, 43,* 582–585.

Derlega, V., Winstead, B., & Wong, P. (1984). *Self-disclosure in an initial encounter: A case where males disclose more intimately than women in opposite-sex pairs.* Paper presented at the meeting of the Southeastern Psychological Association, New Orleans.

de Waal, F. (1996a, June 14). The biological basis of behavior. *The Chronicle of Higher Education,* B1–2.

de Waal, F. (1996b). *Good natured: The origins of right and wrong in humans and other animals.* Cambridge, MA: Harvard University Press.

Dickson, L. (1993). The future of marriage and the family in black America. *Journal of Black Studies, 23,* 472–491.

Dinnerstein, D. (1976). *The mermaid and the minotaur.* New York: Harper & Row.

Dion, K., & Cota, A. A. (1991). The Ms. stereotype: Its domain and the role of explicitness in title preference. *Psychology of Women Quarterly, 15,* 403–410.

Dion, K., & Schuller, R. (1990). Ms. and the manager: A tale of two stereotypes. *Sex Roles, 22,* 569–577.

Doering, C., et al. (1975). Negative affect and plasma testosterone: A longitudinal human study. *Psychosomatic Medicine, 37,* 484–491.

Dohrenwend, B., & Dohrenwend, B. (1976). Sex differences and psychiatric disorders. *The American Journal of Sociology, 81,* 1447–1454.

Dominick, J. (1979). The portrayal of women in prime time, 1953–1977. *Sex Roles, 5,* 405–411.

Doress-Worters, P. B. (1994). Adding elder care to women's multiple roles: A critical review of the caregiver stress and multiple roles literature. *Sex Roles, 31,* 597–616.

Douglas, A. (1977). *The feminization of American culture.* New York: Knopf.

Douglass, J. (1974). Women and the continental reformation. In R. Reuther (Ed.), *Religion and sexism.* New York: Simon & Schuster.

Douvan, E., & Adelson, J. (1966). *The adolescent experience.* New York: Wiley.

Doyle, J. (1995). *The male experience* (3rd ed.). Dubuque, IA: Brown & Benchmark.

DuBois, E. (1978). *Feminism and suffrage.* Ithaca, NY: Cornell University Press.

du Plessix Grey, F. (1989). *Soviet Women: Walking the tightrope.* New York: Doubleday.

Dweck, C. (1975). The role of expectations and attributions in the alleviation of learned helplessness. *Journal of Personality and Social Psychology, 31,* 674–685.

Dweck, C., et al. (1978). Sex differences in learned helplessness: II. The contingencies of evaluative feedback in the classroom and III. An experimental analysis. *Developmental Psychology, 14,* 268–276.

Dworkin, A. (1981). *Pornography.* New York: Perigee Books.

Dworkin, A. (1983). *Right-wing women.* New York: Putnam.

Dye, N. (1980). *As equals and as sisters.* Columbia: University of Missouri Press.

Dyer, G., & Tiggermann, M. (1996). The effect of school environment on body concerns in adolescent women. *Sex Roles, 34,* 127–138.

Eagly, A. (1995). The science and politics of comparing women and men. *American Psychologist, 50,* 145–158.

Eagly, A., & Carli, L. (1981). Sex of researchers and sex-typed communications as determinants of sex differences in influenceability: A meta-analysis of social influence studies. *Psychological Bulletin, 90,* 1–20.

Eakins, B., & Eakins, G. (1978). *Sex differences in human communication.* Boston: Houghton Mifflin.

Edelbrock, C., & Sugawara, A. (1978). Acquisition of sex-typed preferences in preschool-aged children. *Developmental Psychology, 14,* 614–623.

Ehrhardt, A. E., & Baker, S. (1978). Fetal androgens, human central nervous system differentiation, and behavior and social dominance in man. *Psychosomatic Medicine, 36,* 469–475.

Ehrhardt, A. E., & Meyer-Bahlberg, H. (1975). Psychological correlates of abnormal pubertal development. *Clinics in Endocrinology and Metabolism, 4,* 207–222.

Eisenstein, A. (1982). The sexual politics of the New Right: Understanding the "crisis of liberalism for the 1980s." *Signs, 7,* 567–588.

El Guindi, F. (1981). Veiling infitah with Muslim ethic: Egypt's contemporary Islamic movement. *Social Problems, 28,* 465–485.

Elizondo, V., & Greenacher, N. (Eds.). (1980). *Women in a men's church.* New York: The Seabury Press.

Eller, C. (1993). *Living in the lap of the goddess: The feminist spirituality movement in America.* New York: Crossroad.

Erikson, E. (1963). *Childhood and society.* New York: Norton.

Erikson, E. (1968). *Identity: youth and crisis.* New York: Norton.

Fagot, B. (1978). The influence of sex of child on parental reactions to toddler children. *Child Development, 49,* 459–465.

Fagot, B. (1988). *Gender role development in young children.* Paper presented at the Gender Roles through the Lifespan Conference, Muncie, IN.

Faludi, S. (1991). *Backlash.* New York: Crown.

Farah, B. (1976). Climbing the political ladder: The aspirations and expectations of partisan elites. In D. McGuigan (Ed.), *New research on women and sex roles.* Ann Arbor: University of Michigan Press.

Farrell, W. (1974). *The liberated man.* New York: Random House.

Fernberger, S. (1948). Persistence of stereotypes concerning sex differences. *Journal of Abnormal and Social Psychology, 43,* 97–101.

Fillmer, H., & Haswell, L. (1977). Sex-role stereotyping in English usage. *Sex Roles, 3,* 257–263.

Finkelhor, D., & Dziuba-Leatherman, J. (1994). Victimization of children. *American Psychologist, 49,* 173–183.

Finkler, K. (1981). Dissident religious movements in the service of women's power. *Sex Roles, 7,* 481–495.

Fisher, J., Rytling, M., & Heslin, R. (1976). Hands touching hands: Affective and evaluative effects of an interpersonal touch. *Sociometry, 39,* 416–421.

Fitzgerald, L. F., Shullman, S., Bailey, N., Richards, M., Swecker, J., Gold, Y., Ormerod, M., & Weitzman, L. (1988). The incidence and dimensions of sexual harassment in academia and the workplace. *Journal of Vocational Behavior, 32,* 152–175.

Fitzgerald, L. F., & Weitzman, L. (1990). Men who harass: Speculation and data. In M. Paludi (Ed.), *Ivory power: Sexual harassment on campus.* New York: State University of New York Press.

Fitzgerald, L. F., Weitzman, L., Gold, Y., & Ormerod, M. (1988). Academic harassment: Sex and denial in scholarly garb. *Psychology of Women Quarterly, 12,* 329–340.

Flanagan, S. (1989). *Hildegard of Bingen, 1098–1179: A visionary life.* New York: Routledge.

Flax, J. (1987). Postmodernism and gender relations in feminist theory. *Signs, 12,* 621–643.

Fleming, J. (1996). *Who are the proteges? The relationship between mentoring experiences, self-efficacy, career salience, attachment style, and Eriksonian life stage.* Doctoral dissertation submitted to the School of Arts and Sciences, Columbia University.

Flexner, E. (1971). *Century of struggle.* New York: Atheneum.

Fodor, I. G., & Thai, J. (1984). Weight disorders: Overweight and anorexia. In E. A. Blechman (Ed.), *Behavior Modification with Women.* New York: Guilford.

Forden, C. (1981). The influence of sex-role expectations on the perception of touch. *Sex Roles, 7,* 889–894.

Forgey, D. (1975). The institution of berdache among the North American Indian Plains Indians. *Journal of Sex Research, 11,* 1–15.

Forisha, B. (1981). The inside and the outsider: Women in organizations. In B. Forisha & B. Goldman (Eds.), *Outsiders on the inside*. Englewood Cliffs, NJ: Prentice Hall.

Frank, R. (1931). The hormonal causes of premenstrual tension. *Archives of Neurology and Psychiatry, 26,* 1053–1057.

Freeman, J. (1975a). *The politics of women's liberation*. New York: David McKay.

Freeman, J. (1975b). How to discriminate against women without really trying. In J. Freeman (Ed.), *Women*. Palo Alto, CA: Mayfield.

Freeman, J. (Ed.). (1983). *Social movements of the sixties and seventies*. New York: Longman.

Freeman, J. (1984). The women's liberation movement: Its origins, structures, impact, and ideals. In J. Freeman (Ed.), *Women*. Palo Alto, CA: Mayfield.

French, J., & Raven, B. (1959). The bases of social power. In D. Cartwright (Ed.), *Studies in social power*. Ann Arbor: University of Michigan, Institute for Social Research.

Freud, S. (1927). Some psychical consequences of the anatomical distinction between the sexes. *International Journal of Psychoanalysis, 8,* 133–142.

Freud, S. (1948). Some psychological consequences of the anatomical distinction between the sexes. In *Collected papers* (Vol. 5). London: Hogarth.

Freud, S. (1959a). Female sexuality. In J. Strachey (Ed.), *Sigmund Freud: Collected Papers* (Vol. 5). New York: Basic Books.

Freud, S. (1959b). "Civilized" sexual morality and modern nervousness. In J. Strachey (Ed.), *Sigmund Freud: Collected papers*. New York: Basic Books.

Freud, S. (1965). *New introductory lectures on psychoanalysis*. New York: Norton.

Freud, S. (1968). Femininity. In J. Strachey (Ed.), *The complete introductory lectures on psychoanalysis*. New York: Norton.

Friedan, B. (1963). *The feminine mystique*. New York: Norton.

Friedl, E. (1978, April). Society and sex roles. *Human Nature*, p. 70.

Friedman, R. C., Hurt, S. W., Arnoff, M. S., & Clarkin, J. (1980). Behavior and the menstrual cycle. *Signs, 5,* 719–738.

Frieze, I. H. (1997). Battering in intimate relationships. In M. Paludi (Ed.), *Psychology of sexual victimization: A handbook*. Westport, CT: Greenwood Press.

Frisch, R. (1984). Fatness, puberty, and fertility. In B. Gunn & A. Petersen (Eds.), *Girls at puberty: Biological, psychological, and social perspectives*. New York: Plenum.

Fruch, T., & McGhee, P. (1975). Traditional sex role development and amount of time watching television. *Developmental Psychology, 11,* 109.

Gardiner, A. (1976). *Women and Catholic priesthood*. New York: Paulist Press.

Gardner, J. (1970). Sesame Street and sex role stereotypes. *Women, 1,* 42.

Garnets, L. (1996). Life as a lesbian: What does gender have to do with it? In J. Chrisler, C. Golden, & P. Rozee (Eds.), *Lectures on the psychology of women*. New York: McGraw-Hill.

Garrett, C. (1977). Women and witches: Patterns of analysis. *Signs, 3,* 461–470.

Garvey, C. (1977). *Play.* Cambridge, MA: Harvard University Press.

Geer, C., & Shields, S. (1996). Women and emotion: Stereotypes and the double bind. In J. Chrisler, C. Golden, & P. Rozee (Eds.), *Lectures on the psychology of women.* New York: McGraw-Hill.

Geis, F., Brown, V., Jennings (Walstedt), J., & Porter, N. (1984). TV commercials as achievement scripts for women. *Sex Roles, 10,* 513–525.

Gerdes, E., Gehling, J., & Rapp, J. (1981). The effects of sex and sex-role concept on self-disclosure. *Sex Roles, 7,* 989–998.

Gielen, U. (1979). Naturalistic observation of sex and race differences in visual interactions. *International Journal of Group Tensions, 9,* 211–277.

Gilligan, C. (1982). *In a different voice.* Cambridge, MA: Harvard University Press.

Ginorio, A., Gutierrez, L., Cauce, A., & Acosta, M. (1995). Psychological issues for Latinas. In H. Landrine (Ed.), *Bringing cultural diversity to feminist psychology: Theory, research and practice.* Washington, DC: American Psychological Association.

Glen, E., & Feldberg, R. (1977). Degraded and deskilled: The proletarianization of clerical work. *Social Problems, 25,* 52–64.

Gold, Y. (1987, August). *The sexualization of the workplace: Sexual harassment of pink-, white- and blue-collar workers.* Paper presented to the annual conference of the American Psychological Association, New York.

Golden, C. (1987). Diversity and variability in women's sexual identities. In Boston Lesbian Psychologies Collective (Ed.), *Lesbian psychologies: Explorations and challenges.* Urbana: University of Illinois Press.

Golub, S. (1992). *Periods: From menarche to menopause.* Newbury Park: Sage.

Gonen, J., & Lansky, L. (1968). Masculinity, femininity, and masculinity-femininity: A phenomenological study of the Mf scale of the MMPI. *Psychological Reports, 23,* 183–194.

Goodman, L., Koss, M., Fitzgerald, L., Russo, N. F., & Keita, G. P. (1993). Male violence against women: Current research and future directions. *American Psychologist, 48,* 1054–1058.

Goodwin, B. (1996). The impact of popular culture on images of African American women. In J. Chrisler, C. Golden, & P. Rozee (Eds.), *Lectures on the psychology of women.* New York: McGraw-Hill.

Gould, R. (1974). Measuring masculinity by the size of a paycheck. In J. Pleck & J. Sawyer (Eds.), *Men and masculinity.* Englewood Cliffs, NJ: Prentice Hall.

Gould, S. (1976, May). Biological potential vs. biological determinism. *Natural History Magazine,* pp. 12–22.

Goy, R. (1978). Development of play and mounting behavior in female rhesus monkeys virilized prenatally with esters of testosterone of dihydrotestosterone. In D. Chivers & J. Herbert, (Eds.), *Recent advances in primatology* (Vol. 1). New York: Academic Press.

Grady, K. (1988). Older women and the practice of breast self-examination. *Psychology of Women Quarterly, 12,* 473–487.

Graham, D., & Rawlings, E. (1997). Battering. In M. Paludi (Ed.), *Psychology of sexual victimization: A handbook.* Westport, CT: Greenwood Press.

Grant, B. (1980). Five liturgical songs by Hildegard von Bingen (1098–1179). *Signs, 5,* 557–567.

Gray, J. (1996). *Mars and Venus together forever.* New York: Harper Perennial.

Gray-Little, B., & Burks, N. (1983). Power and satisfaction in marriage: A review and critique. *Psychological Bulletin, 93,* 513–538.

Greenberg, M., & Morris, N. (1974). Engrossment: The newborn's impact upon the father. *American Journal of Orthopsychiatry, 44,* 520–531.

Griffin, S. (1979). *Rape: The power of consciousness.* San Francisco: Harper & Row.

Gross, A., Smith, R., Wallston, B. (1983). The men's movement: Personal vs. political. In J. Freeman (Ed.), *Social movements of the sixties and seventies.* New York: Longman.

Gruberg, M. (1968). *Women in American politics.* Oshkosh, WI: Academia Press.

Gunn, B., & Petersen, A. (Eds.). (1984). *Girls at puberty: Biological, psychological, and social perspectives.* New York: Plenum.

Gupta, L. (1994). Kali, the savior. In P. Cooey, W. Eakin, & J. McDaniel (Eds.), *After patriarchy: Feminist transformation of the world religions.* Maryknoll, NY: Orbis Books.

Gutek, B. (1985). *Sex and the workplace.* San Francisco: Jossey-Bass.

Gutmann, M. C. (1994). The meanings of macho: Changing Mexican male identities. *Masculinities, 2,* 21–33.

Gutmann, M. C. (1996). *The meaning of macho: Being a man in Mexico City.* Berkeley: University of California Press.

Guttentag, M., & Secord, P. (1983). *Too many women? The sex ratio question.* Newbury Park, CA: Sage.

Hacker, H. (1975). Gender roles from a cross-cultural perspective. In L. Duberman (Ed.), *Gender and sex in society.* New York: Praeger.

Hall, R., & Sandler, B. (1982). *The classroom climate: A chilly one for women.* Washington, DC: Project on the Status and Education of Women.

Halpern, D. (1995). Cognitive gender differences: Why diversity is a critical research issue. In H. Landrine (Ed.), *Bringing cultural diversity to feminist psychology: Theory, research and practice.* Washington, DC: American Psychological Association.

Hamburg, B. (1978). The psychobiology of sex differences: An evolutionary perspective. In R. Friedman et al., (Ed.), *Sex differences in behavior.* Huntington, NY: Krieger Publishing.

Hamerton, J., et al. (1975). A cytogenetic survey of 14,069 newborn infants. *Clinical Genetics, 8,* 223–243.

Hansen, C., & Hansen, R. (1988). How rock music videos can change what is seen when boy meets girl: Priming stereotypic appraisal of social interactions. *Sex Roles, 19,* 287–316.

Hanson, M. (1994). Sociocultural and physiological correlates of cigarette smoking in women. *Health Care for Women International, 15,* 549–562.

Hare-Mustin, R. (1978). A feminist approach to family therapy. *Family Process, 17,* 181–194.

Hare-Mustin, R. (1983). An appraisal of the relationship between women and psychotherapy: 80 years after the case of Dora. *American Psychologist, 38,* 593–601.

Hare-Mustin, R., & Marecek, J. (1988). The meaning of difference: Gender theory, postmodernism, and psychology. *American Psychologist, 43,* 455–464.

Haring-Hidore, M., & Paludi, M. A. (1989). Sex and sexuality in mentoring and tutoring: Implications for opportunities and achievement. *Peabody Journal of Education, 64,* 164–172.

Harrigan, R. (1982). The German women's movement and ours. *Jump Cut, 27,* 42–44.

Harrison, A. O. (1977). Black women. In V. E. O'Leary (Ed.), *Toward understanding women.* Monterey, CA: Brooks/Cole.

Hartsock, N. (1983). *Money, sex, and power.* New York: Longman.

Hassan, R. (1994). Muslim women and post-patriarchal Islam. In P. Cooey, W. Eakin, & J. McDaniel (Eds.), *After patriarchy: Feminist transformations of the world religions.* Maryknoll, NY: Orbis.

Hatfield, E., & Sprecher, S. (1986). Measuring passionate love in intimate relationships. *Journal of Adolescence, 9,* 383–410.

Hathaway, S., & McKinley, J. (1943). *The Minnesota Multiphasic Personality Inventory.* New York: Psychological Corporation.

Haynes, S. G., & Feinleib, M. (1980). Women, work, and coronary heart disease: Prospective findings from the Framingham Heart Study. *American Journal of Public Health, 70,* 133–141.

Heinrich, P., & Triebe, J. K. (1972). Sex preferences in children's human figure drawings. *Personality Assessment, 36,* 263–267.

Helgeson, V. (1994). Prototypes and dimensions of masculinity and femininity. *Sex Roles, 31,* 653–682.

Henley, N. (1973). Status and sex: Some touching observations. *Bulletin of the Psychonomic Society, 2,* 91–93.

Henley, N. (1977). *Body politics.* Englewood Cliffs, NJ: Prentice Hall.

Henley, N. (1995a). Ethnicity and gender issues in language. In H. Landrine (Ed.), *Bringing cultural diversity to feminist psychology: Theory, research, and practice.* Washington, DC: American Psychological Association.

Henley, N. (1995b). Body politics revisited: What do we know today? In P. Kalbfleisch & M. Cody (Eds.), *Gender, power, and communication in human relationships.* Hillsdale, NJ: Lawrence Erlbaum Associates, Inc.

Herberle, R. (1951). *Social movements.* New York: Appleton-Century-Crofts.

Herdt, G. (Ed.). (1994). *Third sex, third gender: Beyond sexual dimorphism in culture and history.* New York: Zone Books.

Herlihy, D. (1973). Life expectancies for women in medieval society. In R. Morewedge (Ed.), *The role of woman in the middle ages.* Albany: State University of New York Press.

Herman, J. (1981). *Father-daughter incest*. Cambridge, MA: Harvard University Press.

Hill, M. (1988). Child-rearing attitudes of black lesbian mothers. In Boston Lesbian Psychologies Collective, (Ed.), *Lesbian psychologies: Explorations and challenges*. Urbana: University of Illinois Press.

Hilpert, F., Kramer, C., & Clark, R. (1975). Participants' perception of self and partner in mixed-sex dyads. *Central States Speech Journal, 26* (Spring), 52–56.

Hine, D. (Ed.) (1993). *Black women in America: An historical encyclopedia*. Boston: South End Press.

Hines, D. C. (1989). Rape and the inner lives of black women in the Middle West. *Signs, 14*, 912–920.

Hoffman, L. W. (1989). Effects of maternal employment in the two-parent family. *American Psychologist, 44*, 283–292.

Hole, J., & Levine, E. (1984). The first feminists. In J. Freeman (Ed.), *Women*. Palo Alto, CA: Mayfield.

Hollingworth, H. (1943). *Leta Stetter Hollingworth*. Lincoln, NE: University of Nebraska Press.

Hopson, J., & Rosenfeld, A. (1984, August). PMS: Puzzling monthly symptoms. *Psychology Today*, pp. 30–35.

Horner, M. S. (1968). *Sex differences in achievement motivation and performance in competitive and noncompetitive situations*. Unpublished doctoral dissertation, University of Michigan.

Huber, J. (1976). On the generic use of male pronouns. *American Sociologist, 11*, 89.

Hughes, J., & Sandler, B. (1988). *Peer harassment: Hassles for women on campus*. Washington, DC: Project on the Status and Education of Women.

Hunter College Women's Studies Collective. (1983). *Women's realities, women's choices*. New York: Oxford University Press.

Hurwitz, E. (1978). Carrie C. Catt's "suffrage militancy." *Signs, 3*, 739–743.

Hutt, C. (1978). Biological bases of psychological sex differences. *American Journal of Diseases of Children, 132*, 170–177.

Hyde, J. (1981). How large are cognitive differences? *American Psychologist, 36*, 892–901.

Hyde, J. S. (1984). Children's understanding of sexist language. *Developmental Psychology, 20*, 697–706.

Hyde, J. S. (1985). *Psychology of women*. Lexington, MA: Heath.

Hyde, J. (1990). Meta-analysis and the psychology of gender differences. *Signs, 16*, 55–73.

Hyde, J., & Frost, L. (1993). Meta-analysis in the psychology of women. In F. L. Denmark & M. A. Paludi (Eds.), *Handbook on the psychology of women*. Westport, CT: Greenwood Press.

Hyde, J., & Linn, M. (1988). Gender differences in verbal ability: A meta-analysis. *Psychological Bulletin, 104*, 53–69.

Ibsen, H. (1957). *Hedda Gabler: Six plays* (trans. Le Gallienne). New York: Random House.

Inhelder, B., & Piaget, J. (1958). *The growth of logical thinking from childhood to adolescence*. New York: Basic Books.

Intons-Peterson, M., & Crawford, J. (1985). The meanings of marital surnames. *Sex Roles, 12,* 1163–1171.

Jacklin, C. N. (1989). Female and male: Issues of gender. *American Psychologist, 44,* 127–133.

Jacklin, C. N., & Maccoby, E. E. (1982). Length of labor and sex of offspring. *Journal of Pediatric Psychology, 7,* 355–360.

Jackson, L. (1992). *Physical appearance and gender.* Albany: State University of New York Press.

Jackson, L., Fleury, R., Girvin, J., & Gerard, D. (1995). The numbers game: Gender and attention to numerical information. *Sex Roles, 33,* 559–568.

Jackson, L., Sullivan, L., and Rostker, R. (1988). Gender, gender role, and body image. *Sex Roles, 19,* 429–443.

Jacobs, P., et al. (1965). Aggressive behavior, mental subnormality and the XYY male. *Nature, 208,* 1351–1352.

Jacobs, S. (1968). Berdache: A brief review of the literature. *Colorado Anthropologist, 1,* 25–40.

Jacobson, M. (1983). Attitudes toward the Equal Rights Amendment as a function of knowing what it said. *Sex Roles, 9,* 891–896.

Janowsky, D., Berens, S., & Davis, J. (1973). Correlations between mood, weight, and electrolytes during the menstrual cycle: A renin-angiotensin-aldosterone hypothesis of premenstrual tension. *Psychosomatic Medicine, 35,* 143–154.

Janssen-Jurreit, M. (1982). *Sexism.* V. Moberg, trans. New York: Farrar Straus Giroux.

Jennings, M., & Farah, B. (1978). *Social roles and political resources: An over-time study of men and women in party elites.* Paper presented at the Midwest Political Science Association, Chicago.

Johnson, J., Adams, M., Ashburn, L., & Reed, W. (1995). Differential gender effects of exposure to rap music on African American adolescents' acceptance of teen dating violence. *Sex Roles, 33,* 597–605.

Johnson, M. (1980). Mental illness and psychiatric treatment among women: A response. *Psychology of Women Quarterly, 4,* 363–371.

Johnson, P. (1976). Women and power: Toward a theory of effectiveness. *The Journal of Social Issues, 32,* 99–110.

Johnson, P. (1978). Women and interpersonal power. In I. Frieze et al. (Eds.), *Women and sex roles.* New York: Norton.

Jourard, S. (1964). *The transparent self.* Princeton, NJ: Van Nostrand.

Jourard, S. (1971). *Self-disclosure.* New York: Wiley.

Jourard, S. (1974). Some lethal aspects of the male role. In J. Pleck (Ed.), *Men and masculinity.* Englewood Cliffs, NJ: Prentice Hall.

Kahn, A., & Gaeddert, W. (1985). From theories of equity to theories of justice: The liberating consequences of studying women. In V. O'Leary, R. K. Unger, & B. S. Wallston, (Eds.), *Women, gender, and social psychology.* Hillsdale, NJ: Erlbaum.

Kalis, L. (1996, April). What matters more to women voters—Party or gender? *Working Women*, p. 17.

Kalisch, P., & Kalisch, B. (1984). Sex role stereotyping of nurses and physicians on prime-time television: A dichotomy of occupational portrayals. *Sex Roles, 10*, 533–554.

Kanowitz, L. (1969). *Women and the law*. Albuquerque: The University of New Mexico Press.

Kanter, R. (1984). *Men and women of the corporation* (2nd. ed.). New York: Basic Books.

Kaplan, A., & Sedney, M. (1980). *Psychology and sex roles: An androgynous perspective*. Boston: Little, Brown.

Kaplan, M. (1983a). A woman's view of DSM-III. *American Psychologist, 38*, 786–792.

Kaplan, M. (1983b). The issue of sex bias in DSM-III: Comments on the articles by Spitzer, Williams, and Kass. *American Psychologist, 38*, 802–803.

Karraker, K. H., Vogel, D. A., & Lake, A. (1995). Parents' gender-stereotyped perceptions of newborns: The eye of the beholder revisited. *Sex Roles, 33*, 687–701.

Kassell, P. (1984). Ordeal by the press. *New Directions for Women, 13*, 2.

Katchadorian, H. (1977). *The biology of adolescence*. San Francisco: Freeman.

Katz, P., Boggiano, A., & Sihern, L. (1993). Theories of female personality. In F. L. Denmark & M. A. Paludi (Eds.), *Psychology of women: A handbook of issues and theories*. Westport, CT: Greenwood Press.

Kaufman, M. (1989). A tomb of one's own: *Hedda Gabler:* Ibsen's diary of a mad housewife. In D. Kaufman (Ed.), *Public/private spheres: Women past and present*. Boston: Northeastern Custom Book Program.

Kaufman, P. (1984). *Women teachers on the frontier*. New Haven, CT: Yale University Press.

Kaufman-McCall, D. (1983). Politics of difference: The women's movement in France from May 1968—to Mitterand. *Signs, 9*, 282–293.

Keller, E. F. (1982). Feminism and science. *Signs, 7*, 589–602.

Kelly, M. (1981). Development and the sexual division of labor: An introduction. *Signs, 7*, 268–278.

Kennedy, M. (1993). Clothing, gender, and ritual transvestism: The Bissu of Sulawesi. *The Journal of Men's Studies, 2*, 1–13.

Keohane, N. (1981). Speaking from silence: Women and the science of politics. *Soundings, 64* (4), 422–436.

Kerber, L. (1980). *Women of the Republic*. Chapel Hill: University of North Carolina Press.

Ketter, P. (1952). *Christ and womankind*. Westminister, MD: Newman Press.

Key, M. (1975a). *Male/female language*. Metuchen, NJ: Scarecrow Press.

Key, M. (1975b). The role of male and female in children's books— Dispelling all doubt. In R. Unger & F. Denmark (Eds.), *Woman*. New York: Psychological Dimensions.

Kingston, M. H. (1976). *The woman warrior*. New York: Vintage Books.

Kirkpatrick, J. (1974). *Political women*. New York: Basic Books.

Kirkpatrick, J. (1976). *The new presidential elite*. New York: Russell Sage Foundation.

Kitcher, P. (1987). *Vaulting ambition: Sociobiology and the quest for human nature*. Cambridge, MA: MIT Press.

Klonoff, E., Landrine, H., & Scott, J. (1996). Double jeopardy: Ethnicity and gender in health research. In H. Landrine (Ed.), *Bringing cultural diversity to feminist psychology: Theory, research, and practice*. Washington, DC: American Psychological Association.

Klumas, A., & Marchant, T. (1994). Images of men in popular sitcoms. *The Journal of Men's Studies, 2,* 269–285.

Knopf, I. J. (1979). *Childhood psychopathology*. Englewood Cliffs, NJ: Prentice Hall.

Kohlberg, L. (1963). The development of children's orientations toward a moral order: Sequence in the development of human thought. *Vita Humana, 6,* 11–33.

Kohlberg, L. (1966). A cognitive-developmental analysis of children's sex-role concepts and attitudes. In E. Maccoby (Ed.), *The development of sex differences*. Stanford: Stanford University Press.

Kohlberg, L. (1976). Moral stages and moralization: The cognitive-developmental approach. In T. Lickona (Ed.), *Moral development and behavior*. New York: Holt, Rinehart & Winston.

Kohlstedt, S. (1978). In from the periphery: American women in science, 1830–1880. *Signs, 4,* 81–96.

Kolbe, R., & LaVoie, J. (1981, December). Sex-role stereotyping in preschool children's picture books. *Social Psychology Quarterly,* pp. 369–374.

Komarovsky, M. (1964). Cultural contradictions and sex roles. *American Journal of Sociology, 52,* 182–189.

Komarovsky, M. (1976). *Dilemmas of masculinity*. New York: Norton.

Komisar, L. (1971). The image of woman in advertising. In V. Gornick (Ed.), *Woman in sexist society*. New York: New American Library.

Koss, M. (1993). Rape: Scope, impact, inteventions, and public policy. *American Psychologist, 48,* 1062–1069.

Kraditor, A. (1971). *The ideas of the woman suffrage movement, 1890–1920*. New York: Doubleday.

Kramer, C., Thorne, B., & Henley, N. (1978). Perspectives on language and communication. *Signs, 3,* 638–651.

Kreuz, L., & Rose, R. (1972). Assessment of aggressive behavior and plasma testosterone in a young criminal population. *Psychosomatic Medicine, 34,* 321–322.

Kristeva, J. (1975). On the women of China. *Signs, 1,* 57–82.

Kuhn, T. (1962). *The structure of scientific revolutions*. Chicago: University of Chicago Press.

Kuhn, D., Nash, S., & Brucken, L. (1978). Sex role concepts of two- and three-year-olds. *Child Development, 49,* 445–451.

Kukla, A. (1982). Logical incoherence of value-free science. *Journal of Personality and Social Psychology, 43,* 1014–1017.

Kunen, McNeil, & Waggoner. Cited in Paludi, M. A. (1992). *Psychology of women.* Dubuque, IA: Wm. C. Brown.

Kupers, T. A. (1995). The politics of psychiatry: Gender and sexual preference in DSM-IV. *Masculinities, 3,* 597–605.

Kutner, N., & Levinson, R. (1978). The toy salesperson: A voice for change in sex-role stereotypes? *Sex Roles, 4,* 1–7.

LaFrance, M. (1988). *Paradoxes in mentoring.* Paper presented at the International Interdisciplinary Congress on Women, Dublin, Ireland.

LaFromboise, T., Choney, S., James, A., & Wolf, P. (1995). American Indian women and psychology. In H. Landrine (Ed.), *Bringing cultural diversity to feminist psychology.* Washington, DC: American Psychological Association.

Lakoff, R. (1973). Language and woman's place. *Language in Society, 2,* 45–79.

Lamb, M. (1982, October). Why Swedish fathers aren't liberated. *Psychology Today,* pp. 4–77.

Landrine, H. (Ed.) (1995). *Bringing cultural diversity to feminist psychology: Theory, research, and practice.* Washington, DC: American Psychological Association.

Landrine, H., Klonoff, E., & Brown-Collins, A. (1995). Cultural diversity and methodology in feminist psychology: Critique, proposal, empirical example. In H. Landrine (Ed.), *Bringing cultural diversity to feminist psychology: Theory, research, and practice.* Washington, DC: American Psychological Association.

Lansky, L., & McKay, G. (1963). Sex-role preference of kindergarten boys and girls: Some contradictory results. *Psychological Reports, 13,* 415–421.

Lapidus, G. (1978). *Women in Soviet society.* Berkeley: University of California Press.

Lawrence, D. H. (1957). *Lady Chatterley's lover.* New York: Grove Press.

Leavitt, R. (1971). Women in other countries. In V. Gornick & B. Moran (Eds.), *Woman in sexist society.* New York: New American Library.

Lemons, J. (1973). *The woman citizen.* Champaign: University of Illinois Press.

Lerman, H., & Porter, N. (1990). *Feminist ethics in psychotherapy.* New York: Springer.

Lerner, G. (1975). Sarah M. Grimke's "Sister of Charity." *Signs, 1,* 246–256.

Lerner, H. (1976). Girls, ladies, or women? The unconscious dynamic of language choice. *Comprehensive Psychiatry, 17,* 295–299.

Levant, R. F., & Pollack, W. S. (Ed.). (1995). *A new psychology of men.* New York: Basic Books.

Levin, W. (1984). *Sociological ideas.* Belmont, CA: Wadsworth.

Levy, A., & Paludi, M. (1997). *Workplace sexual harassment.* Englewood Cliffs, NJ: Prentice Hall.

Libra, T. S. (1987). The cultural significance of silence in Japanese communication. *Multilingua, 6,* 343–357.

Liebowitz, L. (1989). Origins of the sexual division of labor. In D. Kaufman (Ed.), *Public private spheres: Women past and present.* Boston: Northeastern Custom Book Program.

Lipman-Blumen, J., Handley-Isaksen, A., & Leavitt, H. J. (1983). Achieving styles in men and women: A model, an instrument, and some findings. In J. T. Spence (Ed.), *Achievement and achievement motives.* San Francisco: Freeman.

Lippert-Martin, K. (1992). The classroom climate: What has changed, what has made a difference? In Association of American Colleges (Ed.), *On campus with women, 21,* 1–5, 10.

Lipton, J., & Hershaft, A. (1984). "Girl," "woman," "guy," "man": The effects of sexist labeling. *Sex Roles, 10,* 183–194.

Lombardo, J., & Lavine, L. (1981). Sex-role stereotyping and patterns of self-disclosure. *Sex Roles, 7,* 403–411.

Lopata, H. (1971). *Occupation: Housewife.* New York: Oxford University.

Lopez, S. R., Smith, A., Wolkenstein, B. H., & Charlin, V. (1993). Gender bias in clinical judgement: An assessment of the analogue method's transparency and social desirability. *Sex Roles, 28,* 35–45.

Lorber, J. (1984). Trust, loyalty and the place of women in the informal organization of work. In J. Freeman (Ed.), *Women.* Palo Alto, CA: Mayfield.

Lorber, J. (1994). *Paradoxes of gender.* New Haven, CT: Yale University Press.

Lott, B. (1981). A feminist critique of androgyny: Toward the elimination of gender attributions for learned behavior. In C. Mayo & N. Henley (Eds.), *Gender and nonverbal behavior.* New York: Springer.

Lott, B., & Reilly, M. E. (1996). *Combatting sexual harassment in higher education.* Washington, DC: National Education Association.

Lundberg-Love, P. (1997). Adult survivors of incest. In M. Paludi (Ed.), *Psychology of sexual victimization: A handbook.* Westport, CT: Greenwood Press.

Lynn, D. (1959). A note on sex differentiation in the development of masculinity and femininity. *Psychological Review, 64,* 126–135.

Lynn, N. (1975). Women in American politics: An overview. In J. Freeman (Ed.), *Women.* Palo Alto, CA: Mayfield.

Lynn, N. (1984). Women and politics: The real majority. In J. Freeman (Ed.), *Women* (3rd ed.). Palo Alto, CA: Mayfield.

Lynn, N., & Flora, C. (1977). Societal punishment and aspects of female political participation: 1972 National Convention delegates. In M. Githens & J. Prestage (Eds.), *A portrait of marginality.* New York: Longman.

Maccoby, E. E., & Jacklin, C. N. (1974). *The psychology of sex differences.* Stanford, CA: Stanford University Press.

Machover, K. (1949). *Personality projection in the drawing of the human figure.* Springfield, IL: Thomas.

MacKay, W. R., & Miller, C. A. (1982). Relations of socio-economic status and sex variables to the complexity of worker functions on the occupational choices of elementary school children. *Journal of Vocational Behavior, 20,* 31–37.

Maimon, A. (1962). *Women built a land.* New York: Herzl Press.

Malamuth, N., & Check, J. (1981). Penile tumescence and perceptual responses to rape as a function of victim's perceived reactions. *Journal of Applied Social Psychology, 10,* 528–547.

Malamuth, N., & Donnerstein, E. (1982). The effects of aggressive-pornographic mass media stimuli. In L. Berkowitz (Ed.), *Advances in experimental social psychology* (Vol. 15). New York: Academic Press.

Marecek, J. (1978). Psychological disorders in women: Indices of role strain. In I. H. Frieze, J. Parsons, P. Johnson, D. Ruble, & G. Zellman (Eds.), *Women and sex roles: A social psychological perspective.* New York: Norton.

Marecek, J., & Hare-Mustin, R. T. (1991). A short history of the future: Feminism and clinical psychology. *Psychology of Women Quarterly, 15,* 521–536.

Margold, J. (1994). Migrant masculinity in the transnational workplace. *Masculinities, 2,* 33–36.

Marks, J. (1996, July 19). The credibility of sociobiology. *The Chronicle of Higher Education,* B3. [Letters to the Editor]

Marsh, H. W., Antill, J. K., & Cunningham, J. D. (1989). Masculinity and femininity: A bipolar construct and independent constructs. *Journal of Personality, 57,* 625–663.

Marshall, D. (1971). Sexual behavior on Mangaia. In D. Marshall & R. Suggs (Eds.), *Human sexual behavior.* New York: Basic Books.

Martin, K., & Voorhies, B. (1975). *Female of the species.* New York: Columbia University Press.

Martyna, W. (1980). Beyond the "he/man" approach: The case for nonsexist language. *Signs, 5,* 482–493.

Masters, M., & Sanders, B. (1993). Is the gender difference in mental rotation disappearing? *Behavior Genetics, 23,* 337–341.

Matsumoto, D., & Fletcher, D. (1996). Cross-national differences in disease rates as accounted for by meaningful psychological dimensions of cultural variability. *Journal of Gender, Culture, and Health, 1,* 71–82.

Mazumdar, V. (1978). Comment on suttee. *Signs, 4,* 269–273.

McBride, A. (1990). Mental health effects of women's multiple roles. *American Psychologist, 45,* 381–384.

McCann, I., & Pearlman, L. (1990). *Psychological trauma and the adult survivor: Theory, therapy, and transformation.* New York: Brunner/Mazel.

McClelland, D., Atkinson, J., Clark, R., & Lowell, F. (1953). *The achievement motive.* New York: Appleton-Century-Crofts.

McConnell, E. (1969). *The Beguines and beghards in medieval culture.* New York: Octagon Books.

McCreary, D. (1994). The male role and avoiding femininity. *Sex Roles, 31,* 517–531.

McHugh, M., Koeske, R., & Frieze, I. H. (1986). Issues to consider in conducting nonsexist psychological research: A guide for researchers. *American Psychologist, 41,* 879–890.

McKee, J., & Sheriffs, A. (1957). The differential evaluation of males and females. *Journal of Personality, 25,* 356–371.

McKee, J., & Sheriffs, A. (1959). Men's and women's beliefs, ideals, and self-concepts. *American Journal of Sociology, 64,* 356–363.

McLaughlin, E. (1974). Equality of souls, inequality of sexes: Woman in medieval theology. In R. Ruether (Ed.), *Religion and sexism.* New York: Simon & Schuster.

McNeer, A., Johnson, V., Harbowy, I., & Paludi, M. A. (1984). *Children's causal attributions of successful performance: Replication and refinement.* Paper presented at the Southwestern Society for Research in Human Development, Denver.

Mead, M. (1935/1963). *Sex and temperament in three primitive societies.* New York: Norton.

Mednick, M. (1975). Social change and sex-role inertia: The cause of the kibbutz. In M. Mednick, S. Tangri, & L. Hoffman (Eds.), *Women and achievement.* New York: Halstead Press.

Mednick, M., & Thomas, V. (1993). Women and achievement. In F. Denmark & M. Paludi (Eds.), *Psychology of women: A handbook of issues and theories.* Westport, CT: Greenwood Press.

Mehrabian, A. (1971). Verbal and nonverbal interaction of strangers in a waiting room. *Journal of Experimental Research in Personality, 5,* 127–138.

Melich, T. (1995). *The Republican war against women.* New York: Bantam.

Mernissi, F. (1975). *Beyond the veil.* New York: Schenkman.

Merritt, S. (1982). Sex roles and political ambition. *Sex Roles, 8,* 1025–1036.

Merton, R. (1968). *Social theory and social structure.* New York: Free Press.

Messenger, J. (1971). Sex and repression in an Irish folk community. In D. Marshall & R. Suggs (Eds.), *Human sexual behavior.* New York: Basic.

Miedzian, M. (1991). Boys will be boys: Breaking the link between masculinity and violence. New York: Doubleday.

Mihalik, G. J. (1989). More than two: Anthropological perspectives on gender. *Journal of Gay and Lesbian Psychotherapy, 1,* 105–118.

Miller, C., & Swift, K. (1988). *The handbook of nonsexist writing.* New York: Harper & Row.

Miller, J. B. (1976). *Toward a new psychology of women.* Boston: Beacon Press.

Money, J. (1964). Two cytogenetic syndromes: Psychologic comparisons. 1. Intelligence and specific-factor quotients. *Journal of Psychiatric Research, 2,* 223–231.

Money, J. (1975a). Ablatio penis: Normal male infant sex-reassigned as a girl. *Archives of Sexual Behavior, 4,* 65–72.

Money, J. (1975b). Hormones, gender identity and behavior. In B. Eleftheriou & R. Spratt (Eds.), *Hormonal correlates of behavior*. New York: Plenum.

Money, J. (1987). Propaedeutics of diecious G-1/R: Theoretical foundations for understanding dimorphic gender-identity/role. In J. M. Reinisch, L. A. Rosenblum, & S. A. Sanders (Eds.), *Masculinity/femininity: Basic perspectives*. New York: Oxford University Press.

Money, J., & Ehrhardt, A. (1972). *Man and woman, boy and girl*. Baltimore: Johns Hopkins University Press.

Money, J., & Granoff, D. (1965). IQ and the somatic stigmata of Turner's syndrome. *American Journal of Mental Deficiency, 70,* 69–77.

Money, J., & Tucker, P. (1975). *Sexual signatures*. Boston: Little, Brown.

Moore, M. (1992). The family as portrayed on prime-time television, 1947–1990: Structure and characteristics. *Sex Roles, 26,* 41–61.

Moore, R. (1988). Racist stereotyping in the English language. In P. Rothenberg (Ed.), *Racism and sexism: An integrated study*. New York: St. Martin's Press.

Morgan, R., & Steinem, G. (1980, March). The international crime of genital mutilation. *Ms.* pp. 65–68.

Morgan, T. O., Jacobsen, S., McCarthy, W., Jacobson, D., McLeod, D., & Moul, J. (1996). Age-specific reference ranges for serum prostate-specific antigen in black men. *The New England Journal of Medicine, 335,* 304–310.

Morrison, T. (1970). *The bluest eye*. New York: Holt, Rinehart & Winston.

Moses, Y. (1988). *Black women in the academy*. Washington, DC: Project on the Status and Education of Women.

Murdock, G. (1937, May). Comparative data on the division of labor by sex. *Social Forces,* pp. 551–553.

Murdock, G. (1945). The common denominator of cultures. In R. Linton (Ed.), *The science of man in the world crisis*. New York: Columbia University Press.

Mussen, P., Conger, J., & Kagen, J. (1974). *Child development and personality*. New York: Harper & Row.

Myrdal, A. (1971). Forward. In E. Dahlstrom (Ed.), *The changing roles of men and women*. Boston: Beacon Press.

Myrdal, A., & Klein, V. (1956). *Women's two roles: Home and work*. London: Routledge.

Nanda, S. (1986). *Neither man nor woman: The hijras of India*. Belmont, CA: Wadsworth.

Nanda, S. (1990). The hijras of India: Cultural and individual dimensions of an institutionalized third gender role. *Journal of Homosexuality, 11,* 35–54.

Neal, M. (1979). Women in religious symbolism and organization. *Sociological Inquiry, 49,* 218–250.

Neel, C. (1989). The origins of the Beguines. *Signs, 14,* 321–341.

Nelson, J. A. (1996a, June 28). The masculine mindset of economic analysis. *The Chronicle of Higher Education,* B3.

Nelson, J. A. (1996b). *Feminism, objectivity and economics*. New York: Routledge.

New York Times. (1984, November 17, 18). Women voters, winners and losers. *The New York Times*.

New York Times/CBS Poll. (1984, November 8, 11). Portrait of the electorate. *The New York Times*.

Nichols, P. (1983). Linguistic options and choices for black women in the rural south. In B. Thorne, C. Kramarae, & N. Henley (Eds.), *Language, gender and society*. Rowley, MA: Newbury House.

Nielsen, J., & Christensen, A. (1974). Thirty-five males with double-Y chromosome. *Journal of Psychological Medicine, 4,* 37–38.

Nieva, V., & Gutek, B. (1982). *Women and work*. New York: Praeger.

Nightingale, F. (1979). In M. Stark (Ed.), *Cassandra*. Old Westbury, NY: Feminist Press.

Nilsen, A., et al. (1977). *Sexism and language*. Urbana, IL: National Council of Teachers of English.

Noel, B., et al. (1974). The XYY syndrome: Reality or myth? *Clinical Genetics, 5,* 387–394.

Norton, M. (1980). *The revolutionary experience of American women*. Boston: Little, Brown.

Norton, M., et al. (1982). *A people and a nation* (Vol. I). Boston: Houghton Mifflin.

Nugent, C. (1994). Blaming the victims: Silencing women sexually exploited by psychotherapists. *Journal of Mind and Behavior, 15,* 113–138.

Number of women Ph.D.s reach all-time high. 1996. *The Monthly Forum on Women in Higher Education, 1,* 4.

Oakley, A. (1972). *Sex, gender, and society*. New York: Harper & Row.

Oesterling, J. (1996). Age-specific reference ranges for serum PSA. *The New England Journal of Medicine, 335,* 345–346.

Olien, M. (1978). *The human myth*. New York: Harper & Row.

Owen, D. (1972). The 47, XYY male: A review. *Psychological Bulletin, 78,* 209–233.

Pagels, E. (1976). What became of God the mother? Conflicting images of God in early Christianity. *Signs, 2,* 293–303.

Pagels, E. (1988). *Adam, Eve, and the serpent*. New York: Random House.

Paige, K. (1973, April). Women learn to sing the menstrual blues. *Psychology Today,* pp. 41–46.

Paige, K. (1983). Virginity rituals and chastity control during puberty: Cross-cultural patterns. In S. Golub (Ed.), *Menarche*. Lexington, MA: Lexington Books.

Palkovitz, R. (1985). Fathers' birth attendance, early contact, and extended contact with their newborns: A critical review. *Child Development, 56,* 392–406.

Palm, G. F. (1993). Involved fatherhood: A second chance. *The Journal of Men's Studies, 2,* 139–155.

Paludi, M. A. (1981a). Masculinity and femininity preferences in children: Development of the children's sex role preference scale. Paper presented at the Midwestern Psychological Association, Detroit.

Paludi, M. A. (1981b). Sex role discrimination among girls: Effect on IT Scale for Children scores. *Developmental Psychology, 17,* 851–852.

Paludi, M. A. (1982). The misuse of the chi square statistic in research with the IT Scale for Children. *Sex Roles, 8,* 791–793.

Paludi, M. A. (1984). Psychometric properties and underlying assumptions of four objective measures of fear of success. *Sex Roles, 10,* 765–781.

Paludi, M. A. (Ed.). (1990). *Ivory power: Sexual harassment on campus.* Albany: State University of New York Press.

Paludi, M. A. (1992). *The psychology of women.* Dubuque, IA: Brown & Benchmark.

Paludi, M. A. (1993). Ethnicity, sex, and sexual harassment. *Thought and Action: The National Education Association Higher Education Journal, 8,* 105–116.

Paludi, M. A. (1995, November). *Sexual harassment in higher education: Abusing the ivory power.* Keynote address for the Canadian Association Against Sexual Harassment in Higher Education, Saskatchewon, CA.

Paludi, M. A. (Ed.) (1996). *Sexual harassment on college campuses: Abusing the ivory power.* Albany: State University of New York Press.

Paludi, M. A. (Ed.) (1997). *Psychology of sexual victimization: A handbook.* Westport, CT: Greenwood Press.

Paludi, M. A., & Barickman, R. B. (1991). *Academic and workplace sexual harassment: A resource manual.* Albany: State University of New York Press.

Paludi, M. A., & Barickman, R. B. (1997). *Sexual harassment, work, and education: A manual for prevention.* Albany: State University of New York Press.

Paludi, M. A., & Bauer, W. D. (1979). Impact of sex of experimenter on the Draw-A-Person Test. *Perceptual and Motor Skills, 40,* 456–458.

Paludi, M. A., & DeFour, D. C. (1992). The Mentoring Experiences Questionnaire. *Mentoring International, 6,* 19–23.

Paludi, M. A., DeFour, D. C., Chen, B., Tedesco, A. M., & Brathwaite, J. (1991, August). *Balancing psychological statistics texts for gender.* Paper presented at the annual meeting of the American Psychological Association, San Francisco.

Paludi, M. A., DeFour, D. C., & Roberts, R. (1994). *Academic sexual harassment of ethnic minority women.* Research in progress.

Paludi, M. A., DeFour, D. C., Schneider, P., Gover, S., West, R., & Dekelbaum, D. (1990, August). *The Mentoring Experiences Questionnaire: Initial psychometric analyses.* Paper presented at the American Psychological Association, Boston.

Paludi, M. A., & Fankell-Hauser, J. (1986). An idiographic approach to the study of women's achievement strivings. *Psychology of Women Quarterly, 10,* 89–100.

Paludi, M. A., & Gullo, D. F. (1986). Effect of sex label on adults' knowledge of infant development. *Sex Roles, 16,* 19–30.

Paludi, M., & Steuernagel, G. (Eds.) (1990). *Foundations for a feminist restructuring of the academic disciplines.* New York: Haworth.

Paludi, M. A., & Strayer, L. (1985). What's in an author's name? Differential evaluations of performance as a function of author's name. *Sex Roles, 12,* 353–361.

Papalia, D., & Olds, S. W. (1990). *A child's world.* New York: McGraw-Hill.

Parke, R., & O'Leary, S. (1975). Father-mother-infant interaction in the newborn period. In K. Riegel & J. Meacham (Eds.), *The developing individual in a changing world* (Vol. II). The Hague: Mouton.

Parlee, M. B. (1975). Psychology. *Signs, 1,* 119–138.

Parlee, M. B. (1993). Psychology of menstruation and premenstrual syndrome. In F. L. Denmark & M. A. Paludi (Eds.), *Handbook on the psychology of women.* Westport, CT: Greenwood.

Parvey, C. (1974). The theology and leadership of women in the New Testament. In R. Ruether (Ed.), *Religion and sexism.* New York: Simon & Schuster.

Pegalis, L., Shaffer, D., Bazzini, D., & Greenier, K. (1994). On the ability to elicit self-disclosure: Are there gender-based and contextual limitations on the opener effect? *Personality and Social Psychology Bulletin, 20,* 412–420.

Peplau, L., Rubin, Z., & Hill, C. (1976). The sexual balance of power. *Psychology Today, 10,* 142–147.

Persky, H., Smith, K., & Basu, G. (1971). Relation of psychologic measures of aggression and hostility in chronic alcoholics. *American Journal of Psychiatry, 134,* 621–625.

Persky, H., et al. (1977). The effect of alcohol and smoking on testosterone function and aggression in chronic alcoholics. *American Journal of Psychiatry, 134,* 621–625.

Petersen, A., & Taylor, B. (1980). The biological approach to adolescence. In J. Adelson (Ed.), *Handbook of adolescent psychology.* New York: Wiley.

Petty, R., & Mirels, H. (1981). Intimacy and scarcity of self-disclosure: Effects on interpersonal attraction for males and females. *Personality and Social Psychology Bulletin, 7,* 490–503.

Pheterson, G., Kielser, S., & Goldberg, P. (1971). Evaluation of the performance of women as a function of their sex, achievement, and personal history. *Journal of Personality and Social Psychology, 19,* 114–118.

Phoenix, C. (1978). Prenatal testosterone in the nonhuman primate and its consequences for behavior. In R. Friedman et al. (Eds.), *Sex differences in behavior.* Huntington, NY: Krieger Publishing.

Piliavin, J., & Martin, R. (1978). The effects of the sex composition of groups on style of social interaction. *Sex Roles, 4,* 281–296.

Piliavin, J., & Unger, R. K. (1985). The helpful but helpless female: Myth or reality? In V. O'Leary, R. Unger, & B. Wallston (Eds.), *Women, gender, and social psychology.* Hillsdale, NJ: Erlbaum.

Pines, M. (1978, May). Is sociobiology all wet? *Psychology Today,* pp. 23–24.

Pipher, M. (1994). *Reviving Ophelia: Saving the selves of adolescent girls.* New York: Ballantine Books.

Pizzey, E. (1974). *Scream quietly or the neighbors will hear.* Baltimore: Penguin.

Pleck, J. (1981). *The myth of masculinity.* Cambridge, MA: The MIT Press.

Pleck, J. (1974, April 11). My male sex role—and ours. *WIN Magazine,* 8–12.

Pleck, E., & Pleck, J. (1980). *The American man.* Englewood Cliffs, NJ: Prentice Hall.

Podrouzek, W., & Furrow, D. (1988). Preschoolers' use of eye contact while speaking: The influence of sex, age, and conversational pattern. *Psycholinguistic Research, 17,* 89–98.

Pomazal, R., & Clore, G. (1973). Helping on the highway: The effects of dependency and sex. *Journal of Applied Social Psychology, 3,* 150–164.

Porter, N. (1995). Supervision of psychotherapists: Integrating anti-racist, feminist, and multicultural perspectives. In H. Landrine (Ed.), *Bringing cultural diversity to feminist psychology: Theory, research, and practice.* Washington, DC: American Psychological Association.

Provost, Fr. John (1993). Personal communication.

Pryor, J. (1987). Sexual harassment proclivities in men. *Sex Roles, 17,* 269–290.

Quina, K. (1996). Sexual harassment and rape: A continuum of exploitation. In M. Paludi (Ed.), *Sexual harassment on college campuses: Abusing the ivory power.* Albany: State University of New York Press.

Rabin, A. (1970). The sexes: Ideology and reality in the Israeli kibbutz. In G. Seward & R. Williamson (Eds.), *Sex roles in a changing society.* New York: Random House.

Rabinowitz, V., & Sechzur, J. (1993). Feminist perspectives on research methods. In F. L. Denmark & M. A. Paludi (Eds.), *Psychology of women: A handbook of issues and theories.* Westport, CT: Greenwood Press.

Rapoport, T., Lomski-Feder, E., & Masalha, M. (1989). Female subordination in the Arab-Israeli community: The adolescent perspective of "social veil." *Sex Roles, 20,* 255–269.

Rathus, S. (1983). *Human sexuality.* New York: Holt, Rinehart, & Winston.

Rathus, S. (1988). *Human sexuality.* New York: Holt, Rinehart, & Winston.

Raven, B. (1965). Social influence and power. In I. Steiner & M. Fishbein (Eds.), *Current studies in social psychology.* New York: Holt, Rinehart & Winston.

Rawlings, E., & Carter, D. (Eds.). (1977). *Psychotherapy for women.* Springfield, IL: Thomas.

Red Horse, J. (1980). Family structure and value orientation in American Indians. *Social Casework, 61,* 462–467.

Reed, B., & Garvin, C. (Eds.). (1983). *Groupwork with women/groupwork with men.* New York: Haworth Press.

Reid, P. (1984). Feminism vs. minority group identity: Not for black women only. *Sex Roles, 10,* 247–255.

Reid, P., Haritos, C., Kelly, E., & Holland, N. (1995). Socialization of girls: Issues of ethnicity in gender development. In H. Landrine (Ed.), *Bringing cultural diversity to feminist psychology: Theory, research, and practice.* Washington, DC: American Psychological Association.

Reid, P., & Paludi, M. A. (1993). Psychology of Women: Conception to Adolescence. In F. L. Denmark & M. A. Paludi (Eds.), *Psychology of women: A handboook of issues and theories.* Westport, CT: Greenwood Press.

Rhodes, A. (1983). Effects of religious domination on sex differences in occupational expectations. *Sex Roles, 9,* 93–108.

Ricciardelli, L., & Williams, R. (1995). Desirable and undesirable gender traits in three behavioral domains. *Sex Roles, 33,* 637–655.

Rodin, J., & Ickovics, J. R. (1990). Women's health. *American Psychologist, 45,* 1018–1034.

Rogan, A. (1978). The threat of sociobiology. *Quest, 4,* 85–93.

Rohrbaugh, J. (1979). *Women.* New York: Basic Books.

Romero, G. J., Castro, F., & Cervantes, R. (1988). Latinas without work: Family, occupational, and economic stress following unemployment. *Psychology of Women Quarterly, 12,* 281–297.

Romero, G., & Garza, R. (1986). Attributions for the occupational success/failure of ethnic minority and nonminority women. *Sex Roles, 14,* 445–452.

Root, M. P. P. (1995). The psychology of Asian American women. In H. Landrine (Ed.), *Bringing cultural diversity to feminist psychology: Theory, research, and practice.* Washington, DC: American Psychological Association.

Rosaldo, M., & Lamphere, L. (Eds.). (1974). *Woman, culture, and society.* Stanford, CA: Stanford University Press.

Rosenblatt, M. E., & Witherup, R. (1996, April). Was St. Paul sexist? *Catholic Update,* pp. 1–4.

Rosenfield, S. (1980). Sex differences in depression. Do women and men always have higher rates? *Journal of Health and Social Behavior, 21,* 33–42.

Rosenkrantz, P., et al. (1968). Sex-role stereotypes and self-concepts in college students. *Journal of Consulting and Clinical Psychology, 32,* 287–295.

Rosenthal, R. (1976). *Experimenter effects in behavioral research.* New York: Halstead Press.

Rosenthal, R. (1979). The "file drawer problem" and tolerance for null results. *Psychological Bulletin, 86,* 638–641.

Rosewater, L. B. (1984). Feminist therapy: Implications for practitioners.

Rossi, A. (1977). A biosocial perspective on parenting. *Daedalus, 106,* 1–31.

Rossi, A. (1982). *Feminists in politics.* New York: Academic Press.

Rossi, A. (1983). Beyond the gender gap: Women's bid for political power. *Social Science Quarterly, 64,* 718–733.

Rothblum, E., & Cole, E. (Eds.). (1986). *Another silenced trauma.* New York: Haworth Press.

Rotundo, E. A. (1993). *American manhood*. New York: Basic Books.

Rowbotham, S. (1973). *Women's consciousness: Man's world*. Baltimore: Penguin Books.

Rozee, P. (1993). Forbidden or forgiven: Rape in cross-cultural perspective. *Psychology of Women Quarterly, 17,* 499–514.

Rozee, P. (1997). Rape. In M. Paludi (Ed.), *Psychology of sexual victimization: A handbook*. Westport, CT: Greenwood Press.

Rubin, J., Provenzano, F., & Luria, Z. (1974). The eye of the beholder: Parents' views on sex of newborns. *American Journal of Orthopsychiatry, 44,* 512–519.

Ruether, R. (Ed.). (1974a). *Religion and sexism*. New York: Simon & Schuster.

Ruether, R. (1974b). Misogynism and virginal feminism in the fathers of the church. In R. Ruether (Ed.), *Religion and sexism*. New York: Simon & Schuster.

Ruether, R., & Bianchi, E. (1976). *From machismo to mutuality*. New York: Paulist Press.

Russell, D. (1973). *Rape and the masculine mystique*. Paper presented at the American Sociological Association, New York.

Russell, L. (1974). *Human liberation in a feminist perspective*. Philadelphia: Westminister Press.

Russo, N. (1975). Eye contact, interpersonal distance, and the equilibrium theory. *Journal of Personality and Social Psychology, 31,* 497–502.

Russo, N. F. (1976). The motherhood mandate. *Journal of Social Issues, 32,* 143–153.

Russo, N. F. (1984). *Women in the American Psychological Association*. Washington, DC: Women's Program Office, American Psychological Association.

Russo, N. F. (1993). Women and mental health. In F. Denmark & M. Paludi (Eds.), *Psychology of women: A handbook of issues and theories*. Westport, CT: Greenwood Press.

Russo, N. F., & Green, B. (1993). Women and work. In F. Denmark & M. Paludi (Eds.), *Psychology of women: A handbook of issues and theories*. Westport, CT: Greenwood Press.

Sadker, M., and Sadker, D. (1994). *Failing at fairness: How America's schools cheat girls*. New York: Charles Scribner's Sons.

Sanday, P. (1973). Toward a theory of the status of women. *American Anthropologist, 75,* 1682–1700.

Sandler, B., & Paludi, M. (1993). *Educator's guide to controlling sexual harassment*. Washington, DC: Thompson.

Sapp, S. (1977). *Sexuality, the Bible and science*. Philadelphia: Fortress Press.

Scanzoni, J. (1972). *Sexual bargaining*. Englewood Cliffs, NJ: Prentice Hall.

Scanzoni, L., & Scanzoni, J. (1981). *Men, women, and change* (2nd ed.). New York: McGraw-Hill.

Schaef, A. (1981). *Women's reality*. Minneapolis: Winston Press.

Scharf, L. (1980). *To work and to wed*. Westport, CT: Greenwood Press.

Schneider, J., & Hacker, S. (1973). Sex role imagery and the use of the generic "man" in introductory texts. *American Sociologist, 8,* 12–18.

Schockett, M., & Haring-Hildore, M. (1985). Factor analytic support for psychosocial and vocational mentoring functions. *Psychological Reports, 57,* 627–630.

Schockett, M., Yoshimura, E., Beyard-Tyler, K., & Haring, M. (1983, April). *A proposed model of mentoring.* Paper presented at the meeting of the American Educational Research Association, Anaheim, CA.

Schowalter, E. (1985). *The female malady: Women, madness, and English culture, 1830–1980.* New York: Penguin.

Schowalter, J., & Anyan, W. (1981). *Family handbook of adolescence.* New York: Knopf.

Schulenberg, J. T. (1989). Women's monastic communities, 500–1100: Patterns of expansion and decline. *Signs, 14,* 261–292.

Schwabacher, S. (1972). Male vs. female representation in psychological research: An examination of the Journal of Personality and Social Psychology, 1970, 1971. *JSAS Catalog of Selected Documents in Psychology, 2,* 20–21.

Scott, A. (1970). *The southern lady.* Chicago: University of Chicago Press.

Seavey, C., Katz, P., & Zalk, S. R. (1975). Baby X: The effect of gender labels on adult responses to infants. *Sex Roles, 1,* 103–109.

Sedugin, P. (1973). *New Soviet legislation on marriage and the family.* Moscow: Progress Publishers.

Segal, E. (1988). *Tomboy taming and gender role socialization: The evidence of children's books.* Paper presented at the Gender Roles Through the Lifespan Conference, Muncie, IN.

Serbin, L., et al. (1973). A comparison of teacher response to the preacademic and problem behavior of boys and girls. *Child Development, 44,* 796–804.

Setta, S. (1989). Empowering women from the sanctuary to the cosmos: Reflections on the nature of gender. In D. Kaufman (Ed.), *Public/private spheres: Women past and present.* Boston: Northeastern Custom Book Program.

Sharma, U. (1978). Women and their affairs: The veil as a symbol of separation. *Man, 13,* 218–233.

Sher, M., & Lansky, L. (1968). The IT Scale for Children: Effects of variations in the specificity of the IT figure. *Merrill-Palmer Quarterly, 14,* 323–330.

Sherif, C. W. (1982). Needed concepts in the study of gender identity. *Psychology of Women Quarterly, 6,* 375–398.

Sherman, A., Hutchens, T., Marsh, J., & Williams, R. (1996). Gender differences in social support: Is there a biological basis? *Journal of Gender, Culture, and Health, 1,* 51–69.

Sherman, J. (1978). *Sex-related cognitive differences.* Springfield, IL: Thomas.

Sherman, J. (1980). Therapist attitudes and sex-role stereotyping. In A. Brodsky & R. Hare-Mustin (Eds.), *Women and psychotherapy.* New York: Guilford.

Sherman, J., Koufacos, C., & Kenworthy, J. (1978). Therapists: Their attitudes and information about women. *Psychology of Women Quarterly, 2,* 299–313.

Shields, S. (1975). Functionalism, Darwinism, and the psychology of women: A study in social myth. *American Psychologist, 30,* 739–754.

Shields, S. (1982). The variability hypothesis: The history of a biological model of sex differences in intelligence. *Signs, 7,* 769–797.

Sidorowicz, L., & Lunney, C. (1980). Baby X revisited. *Sex Roles, 6,* 67–73.

Silverstein, B., Caceres, J., Perdue, L., & Cimarilli, V. (1995). Gender differences in depressive symptomatology: The role played by "anxious somatic depression" associated with gender-related achievement concerns. *Sex Roles, 33,* 621–636.

Sinnott, J. (1984). Older men, older women: Are their perceived sex roles similar? *Sex Roles, 10,* 847–856.

Smith, A. (1983). Nonverbal communication among black female dyads: An assessment of intimacy, gender, and race. *Journal of Social Issues, 39,* 55–67.

Smith, C. (1996). Women, weight, and body image. In J. Chrisler, C. Golden, & P. Rozee (Eds.), *Lectures on the psychology of women.* New York: McGraw-Hill.

Smith, M. (1980). Sex bias in counseling and psychotherapy. *Psychological Bulletin, 87,* 392–407.

Snodgrass, J. (1977). *For men against sexism.* Albion, CA: Times Change Press.

Sparks, C. (1985). *Preliminary comment on the DSM-III proposed revision.* Bethesda, MD: Feminist Institute.

Spence, J. T., Helmreich, R., & Stapp, J. (1974). The personal attributes questionnaire. *JSAS Catalog of Selected Documents in Psychology, 4,* 127.

Spiro, M. (1971). *Kibbutz.* New York: Schocken Books.

Stacy, J. (1975). When patriarchy kowtows: The significance of the Chinese family revolution for feminist theory. *Feminist Studies, 2,* 64–112.

Stanley, J. (1977). Paradigmatic woman: The prostitute. In D. Shores (Ed.), *Papers in language variation.* Birmingham: University of Alabama Press.

Stanovich, K. E. (1986). *How to think straight about psychology.* Glenview, IL: Scott, Foresman.

Stein, D. (1978). Women to burn: Suttee as a normative institution. *Signs, 4,* 253–268.

Steinem, G. (1986). Men and women talking. In *Outrageous acts and everyday rebellions.* New York: Holt, Rinehart & Winston.

Steinmetz, S. (1978). Violence between family members. *Marriage and Family Review, 1,* 3–16.

Stericker, A. (1981). Does this "he or she" business really make a difference? The effect of masculine pronouns as generics on job attitudes. *Sex Roles, 7,* 637–641.

Sterling, D. (1988). *Black foremothers: Three lives.* New York: The Feminist Press.

Steward, M., Steward, D., & Dary, J. (1983). Women who choose a man's career: A study of women in ministry. *Psychology of Women Quarterly, 8,* 166–173.

Stewart, D. (1980). The women's movement in France. *Signs, 6,* 350–354.

Stier, D., & Hall, J. (1984). Gender differences in touch: An empirical and theoretical review. *Journal of Personality and Social Psychology, 47,* 440–459.

Stites, M. C. (1996). What's wrong with faculty-student consensual sexual relationships? In M. Paludi (Ed.), *Sexual harassment on college campuses: Abusing the ivory power.* Albany: State University of New York Press.

Straus, M., Gelles, R., & Steinmetz, S. (1980). *Behind closed doors.* New York: Doubleday.

Strickland, B. (1988). Sex-related differences in health and illness. *Psychology of Women Quarterly, 12,* 382–399.

Strodtbeck, F. (1951). Husband-wife interaction over revealed differences. *American Sociological Review, 16,* 468–473.

Summerfield, P. (1980). *Women workers in the second world war: Production and patriarchy in conflict.* New York: Routledge.

Swacker, M. (1975). The sex of the speaker as a sociolinguistic variable. In B. Thorne & N. Henley (Eds.), *Language and sex.* Rowley, MA: Newbury House.

Swenson, C. H. (1968). Empirical evaluations of human figure drawings: 1957–1966. *Psychological Bulletin, 70,* 20–44.

Swidler, L. (1976). *Women in Judaism.* Metuchen, NJ: Scarecrow Press.

Swidler, L. (1971, January). Jesus was a feminist. *Catholic World,* pp. 177–183.

Swidler, L., & Swidler, A. (1977). *Women priests.* New York: Paulist Press.

Swoboda, M. J., & Millar, S. B. (1986). Networking-mentoring: Career strategy of women in academic administration. *Journal of NAWDAC, 49,* 8–13.

Taal, M. (1994). How do mathematical experiences contribute to the choice of mathematics? *Sex Roles, 31,* 757–769.

Tabory, E. (1984). Rights and rites: Women's roles in liberal religious movements in Israel. *Sex Roles, 11,* 155–166.

Talmon, Y. (1972). *Family and community in the kibbutz.* Cambridge, MA: Harvard University Press.

Tangri, S., Burt, M., & Johnson, L. (1982). Sexual harassment at work: Three explanatory models. *Journal of Social Issues, 38,* 33–54.

Tannen, D. (1990). *You just don't understand: Women and men in conversations.* New York: William Morrow & Co.

Tannen, D. (1994). *Talking from 9 to 5: Women and men in the workplace, Language, sex, and power.* New York: Avon.

Tanner, J. (1962). *Growth at adolescence.* Oxford: Blackwell.

Tedisco, J. N., & Paludi, M. A. (1996). *Missing children.* Albany: State University of New York Press.

Terman, L., & Miles, C. (1936). *Sex and personality.* New York: McGraw-Hill.

Terrien, S. (1976). Toward a biblical theology of womanhood. In R. Barnhouse & V. Holmes, III (Eds.), *Male and Female*. New York: The Seabury Press.

Tewksbury, R., & Gagne, P. (1996). Transgenderists: Products of non-normative intersections of sex, gender and sexuality. *The Journal of Men's Studies, 5,* 105–130.

Thomas, S. (1979). *Adolescent sex role inventory*. Paper presented at the Special Interest Group on Research on Women and Education, Cleveland.

Thompson, S., Sargent, R., & Kemper, K. (1996). Black and white adolescent males' perceptions of ideal body size. *Sex Roles, 34,* 391–406.

Tiefer, L. (1990). *Gender and meaning in the DSM-III-R sexual dysfunctions*. Paper presented at the meeting of the American Psychological Association, Boston.

Tieger, T. (1980). On the biological basis of sex differences in aggression. *Child Development, 51,* 943–963.

Tiger, L. (1969). *Men in groups*. New York: Random House.

Tiger, L., & Fox, R. (1971). *The imperial animal*. New York: Holt, Rinehart & Winston.

Tiger, L., & Shepher, J. (1975). *Women in the kibbutz*. New York: Harcourt Brace Jovanovich.

Tobach, E., & Rosoff, B. (Eds.). (1978). *Genes and gender*. New York: Gordian Press.

Travis, C. (1993). Women and health. In F. L. Denmark & M. A. Paludi (Eds.), *Psychology of women: A handbook of issues and theories*. Westport, CT: Greenwood Press.

Tronto, J. (1987). Beyond gender difference to a theory of care. *Signs, 12,* 644–663.

Udry, J. R., & Talbert, L. M. (1988). Sex hormone effects of personality at puberty. *Journal of Personality and Social Psychology, 54,* 291–295.

Unger, R. K. (1979). Toward a redefinition of sex and gender. *American Psychologist, 34,* 1085–1094.

Unger, R. K. (1983). Through the looking glass: No wonderland yet! (The reciprocal relationship between methodology and models of reality). *Psychology of Women Quarterly, 8,* 9–32.

Unger, R. (1995). Cultural diversity and the future of feminist psychology. In H. Landrine (Ed.), *Bringing cultural diversity to feminist psychology: Theory, research, and practice*. Washington, DC, American Psychological Association.

Unger, R., & Saundra (1993). Stereotypes about women. In F. L. Denmark & M. A. Paludi (Eds.), *Psychology of women: A handbook of issues and theories*. Westport, CT: Greenwood Press.

U.S. Commission on Civil Rights. (1977). *Window dressing on the set: Women and minorities in television*. Washington, DC: U.S. Government Printing Office.

U.S. Commission on Civil Rights. (1979). *Window dressing on the set: An update*. Washington, DC: U.S. Government Printing Office.

U.S. Merit Systems Protection Board. (1981). *Sexual harassment of federal workers: Is it a problem?* Washington, DC: U.S. Government Printing Office.

U.S. Merit Systems Protection Board. (1987). *Sexual harassment of federal workers*. Washington, DC: U.S. Government Printing Office.

van den Berghe, P. (1978). *Man in society*. New York: Elsevier.

Wade, J. C. (1996). African American men's gender role conflict: The significance of racial identity. *Sex Roles, 34*, 17–33.

Wadley, S. (1977). Women and the Hindu tradition. *Signs, 3*, 113–125.

Wagenvoord, J., & Bailey, J. (1978). *Men*. New York: Avon.

Wagner, S. (1984). The world anti-slavery convention of 1840: Three antisexist men take a stand. *M., 12*, 35, 41.

Waite, B., & Paludi, M. A. (1987). *Sex role stereotyping in popular music videos*. Paper presented at the Midwestern Psychological Association, Chicago.

Walker, L. (1991). Post-traumatic stress disorder in women: Diagnosis and treatment of battered women's syndrome. *Psychotherapy, 28*, 1–9.

Wallace, J. (1982, June 28). Chinese men and women are equal—but men are more equal. *U.S. News & World Report*, p. 54.

Wallston, B. S., & Grady, K. E. (1985). Integrating the feminist critique and the crisis in social psychology: Another look at research methods. In V. O'Leary, R. Unger, & B. S. Wallston (Eds.), *Women, gender, and social psychology*. Hillsdale, NJ: Erlbaum.

Walsh, M. R. (1977). *Doctors wanted: No women need apply: Sexual barriers in the medical profession, 1835–1975*. New Haven: Yale University Press.

Walstedt, J. (1977). The altruistic other orientation: An exploration of female powerlessness. *Psychology of Women Quarterly, 2*, 162–176.

Walstedt, J. (1978). Reform of women's roles and family structures in the recent history of China. *Journal of Marriage and the Family, 40*, 379–392.

Walters, W. A. W., & Ross, M. W. (Eds.). (1986). *Transsexualism and sex reassignment*. New York: Oxford University Press.

Ware, S. (1981). *Beyond suffrage*. Cambridge, MA: Harvard University Press.

Warshaw, R. (1988). *I never called it rape*. New York: Harper & Row.

Weathers, D., & Lord, M. (1979, December 3). Can a Mormon support ERA? *Newsweek*, p. 88.

Weir, E. (1996). The '96 vote: Listening to America, hope amid the anger. *The National Voter, 45*, 4–8.

Weissman, M., & Klerman, G. (1977). Sex differences in the epidemiology of depression. *Archives of General Psychiatry, 34*, 98–111.

Weisstein, N. (1971). Psychology constructs the female. In V. Gornick & B. Moran (Eds.), *Women in sexist society*. New York: New American Library.

Weithorn, C. (1975). Woman's role in cross-cultural perspective. In R. Unger & F. Denmark (Eds.), *Woman*. New York: Psychological Dimensions.

Weitzman, L., et al. (1972). Sex role socialization in picture books for preschool children. *American Journal of Sociology, 77*, 1125–1150.

Weitzman, L. (1979). *Sex role socialization*. Palo Alto, CA: Mayfield.

Welch, S. (1978). Recruitment of women to public office: A discriminant analysis. *Western Political Quarterly, 31,* 372–380.

Welter, B. (1974). The feminization of American religion: 1800–1860. In M. Hartman & L. Banner (Eds.) *Clio's consciousness raided.* New York: Harper & Row.

West, C., & Zimmerman, D. (1977). Women's place in everyday talk: Reflections on parent-child interaction. *Social Problems, 24,* 521–529.

West, P. (1994). Do men make the rules or do the rules make men? Growing up male in an Australian country town. *Masculinities, 2,* 46–59.

White, L., & Brinnerhoff, D. (1981). The sexual division of labor: Evidence from childhood. *Social Forces, 60,* 170–181.

White, M. (1975). Women in the professions: Psychological and social barriers to women in science. In J. Freeman (Ed.), *Women.* Palo Alto, CA: Mayfield.

Wikan, U. (1982). *Behind the veil in Arabia: Women in Oman.* Baltimore: Johns Hopkins University Press.

Will, J., Self, P., & Datan, N. (1976). Maternal behavior and perceived sex of infant. *American Journal of Orthopsychiatry, 46,* 135–139.

Williams, J. (1983). *Psychology of women: Behavior in a biosocial context.* New York: Norton.

Williams, J., & Spitzer, R. (1983). The issues of sex bias in DSM-III: A critique of "a woman's view of DSM-III" by Marcie Kaplan. *American Psychologist, 38,* 793–798.

Williams, S. (1978). *Riding the nightmare.* New York: Atheneum.

Williams, W. L. (1986). *The spirit and the flesh: Sexual diversity in American Indian culture.* Boston: Beacon Press.

Wilson, E. (1978). *On human nature.* Cambridge, MA: Harvard University Press.

Winslow, D. (1976). Sex and anti-sex in the early church fathers. In R. Barnhouse & U. Holmes, III (Eds.), *Male and female.* New York: The Seabury Press.

Witkin, H., et al. (1976). Criminality in XYY and XXY men. *Science, 193,* 547–555.

Wolf, M. (1980). Uterine families and the women's community. In J. Spradley & D. McCurdy (Eds.), *Conformity and conflict* (4th ed.). Boston: Little, Brown.

Wollstonecraft, M. (1792/1975). *A vindication of the rights of women.* New York: Norton.

Wong, M. (1978). Males in transition and the self-help group. *The Counseling Psychologist, 7,* 46–50.

Woo, D. (1992). The gap between striving and achieving: The case of Asian American women. In P. Rothenberg (Ed.), *Race, class, and gender in the United States: An integrated study.* New York: St. Martin's Press.

Wooley, S., & Wooley, O. W. (1980). Eating disorders: Obesity and anorexia. In A. Brodsky & R. Hare-Mustin (Eds.), *Women and psychotherapy.* New York: Guilford.

Worell, J. (1980). New directions in counseling women. *Personnel and Guidance Journal, 58,* 477–484.

Worell, J. (1990). Women: The psychological perspective. In M. A. Paludi & G. Steuernagel (Eds.), *Foundations for the feminist restructuring of the academic disciplines.* New York: Haworth.

Wu, X., & DeMaris, A. (1996). Gender and marital status differences in depression: The effects of chronic strains. *Sex Roles, 34,* 299–319.

Yinger, M. (1982). *Counterculture.* New York: Free Press.

Youngstrom, N. (1990, October). Issue of sex misconduct discussed at convention. *APA Monitor,* pp. 20–21.

Zalk, S. R. (1996). Psychological profiles of men who harass. In M. Paludi (Ed.), *Sexual harassment on college campuses: Abusing the ivory power.* Albany: State University of New York Press.

Zalk, S. R., Paludi, M., & Dederich, J. (1991). Women's students' assessment of consensual relationships with their professors: Ivory power revisited. In M. Paludi & R. Barickman, *Academic and workplace sexual harassment: A resource manual.* Albany: State University of New York Press.

Zellman, G. (1978). Politics and power. In I. Frieze et al. (Eds.), *Women and sex roles.* New York: Norton.

Zimmerman, D., & West, C. (1975). Sex roles, interruptions and silences in conversations. In B. Thorne & N. Henley (Eds.), *Language and sex.* Rowley, MA: Newbury House.

Zuckerman, M. (1982). Masculinity-femininity and encoding of nonverbal cues. *Journal of Personality and Social Psychology, 42,* 548–556.

Zuckerman, M., DePaulo, B., & Rosenthal, R. (1981). Verbal and nonverbal communication of deception. In L. Berkowitz (Ed.), *Advances in experimental social psychology.* New York: Academic Press.

Name Index

A

Abbott, S., 276
Abramowitz, S., 238
Abu-Lughod, R., 102
Acosta, M., 50, 71, 86, 186, 234
Adams, M., 236
Adelson, J., 64
Aiello, J., 164
Al-Issa, I., 228
Albee, G., 211
Albin, R., 126
Allan, K., 81
Allen, I., 173
Altbach, E., 275
Amaro, H., 186, 229
American Association of University Women, 64, 86, 138, 139
American Psychiatric Association, 232
American Psychological Association, 19, 20, 170
Antill, J. K., 48, 76
Anyan, W., 33
Arch, E. C., 178
Arnoff, M. S., 38
Ashburn, L., 236
Ashmore, R., 48
Association of American Colleges, 182
Atkinson, J., 8

B

Baenninger, M., 54
Bailey, J., 166
Bailey, N., 136, 137, 140, 141
Bailey, R. F., 171
Baker, N., 138
Baker, S., 29
Bandura, A., 56, 57

Bar-Yosef, R., 112
Barickman, R. B., 142, 182, 197
Bartlett, J., 217
Basow, S., 75, 84, 236
Basu, G., 36
Baude, A., 110
Bauer, W. D., 47, 172
Baxter, S., 221
Bazzini, D., 158
Beale, F., 186, 276
Beck, L., 102
Bell, S., 261
Belle, D., 229
Bem, S. L., 16, 33, 48, 58, 59, 65, 75, 84
Benally, H. J., 216
Beneke, T., 235
Bentzen, F., 33
Berens, S., 38
Bergmann, B., 82, 189
Bernard, J., 70, 123, 230
Bertilson, H., 168
Berzins, J., 48
Betz, N., 76, 77, 89, 90, 100, 122, 176, 186, 188, 189, 190, 191, 193, 197, 198, 237
Beyard-Tyler, K., 89
Beyene, Y., 39
Bianchi, E., 212
Biden, J., 145, 146
Billingsley, D., 238
Bird, P., 202
Blackwood, E., 104, 105, 106
Blau, F., 189
Block, J., 13
Blood, R., 124
Blumberg, R., 101, 111
Boggiano, A., 234
Bond, M., 140
Bouhoutsos, J., 239
Boyd, S. B., 211

Subject Index

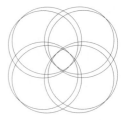

Bolded page numbers preceded by **b** or **p** refer to pages that contain a box or a picture.